COLLECTION OF INTERCULTURAL STUDIES

Interrelations of Cultures

THEIR CONTRIBUTION
TO
INTERNATIONAL UNDERSTANDING

GREENWOOD PRESS, PUBLISHERS
WESTPORT, CONNECTICUT

CONTENTS

Introduction

Four years' ago, Unesco initiated a series of studies and enquiries, which are not yet concluded or near being so, on the present stage of the indigenous cultures of the various peoples of the world and on the relations existing between these cultures. A number of scientists, historians, ethnologists, humanists and philosophers have contributed their personal views on the culture either of their own country or of countries with which they are particularly well acquainted.

This mass of documentation was submitted at the end of 1949 to the examination of a committee of experts composed of: Messrs. C. C. Berg (Netherlands), S. Buarque de Hollanda (Brazil), M. Castro Leal (Mexico), L. Febvre (France), M. Griaule (France), R. McKeon (United States of America), Mei Yi Chi (China), Mostafa Amer Bey (Egypt), J. M. Romein (Netherlands), N. K. Sidantha (India).

This committee drew up a joint statement, which forms the conclusion of the present volume. It was of the opinion that a useful purpose would be served by publishing part, at least, of the material collected, such contributions as by their character and form were best suited to appear in a symposium. A small sub-committee, formed of Messrs. C. C. Berg, M. Castro Leal, M. Griaule and R. McKeon, undertook to prepare this publication. Mr. Marcel Griaule, with the agreement of his colleagues, was responsible for the final choice and for making the necessary cuts and adaptations, with the authors' consent.

The volume which Unesco puts before the public today includes only some of the essays selected by the committee of experts. Nor has there been any deliberate plan behind this selection, for the editors had frequently to be guided by certain practical considerations of length and coherence of the whole.

Some of the papers which it was not possible to include in this volume will undoubtedly appear in other collections or find some other use. The Unesco enquiry, as stated above, is continuing in various forms. For example, in December 1951, meeting between thinkers of different countries took place in a New Delhi, with a view to investigating aspects of the cultural relations between East and West. A preliminary enquiry had been carried out among National Commissions, learned bodies and a number of experts in this field. The contributions which Unesco collected in this way and the conclusions of the New Delhi meeting will be published in a second volume. Other subjects will be studied as time goes on, and the results of these successive investigations will complement the collection inaugurated by the present work.

The incomplete and provisional character of this first compilation or the disparity apparent in the very conception of the problems under study should be no cause for surprise. The novelty and complexity of the subject, the varying viewpoints and methods of the approach adopted to it by specialists of the disciplines concerned, and the necessity of allowing full independence to the authors imposed this diversity of expression, which does not, of course, exclude a very large measure of agreement on the basic conclusions. Taken as it is, and incomplete by its nature and its purpose, this volume forms the first foundations of an edifice which it is hoped to build up, stone by stone, in the years that lie ahead.

The objective common to these studies exceeds their mere scientific or speculative interest. It concerns in a very concrete way more than one of the most urgent tasks of Unesco and of the other United Nations agencies. The extension of education, the general raising of the level of culture, the improvement of living conditions, technical assistance with a view to the economic development of less favoured nations or the application of the principles enshrined in the Universal Declaration of Human Rights—all such international activity runs the risk of being fruitless or even harmful unless it makes the widest allowances for the diversity and independence of civilizations and for the relations which have sprung up in the course of history between peoples of different cultures. Ignorance or misunderstanding of the intellectual, moral or spiritual values inherent in each culture would not only impair the efficiency of international co-operation: it would expose the most praise-worthy endeavours to the worst mistakes or to irreparable disaster. It is hoped that the studies whose publication this volume inaugurates, may make their modest contribution to this important task.

Unesco takes this opportunity of expressing its deep obligation to those who have contributed essays, to the members of the committee of experts, and especially to Mr. Marcel Griaule.

Opinions expressed are those of the authors and do not necessarily reflect the views of Unesco.

Philosophy and the Diversity of Cultures

by

RICHARD McKEON

Cultures may be described in terms of historically derived patterns and socially valued habits for which data may be found in all human activities and functions including political institutions and rules of law, constructions and influences of the fine arts, religious rites and dogmas and all forms of intellectual enquiry and speculation. Political problems, enlarged from national to world dimensions, involve these same data. The establishment of peace and security is a problem, not merely of bolstering the *status quo* and elaborating measures calculated to avoid armed hostilities, but of establishing an order extended to all peoples and fitted to their just expectations. A peaceful order must be adjusted to their needs and resources, and it must reflect and in turn influence their character, that is, their habitual attitudes and understandings. The establishment of such world order depends on using available knowledge and providing for its increase and dissemination, and on broadening the applications of wisdom. The cultural heritage, finally, is determined in patterns which have resulted from innovations in action, thought, or expression of individual human beings engaged in the solution of social, economic, religious, aesthetic, ethical, philosophic or scientific problems. The conscious critical examination of these activities and their clarification relative to the ends they serve depends, not on social conditions from which they arose or on political power and controls by which their external manifestations might be inhibited or advanced, but on standards of aesthetic, ethical and scientific judgment.

The characteristics of cultures may be discerned, in the first place, in the social aspects of human action and co-operation—in the patterns, recognizable as forms of conduct and transmissible from generation to generation, which appear in the

behaviour of men and the determination of their functions.
Forms of group behaviour are, however distinguishable from
the cultures of which they are signs, and anthropologists sometimes differentiate "society", in the sense of a group of people
who have learned to live together, from "culture", in the sense
of the distinctive ways of life of such a group of people.[1] The
distribution of functions and the division of labour required
for the production and exchange of goods and for the common
life constitute the organization of societies, while the customs
and beliefs which hold societies together and enable them to
survive are expressions of their cultures. The distinction is
seen in its limiting case in sub-human societies, like those of
the social insects, which are cultureless, whereas every human
society is possessed of a characteristic culture. Every culture
presupposes a society, but the converse of this formula is not
true.[2]

I

Cultures may therefore be studied in the conduct of peoples
and in the cumulative traditions of the transmission of patterns
of conduct with their lags, interruptions, and intrusions of
novelty. So viewed, cultures are the material traces of ideas
and ideals in the habits of men. An analysis of the actions,
productions and convictions by which men adjusted themselves to the conditions in which they found themselves (or
which they continued from some earlier adjustment of the
group after the utility of the habit or the truth of the conviction
had ceased), can supply information, not about the circum-

---

[1] C. Kluckhohn and W. H. Kelly, "The Concept of Culture", *The Science of Man in the World Crisis*, ed. R. Linton, New York, 1945, p. 79. The author refers to a long treatment of the distinction between the "social" and the "cultural" which was omitted from the published form of
their essay (op. cit. p. 102). Cf. R. Linton, "Present World Conditions in Cultural Perspective",
op. cit. p. 203: "The culture of a society is the way of life of its members; the collection of ideas
and habits which they learn, share and transmit from generation to generation. Culture provides the members of each generation with effective, ready made answers to most of the problems
with which they are likely to be confronted. These problems, in turn, stem from the needs of
individuals living as members of organized groups."

[2] Cf. A. L. Kroeber, "The Concept of Culture in Science", *The Journal of General Education*–III
(1949), p. 183: "That non-differentiation of the two aspects should continue up to a certain
point is expectable, since culture by definition includes, or at least presupposes, society. As
something shared and supra-individual, culture can exist only when society exists; and conversely
every human society is accompanied by a culture. This converse, to be sure, is not complete: it
applies only to *human* societies. In principle, however, the limitation is extremely important. The
existence of cultureless or essentially cultureless sub-human societies, especially the highly
elaborate ones of the social insects, serves as an irrefutable touchstone for the significant discrimination of the concepts of the social and the cultural: they *can* exist separately. At any rate,
one of them does exist separately."

stance and materials to which they were applied, but about the group. The categories of explanation and interpretation of the regularities or dynamic interrelations of cultural forms and significances are found in the sub-cultural social grounds and conditions of those forms. As Kroeber puts it, "cultural constants", like family, religion, war and communication, appear to be bio-psychological frames variably filled with cultural content, and "custom is a psycho-biological habit on a social scale carrying cultural values".[1] The cultural content is not determined by the container, nor again is it determined by abstractly conceived standards of survival value, utility, or moral good. Social life depends on "conventional understandings"[2] which in turn depend on criteria later uncovered in critical inquiry. The ideas which influence social and cultural relations do not first come into existence, or begin to operate, at the moment when they are given abstract expression. On the contrary, abstract expressions of such ideas may be viewed as the results of analysis of the concrete experiences which the ideas rendered possible in the group, and intelligent interest in the social expectations of conventional morality may in this manner yield either the philosopher's principles of ethical judgment or the anthropologist's description of national character, depending on whether the ideas are related to the motivations of persons or to the internal pressures of groups.

Cultures are dependent on man's capacity for conceptual thought and articulate speech. Primitive cultures no less than technologically advanced civilizations are compendent bodies of beliefs and interrelated devices for the communication of meanings adapted to the ends of the society or derived from traditions which were once adapted, or seemed to be adapted, to those ends. They are tested, when questions or conflicts arise, by the consequences to which they have been related and for which they should account, against rival meanings and beliefs suggested by the internal movements and the external contacts of the culture.

II

The development of internal tensions and the danger of external aggression in a society lead to the differentiation of

1 Kroeber, op. cit., p. 186.
2 Kluckhohn and Kelley, op. cit., p. 103.

political institutions and political authority from other forms of social structure and other forms of social sanction. The characteristics of cultures may therefore be discerned and studied, in the second place, in the political aspects of human association and co-operation. The political aspects of culture are those pertinent to the regulation of common life by the control of the material and indirect consequences of personal or group transactions. They are found in the external actions that can be controlled by law and in the motives by which adherence to the law may be induced; they are marked by the establishment of clearly defined agencies of enforcement and by an effort to achieve clear communication and definite attachment to principles of regularity. The distinction between the political and the social aspects of cultures is not a separation of entities, but a differentiation of traits in the complex of human associations according to modes of associations which evolve in the development of society and co-exist in the more advanced forms of national States. Law cannot be separated sharply from custom in primitive societies, and even in the modern State the public is not easily differentiated from the numerous forms of private association. Yet the signs of the emergence of the public, or of the need for it, are unambiguous; in the social examination of the conduct of a group, including its political institutions, actions and decision are related to the characteristic "way of life" of the group and to the problems which that way of life solves or raises; in the political examination of the conduct of a group, including the behaviour of individuals and private groups, actions and decisions are related to their consequences which are judged according to a certain definition of the "common good".

The differentiation of functions, characteristic of these two aspects of cultures, appears even in the analyses of philosophers who do not depend on distinguishing "society", "cultures", and "state", and who depart from widely different data and assumptions. John Dewey distinguishes the state from other forms of social organization by the consequences which flow from it and by the instruments of control which it employs. All forms of association—religious, artistic, scientific, educational, industrial, commercial, recreational, even in such varied manifestations as political parties, trade unions, and pressure groups—produce distinctive consequences. When these consequences are recognized as sound from the intellectual and emotional points of view, a shared interest is generated, which in turn transforms the nature of the interconnected behaviour. The distinction between patterns of co-operative action and forms of shared interest goes beyond the distinction between society and culture, since it is possible to have a human society without that conscious appreciation of shared interests which constitutes a community, while all human societies have a minimum culture. In any complex society, the community and the public emerge at the same time. Since all modes of associated behaviour have extensive and enduring consequences which involve others beyond those participating, the state is necessary as a form of association to regulate those consequences by the actions of public officials. Rules of law are then the institution of conditions under which persons make their arrangements with one another, and the problem of the public is fundamentally a problem of communication.[1]

Similar distinctions enter a totally different philosophic context and structure when Plato analyses the formation of the state in three stages:[2] first, the association of artisans, husbandmen, and tradesmen, determined by the division of labour in order to provide a minimum standard of life, in which justice and injustice are found in the relations of citizens with one another; second, the luxurious state enlarged to provide the amenities of life, which leads as a consequence of this enlargement to wars and to almost all the other evils, private as well as public, found in states;[3] and, third, the further enlargement to provide guardians, still according to the principle of the division of labour, for the defence of possessions against external invaders and of values against internal dangers. Plato's construction, like Dewey's analysis, finds the state first in the functions of officials in the control of external actions, and encounters problems of meaning, communication, and value in the examination of the consequences of those actions. In the perfect state, which Plato was convinced never existed and never will exist, the wisdom of the philosopher-king would provide an answer to these problems, based on true principles and sound demonstration; but in actual states they

---

[1] John Dewey, *The Public and Its Problems*, New York, 1927, pp. 15–16, 69–74, 96–98, 151–59.
[2] *Republic*, II, 469 B ff.
[3] ibid., 373 D.

must be met by two related devices, the provision in the promulgation of law of adequate power for its enforcement combined with persuasion in the prelude to the law suited to win approval for the law by the citizen.[1] Cicero establishes the same distinctions, but he begins with the importance of speech and communication in the development of society, culture, and the state. Speech and articulate thought differentiate men from brutes, and the enquiry after truth leads not only to knowledge and the arts but to the virtues and the associations of men in society and the state. The eloquence cultivated by the orator is merely the art of using this faculty of communication among men and of reproduction of thought in words. But the highest achievement of eloquence is to have gathered "scattered humanity in one place", to have led mankind "out of its brutish and rude existence to our present condition of culture as men and as citizens (*ad hunc humanum cultum civilemque deducere*)", and to have given shape, "after the establishment of states, to laws, tribunals and civic rights".[2]

"Society" and the "state" serve to isolate aspects of cultures which are closely related in their factual bases but distinct in their functional operations. A society is a structure of behaviour and functions of men associated in action and in life; a state is a structure of officers and laws established to maintain conditions necessary for communication and the existence of a community by the control of consequences of actions. A culture is a structure of customs and beliefs uniting men in societies and determining, both within societies and in the relations of societies to each other, attitudes and expectations which require for their harmonious adjustment the controls of the state. The social aspects of cultures are the material traces of ideas and ideals in the habits and associations of men; the political aspects of cultures are the instrumental uses of ideas and ideals in order to establish, preserve, or transform the human community. Political organization depends on instrumentalities to control the actions of individuals and groups rendered effective by common habits or recognition of common interests. Despite recurrent efforts in the political history of states to control the attitudes, intentions, and beliefs of men, the effective operation of political institutions is

---

1 Laws, IV, 722 A–723 D; X, 886 E–887 D.
2 Cicero, *De Oratore*, I. 8. 33.

limited to sanctioning by rewards or penalties their overt actions with respect to their external consequences on others.

The differentiation of the political from the social aspects of cultures, consequently, has important bearings both on theory and on practice. In theory the broadened scope of world political problems has given a new relevance and practical importance to the subordination to the state of all other forms of association and of all cultural values, principles affirmed in philosophies as diverse as those of Plato and Hegel. In practice not only has the control of all actions, including thought and expression, been undertaken in states as different in their ideologies and social structures as Nazi Germany and the Communist Soviet Union, but also the opposition of the Western democracies to communism (or, according to the communists, economic interest) causes them in turn to make efforts to control thought, expression, and the right of association. When, in the amenities of international political discussions, criticisms of the totalitarian methods of the "police state" are set against criticisms of the insidious aggression of "economic and cultural imperialism" the clash arises because in formulating political problems each has a different method of reducing the cultural relations of peoples to economic terms.

Society and the state—the law of opinion and positive law— are closely related to each other, and each exercises a crucial influence in determining the other. The state and positive law are adjusted to social circumstances and to the current opinions which interpret them. Both the state and the social circumstances may be modified, despite the conservative character of law and custom—positive law and the constitution of the state by legal enactment, by judicial interpretation, or by violent revolution; the law of opinion by internal change within the society or by external influence—and changes in the one may cause changes in the other. Political action to carry out or resist such changes encounters, on the one hand, those social aspects of culture which determine the necessities within which political operations work and the attitudes which motivate them and, on the other hand, those humanistic aspects of culture which guide the decision concerning alternative possible courses of action.

17

In its minimum form this third aspect of cultures is found in the moral dimension in the regulation and communication which are essential to any political community. Recognition of the reciprocal character of communication and regulation in a genuine community—that is, communication in which there is exchange and mutual influence, and regulation in which citizens rule and are ruled—is as old as Aristotle's definition of the state in terms of the functions of citizens which, he points out, is adapted best to democracy,[1] and as new as Dewey's argument that the idea of democracy is identical with the ideal of community life.[2] The moral distinction appears in the very terms applied to the instruments of political control; the distinction between education and indoctrination, information and propaganda, police regulation and totalitarian control depends on moral judgments which cannot be reduced to differences of opinion and mores or of techniques and attitudes. Moral interests, artistic preferences, and doctrinal convictions are implicit in cultures. They depend for their material and for their exercise on the recognized forms and rules of conduct of a society and a state. Just as the laws of opinion presuppose a social fabric supported by positive laws, so in turn the patterns of social life and the controls of political agencies are embodiments of, and instrumentalities for, ideals which are expressed, explained, and justified in arts, sciences, philosophies, and religions. Morality, taste, and opinion have their bases in society, their material support and use in the state; but their expression constitutes the humanistic aspects of cultures, and their theory and justification are sought in ethics, æsthetics, and science.

The humanistic aspects of cultures found in arts and sciences and other expressions of values undergo in the operations of the state and in the problems of the statesman a transformation similar to that which characterized the shift from the social to the political aspects of cultures. As the complex of relations which constitutes the social aspects of cultures tends

---

[1] Aristotle, *Politics*, III. 1. 1275 b, 5–7, 17–21.

[2] Dewey, *The Public and Its Problems*, p. 146: "Nevertheless the current has set steadily in one direction: toward democratic forms. That government exists to serve its community, and that this purpose cannot be achieved unless the community itself shares in selecting its governors and determining their politics, are a deposit of fact left, as far as we can see, permanently in the wake of doctrines and forms, however transitory the latter. They are not the whole of the democratic idea, but they express it in its political phase." Cf. p. 148: "Regarded as an idea, democracy is not an alternative to other principles of associated life. It is the idea of community life itself."

to be translated into external material aspects of actions and organized expressions of attitudes available for purposes of political control, so too the complex of values pursued in arts, religions, and sciences tends to be translated into the moral judgments which underlie public policy in the political ordering of the life of a community. Religious observation, scientific explanation, and aesthetic expression are, like political structure and regulations, indistinguishable parts of social forms in primitive societies,and their separation may be traced as an evolutionary process in which the first emergence of religion, art, and science coincided with the appearance of a class freed from the necessities of life and from the mechanical arts to devote its leisure to non-utilitarian pursuits. One of the basic political problems in advanced societies is to bring the value judgments implicit in these humanistic aspects of culture to bear on the solution of problems of political community, and the relation of ethical, aesthetic, and scientific judgments to each other and to political action is a problem in all philosophies whether they distinguish, relate, or identify theory and practice. . . .

The marks of these differences in the aspects of cultures are apparent even in philosophies which do not separate "society", "state" and the "humanities". Statements of the differences frequently take one of two exaggerated forms—the attempt to treat humanistic values apart from consideration of political or social aspects of culture, or the attempt to reduce all aspects of culture to one by explaining them in terms of society, or the state, or the conclusions of some science, or religion, or philosophy. But the aspects of cultures are also recognized and distinguished by means of historical or dialectical devices which stress their interpenetrations rather than their parallelisms and distinctive contributions to the common life. Burke, thus, uses "society" and "state" as equivalent terms and conceives them as "contracts" rather than "associations", but his conception of the state depends on a contrast he establishes between humanistic and material aspects of culture. "Society is indeed a contract. Subordinate contracts for objects of mere occasional interest may be dissolved at pleasure; but the state ought not to be considered nothing better than a partnership agreement in a trade of pepper and coffee, calico or tobacco, or some other low concern, to be taken up for a little temporary interest, and to be dissolved by the fancy of the parties. It is to be looked on with other reverence; because it is not a partnership in things subservient only to the gross animal existence of a temporary and perishable nature. It is a partnership in all science; a partnership in all art; a partnership in every virtue and in all perfection". Hegel, on the other hand, differentiates civil society from the state, but the state is absolutely rational, the actuality of the ethical idea, and the true ground of society and all human association. "Since the state appears as a result of the advance of the philosophic concept through displaying itself as the true ground (of the earlier phases) that show of mediation is now cancelled, and the state has become directly present before us. Actually, therefore, the state as such is not so much the result as the beginning. It is within the state that the family is first developed into civil society, and it is the idea of the state itself which disrupts itself into these two moments".[1] Not only are the patterns of social relations and of the tenure and use of property based on the state, but also freedom of thought and science have their origin in the state.[2]

The humanistic aspects of cultures are expressions of values and ideals found in man's effort to understand his environment and himself, to determine his career among the forces of nature and with the co-operation of men, to control nature and his own actions and expressions and adapt them to the values and ends which he discovers. The social, economic, political, and cultural situation influences thought and expression, but the influence is universal and does not serve to differentiate magic from science, superstition from religion, or skill from art. Statesmen, demagogues, and politicians arise from the same social conditions, and with the shift of political circumstances and the exchange of compliments in political debate the titles are exchanged indiscriminately. Common problems are treated, common terms are used, and common ideals are evoked or condemned by the spiritual leaders, the obscurantists, and the sectarians of an age, and by the philosophers, the scholastics, and the sophists. Scientists, tinkerers, and charlatans, like artists, dabblers, and hacks, are distinguished from each other by the contribution which the individual worker

1 Hegel, *Philosophy of Right*, trans. by T. M. Knox, Oxford, 1942, par. 256, p. 155.
2 ibid., par. 270, p. 172.

makes in each case in his treatment of common materials, common problems, and common forms. These humanistic aspects are so conspicuous in great original work in all fields that it is easy to ignore the social and cultural influences that conditioned the work of an artist who first uses a form which departs from earlier modes of expression, or of a thinker who first formulates a problem and resolves it in a way which reveals the errors or insufficiencies of earlier approaches to the problem. None the less, the artist and the thinker draw on the materials prepared in previous formulations, on the interest centred on the problems they treat, and on contemporary effort, awareness, need, and appreciation. The preparation of the scene for the individual effort is, indeed, so important that innovations, inventions, and discoveries are often made simultaneously by several men, and great original departures usually become the common property and characteristic of the age succeeding that of their discovery.

The recognition of special "climates of opinion" character-istic of certain times and places and the search for the "spirit" of an age and the "character" of a culture in the common concepts, symbols, and attitudes revealed in the social aspects of cultures should not, however, obscure the contemporary differences of meanings expressed by philosophers in those symbols, the varieties of presentations evolved by artists, the fruitful divergences of scientists by which they develop the implications of previous stages of enquiry, or even the oppo-sitions of historians and sociologists interpreting the spirit and evolution of previous ages. The contribution of the artist, the philosopher, and the scientists to communication between social groups, national states, and cultures and to the establish-ment of more inclusive communities is not found in the com-mon symbols they employ or the common materials they treat but in the uses they make of them. Art is intelligible across cultural and national boundaries, but the effectiveness of artists in communication must be found in the aesthetic quali-ties of their works rather than in the attitudes and prejudices of particular audiences to which propagandists appeal or in the dominant tastes and sentiments of groups or classes on which hacks depend. The influence of science, philosophy, and religion is not limited to the common symbols which bind to-gether the men who use them, but derives its vitality from the significances imparted to those symbols by the insights of individual men.

The form or content of great expressions of art, science, or philosophy may profoundly alter the society, the culture, and the nation. The artists and thinkers of the Renaissance, thus, built a contemporary culture by reinterpreting the cultures of Greek and Roman antiquity. The readiness of the times and the availability of the materials conditioned, but did not determine, the creative expression. Shakespeare's rendering of the past departs often from the historical facts, and it would be difficult to determine how accurately he expressed the attitudes and aspirations of his contemporaries, since his writings constitute an important part of the evidence and since he contributed to forming the national character of his countrymen by writing lines in which they later expressed or exemplified their ideas and ideals. The use of Homer by Greek philosophers and critics is indication of the influence of the poet on the national character, conduct, and spirit, and the Romans felt the need of a native *Iliad* even before the *Aenead* was produced to be adapted to their cultural and educational needs and uses, and to afford guidance to future Dantes in their exploration of new cultural regions.

The humanistic aspects of cultures may be distinguished from the social aspects only by critical judgment and evaluation. If the effects of communication are sought in the behaviour of men and in their associations, no sharp line separates one form of communication from another. Verifiable truth and artistic form are not necessary when the purpose is to achieve wide and forceful effects. The methods used by primitive man to control the forces that surrounded him are broadly similar to the scientific method; art originated in religious observances and in practical functions; and philosophy grew from speculation on values and objectives embodied in cultures; yet, in the process, the advantages of science over taboo, the characteristics of artistic expression, and the critical evaluation of standards of action became apparent in spite of the difficulties men encountered in formulating principles and criteria or agreeing on any one formulation. Human values depend on the intrinsic qualities for which they are valuable and on the extrinsic circumstances which make them available and accessible to appreciation. Differences in preferences are due to differences in circumstances which make all values relative, but that relativity in turn is discovered by recourse to ethical, aesthetic, and scientific methods and criteria which go beyond mere considerations of circumstance and serve to guide action and mould social forms. The paradox of cultures is in the fact that values are relative to cultures and that cultures progress in their pursuit of values: intelligent action, individual or social, depends on the discernment of values and their translation into policies of action.

III

The three aspects of cultures—social, political, and humanistic —though distinguishable, are inseparably interconnected. The adjustments of human beings to conditions and problems are not determined by their biological adaptation alone, and the individual characteristics of men result from their nurture, training, and education in the groups in which they partici- pate. Individual men are consequently characterized by their habits, and these include all socially acquired responses to stimuli—political attitudes, virtues, skills, and knowledge, as well as personal character traits. But since conditions affect habits by inducing activities which modify, inhibit, or strengthen prior habits, and since habits affect conditions by the actions to which they lead, force and justice are needed to control the consequences of actions and the formation of habits. To understand and to judge social relations and political actions in their relation to the choice of means to the good life, is to make explicit and to judge criteria which determine fact, action, and purpose. Man is a social animal, adapting himself to a natural and human environment by forming habits; he is a political animal, ruling and being ruled; he is a human animal, creating and appreciating values.

The movements of cultures reflect both an attachment to the particular sources of the values of a culture and a striving for the realization of those values in universal and communi- cable forms. As structures of communication and action, the patterns of cultures depend on establishing modes of action on bases of habitual behaviour, and modes of thought on bases of traditional belief. The survival of the group depends on adherence to the structure of beliefs that constitute it a group: cultures are therefore both conservative in their resistance to change and exclusive of each other in their tendency to diversity and multiplicity. Yet communication and action are sensitive to alteration within the group and without, and the mechanisms by which the group is preserved make it readily susceptible to change. The conservative character of custom, which contributes to the preservation of the group, is a source of danger when the mode of behaviour has lost its adaptive value; the variable character of custom, which contributes to the adjustment of the group, is a source of danger when the acquisition of novel modes of behaviour impedes pursuit of common values which unite the group.

This pull between the particular and the universal poles of culture, and the tumbling sequence in which problems are considered under their social, political, and humanistic aspects and in which they influence each other reciprocally and are successively dominant as causes, are illustrated in the histories of all nations which have achieved high civilizations and wide contacts with other nations.

The social aspects of cultures are based on a division of labour and functions which tends, as it becomes more efficient in the production of goods, to divide the society into conflicting parts and to set its members to the pursuit of ends destructive of the purposes and amenities to which the society was earlier directed. The division of functions and the exchange of products instituted to secure common interests more effectively become the basis for a separation of economic classes whose members recognize common interests and common opponents. Values are sought by group action in opposition to other groups and classes, and value is attached to membership in respective groups. The possibility of pursuing values beyond the limited objectives of bare subsistence afforded by the establishment of media of exchange endangers the ability of some members of society to secure bare subsistence, while it permits the unlimited accumulation of material goods by other. The traditional customs and beliefs which are the bond of society come into conflict with the more refined beliefs of subtler and more sceptical minds and, as beliefs become better and more accurately adjusted to the nature of things by their increase in scientific precision, they are more easily perverted or removed from their social functions in relation to human activities.

These oppositions and movements have been accentuated by the advance of technology and the growth of industrial society, but they were recognized as fundamental forces in the earliest speculations on social problems. Plato and Aristotle both treated the problems of practical politics in terms of the oppositions and adjustments of the "rich" and the "poor" and of the mediating devices that could be found to regulate such oppositions in view of common interests; both looked upon money, property, and the arts of acquisition as devices for the achievement of the common good, which are in themselves "infinite" or "undefined" unless limited by political control and moral insight; both looked for solutions to science and to values which might regulate a more equitable distribution of material goods and set limits on their accumulation, but they recognized that the regulation of property and of passions depends on putting them in the perspective of the goods which, unlike material goods, are enhanced rather than lessened by being shared and are increased rather than divided by competition. Progress in science, technology, and industry has, owing to the opposition of their respective interests, sharpened the division between proletariat and entrepreneur, between labour and management; it has infinitely increased the possibility of accumulating wealth and economic power without making the increased production of goods more easily available to relieve penury, famine, disease, and insecurity; it has made more difficult and unwieldy the intelligent application of scientific methods, which provided new material resources and opportunities, to the solution of moral and religious problems, and it has shaped the common forms of life in patterns not easily influenced by spiritual, ethical, and aesthetic values.

In its political aspects justice in operation is the order in which the citizens are unified in a state by the pursuit of common interests, and the end of the state, as St. Augustine pointed out, is not justice in any transcendental sense, but the preservation of the state. To achieve even that end, however, the constitution and the laws must be effective as instruments of common interests and as embodiments of a justice which reflects the conditions, potentialities, and aspirations of the citizens and subjects of the state. When the political constitution ceases to be adjusted to the social circumstances which it was designed to control, violent or gradual revolutions alter the constitution or change the groups who exercise power under it.

Political actions operate between two extremes: the necessary conditions by which they are determined—the characters of peoples, their circumstances and their resources, the stage of their arts and sciences, their tensions and ambitions; and the ways of life to which they are devoted and the ideals which they seek. But the ideals are assimilated to the character of each nation, and movements which split established political structures assimilate to themselves other universal ideals. Traditional forms of nationalism depended on the claim that a particular universal ideal was the particular possession of a people inhabiting a particular area. The ancient Jews regarded themselves as the chosen people and the custodians of the true religion. The Greeks differentiated themselves from the barbarians by the possession of freedom and a cultivated life of art and thought, and the Romans were law-givers who extended universal peace to the peoples of the world. The English have in modern times been proponents of Protestantism and of parliamentary practices and institutions; the French, since the Revolution, have been the promulgators of democratic freedoms, the rights of men, and intellectual enlightenment; the Americans have appeared as the defenders of the common man and common sense and have exemplified technological skill and industrial organization; the Russians have assumed the role of partisans of the equality of men and the solidarity of the workers of the world against exploitation and oppression. The claims presented by those who suffer from want and need, racial discrimination, and imperial domination, have led to new delusive attributions—to one race, one economic class, one economic system, one party, one creed—of universal values by which to organize the world more justly.

The particular circumstances and universal ideals embodied in the constitutions of states, no less than those of groups and parties in revolt are means simultaneously to unify and to divide. The revolutions of our times are motivated by efforts to secure political self-determination, economic security, and human equality. The new nationalism differs from the traditional nationalism which developed with the spread of industrialism, since the new nationalism is an expression of the responsive demand for industrialization in regions where it has not yet taken root. The forms in which this nationalism expresses itself range from the exercise of the newly acquired independence of the Philippines, India, Pakistan, Indonesia and Burma, and the aspirations to self-government of colonial peoples like those of Ceylon, Nepal, and Indo-China, to the establishment of Israel as the homeland of a people, to the jealously guarded cultural autonomy and sealed borders which are instruments of economic and political change in the Balkan states, to the efforts of nations long established to solve their economic and social problems. In the political context, cultural problems are translated still into terms of property and the external consequences of actions on security, possessions, and honour. The necessary conditions within which political action operates and the ideals to which it is directed are both stated in terms of the distribution of goods: the necessary conditions are set by needs and resources and the choice of actions for the resolution of needs is thrown into stultifying confusion by the ideological conflict which affects the discussion of facts, actions, and the very theories involved in analysing the conflict. Ideals and purposes are economically determined in that conflict according to both extremes of theory, for it is held at one extreme that the conflict will be stopped only by the elimination of exploiter classes and at the other extreme that it will be resolved only by the elimination of those who oppose free enterprise and individual rights.

IV

The humanistic aspects of cultures are based on the arts, the sciences, the philosophies, and the religions which express values and seek knowledge and control of man's destiny. Arts and sciences, ideas and ideals, have their roots in social situations and are affected by political institutions and regulations; they are in turn powerful instruments in moulding the social situation and in altering political structures and the operation of laws. But progress in knowledge, in artistic expression, and in spiritual insight depends on a double movement: first, science is separated from magic, fine arts from mechanical and banausic, religion from superstition, since they are subject to improvement and refinement, and those who practise the more advanced forms of each, as well as those who appreciate them, are separated in their preferences and their understandings from other groups in society; then, since science, art and religion have an effect on life, reformers and practical men try to make religion effective as motivating beliefs in the practices of men, to restore to fine arts an influence equal to that of mechanical arts in men's lives, and to rejoin theory and practice. Science, art and religion as modes of communication, acquire breadth, power, and precision in the development of common symbols relative to common ideals and common subjects, but in the process they become inaccessible to those who do not share those symbols, and the organized efforts of groups or governments to bring them to bear on the attitudes, understanding, and emotions of larger groups run the risk of reducing them to the level of propaganda. Although they have profound influences in the creation and solution of political problems, nations which, like the Soviet Union, undertake to control them and in so doing recognize their importance, inhibit the possibility of their achieving their distinctive values; whereas, nations which, like the United States, provide the possibility for their free development, have not found means by which to take serious account of their possible social applications and consequences. The manipulation and control of scientific, aesthetic, and spiritual values and the separation of those values from social and political problems have equally stultifying effects, for the one makes them socially pertinent but sterile, while the other fosters their development in directions removed from all effective relevance.

The division of mankind into groups in the pursuit of ideas and values, like the divisions of men according to social function and political power, may be the cause of tension or of progress. Differences and even conflicts in ideas and values have contributed to the advancement of knowledge, art and society; and they have in turn been affected by the divisions of men. But the basis of universality and particularity in the communication of ideas is different than in the exchange of goods. Science consists in the formulation and solution of problems, and its universality consists in a uniformity of communication in which results are susceptible of independent test; it is particularized by reference, not to subject matter, but to rival groups, schools, or nations. The universality of religion is found in values experienced by men and shared by the great religions of the world; it is particularized by reference to rival groups, creeds, or nations. Great art is universally intelligible and is enclosed in particularity only by the mannerisms and exclusiveness of groups, styles, and nations. All these forms of value differ from material goods, since the possession of property, whether held in common or privately, is exclusive, and the consumption of goods destroys them; whereas art, science, and religion are not restricted in the number of possible possessors, are not destroyed by use, and their appreciation and enjoyment are enhanced by sharing. Yet they can be reduced to objects of ownership, causes of division, and instruments of power rivalry. Their universality is preserved against such appropriation to groups by the standards which are discovered in ethical, aesthetic, spiritual and scientific judgments, and which are tested in the philosophical scrutiny of the principles and methods of such judgments. Value judgments are not determined by the practices of current morality, the preferences of actual taste, the dogmas of prevailing creeds, or the consensus of men in general or of experts in particular concerning the nature of things. Not only do great accomplishments in arts, science, and philosophy transcend and transform current judgments of value, but they affect attitudes toward economic circumstances and material goods. The ascetic ideals or religious communities have lessened the domination of other values in the group and have introduced new cultural forms; and the programme of Gandhi, by freeing his followers from fear of loss of property and even of life, prepared a political revolution designed to secure for India not only self-government but economic advancement. Conversely, the discipline of parties—fascist, nazi, or communist—can impose standards by force and transform economic relations, political institutions and cultural values by fear. The great problem of democracy, within nations and between nations, is to form policies based on ethical, aesthetic, and scientific judgments and to secure co-operation in them, by agreement rather than by force, in the solution of economic, social, and political problems.

The new problems in the relations of cultures may be stated in their bearing on all three aspects of cultures. The division of labour and functions in the production of goods and in common life leads to the separation and antagonism of groups, classes, races, and nations, unless it is accompanied by co-operation and mutual respect born of understanding of social interdependences and values. The distribution of power and prestige in political organization leads to the reduction of justice to what can be secured by power, unless there are standards of justice by which to guide the exercise of power and the distribution of goods and functions. Finally it is the cultivation of the values of art, science, and philosophy which contributes standards essential to the solution of social, economic, and political problems.

<h1 style="text-align:center">V</h1>

Communication between cultures and the establishment of world community and world understanding depends on the creation of values which are not peculiar to any existing culture, and on the preservation of values which are the forms assumed by common values in particular cultures. Yet the relations of cultures has become a problem of the relations of nations and—within nations and across national lines—of classes, races, churches, and parties. In both forms, national and international, the political problem assumes primacy since cultural relations uncover differences and oppositions of economic and social needs and involve the clashes of interests and powers. The source of differences is found, however, not in the needs which are widely recognized, or in the resources and knowledge which are available, but in the opposing ideologies, political forms, and economic systems adopted to consider means to remedy the situation. This problem of analysis of problems and of communication concerning actions has been little considered. There has arisen, consequently, a widespread sense of an unreal separation of fact from value, and of knowledge of fact from knowledge of value, which is criticized as anti-intellectual and anti-rational and for which remedies are sought by "realistic" and "practical" assertions that values are facts and are found among facts.

The suspicion of argument in all forms, especially argument based on abstract concepts, which is a characteristic of our times, and the effort to relate it to particular situations assume their most paradoxical form in the political discussions and actions. The flight from generalized argument leads philosophers to substitute for the principles of proof the concrete phenomenology of thought, or the specific difficulties and adjustments of experience, or the dialectical oppositions of nature, or the arbitrary determinations of symbols. In politics, and in the legal and moral disciplines related to political action, the distrust of proof takes two complementary forms: the discrediting of arguments to permit recourse to facts and the manipulation of facts to establish the cogency of arguments.

The suspicion of arguments has reached its heights in jurisprudence, where the historically effective use of argument has been questioned because the applications of rules of law evolve in successive interpretations and because the reasons alleged by judges as grounds for their decisions do not express the processes of thought which led them to their conclusions. In political philosophy, in general, an escape from the complexities of argument is sought in the hope that scientifically verified facts or established principles from some region of scientific enquiry will remove the ambiguities and uncertainties of social and political discussions. But political experience proves that hope illusory, in view of the vulnerability of scientific pursuits to social and political influence and interference. Even if the scientists of the Soviet Union and the West are in some sense in agreement concerning the scientific principles and facts of physics and biology (if not of psychology and anthropology) despite differences concerning dialectical materialism and naturalistic empiricism, that agreement does not supply criteria by which to bring them to agreement concerning the respective virtues of common or private possession of the means of production. The complementary forms of these devices to avoid the deceptions of argument are even more sinister, for inasmuch as arguments are conditioned by the convictions of the thinker, the silencing or elimination of the class or the party committed to erroneous arguments is an effective substitute for refutation, as a means of bringing attitudes and actions into more precise relation and contact with facts.

In this argument about arguments, which arises at all levels of political problems, both parties profess attachment to moral ends, an attachment which each thinks to be lacking in the other; and both find proper employment for the scientific

31

method, which each argues is neglected or misused in the other.

VI

Contemporary philosophic discussion exhibits awareness of the different aspects and influences of cultures in a variety of ways. The predominant emphasis on experience in the philosophic schools of the West is a symptom of a common effort to discover the problems and subject matter of philosophy in the cultural milieu. Philosophic terminology, methodology, and subject matter have been broadened by borrowings from the sciences, arts, history, and practical experience. In the West this broadening has taken two forms: (a) an effort, in philosophies like pragmatism and logical positivism, to refine by direct philosophic analysis the methods, devices, and terms of science, art, or practice, and (b) an effort, in philosophies like phenomenology, existentialism, and dialectical materialism, to employ common techniques and distinctions in sciences, arts, theories to practice, and philosophic discussions. Such efforts encounter two sorts of difficulties arising, respectively, in relation to the new techniques and subject matters and in relation to efforts of other philosophies to accomplish similar tasks. The refinements in the symbolism of mathematics attempted by philosophers and their statement of scientific, artistic, and political problems have not been conspicuously useful to workers in those fields, nor have the phenomenological or dialectical explorations of the intentionalities of mind or the contrarieties of nature yielded greater literal precision than the literary, scientific, or practical expressions of like ideas—or indeed much difference in formulation. Philosophers in the East—in Islam, India, and China—have had more opportunity to meditate on the relations of philosophic trends, to discover basic similarities in the fundamental principles of Eastern and Western philosophy, and to recognize the cultural changes consequent on the introduction of science and technology in the East, even to the nicety of detecting existentialist trends in Arabic philosophy and pragmatic strands in Chinese thought. These differences among philosophers employing and explaining science, art, and the practical, coupled with their reluctance to find sound scientific bases or practical application in the doctrines of other schools than their own, constitutes the second problem, that of achieving communication in the confused and contradictory movements which constitute now, as in the past, the external aspect of philosophic discussions. The confusion of present-day problems, in so far as it is ideological, is a reflection of that philosophic confusion, and it would seem probable, were it not for the reorientation afforded by the juxtapositions of cultures and of philosophies, that disputes would be heightened rather than moderated by making the basic differences explicit.

The common and related derivation of the philosophies of the regions of the world and the particular forms which they take in different regions and ages suggest a first series of questions. The philosophies of the West derive from a common and continuous tradition in which the influence of Greece and Rome has been a constant but variable element, and the conditions and problems of successive periods have determined the form and development of the oppositions and sequences of schools. For one long period—during the Abbasid dynasty—Islam was the custodian of this tradition, and some of the basic ideas of Greek thought penetrated to India with the spread of Mohammedanism. Conversely, the influence of Hindu and Chinese ideas on Western thought during the nineteenth and twentieth centuries has been greater than would seem probable from the slight contacts of philosophers of East and West. Viewed in terms of their historical derivation the philosophies of the nations of the world today are characterized primarily by two facts: (a) they have been formed under the influence of different historical periods while at the same time they derive in general from a common heritage, and (b) philosophies derived from the same philosophic tendency assume different forms in different cultures. The dislocation of chronological sequence and the difference of cultural influence is strikingly illustrated in the philosophic trends in the United States and in Latin America. The beginnings of philosophy were derived in both regions from European philosophy, but the influences dominant in the one region in any period were seldom conspicuous in the other, and the uses which philosophy found in the cultural development of the two regions were different.

Consciousness of a distinctive approach to philosophy emerged in the United States during the twentieth century in

33

the reactions to the widely prevalent "idealism" of academic philosophers, and took a variety of forms in pragmatism, realism, and naturalism. More recently, and as a consequence of the development of these characteristic philosophic attitudes, a new interest in the history of North American philosophy has grown with the recognition that earlier movements in the United States are not explained simply by the European influences from which they originated. Even in their early and simple forms philosophic doctrines reflected and influenced the social and the political as well as the humanistic aspects of North American culture. The doctrines of seventeenth- and eighteenth-century English and French philosophers entered into the framing of the Constitution and into the development of churches and theological doctrines, and their influence in determining political organization and religious life was more direct than in Europe. The opposition was not between long established interests or widely separated classes, and the open frontier provided the constant possibility of socially approved or even politically institutionalized continuations of dissentient opinions. The experimentalism and individualism which have come to characterize American philosophic tendencies were developed under the influence of conditions which permitted differences to continue and to be tested by experience of consequences implicit in the European conceptions from which these philosophic tendencies derived.

Latin American philosophy is likewise derived from European sources and adapted to broadly comparable conditions. The fundamental Spanish and Portuguese culture, however, was not characterized by strong or original philosophic movements after the sixteenth century, and the use which was made of eighteenth- and nineteenth-century philosophies in Latin America was in revolt against scholasticism and colonialism. Destutt de Tracy and the French *ideologues* had a profound influence on Jefferson, and their ideas entered easily into the amalgam of reasons and justifications for North American political institutions and attitudes of mind; but they had a specific influence in providing an intellectual vocabulary for the reorientation of man to his environment and to human associations in Latin America. The positivism of Comte had little lasting effect in North America, whereas it was an instrument of communication, education, and revolt in Latin

34

America. The philosophies of Vasconcelos and Caso are part of the Mexican liberation; while the philosophies of James and Dewey are part of a revolt against idealism based on science and a long tradition of political independence.

Communication between Latin American and North American philosophers is complicated by the fact that historical circumstances have led them to use different aspects of a common tradition and to use what they borrowed differently.

The differences uncovered in even an off-hand exploration of the present position of philosophies influenced by a common tradition suggests a second series of questions. If there is such diversity and controversy within each tradition and such lack of adjustment and communication between traditions, where is that element of universality to be found among philosophies which each philosophy claims not only for its systematic explanations but also for its cultural consequences? The answers to questions in that form are one more illustration of the pull and interplay between particularity and universality in cultural phenomena. The relation between the unifying and divisive influences of philosophy becomes intelligible when one examines how a culture may be homogeneous and have nevertheless a philosophy which is expressed in the oppositions of cultural tendencies and philosophic schools. A culture is unified by a philosophy without prejudice to the philosophic differences which lead to continual exploration of different approaches to the facts and problems of the culture.

Underlying the diversity of forms taken by recent revolts against idealism and absolutism there is a basic identity of significance which is expressed in a vast variety of ways and in terms of arguments and principles which are otherwise antagonistic. Yet the avowed purposes of present-day philosophies are strikingly similar. They have in common an intention to avoid the abstract and the static, and to base principles and arguments on the concrete in existence and experience. They choose, as subjects of discussion suited to those purposes, "relation", "processes", and "activities" rather than "entities", and they stress interrelations and organic wholes in which arbitrary distinctions or separations must be avoided. Whether or not the philosophies on which contemporary movements have turned their backs were guilty of the errors for which they have been summarily criticized, is proper subject for historical

35

doubt, but the present philosophic dispute concerns the means by which abstraction is to be avoided, and the existential, experiential, and organic reality is to be achieved. Pragmatism and positivism find the concrete in the problems presented in experience and the relations imposed on symbols as a result of the use of the scientific method. Latin American philosophers have turned their attention to the concreteness that can be found in a philosophy of man which avoids extraneous and fictive additions to or distortions of what is human. Phenomenology and existentialism begin with human apperception as a device by which to detect and avoid erroneous constructions and additions, and they differ primarily in the recognition of metaphysical and scientific objectives in some varieties of existentialisms. Dialectical materialism seizes on the concrete in nature, by means of the recognition of the coexistence of contraries and contradictories.

Despite their differences, contemporary philosophies tend to share the common objective of closer adherence to the peculiarities and intricacies of experience and existence, as it has been explored by science and as it impinges on the life of man. This identity of purpose is relevant to the oppositions and exclusivism of philosophic systems, for the nature of philosophic communication is explained by the interplay of the technical elaboration, by which philosophies are developed in their exclusive claims to adequacy and pertinence, and of the common bases of meanings and methods, by which universal significances and values are translated from one set of terms to others. But the same identity of purpose is relevant to the applications of philosophy to cultural life, both because the philosophic aspects of cultures are conditioned by and reflect a like striving in other aspects—social, economic, political—and because those aspects of cultures are influenced and explained by each of the variety of philosophies competing in the culture. The fact was recently observed by a committee of experts analysing data collected by Unesco in an enquiry into the nature of democracy and the ambiguities arising in discussion of it, that no major party or nation professes to be undemocratic today, whereas the political disputes during the period between the two world wars involved an opposition of democratic and anti-democratic theories. This is indication at once of the relation of social changes, consequent on the advance of science and industrialization, to "democracy", and of the diversity of interpretations and significances which extend throughout the lives of men from differences concerning democracy. Resolution of the ideological conflict centering about democracy can come only in one of two ways, by agreement on one interpretation and on one philosophy, or by discovery of common consequences of independent philosophies which permit a commonly conceived democratic way of life. The "dignity of man", the "democratic way of life", "freedoms", and "rights" do not constitute such a philosophy: they are conceptions common to many philosophies and claimed by more, and they become unambiguous points of agreement only when their significances are defined by reference to the principles of the philosophies to which they are appropriated and to the consequences in action and control which follow from them. Agreements on statements and verbal formulations are indispensable parts of agreements about meanings, even when they have consequences in action, and about actions and beliefs, even when their principles have not been asserted.

The similarity of intention and purpose which can be detected in philosophies which have been in contact with each other is a guide to the portions of philosophy which are cultivated most assiduously to achieve such ends. The search for the concrete, the press of practical problems, and the influence attributed to science combine to focus attention on problems of method, of practical action, and of the nature of reality. In those enquiries a thread of universality and underlying agreement even on details of doctrines and devices of method runs through philosophic traditions which have no detectable common roots or direct communication. Hindu analyses of concepts and methods of logic have surprising analogies to treatments of similar problems in the West; the aphoristic moral philosophy of China explores intricacies and profoundities of human motivations and conduct along paths that have also been followed in the Western tradition. The mysticism, the metaphysics, and the wisdom of the East have affinities with the doctrines of sages, prophets, and metaphysicians in the West, although their influence and prestige has grown less conspicuous with the prosecution of the search for the concrete.

A third series of questions arises in connexion with the examination of problems of translation and compatibility among philosophic systems, and particularly concerning the blocks to communication and to the resolution of problems imposed by erroneous or limited conceptions. The nature of the difficulty of passing from one philosophic language, or from one set of philosophic assumptions, to others is illustrated in each of the foci of present-day philosophic interest. Investigation of logical problems has been stimulated by the advances of science and the elaborations of scientific method, but the development of systems of logic leads to very diverse conceptions of scientific method: symbolic logicians have concentrated on the characteristics of symbols and the rules for combining them in languages; pragmatic logicians have postponed the construction of languages in order to enquire into the solution of problems which would determine the significances to be given symbols; phenomenologists seek a basis and structure of scientific concepts in the intentionality of the mind; dialectical materialists claim unique possession of the scientific method in their use of the contrarieties of nature. There is little ground to doubt that "scientific method" is a single procedure which is coherent and unambiguous enough to afford effective guidance to scientists; but scientific problems are tested in varieties of circumstances which require varieties of methodological approaches, and the pursuit of science involves operations of enquirers, symbols of formulae, motions of things, thoughts of minds, and even circumstances of inquiry. Further, any of the varieties of methodological approach or appurtenances of scientific development may be made the point of departure of a study of scientific method. Yet there is little communication between these approaches: even sympathetically inclined symbolic logicians think pragmatic logic misnamed "logic", dialectical materialists who sought to express the relations of contrariety symbolically would doubtless be condemned for formalism, and in general each approach to the scientific method has ready-made reasons for ignoring the others and for confining attention to the numerous differences and disputes within the confines of its orthodoxy.

Moreover, the problem of method is not limited to the differences of logicians, but includes also oppositions of philosophers to the methods of logic, or at least to the exclusive use of the formal methods of logic, for contact with and knowledge of reality and thought. The problems of logic shade therefore into the problems of metaphysics. Even the denial of metaphysics and the equation of philosophy to logic involve assumptions concerning the nature of things and the principles of proof, which constitute a minimal utilization of the science of being and of first principles. The differences in metaphysics reduplicate the differences in logic, for they likewise are of two kinds: (a) the differences between metaphysicians who limit their metaphysics to the principles assumed in their sciences and in their methods, and metaphysicians who separate metaphysics from science; and (b) the differences among the metaphysicians of the logical variety and among the metaphysicians of the ontological variety. The problems of practical action are affected by like differences. There are moralists who seek to apply the methods of science to the problems of human action. There are moralists who seek a basis for the determination of values in the nature of things, or of men, or of their minds, passions, or bodies. There are, finally, moralists who detect a particular method in the formation of moral character and political institutions, which is to be distinguished from the method of the natural sciences no less than from the imaginative insights of the arts, and who find a particular subject of study in the associations of men, which is not reducible to its parts or assimilable to transcendent purposes.

Differences of philosophic attitude and difficulties of communication and understanding arise from the nature of philosophic enquiry. Differences in principle and terminology are the sources, sometimes of fruitful stimulation in enquiry, sometimes of blank unperceptive controversies. Identities in purpose and principle are the causes, sometimes of co-operative extensions of meanings, sometimes of blank reductions to neutral common meanings or distortions to single poles of possible meanings. In their influence on cultures, philosophic distinctions—even those of logic and metaphysics, æsthetics and epistemology—are transmuted into moral and political forms, which are manifested in actions of men and in control of their material circumstances. In that form, the interrelations of different philosophies are considered relative to the possibility of agreement concerning action, rather than relative to the possibility of agreement concerning doctrine. Such agreement is somewhat more than compromise, since it

39

depends on the discovery of modifications of policy which do not abandon essential principles; it is somewhat less than persuasion, since it depends on the justification and formulation of the common action in terms of the divergent principles held by those who agree on the action.

Blocks to communication and particularization of principles to the parties opposed stand in need of investigation by means of two additional related sets of questions. The three sets of questions concerning the historical derivation of philosophic positions, the elements of universality that might join them, and the blocks that might set them in opposition are completed by enquiry into the misconceptions formed of one philosophy or culture from the vantage point of others, and, conversely of the contribution which traits of analysis and doctrine which are conspicuous and highly developed in one philosophy or culture might make to broader understanding and communication. The misconceptions of a philosophy depend on a double movement in which the statements of philosophers are simplified and are then interpreted by appeal to other aspects of the culture, usually also presented in highly simplified terms. Thus it is easy to dispose of American philosophy if it is supposed that American philosophy is pragmatic, and that pragmatism seeks the standards of prudence and science in successful accumulations of material goods. The principles are examined here, not in their explicit formulations nor in their implications, but in the character of the people to whom they are attributed; and the culture of this people, conversely, is characterized by those principles. The discussion of problems is then lost in exercises of self-explanation and self-defence, whereas access to common elements and purposes underlying the diversity might make it possible not only to understand and tolerate the highly developed tendencies of analysis peculiar to certain cultures, but also to adapt them to wider common uses. It is probable that the outstanding quality of contemporary American philosophy is its precision in the interpretation of processes and operations, of symbols and actions; there has doubtless been a lack of speculative audacity in recent American thought, and in its flight from claims of certainty it has failed to find important or practical uses for its precisions. But the generation which has followed the philosophers who reacted against absolutisms and ideal-

isms finds it difficult to attach meaning to much of the speculation on questions which it recognizes as important, and it is
acutely aware of the danger of claims of certainty in regions
in which the tests of knowledge and even of existence are
dubious.

To suppose that co-operation among philosophers can take
the form of the mixture of methods and technical precisions
contributed by the West or by portions of the West and contemplative and intuitive insight borrowed from the East or
from traditions in Europe, like the ingredients of a co-operative cake, is to neglect both the nature of thought and the
history of philosophic discussions. Methods are borrowed from
other philosophies and appropriated to new principles;
objectives and structures are adjusted to new methods; but
philosophies multiply even among the faithful interpreters of
a single master and a common orthodoxy. Yet philosophic
means may contribute to the community of men, as they have
contributed to the consolidation of human associations in the
past, by the clarification of social, political, and humanistic
aspects of cultures; and investigation of the effects of philosophies in human relations, actions, and expressions may in
turn facilitate communication and co-operation in speculative
thought.

Philosophic enquiry is implicit in each of the aspects of
cultures, and the contribution of philosophy to cultural community and communication is found in a form adapted to
each of the aspects. With respect to the social aspects of cultures, the contribution of philosophy is to the understanding
and appreciation of the values and aspirations of peoples. The
philosophies of peoples constitute information concerning the
cultures of the world, to be found in part in explicit statements
and in part in common images, symbols, and scales of pre-
ference; they are embodied in the external civilization and
they determine the uses that are made of material resources
and technical skills. With respect to the political aspects of
cultures, the contribution of philosophy is to the motivation
of peoples in their co-operative activities. The statesman
should find the resources of philosophy available for his use
in two forms, derived respectively from the social and the
humanistic aspects of cultures; he should be able to recognize
the existing customs, beliefs, and capabilities, and he should

be able to formulate policies which reflect practicable ideals. Political communication should lead to agreement on common courses of action enforced by the imposition of penalties on actions which endanger the common action and the community. With respect to the humanistic aspects of cultures, the contribution of philosophy is in the critical clarification of values and of means employed for their achievement in arts, sciences, social structures, and religious observances.

In all three forms, the contribution of philosophy is made ordinarily without the need of technical philosophy or the ministrations of technical philosophers. Philosophy emerges when an awareness is reached of basic principles or values as they exist in the relations of men, in their instrumental activities, or in their enquiries and free expressions. All three depend, therefore, on a fourth contribution of philosophy to culture, which consists in the achievement of the proper purposes of philosophy, recognizable in great philosophies however variously the purposes of philosophy are stated in those philosophies. The present juxtaposition of philosophies in the juxtaposition of cultures, and the pressing importance of the practical consequences of philosophic differences in the ideological conflict concerning the relations of cultures and nations, has set problems for philosophers which may illuminate the relations between their respective methods of performing the proper tasks of philosophy. Any degree of success in treating the social, political, and humanistic aspects of cultures must contribute somewhat to such intellectual communication, for philosophy is not only a subject, a means, and a test of communication and community, but it is also in itself a form of communication, and the development of philosophy is one of the marks by which progress in world civilization will be recognized. Intelligent resort to analysis and principles should contribute instruments to move the complex parts of world culture, but the functioning of world community must eventually depend on a common spirit and force which is diffused in various forms throughout the whole.

The Cultural Essence of Chinese Literature

by

SHIH-HSIANG CHEN

The Chinese word for literature, *wen*, denoted originally nothing less than the totality of human civilization as conceived by the Chinese people. This conception may be regarded as fundamentally aesthetic. The earliest known ideograph of *wen* appears as an intricate symmetry of intersecting lines. Whether this symmetry was suggested by the splendid markings of the tiger, as some have thought, or derived from a more ample vision inspired by the observation of similar patterns on earth and in the firmament, it is impossible to determine. Both explanations may be supported, metaphorically speaking, by the tradition of ancient texts, from the *Yi Ching (Book of Change)*, to the works of the great sixth-century literary critic, Liu Hsieh. We know that no single cause can account for the creation of a word of such complex connotation; nevertheless, all words being emblems, we feel justified in affirming that the Chinese word for literature, *wen*, as well in its etymological graph as in its primary acceptation, symbolizes the apprehension of that formative intelligence which reduces shapeless parts to an organic whole, opposites to harmony, chaos to order, and by making thus manifest the good and the beautiful achieves the end of all art sprung from the creative energy of man.

This notion, whereby all human accomplishments may be expressed in terms of literary art, is eloquent at least of the supreme importance attributed to literature by Chinese cultural tradition. It is a notion which was evolved at a very remote period and which has been maintained throughout the centuries. For us, therefore, it raises not only points of great interest for the study of modern culture and literary criticism, but very complex problems as well. For the Chinese the supreme object of veneration has always been the Ideal Man

43

of Confucius, personified by such ancient emperor-sages as Yao and Shun, veritable Sons of Man incarnate, or at a later period by the idealization of Confucius himself, exemplifying more specifically the flower of man's moral qualities. And the supreme object of their speculation is the Taoist way of nature, the selfsame, in the midst of which man lives, breathes and has his being and of which the marvellous order of the physical universe is the visible and tangible expression. From the combination of these two ideals, the Confucian and the Taoist, implicit in the inspiration of the great majority of Chinese poets and writers, the formulation of their literary philosophy proceeds as it were necessarily: man in his essence is supreme in the universe, and the cosmos, partaking of that nature which is the selfsame, is conceived as subordinate to no higher will or power than man's and as serving no higher purpose than that of a gratuitous revelation to man. Whence it readily follows that literature, created by man to manifest his supremacy, is exalted as coequal with the cosmos, in order and in splendour.

It is thus easy to understand how the word *wen*, referring to literature, came to be overburdened with such pretentious excess of significance, and literature itself, throughout the ages of Chinese tradition, to be overestimated. The consequences of this may sometimes appear to us regrettable; and they involve, for the student of Chinese literature, many grave problems, of which not the least is that of methodology. The irritation and discouragement of many critics, as well in China as in the West, have no other cause. And often the issue is evaded, in well-meaning and superficial generalizations. Whether there exists a Chinese word for literature or poetry has been the occasion of indefatigable quibbling. One might just as well try to find, in English or in any language other than German, an exact equivalent for *dichtung*. Even the French *poésie* has not quite the same meaning as "poetry".

Every literature has its specific national characteristics and categories of worth. The homogeneity of Chinese literature is doubtless the source of one of its most important functional values. By this homogeneity we naturally do not mean its complete autochthony. It consists on the contrary in a profoundly organic faculty, whereby adventitious elements are continually assimilated and the growth of the Chinese national

44

character constantly sustained. It is in this sense that Chinese literature may be regarded as one of the great unifying forces of Chinese history and civilization and as perhaps meriting after all the grandiose role assigned to it, however uncritically, by ancient Chinese tradition.

A brief survey of this unifying force, considered both geographically and historically, will enable us to grasp its scope and limits, its merits and demerits. Geographically speaking Chinese literature, written in logographic characters practically impermeable to all dialectal and phonetic variations, unifies reading and writing over a vast area presenting as many different idioms as its natural barriers of hills and rivers. Thus literature tends to become a great leveller of local expressions. From Manchuria to Canton men of very different stock, debarred from converse by their diversity of tongues, may meet and commune in the domain of literature, in the national expression of their aspirations and emotions. This unification has no doubt detracted from that richness and diversity of interest which Chinese literature, after its long millenniums of growth, might otherwise have offered; but it has also prevented the Chinese nation from breaking up, with dubious benefit for humanity, into as many separate peoples as in Europe. Historically speaking, Chinese literature marks a unification of the sense of time. Thanks to the strength of Chinese traditionalism, to the close identification of literature with history and to the conservative evolution of the written language, poetry of three thousand years ago not only continues to be read, but strikes on the mind of Chinese men of letters with as much freshness as that of the nineteenth century. Furthermore, there has been as little of rivalry between literary movements and doctrines at different times as of religious controversy or persecution in their more violent forms. What we lose, as a result, in interest and variety of conflicting literary theories, is offset by this unification, on the temporal plane, both of literature and of history by means of literature. It is no exaggeration to say that in these texts, ancient and modern, the whole of history comes to life with a kind of timeless immediacy. Such a judgment as only a European of Mr. T. S. Eliot's acuteness could formulate: "the whole of the literature of Europe from Homer has a simultaneous existence and composes a simultaneous order",

45

seems almost a self-evident truth to the Chinese literary historian.

But in order to see Chinese literature as a unifying force, it is necessary to take certain other considerations into account. Its practical value is another matter. The process of unification entails certain sacrifices. The long unification of which Chinese literature was, as we believe, not only the reflection, but a contributory factor, has been very diversely appreciated. For unification, whether literary or national, while valuable as conducive to stability, tends also to arrest, or at least to retard, those developments which would normally accrue from the emulation and interpenetration of rival cultures—though grave doubts have been expressed, in recent times, as to the value and reality of a progress obtained, in the name of humanity, from the agitation of incessant competition and enterprise. And we must not forget that Chinese literature, considered as a unifying influence, is a mere superstructure in every sense of the word. Its vehicle, the graphic symbol, effective as a leveller of local differences, was no less so in maintaining in a state of illiteracy an astonishing proportion of the national population. Thus slowly evolved, behind the façade of unification, those problems of cultural reform, modernization and diffusion which confront us in China to-day. And in these problems Chinese literature is involved, both as an object and as a means. It is not our purpose here to suggest a solution, but merely to state the facts.

It is certain that contemporary China, in all her efforts towards social, political and economic modernization, is at grips with a very ancient and highly complex situation which she cannot efface, but must accept as her inheritance. The fact is, as we are told by such distinguished modern thinkers as Bertrand Russell and the Chinese philosopher Liang Su-Ming, that traditional China is a whole body of civilization, or a great cultural society, but not properly speaking a nation or state. This thesis is confirmed by the recent writings of the Chinese historian Lai Hai-tsung who points out that true states, comparable in nature and structure to those of modern Europe, did exist in China two thousand years ago during the period of the *Chan Kuo* (warring states), but that they disappeared with the unification of the Han empire at the end of the third century B.C. Some years ago a Japanese scholar,

Hasegawa Myoze Kan, considering Chinese culture from this same viewpoint, declared: "Some modern British thinkers regard the state as a necessary evil; but the Chinese had already realized, two thousand years ago, that the state is an *unnecessary* evil."

From whatever angle we bring these conceptions to bear upon our problem, the significant fact that emerges is the following: while the Chinese, in such cultural domains as literature, art and philosophy, unmistakeably evince the singleness and oneness of their character, they show but little interest or ability when it comes to other activities better calculated to organize and unify them, practically and formally, as a people and a distinct political entity, by cultivation of the federal spirit or establishment and strict observance of a meticulous code of laws. The federal spirit is replaced by an attachment to human relations, to family and friends; the observance of impersonal law by fidelity to moral and ethical rules with reference to which jurisprudence is a mere auxiliary. And though in China these private and personal moral codes may be found wanting, at least as often as public law in other countries, there is an unshakeable force in values to which a people remains so tenaciously attached and which in its literature it so clearly expresses and proclaims.

Whatever name we chose to give to these characteristics— Chinese national character, tradition, inertia, force of habit— and whether we approve of them or not, they constitute a reality that every reformer of China, every student of world culture, must seriously reckon with. True religious fervour for social organization, inspired by "universal love" and by the fear of God, as advocated by Motism, once coexisted with early Confucianism and Taoism and was almost as influential as these during the early formative age of Chinese culture. The supremacy of law was similarly asserted by the Legalists at about the same period. But in the following two thousand years of Chinese history neither of these doctrines produced any positive effects. Subsequently, and right up to the present day, they have admittedly been admired, from time to time, and intermittent efforts have been made to implement the measures they proposed. But their application always proved a failure and there is no trace of them in Chinese political and social history, just as in Chinese literature, no doubt for analogous reasons, there is no trace of great "tragedies" or "mysteries".

Having noted the main significance, the traditional "grand ideal" of Chinese literature, its deep interest and active participation in human affairs, let us now focus our attention on what may be more properly called, in the language of modern criticism, imaginative or creative literature—due allowance being made for the unavoidable arbitrariness of such distinctions. Before going into details, it may be as well to touch briefly upon certain salient features of Chinese creative literature. In the article I wrote for the *Encyclopaedia Americana*, my account of these features was given in the form of five general remarks. The reproduction of these, in slightly different terms, will best serve, it seems to me, the purposes of our present discussion.

First, though the court was the centre of literary fashion throughout most of the imperial dynasties, all creative writing had its source and inspiration in the Chinese people. Foreign thoughts and ideas remained without effect on creative literature until they were adopted by popular song and legend and "re-experienced" by the fecundating imagination of the people. Only then could they receive recognition and artistic form at the hands of the literati. The relationship between the people and these professional men of letters, to whom the barbarous sociological term "literocracy" is too often applied, is much closer than is commonly thought. In Chinese society the literati do not form a separate class or caste. They had not only to draw on the people for the living substance of their works, but also, as we shall see later, to lose their identity among them.

Secondly, while the mythical spirit was prevalent among the ancient Chinese, they do not seem to have created any high epic poetry. Legendary figures, instead of being glorified epically as heroes and gods, were idealized morally as "great men". And the form of writing they inspired was didactic and historical prose rather than epic poetry. Similarly tragedy, the culmination of early Greek literature, was unknown in ancient China, when culturally speaking she was the equal of her Western contemporary.

Thirdly, literature in praise of war, or characterized by a militant patriotism, is very scarce, whereas anti-militarist literature abounds.

48

Fourthly, the vague term "romantic", applied to numbers of Chinese poets, is perhaps justified by their spontaneity of emotional expression, their unbridled analysis of immediate personal experience and their Taoistic individualism in revolt against convention; but other and perhaps even more essential aspects of romanticism, such as a passionate otherworldliness, the universalized ego of extreme individualism and Wertherian love, are hardly to be found in the representative literature of China. It is true that the unknown has occupied the imagination of many great Chinese writers. But from this land of dream the awakening is never long deferred, nor the return to the everyday world. The eternal inspirations of the Chinese poet are life on earth and the things of earth, this visible, physical world that is the nursery and the texture of spirit. And in their highest emotional flights they seldom exceed the limits of epicureanism or an ardent love of nature.

Finally, the peculiar properties of the Chinese language, such as the ideograph, monosyllabism and the determination of meaning by means of specific tonal inflexions, make Chinese literature very akin to music and the fine arts. Thus the metre and rhythm of Chinese poetry, thanks to its monosyllabic characters, have a definitely visual quality, and "soaring" ceases to be a metaphor when applied to the lyricism of Chinese prose, at least in its classical forms.

This brief summary of the characteristics of Chinese literature may serve at least to indicate the main lines of what is to follow. By these we shall be led to investigate the evolution of the principal literary genres in their historical and social contexts, the relative positions of polite and popular literature, the adaptation of spiritual attitudes to the major literary themes and finally the more strictly technical matters of language and literary convention. All these questions, emerging from a background of cultural conditions common to them all, are naturally bound up with one another. We shall nevertheless try to treat them separately.

When we consider the rise of literary genres and the evolution of literary forms, the fact that stands out most clearly is the close relationship between popular literature and the polite literature of the court and the intelligentsia. Every important Chinese literary genre may be clearly traced to the people. And every new form, throughout the long history of Chinese literature, was evolved from popular sources. What is more, every development of popular inspiration in the field of polite literature was preceded by the falling into disuse and decay of an ancient mode or form. More generally speaking, following the fluctuations of history one literary genre was superseded by another, if not in the actual fact of its existence, at least in importance and excellence, as for example, in poetry, the *shih* by the *t'zu* and the *chu*, and, at a later period, poetry by the novel. Popular literature, that vast and ceaseless undercurrent of Chinese society throughout its slow evolution, was the unfailing regenerator of polite literature in its periods of crisis. This revitalizing force embodies the perpetual growth and transformation of social and religious customs in their infinite variety and of language itself; and the expression of all these springs directly from the native genius of the people, from utter simplicity of feeling and sheer love of life. But popular literature is important also as the preserver of the classical tradition. For it "folklorizes", so to speak, such elements as it may have inherited from the polite literature of the past, elements long forgotten by the literati and which they rediscover, in the hour of need, as their rightful due. Foreign customs also and foreign ideas were not regarded by the people as curiosities of merely exotic interest, nor intellectualized after a superficial contact, as they would have been by the *élite*, but assimilated almost unconsciously and cherished in popular ways of life until such time as they might enrich literature with new themes and motifs. It should further be remarked that the salutary and regenerative impulse given by the people to the higher regions of literary creation may invariably be seen to coincide with certain changes in the general course of Chinese history. This is a phenomenon which is perhaps by no means peculiar to China. The necessity of this so-called "rebarbarization" for the regeneration of all literatures, has indeed recently been recognized by a number of writers who, we believe, have invoked above all, in support of their thesis, the evidence of the literary history of the West. But it seems to us that this modern view of literature as a living organism may receive much fresh confirmation from the type of relational pattern which millenniums of history enable us to discern with such vividness in Chinese literary evolution and which is one of the most important keys to an understanding of Chinese culture.

A brief historical survey of this phenomenon is here our immediate concern. Leaving personalities and particular incidents to one side for the moment, we see the periods of Chinese literature as an ample succession of curves rising and falling. Sprung from the common source of popular literature they stand, various in height and span, like a chain of rainbows, as radiant and as transitory. Beneath flows, without ceasing, the vast life-giving stream of popular invention, unpicturesque, unselfconscious, impelled by the vital force of the nation. These periods may be regarded as forming a comparatively simple pattern and as obeying an ostensibly regular rhythm, like those of the dynasties themselves. But they must not be thought of as discontinuous, self-contained cycles. They are, so to speak, dialectically interrelated; they have a common origin; and when one yields its place to another, it yields also some of its qualities.

The first flowering of Chinese poetry is to be found in the *Shih Ching (Book of Odes)* whose composition covers roughly the period stretching from the tenth to the seventh century B.C. Although at that time Chinese urban culture was well developed, the early feudal system firmly established and social classes clearly differentiated, these odes continued to proclaim, in lofty, idyllic strain, what W. B. Yeats called the "unity of being" of mind and body and of collective and individual consciousness. Here music and poetry are indissoluble, a simple and unpremeditated outpouring of heart and soul. No translation can give any idea of this perfect unity which constitutes the real "meaning" of these odes. And though abounding in parables, they do not suffer the least commentary. Their 30 centuries of existence have completely impregnated Chinese literary thought. And even today, thanks to Chinese traditionalism and the conservatism of Chinese language and culture, their recitation, however fragmentary and marred by modern pronunciation, stirs the heart with profound racial memories.

There is no doubt that these odes are for the greater part the work of the people. But they include also a number of courtly and aristocratic imitations, reflecting a polite concern with historical and political events. But even these, at their best, have a musical beauty of language which goes to show

51

that poetry, as ordained by ancient and official prescription, is instinct with that magic virtue from which the traditional conception of the omnipotent *wen*, as we have described it, very possibly derives.

After this first flowering of Chinese poetry, carried to its perfection in the *Book of Odes*, the three following centuries, that is to say from the sixth to the fourth century B.C., witnessed a gradual decline of poetic art, notwithstanding its vogue among the new ruling and aristocratic classes of the rival "nationalisms" then emerging. During this period the *Book of Odes* became a repertory of songs reserved for diplomatic and social festivities. The odes were chanted, declaimed or parodied. In high soceity, where poetry was an affair of fashion or the adornment of a special occasion, the art of its effective presentation replaced that of its creation. It has been noted as a very singular fact in Chinese literary history that the three centuries corresponding to the golden age of Chinese philosophy should have been followed by a virtual blank in the field of poetic composition. For all their "nationalist" spirit and vigour the rival states, engaged in mortal conflict, did not succeed in producing a single national poet. But after all this is perhaps not to be wondered at. Which of our modern warrior nations, with their intense mobilization, has produced a real poet of its own? Better perhaps to sing some of the old odes than to exact, from the "mobilized" poet, bombastic verses that are a derision of poetry. The Chinese poets of the ancient warring states having never written marching songs or martial verses, it was all the more difficult for them to do so at a later time. Such compositions of this kind as they finally adopted had to be borrowed from foreign sources. Just as the Chinese people could with difficulty identify themselves with the state, so the Chinese muse chose either to be silent during wars which were primarily the state's affair, or to protest vigorously against them.

During the three hundred years from the sixth to the fourth century B.C., while poetry lay dormant, both sophistry and philosophy developed in China. With the sophists rhetoric flourished. In a manner typical of the interpendence of Chinese literary cycles, the technical qualities of a declining cycle— wit, pungency, preciousness and rhetorical ability in general— were always handed on to its successor. The fourth century

B.C. marked the close of the ancient or "classical" age of Chinese history, though the dawn of the unified empire was yet to come. As if to set the pattern for all subsequent Chinese literature to be produced under similar historical conditions, there now appeared poets and writers of such individuality and technical ability as made them the heralds of a new and now imminent golden age. In the north the philosopher Hsun Ch'ing (314–217 B.C.), now often compared to Aristotle as having occupied in relation to Confucius and Mencius the same position as the Stagyrite in relation to Socrates and Plato, was also one of the first Chinese men of letters. The author of profound philosophical dissertations written with great rhetorical mastery of exposition and argument, he also wrote some long poems, expostulatory and allegorical, in what he called the *fu* form, later to become one of the most important literary genres of the Han empire (209 B.C. to A.D. 220). Hsun's *fu* poems were less remarkable for literary excellence than for the unprecedented lucidity with which the poet expressed his awareness of a world lapsing in chaos and agony. This consciousness he formulated in two lines:

> *T'ion hsia pu chih*
> *Ch'ing ch'en kuei shih*

which mean literally:

> *The world is in chaos,*
> *I ask to present my* fantastic *poems.*

The word *kuei*, which we have translated by "fantastic", unites the implications of weirdness, danger, ominousness and shock. Here the poet is an individual face to face with the whole of humanity and consciously arrogating, for the first time in Chinese literary history, such importance to his art as to render it capable of shocking back into sanity the chaotic world. Such awareness of poetic individuality could never have been possible in the period of the collective composition of the *Odes*. Then there had been true poetry and bards, but no poet.

But the most remarkable literary achievement of declining classicism was that of the southern poet Chu Yuan (340–278? B.C.), a striking example of the highly conscious poetic individual in conflict with an iron age to which at the same time he is irretrievably committed. His was an accomplishment of such poetic excellence, in the choice and handling of themes, that it opened up the way for the *fu* of the Han period and exercised a profound and lasting influence on all that is best in the subsequent imaginative literature of China. Now Chu's works are unmistakably and demonstrably of popular origin. When popular literature in the north, after its apogee in the *Book of Odes*, entered upon a period of exhaustion, the southern land above the Yangtze valley, with its folk songs, myths and customs as colourful and luxuriant as its jungle and flora, awaited the coming of its poet of genius. It is now certain, in the light of fuller biographical evidence, that Chu Yuan's works consist largely of revised versions of popular religious songs, now known as his *Nine Songs*. We also possess more than a dozen lyrical and descriptive poems of mighty, surging line, ranging from youthful experiments to the impassioned cries of an anguished and despairing soul and profound meditations on the meaning of history and of the universe.

But his most representative and influential work is a long poem of about three thousand words, the *Li Sao (Meeting with Sorrow)*. The *Li Sao* is a rhapsodical medley of autobiography and myth, history and legend, strange and far-flung landscapes, astounding visions of heaven reflecting a tortured and depraved humanity, fragrance of flowers and stench of weeds, virtues and vices, and above all, in an atmosphere of morbid ambiguity, a mixture of politics and erotism dominated by the King symbol—all these elements being developed in such bold juxtaposition that, were it not for our possession of such modern works as Eliot's *Waste Land* and Joyce's *Ulysses*, we could hardly conceive how such a poem ever came to be written. Its unique quality is such that Mr. Waley, applying Goncourt's phrase, described it as issuing from the master's *propre nervosité*. That it should present, across such immensities of space and time, points of resemblance with the modern works just mentioned, affords us in any case ample food for reflection.

The unification achieved by the Han empire at the end of the third century B.C. amounted for the Chinese to a reintegration of their universe. It was the beginning of a new cycle of Chinese literature. The influence of Chu Yuan, Hsun Ch'ing and Chu's disciple Sung Yu on the Han *fu*, soon to impose itself as a literary genre, was decisive and immediate. But strictly speaking this influence was of a kind with that of the rhetoric of the pre-Han sophists, that is to say technical rather than spiritual. This is characteristic of all action exerted on an age of regeneration and growth by a previous period of decadence.

During the four centuries of stability of the Han empire the forms of Chinese culture, such as they have survived to the present day, were gradually established for all time. This does not mean that, in the centuries that followed, all evolution was at a standstill in cultural domains; but their main patterns had been laid down once and for all and those channels determined in which they were henceforward to move. The new triumphant philosophy of Confucianism, tempered as circumstances permitted by Taoist revolts against its dogmas, was to control the entire future development of Chinese ideology. Subsequently Buddhism, though it ostensibly modified certain forms of worship and religious expression, brought about little fundamental change. From the dualistic forces of Confucian humanism and Taoist "naturalism" the Chinese spirit was to receive, in the ensuing millenniums, its every impulse. It is significant that the only comprehensive history of Chinese philosophy written in a modern spirit (by Professor Fung Yu-lan, pub. 1934) should discern in Chinese philosophy only two main periods, the first ending with the first century B.C., the second extending from then on to the end of the nineteenth century. A similar treatment of Chinese literature, with reference to the appearance of new genres and conventions, to its individual representatives and changing social conditions, is by no means such a simple matter. But the main lines of development since the Han age may be charted and shown to present a considerable degree of regularity. They appear as a series of rising and falling curves or cycles, in close dependence on both popular tradition and the works of the literati.

The works of Chu Yuan, popular in origin, but bearing all the marks of his tormented and solitary genius, of his impassioned hyperbolism and great imaginative power, could never fail to be impressive. But it was above all his technical mastery, not to be confused with the cult of technique, that most strongly influenced the *fu* writers of the Han period, representative of a spirit very remote from his. The most distinguished of these writers became the favourites of the visionary and megalomaniacal emperor Wu Ti (157–87 B.C.). In subsequent reigns most of them, at various times in their lives, were court dignitaries of the prosperous and stable empire. The favourite themes of the earlier *fu* writers of the Han period were the splendours of cities, palaces, imperial hunting-grounds, gardens haunted by strange birds and animals, exotic tributes from all parts of the world. And indeed their works were most estimable glorifications of great material achievement and national stability and expansion. They were often introduced, or concluded, in a manner characteristic of this moralizing age, by a passage of an edifying nature, the purpose of which was not so much to exalt the achievements of empire as to exhort the ruler to honour personal merit. Later *fu* works turned towards mystic visions, minute descriptions of natural objects, personal lyricism, philosophic speculation, discussions and expositions. From the point of view of literary craftsmanship it must be allowed that the best *fu* compositions of the Han period were consumate syntheses of all the qualities that the Chinese language, as a living medium, could boast at that time. All its resources, melody, inflexion and ideographic imagery, were exploited to the fullest. The old verbal magic, enchanter of the gods, that same magic which inspired so much of ancient poetry and particularly the works of Chu Yuan himself, appears here as the magnificent instrument of human genius and as a means to the glorification and formal adornment of life on earth. The *fu* writers have given us a few great works; but the *fu* itself, as a conventional form, gradually lapsed into such extravagance, into such a hybrid confusion of verse and prose, that it lost both its moral and its artistic *raison d'être*.

But thanks to fresh impetus received from popular sources, Han literature entered upon a new cycle of vigorous creation lasting nearly seven hundred years, that is to say up to the end of the post-Han age. The emperor who founded the Han dynasty was himself of very humble origin. With the downfall of the brief Ch'in dynasty (221–206 B.C.), militarist and 'legalist' in tendency, and the subsequent annihilation of its successful rivals, the last of the old aristocracy disappeared. Cultural and social life was transformed on a national scale.

Not only was the imperial throne occupied by a commoner, but the chief provinces throughout the empire were governed by generals sprung from the people. Furthermore, the founder of the Han dynasty, as well as being the first commoner to become emperor, was the first southerner to exercise dominion, from the ancient seat of culture in the north, not only over his native state, but over the whole country. This is not to be regarded, however, as a matter of racial or territorial conquest, but rather as the symbol of a united and homogenous culture taking the place of an antiquated multiplicity of states. As far as personal culture was concerned, the emperor was distinguished by little more than the plebeian's solid common sense and possibly a southern accent. He disposed neither of superior military force nor of any political slogan likely to impress, if we except three brief and ingenuous pronouncements against the perniciously elaborate regional laws of the Ch'in dynasty. Yet he found alliances and followers everywhere, in the north as in the south. He was made by the times. And the times were for unification, for peace and security. Thus the demagogic measures that he was led to take after his accession did not exceed the execution of his former associates, risen high in rank and military power. But his general system of government, like that of his immediate successors, was pure and simple *laissez-faire*, joined to a perfunctory belief in the legendary Yellow Emperor and the ancient Taoist "way". The people generally were free to do as they pleased. War had brought them into close contact; now peace was in the land and the possibility of exchanging customs and occupations. All parts of the country communed in a general and positive union, in speech and song. Popular music and manners gave the tone to social life, in conformity with the rustic tastes, in art and culture, of the early rulers.

But the rich and robust creations of the people were even to exercise, through the channel of official institutions, a direct and widespread influence on literature. The earlier Taoist policy of *laissez-faire* and non-interference with the natural course of nature had been an inevitable reaction and a salutary stimulant; but it could not go on for ever. Nor could any far-reaching effect be expected from the "legalist" theory of the omnipotence of law, a theory which the third ruler made strenuous efforts to apply. With the reign of the emperor Wu

57

Ti, as the nation was settling down in a system of common-wealth based on the family, Confucianism triumphed in spite of its exaggerated ethics and their tinge of anthropocentric mysticism. The old Confucian ideal of government by music and ceremony now became, at least ostensibly, a major political principle. And knowledge of the people through their music and songs was regarded as the best means to government and to the improvement of government. The *Yueh-Fu* (Government Music Bureau) now began very actively to collect popular songs and airs all over the country. These were of both native and foreign origin. They were arranged and sung by trained musicians. New words were set to the airs and forms and motifs were imitated by talented men of letters.

From these popular sources was developed the *dolce stile nuovo* characteristic of the spirit of the Han age. It established, more firmly than the *Book of Odes*, the *shih* as the sovereign form of all orthodox Chinese poetry. The metrical schemes of folk songs and poems were as various as their origins. The rhythm of the text scarcely differed from that of the music. But in the process of their refinement to a higher poetic art, the purely musical element was largely sacrificed to the literary. There was so strong a tendency in favour of classical symmetry and regularity of versification that the monotonous pattern of five syllables to each line finally became the norm. These passages, and even entire stanzas, of strictly five-syllable lines, frequent in popular songs, are the origin of the *wu yen shih*, or "pentasyllabic verse" that was to become the dominant metre of Chinese poetry for centuries to come.

In matter, then, as well as in form, the *wu yen shih* remained a powerful and enduring influence on later Chinese poetry. Its vigorous pentasyllabism maintained itself, throughout the following centuries and down to quite recent years, as one of the two predominant metres of Chinese tradition. The other is the line of seven syllables. But this latter metre, established at the end of the Han age, constituted in reality a quantitative elaboration of the same pentasyllabic effect rather than a qualitative change. Whereas the substitution of the pentasyllabic for the quadrisyllabic pattern, that is to say of an uneven for an even number of beats, was of a nature to upset the balanced serenity of the ancient measure, it is obvious that

58

the line of seven syllables amounted to a mere extension of that of five. There resulted an approximation, made possible by the increase in flexibility, to living speech and its inherent prosaism. Thus the Han metres, once they were established, endured throughout the whole course of Chinese poetry and even down to the present day, in the same way as the main features of the written language and literary phraseology. It is true that the *tz'u*, which flourished as a musical and poetic form from the late tenth century onward and rapidly developed into lyric drama, possessed qualities which made it the equal and even the superior of contemporary five-syllable and seven-syllable metres. But these latter persisted, thanks to the devotion of the best poets, as the representative forms of the great tradition.

This absence of fundamental change must not be confused, however, with an absence of evolution. Within this vast and apparently immutable framework the processes of growth, decay and rebirth were at work. The static and all too simple aspect of Chinese poetic forms, like that of Chinese society, is often deceptive. *A priori* it seems almost impossible that a metre composed uniformly of five-syllable lines should be capable of expressing with such variety and over so long a period the multifarious shades of human feeling. When we compare the various translations and interpretations of a given Chinese poem, we realize what kaleidoscopic virtuality of sense and nonsense can be concentrated within a few syllables. But what is a Chinese syllable? The whole secret lies in its complexity. Each monosyllable is a word. This monosyllabism of the language necessarily results in a great number of homophones or quasi-homophones, whence an infinite variety of rhymes and assonances. In traditional Chinese poetry the prescribed rhymed couplet, or the rhyming of alternate lines, gives the poet ample occasion to show his ingenuity in the use of such euphonious abundance; but these devices are too easily recognizable and tend to mask, even for prosodists, those subtle intricacies of oblique rhyme, consonance, assonance and alliteration whose echoes and overtones are so effective and which act as a test of the poet's skill in his striving after perfection. And these monosyllables of Chinese verse, with their tonal differentiations, contrasts and analogies, all possess the complex properties known in Western prosody as pitch-accent, quantity, mobile stress and periodicity, as the case may be. But on the plane of poetic function all these properties must be apprehended as an indissoluble whole.

It is because of this immense complexity and these rich prosodic possibilities that Chinese poetry, in spite of the apparent simplicity, regularity and fixity of its metres, with their lines of only a few syllables, never wanted the faculty of growth and development. Modes of writing flourished and disappeared. Periods of strength alternated with periods of weakness. It seems strange that the possibilities of a domain so pertinaciously explored were not finally exhausted. But the true Chinese poet has never ceased to find, at least until the present century, ample matter for his skill and ingenuity within the limits of the time-honoured tradition.

The persisting influence of the Han poetic tradition appears as clearly in the choice and treatment of themes as in the domain of form itself. True to the humanistic and naturalistic spirit of the age, to its vision of a vast and stable world empire of homogenous culture, the Han *wu yen shih* treated practically all the eternal themes of great poetry with a mastery of matter and of style that was to mark Chinese poetry for ages to come. An examination of some of the more remarkable characteristics of this form is thus revealing of what is best in later Chinese poetry and testifies to the persistence of Han humanism throughout Chinese history. The highest achievement of Han poetry is to be found in the *ku shih shih chiu shou (Nineteen Old Poems)*. One of the greatest and most discriminating critics of Chinese poetry, the sixth-century Chung Hung, commented on these as follows: "Each word gold a thousandfold!" Throughout all the subsequent fluctuations of literary taste and fashion and the changing fortunes of even the greatest poets, this high tribute to the *Old Poems* has never been contradicted.

Even before Chung's time the authorship of these poems was uncertain. They have come down to us shrouded in the same atmosphere of gratuity and anonymity as popular poetry, to which however their supreme refinement makes them vastly superior. This is a highly significant fact. They have definite personality, but it is as it were a collective personality, that of the common humanity of the Han age. Lytton Strachey, commenting on Herbert Gile's translation of hundreds of Chinese poems covering a period of over two thousand years, said of them taken as a whole: "We can perceive in them a unity in their enchantment and, listening to them, we should guess these songs to be the work of one single mind, pursuing through a hundred subtle modulations the perfection which this earth has never known." Though some truth must be allowed to this most elegant statement, justified in part by Chinese classical traditionalism, it may be thought that the impression of its author is due rather to the unifying hand of a single translator. It is none the less impossible to deny this "unity of enchantment" of the *Nineteen Old Poems*. If they are the work of an individual, he represents the universal mind of the Han age; if of more than one, they together constitute that mind. Historically speaking, the specific *quale* of the Han spirit shines through the texture and imagery of these poems. And on the plane more particularly of cultural history, this same Han spirit here reaches such heights of expression that it contains within itself most of what is best in Chinese poetry to come and confers upon it that homogeneity of essence and of form which seems to have struck Strachey as an intuition.

It is naturally difficult to analyse the qualities of these poems in a foreign language. And yet we know, due allowance being made for the inevitable loss of their original music, that they lend themselves better to translation than perhaps any others. This is a further proof, if further proof be required, of their profound and immense humanity. Mr. Arthur Waley, the best English translator—considering the range and quality of his work—of Chinese poetry, has given us a version of these poems distinguished by all his usual felicity. Our quotations, therefore, shall be from his text.

We find here all the great poetic themes—love, death, friendship, attachment to home, the sorrows of separation and the soul grappling with its destiny—treated in a manner that was to become typical of Chinese poetry. A notable quality of these works, in virtue of which even the most trivial human experience is exalted to a high poetic plane, is the grandiose vision of a universe inseparable from the common individual. The immensities of time and space, never before visualized with such clarity and penetration, illuminate the poems with their radiant and vivifying images. Such expressions as "ten thousand *li*", "forever" or "a thousand years of sorrow", are here no longer hyperbolical or hazardous, but correspond to actual facts of poetic experience, quickened by commensurate emotion and passion. The secret of this achievement lies in the absolutely natural and spontaneous juxtaposition, within the space of a few syllables, of the infinitely vast and the most intimate personal circumstances, joined to a wealth of shades and gradations and a freshness of metaphor such as no translation can render. In this poetic art the whole world becomes a single scene, animated by the lonely and anonymous heart beating in passionate unison with the elemental emotions which the whole of humanity feels and understands. Universal significance was given to every individual experience, however intimate and trivial. The anonymous individual, exalted precisely for his aptitude to express the fundamental emotions of humanity, literally embodied, in the great poetry of this great age of humanism, the very meaning of human existence as rooted in the experience and understanding of all men, a meaning in which all space and time seemed to participate. And just as in that age there was coherence in the affective rhythms and urges of humanity, so there was coherence in those which man shared with nature and with natural phenomena. This effective, spontaneous juxtaposition of vast horizons and petty matters, these infinite images of time and space brought to bear on intimate personal experience, may at least partially be illustrated by Mr. Waley's sensitive translations, though what we have said was inspired by the implications and music of the originals. The first poem, as translated by Mr. Waley, begins:

> On and on, always on and on,
> Away from you, parted by "life-parting",
> Going from one another ten thousand "li",
> Each in a different corner of the World.
> The way between is difficult and long,
> Face to face how shall we meet again?

How mere physical distance, thus simply and naturally visualized, breathes all the pathos of separation! This is made possible by such simple and direct expressions of heart-felt personal experience as "life-parting", "face to face", the Chinese savour of which Mr. Wiley has so wisely tried to retain. The vivid and exotic metaphors of the following couplet may seem farfetched; actually they are highly appropriate in their identification of the nature of things with humanity and their exotism is the face of familiar things:

> *The Tartar horse prefers the north wind,*
> *The bird of Yueh nests on the southern branch.*

Vast aspects of nature—sun, clouds, time—are next brought together with extraordinary mastery, immediacy and depth of feeling, in tones at once ingenuous and spontaneous:

> *Since we parted the time is already long,*
> *Daily my clothes hang looser round my waist.*
> *Floating clouds obscure the white sun,*
> *The wandering one has quite forgotten home.*

From here on the poem rises to new heights of intensity and feeling, all the more impressive as apparently tempered and restrained by that resignation to the passage of time which is characteristic of many Chinese masterpieces:

> *Thinking of you has made me suddenly old,*
> *The months and years swiftly draw to their close.*

Time, indeed, as well in Chinese literature as in the Chinese conception of history, has a more positive and active meaning than perhaps in any other nation. Resignation to its omnipotence carries with it an intense feeling of tragedy, but also a solution. And this has been so at least ever since the Han dynasty. The poet closes on the couplet:

> *I'll put you out of my mind and forget for ever,*
> *And try with all my might to eat and thrive.*

Every event has its beginning and its end, for better or for worse. But life must go on.

We cannot here discuss in such detail each one of the *Nineteen Old Poems*. Nor can we consider at length each one of the following periods of Chinese literary history. We must confine ourselves to a brief outline of the rising and falling curves that mark their development. But in view of the fact that Han poetry as a whole initiated and established the main patterns of much of later Chinese poetry, just as the Han age did for much of Chinese cultural and social life in general, it is expedient to give some account of other aspects of Han poetry already referred to and which, *mutatis mutandis*, are equally characteristic of much of subsequent Chinese poetry.

Let us first consider the theme of love. The poem just quoted is typical of many Chinese love poems. Love is never expressed with passionate ardour and hardly ever idealized as an object of contemplation. Now this passion and this idealization are precisely the most valuable features of Western love poetry, particularly at its great romantic period. Passion appears in all its tragic beauty, in the sublimity of its eternal conflicts, as expressed by Keats:

> *What mad pursuit! What struggle to escape!*

And in order to be idealized for contemplation love must be raised high above the contingencies of common life and conceived as a condition of suspense and dissatisfaction. It has to be represented as ever striving towards its goal and ever falling short. At the same time it must be removed from the real conditions of experience. The significance and reality of the 'mad pursuit' reside in its permanence. Its only hope of finality is in "teasing eternity". But even there it is right that

> *Bold lover, never, never canst thou kiss.*

In Chinese poetry, on the contrary, love is not presented as the pursuit of an eternal future, but rather as a thing of the past and in its consequences as such, these consequences being regarded as an immediate expression of present reality. Thus love in Chinese poetry is a matter for reflection, never for speculation. It follows, as we have seen, that Chinese poets are concerned rather with the deep pathos of separation *following* love than with the passionate pursuit of love. Profound and enduring melancholy takes the place of the exaltation and tragic splendour of passion. It is a melancholy resembling, in its expression, that described by Shakespeare as "composed of many simples, extracted from many objects", a melancholy consequently "in which my rumination wraps me in a most humorous sadness". Mother wit and common sense are substituted for a yearning after the impossible. For the Western romantic poet, love is both a paradise to be and a mirror in which to contemplate his image. But the Chinese poet sings as it were from beyond paradise, where his concern is not to see himself, but to obtain a clearer view of the world and all it holds.

Let us next consider the importance of friendship in Chinese poetry. The raptures of intellectual fellowship and the ties of friendship are sung by Chinese poets almost as often as the profound emotion of farewell. This has sometimes been explained by the fact that among the Chinese, as among the ancient Greeks, the low social status of woman tended to reinforce the attachments among men. From the same sociological point of view, the conception of love as a *fait accompli* might be explained by the tradition in virtue of which marriages in China were arranged long in advance, between the families of the parties concerned. But these explanations, even supposing them to be valid, do little more than satisfy our sociological curiosity. They do not in the least increase our capacity to appreciate the intrinsic quality and emotional force of Chinese poetry when it treats of love or friendship. Further, if there exists an analogy between the situations of the men of Greece and the men of China, how is it that the Greeks are as deficient in the poetry of friendship as the Chinese in epics and tragedies? We believe that there is a deeper reason for the Chinese poet's adoption of friendship as one of his most important themes and for the strength with which he reacted to it emotionally. We believe notably that friendship, as an emotional bond, is humanly speaking more general in scope than love between the sexes, the effect of which is necessarily limited to two individuals. And this closer bond by which the Chinese poet feels all men to be united may in its turn be explained by the Chinese attachment to life here below. In the absence from his preoccupations of a future world (or even a platonic world of ideas), a joyous forgathering of friends, here and now, of those friends who are called *chih chi* or *chih hsin*, "knowers of each other's self or heart" (for there is no hope of God's knowing it), such a forgathering is cherished as one of the greatest blessings and realities that this fleeting existence has to offer. And "life-parting", between friends as between lovers, is as heart-rending as death.

The Chinese poet's treatment of other important themes may be examined in the same light. The same mundane and humanistic attitude accounts for his attachment to home. This has inspired very magnificent and very tender poetry. Far back, before the Han age, Chu Yuan, after having travelled the whole "universe", could find no other solution to his problems than to return to this earth and take his ill-fated life by his own hand. Chang Heng, the Han poet, having roamed through all time and the entire cosmos in search of wisdom, finally decided that he could apprehend the whole universe within the four walls of his homestead.

The attitude of the Chinese poet towards life and death may be similarly elucidated. An acute sense of the fortuitousness and fragility of life, on the one hand, and, on the other, a belief in the positive reality of humanity as a whole, as a permanent and absolute fact, give rise respectively to a system of epicurean or hedonistic enjoyment and to a stoical endurance of destiny. But lest these terms of Western classicism should be the cause of a regrettable confusion, not so much by the meaning they possess as by the implications they carry—as they invariably are when applied to an alien culture—a word of explanation is called for. We may say, then, that the epicureanism of the Chinese poet, though less firmly founded on scientific observation than the Greek's and less highly intellectualized and rationalized than the Roman's, contains perhaps more of spontaneous mirth or, in the phrase of Bertrand Russell, speaking of the Chinese temperament, more of "instinctive joy", just as his stoical acceptance of fate is less defiant in its manifestations.

These stock themes of Chinese poetry, and their characteristic developments, were originally established during the Han dynasty. The basis of this establishment was, as we have seen, the collective consciousness of a vast union of mankind in the humanism of a new age, a consciousness to which popular poetry gave its first spontaneous expression. This spontaneous expression, sprung from the deepest strata of society to become the representative mode of Han poetry, is remarkable not only for its salutary and lasting influence on future ages, but for the vigour with which it instinctively and triumphantly asserted itself against certain of its contemporary rivals. In the higher spheres of society, at court and among the intellectuals, the

66

preciocity of the *fu* style was in high favour; and, what is more, the mysticism, bigotry and dogma of the Confucian moralists were imposed from above on Han culture, and superstition flourished. But all this could not prevent the upspring of humanistic poetry to testify to the healthy development of the Chinese people and to the stability of their ancient society. That the age was sound at heart, and its soul pure, is proclaimed by the survival of these aspects of Chinese popular culture which were to endure and develop amid all the vicissitudes of later ages, in spite of tyrants, patrician corruption of ideals and manners, and all the havoc that followed in their train.

In the third century the vigour of the Han period gave unmistakable signs of decay. The decline of this second great literary cycle became evident. But it was to flare up, before its final extinction, in a brief period of splendour. During the period of the Three Kingdoms (220–265), rich in heroism and shaken by the wars which split the empire, literature gave proof, as though suddenly galvanized, of brilliant and romantic qualities. The *wu yen shih*, in spite of its increased individualism, maintained its lofty classical strain. The *fu*, during these few years, flowered anew. Even the solemn and antiquated monotony of strict quadrisyllabism enjoyed a brief revival in the songs of the heroic king Ts'ao Ts'ao, who resuscitated, as it were, a mummified form, by the sheer force of his revolutionary spirit and his insistence on "plain speech". The ardour which animated this brief and splendid period of Chinese literature was derived from the vigorous Taoist rebellion against the long-established Confucianism of the Han age. This revolution, however, was not so much a clearly defined intellectual movement as a general social trend, represented in various domains by a great number of eminent personalities, among the most distinguished of whom we find members of the Ts'ao family. If this period was as feverishly brilliant as it was short-lived, the ensuing Tsin dynasty burned with even briefer and more fitful flame, in its struggle for unification and expansion. The decline of the empire, and with it the decadence of creative literature, were precipitated, early in the fourth century, by tremendous waves of barbarian invasion from the north.

From the fourth to the end of the sixth century, Chinese

literature presented all the symptoms of decadence. Cloistered in the placid and luxuriant sites of the Yangtze valley, the imperial courts and intellectual coteries beguiled their precarious leisure with a literature typically florid, artificial and effeminate. Literary technique, to the exclusion of all else, had never before been so cultivated and emphasized. Poetry became an elaborate filigrane of tone-patterns. Spring wind, autumn cicada, the twittering canary and the silvery moon became its principal motifs. But while this period was marked by the decline of creative literature, it was a golden age for literary criticism, distinguished not only for its conscientious cult of literary craftsmanship, but also for its profound literary philosophy and judicious critical principles.

The purely aesthetic value of literature had never been so clearly recognized and so highly esteemed. It was as though the old general conception of the omnipotence of *wen*, with its symbolic attributes of legislator, governor and civilizing agent, were now interpreted literally and from a predominantly aesthetic point of view. Unlike the ancient semi-legendary emperors to whom the epithet *wen* had been applied in a vague, symbolic sense, a number of emperors of this period were so distinguished, who were nothing more than accomplished men of letters and aesthetes of talent, and otherwise mere victims of the national disasters. But the worship of aesthetics, having been brought to such a pitch, continued indefinitely. In the system of civil examinations inaugurated by the great T'ang dynasty that followed, the high value set on poetry was doubtless due to the tradition of this period. In the ensuing age of victories, the emperor T'ang T'ai Tsung (597–649), a colossus in Chinese history both for his military exploits and the wisdom of his administration, assiduously cultivated poetic composition. A later T'ang emperor, Hsuan Tsug (810–859), so craved the title awarded for distinguished literary talent to successful candidates at the civil examinations, that he secretly hung a tablet in the inner hall of his palace, bearing the inscription written by himself: "Mr. Li, *chin shih*." It was his own name, followed by the title he coveted!

But the literary merit of the decadent period from the sixth to the fourth century was not exhausted by the official recognition of the "literocracy", to employ the modern term too often applied and misapplied, nor by its remarkable achievements in the field of literary criticism. In its earlier phase, after the fall of the heroic Three Kingdoms, such great spiritual rebels as the Seven Worthies of the Bamboo Grove wrote inspired poetry so expressive of their Taoistic unrestraint, of their revolt against social convention in word and deed, that both by their works and by their personalities they may be said to have created a new conception of man and to have reasserted, in a dark chaotic age, the meaning and the value of his individuality. These men, with their prodigious excesses of wine, their fantastic visions of the cosmos, their singularly poignant views on life and nature, their soaring flights of imagination and their spiritual escapades, bequeathed to future rebel poets, pitting their individuality against society and the age, the prototypes of a poetry of sanctuary and protestation. Before all others let us place T'ao Ch'ien (365–427), a poet unique in Chinese history, who alone in an age of chaos attained to a profound harmony between nature and life, between fate and human will, and left behind him, to be the model and despair of future generations, the spontaneous outpouring of his gentle and soul-appeasing muse. Without the great accomplishments of these men, the ensuing T'ang renaissance could not have been what it was.

In more ways than one, indeed, the literature of the post-Han decadence completed and counterbalanced that of the Han period, by a process of reaction and reorientation. Thus were established, for the whole of Chinese literature, the twin dialectical sources of its long and varied development, analogous to Confucianism and Taoism in the domain of Chinese culture generally. The principal characteristics of post-Han literature admittedly constituted a reaction, but at the same time a corollary, to those of Han literature, in such a way as to complete that great medieval cycle in which all the main features of traditional Chinese poetry were already present.

For the greater clarity of our exposition we now propose to examine another aspect of Chinese poetry which, though it first emerged at the period we have been discussing, did not assume its full importance until very much later. The elaboration of literary technique during the post-Han age, combined with the pronounced Taoist beliefs then prevalent, produced a singular result, that unique form of specifically Chinese imagery from which later Chinese poetry was to evolve both its exquisite beauty and its arsenal of clichés. Now an unprejudiced analysis of the clichés peculiar to a given national literature is, in our opinion, one of the best methods that can be used to unravel those complex characteristics which make up its cultural unity.

Taoist "naturalism", regarded as a cultural influence, was the source, in spite of its great ideal of unity in the "one" the "selfsame", of very contradictory practical consequences. This is discernible even in the ancient period. *Tao* originally means the "way", the way of nature, of the selfsame. To return to nature is, or should be, to find freedom, as was well shown by that great Taoist of antiquity, Chuang-tze, both by his works and by his personality. But in the fourth century B.C. the legalists sought and found in the Tao, or "Way", the notion of the absolute supremacy and omnipotence of impersonal law; and this law, so flagrantly opposed to freedom, they codified and applied to government! But the antinomies of Taoism, at this period of its post-Han revival, manifested themselves in other fields than that of jurisprudence. On the one hand the new Taoist philosophers, having attained a high degree of spirituality, evolved a body of abstract metaphysics of extraordinary abstruseness and intricacy. While on the other the naturalistic cult of the Tao, growing ever since the Han age, continued to develop its picturesque ritual practices insisting on the importance of corporal well-being. The life of the body was to be cherished and prolonged by the physical pleasures in nature's gift, not excluding carnal enjoyment. In poetry we find on the one hand an untrammelled spirituality expressed in lofty and visionary strain, well exemplified by the Seven Worthies of the Bamboo Grove. And on the other, under the same Taoist influence, the keen observation and profound intuition of the physical beauty of nature, the joys of sensuous perception and an elaborate literary technique, the union of all which produced that imagery of exquisite fashioning destined to become the principal characteristic of Chinese poetry.

To infuse human emotions into natural objects, which in their turn give tangible form to those emotions, is of course as old as poetry itself. In Chinese poetry the immediate communion of nature and human feeling had been amply demonstrated by the *Book of Odes* and by Chu Yuan. But there had never been such chiselled and polished beauty as in this post-Han period. Most of the images were still taken from the objects invoked by ancient poetry. They were now so exquisitely wrought, endowed with such magic, that they were ever after to haunt the Chinese literary mind, blossoming from season to season until in the tenth century the *t'zu*, approximating still mose closely to *poésie pure*, carried them to a new perfection of poetic form. Rendered into another language these beauties naturally appear as mere preciousness, sentimentality and exotic nonsense. This is no doubt the reason why post-Han poetry of this type has been as rarely translated as the *t'zu* itself, and on those rare occasions their identity completely obscured.

We shall nevertheless try to give a few examples. Considered isolatedly most poetic images are mere cold symbols of objects. It is their context which gives them light and life and which they in their turn irradiate. Their context, that is to say the poet himself, thanks to his gift of observation and his art of enriching objects, not only with his own emotions, but with all the wealth of associations, linguistic and traditional, of which he is capable. In this observation and in this art the post-Han poets excelled. As imaged by them certain objects began to acquire, for Chinese poetic convention, those specific qualities of suggestion and evocation which, it is no exaggeration to say, have become part and parcel of Chinese cultural emotion.

It is to the post-Han poets that one must chiefly attribute the associations peculiar to "kingfisher", "pearl-curtain", "willow", "peach", "jade", "hibiscus", "clouds" and so on indefinitely. The kingfisher *(tz'ui)*, for example, was variously associated with the magic art of provoking rain in time of drought, the emerald colour of certain precious stones, the deep, rich green of vegetation, the dark hair of youthful beauty and sometimes the flight of love-birds. And in an exquisite short poem by Yu Chien-wu (sixth century), describing the grass in a melancholy harem, all these associations are gathered into one and impregnate the poem with simultaneous evocations of the luxurious palace and the anxiety, longing and amorous pining of the girls wasting their fair

Interrelations of Cultures

youth in a life that is like the aimless growth of tender grass.

Similarly in a love-song by Hsieh T'iao (464–499) we read:

> The pearl-curtain glimmers down before the evening hall,
> The glow-worms fly, and then cease:
> The whole night I sew this silken robe,
> How thus my love for you is without end.

We glimpse a momentary shimmer of pearls, in the light of the glow-worms, before the long hours of darkness. Then the lustre of the silken robe gleaming in the candlelight, pulsing like a lovesick heart. This pulsing and gleaming are an echo of the countless scintillating pearls. The curtain, then the robe, enfold the inner glow of love. The room is restless with the tantalizing interplay of light and shadow. But without is spread the all-enveloping night sky, like a garment, studded with stars as innumerable as the curtain's pearls. Even so is love, agleam, endless, innumerable, in the long starry nights. The closely woven texture of this poem is achieved by the tone relations of a score of monosyllables, strung together like a filigree of pearls and fraught with such music and meaning as no translation can convey. We hope, nevertheless, that the foregoing analysis may give some idea of what is involved. After such poems the "pearl-curtain", to be effective, was committed once and for all to the associated themes of twilight, moonlight, stars, love and night. Transposed in terms of English literature, it is as though rainbow and daffodils, having once been associated by Wordsworth with the upleaping and pleasure-filled heart, were to have their power of suggestion limited for all time to this single image.

The same object often evokes, in different languages, very different ideas, expressive perhaps of cultural idiosyncracies. A striking example of this is the reaction of the Chinese to *jade*. The Westerner associates it immediately with the ideas of coldness and hardness and thinks of it as something to be admired from a distance. I have verified this over and over again in conversations with students and friends. But in Chinese its classical epithets are "soft", "smooth" and "warm". Its use as a metaphor for the body and skin of woman is a commonplace. This may perhaps be explained empirically by the

72

Chinese use of jade in numerous objects of personal adornment. However this may be, the direct effect, emotional or
physical, inducive of a kind of empathy, exerted on the
Chinese sensibility by natural objects, can hardly be better
illustrated than by this example of jade and its inseparable
epithets. Examples of even triter metaphors are the "willow-
leaf" for eyebrow and "autumn-waves", which does not describe, but *means* the eyes of a beautiful woman, just as "dark-
clouds" *means* her hair. Such clichés do not perhaps make good
poems. Indeed they often make bad ones. But their ubiquity
in Chinese literature is significant.

Having discussed the literary characteristics of the long
period stretching from the Han to the post-Han age, we shall
now briefly treat of the T'ang age, considered as a new cycle
worthy of the name of renaissance. The grandeur and richness of T'ang culture and particularly of T'ang poetry are
universally acknowledged. It is an age intensely interesting in
and for itself and deserving of close study. But for our present
purpose, which is to show the general characteristics of Chinese
literature, it is convenient to assimilate it to the periods
that went before. There is no doubt that it constitutes, in the
general panorama of Chinese literature, an age of rebirth. But
as such it is more remarkable for having infused new meaning,
purpose and vigour into the old classical forms and ideas than
for having created new ones. Its energy was derived from the
young union of peoples. And it benefited also by the vast
popular treasury accumulated during three hundred years of
indigenous social development and further enriched by the
assimilation of the foreign invaders with their picturesque
customs and barbaric arts. Not to mention the elaborate literary technique inherited from the post-Han age. Li Po (701 to
756) and Tu Fu (712–770), hailed by tradition as the two
greatest T'ang poets, would not have been what they were
but for this immediate heritage, though they both harked back
to a still remoter past in their ambition to revive the ancient
tradition. This was natural. For the China of their day was
a regenerated China. They were brave new youth in search
of their primordial ancestral image, seeking to reconstitute the
family-tree in all its ramifications.

The only epoch-making original creation of the T'ang age
is fiction. That is, fiction consciously developed into an enter-

taining literary form. Its immediate source, as of every other new literary genre, was folklore. It is strongly marked by Buddhism. Stylistically, it owed much to the development of a new prose freed from the artificial parallelism of the past. It is interesting to note that the Buddhist influence on Chinese literary life gained in extent and depth as the religion itself became more characteristically Chinese. And as the expressions of this religion are various, so are the marks of its influence in different fields of Chinese literature. This foreign faith, as reflected in Chinese poetry, was true to its spirit and gave up its life that it might live. To the early zealots of the post-Han period it had inspired sermons and hymns written in traditional Chinese verse forms. But these seldom deserved the name of poetry. It was not until the T'ang period that Buddhism appeared, in the writings of several great poets, as a subtler, more temperate and more pervasive influence. It suffused their works with a strange and insidious light and conferred on their word-painting and word-music, however characteristically Chinese these remained, unique and unspeakable calm and austerity. In ironical contrast to this we find among the Buddhist monks of this period such able poets as Kuan Hsiu and Chi Chi whose writings, in spite of their professed faith, yield to none in secularism. But the enriching Buddhist influence is most clearly to be seen in Chinese folklore and in Chinese fiction.

So far poetry has been the chief source of our evidence as to the general characteristics of Chinese literature. This is inevitable, since the traditional masterpieces of this literature belong to poetry. Fiction did not properly begin until the T'ang dynasty. From the eleventh century on, through the Sung, Yuan and subsequent dynasties, its broader and more popular development, soon accompanied by that of drama, brings us to the next phase, on the threshold of modern times.

This period from the eleventh to the end of the nineteenth century may here be most conveniently discussed from the two following points of view: historically, as a reorientation, and culturally, in its significance for the evolution of literary genres. With the Sung dynasty Chinese history may be said to have entered on a new phase, and Chinese literature along with it. If the T'ang age was a rejuvenation of Chinese culture, the Sung age was a step towards maturity. In the following eras Chinese national life was marked by all the troubles, anxieties and struggles for survival characteristic of adult existence. In order to survive this period of crisis literature was compelled to a more sustained effort of cohesion. If it was to subsist as a unifying force and at the same time as an expression of the state of things, it had a double role to play. It had to assert, on the one hand, an ever stronger traditionalism and, on the other, to adapt itself to new conditions.

During the period of nearly a thousand years following the Sung dynasty, the course of history was free of those internecine tensions and scissions which had marked the Three Kingdoms and the post-T'ang age. The successive dynasties enjoyed, ostensibly at least, long periods of unity and solidarity. But it is well known that during the Sung age the Chinese nation not only ceased to develop territorially, but was very often reduced to the defensive by foreign invasions from the north. As for the only other national dynasty of this millennium, the Ming, its main task consisted in the measures to be taken for the recovery of the historical tradition and in the energetic assimilation of racial groups created by the Mongolian domination. The two powerful dynasties which succeeded, thanks to the might of their arms, in holding China and even in expanding its dominions, were both foreign: the Mongols of Yuan and the Manchus of Ch'ing.

The general effects of these historical events on the Chinese temperament are visible in various domains. To begin with, there was an accentuation of public apathy with regard to state authority, national military glory and federal organization. It is true that drastic measures of reorganization were essayed during the middle Sung dynasty. And it may seem strange that the Chinese, in the ensuing ages, did not rise against foreign domination at the call of some ambitious and energetic leaders, instead of allowing the efforts of these few patriots to degenerate into abject local and clandestine cults. Why, we wonder, did the *élite* of Chinese intellectuals hold aloof for so long from these efforts at organization? The consequences of their failure to revolt are still flagrant. This inertia has been censured over and over again by modern thinkers, both in China and elsewhere; but the heat of stricture will long be cold before a solution is found to this afflicting enigma. Pragmatically we neither can, nor should, justify this desertion. But gesticulating denunciation can only lead either to the despair of self-commiseration or to the futility of rash and subjective judgments. If we wish to understand, we must re-examine without passion the deep historical forces at work. The function of history is rather to give us a better understanding of the past in the light of the present than to encourage us to accept the present as inevitable or to inveigh against historical facts because of their regrettable consequences. And since Chinese national life and cultural development seem to have been preserved by some other means, surely we should try and see in what this means consisted. A survey of the literary trends during this period may help us to understand.

It is a truism to say that what safeguarded the existence and growth of China at this time was the assimilation of the foreign emperors by cultural forces. But if we examine more closely the meaning of this simple conflict between culture and military strength we may find it rich in implications for Chinese history of the last ten centuries. Culture, though a real force, cannot be conscripted and applied with the foresight and strategy proper to a military organization. We have seen how the meaning of culture is distorted, and its true nature and function obscured, when governments "mobilize" national art and literature like so many tanks. The real force of culture, its faculty to maintain in lasting being a given human group, reside precisely, to our mind, in a consciousness exempt from all nationalism, in an integral, undiscriminating, ever widening humanism. And the Chinese, for the past thousand years, have been engaged in attaining this cultural ideal at the expense of their nationalism and with that concomitant disregard for organization which we now deplore, rightly or wrongly. We further notice that this cultural force, in pursuance of its true nature, did not conform—which does not mean that it never can—to any policy of government, but rather on occasion determined such policy. In other words, its action cannot be explained in terms of a conscious leadership, whether of party or of individual. But it was deeply rooted in the common way of life; it was supported and safeguarded by a long tradition; it asserted and developed its values not so much in spite, as in virtue, of the troubled times; and it did so in that spirit of irresistible solidarity which could only spring from a total, undiscriminating consciousness of common humanity.

Further evidence in support of this view may be adduced from the rise of the novel and drama as literary genres, with their specific forms and qualities. The individual consciousness of national tradition was more particularly marked in the upper strata of society, among intellectuals. The great literary tradition was obviously to be sought in the magnificent achievements of ancient poetry. It was here that the great models were preserved, and the great literary moulds. But times had changed. History had taken a new turn. And the cultivated traditionalism of this period did not produce much original poetry. Its voice was the voice of the past, its merit a fostering of the antique strain. The only living prolongation of the old poetic tradition at this period was the *tz'u*. It was an exceedingly musical form akin to *poésie pure*, evolved from popular sources in the T'ang age. It inherited the high technique of the post-Han and following periods and was developed with great sensitivity by the Sung poets. During the Sung-Yuan-Ming-Ch'ing period it was transposed and popularized in the form of drama. For drama and the novel had triumphed as literary forms.

Their rise to pre-eminence from the eleventh century on was a reflection of contemporary historical events, just as the rise of the modern European and American novel to its present predominance is a reflection of nineteenth-century individualism, industrialism and free enterprise. In both cases the form was determined by the times. And the parts they were to play, though very dissimilar, were equally vital. The assertion that the Chinese novel, compared to its modern counterpart, is lacking in art and technique, is as true as it is anachronistic. In encyclopaedias and critical anthologies of world literature it is often to be remarked that ancient and medieval European literature is presented and assessed in terms of its continually shifting social and historical background, whereas Chinese literature is treated as though eternally contemporary and with as little regard for its social and historical references as, when it comes to translation, for its linguistic qualities. It is commonly alleged that the belatedness and primitiveness of the Chinese novel and drama are due to the contempt in which they were held by Chinese literary and social circles. This explanation is very true and may be regarded as highly satisfactory from the view-point of modern sociology. And it has acted as a stimulant on the modern Chinese movement in favour of a vernacular literature and a deserved revival of novel and drama, with results extremely beneficial for modern Chinese literature in general.

But when we relate the traditional Chinese novel and drama to their proper historical circumstances, it becomes clear to us that the important cultural action which they exercised on their epoch was only possible in virtue of the specific characteristics with which that epoch had endowed them. Their effectiveness as a unifying factor of Chinese culture, during this long and troubled period of foreign conquest and domination, was due precisely to their maintenance on a level with the people, whence their low social status and naïve technique. This does not mean that they never rose above the level of folklore, nor were even given artistic form by the more gifted men of letters. But unlike Chinese poetry they never abandoned, even in their final "literary" form, the structure, subject-matter, language and tone of their popular origins. The merit of the literati, particularly as novelists, often of great talent, consisted in their willingness to lose their identity among the people. This may be explained negatively by the fact that these writers, jealous of their freedom of expression and fearful of persecution at a time of foreign domination and tyranny, preferred to remain anonymous. But the real reason is rather to be sought in the decline of literature among the upper classes, as a result of their chauvinistic nationalism and of a perfunctory and scholastic classicism encouraged by foreign rule, and in the corresponding concentration of creative vigour and originality among the people. This close union of the highest literary talent with the people resulted in a refinement and widespread diffusion of popular literature. Sprung from the people, it was faithful to the people's modes of thought and expression, while remaining more familiar to them in the form of oral relation than through the medium of reading.

This result of the conflict between culture and militarism contributed powerfully to the maintenance of Chinese literary life. It must be regarded as one of the most important factors whereby, despite perpetual menace from abroad, the Chinese people were held together and their general cultural life preserved intact. It also played a decisive role in the assimilation of alien peoples and their inclusion in the consciousness of a collective humanity proper to Chinese popular tradition. This may further serve to explain, in functional terms, the special characteristics of the Chinese novel and drama. Unlike the modern novel, they were deficient in personal originality and technical invention. This was inevitable. For these works to be convincing it was necessary for the author to forego all personality. What they had to convey was not the calculated pronouncements of an individual, but, with careless and spontaneous persuasiveness, the vague content of everyday existence. It was a thankless task and conducive neither to personal fame nor to that supreme desideratum of modern novelists, royalties. We must add that such works were not prompted by an exclusive concern with the preservation of national culture, but rather by a genuine artistic urge in harmony with the exigencies of the time. The result is a memorial that transcends its artificers.

The language of the traditional novel had to be colloquial, and even uncouth, in order that the people might easily recognize their own speech and their own images, however these might be transformed—grossly, idealistically or fantastically—in the figures of great lovers, supermen or heroes. Here Quixote is born of Sancho's imaginings. For the same reasons plausibility of plot is required, and the observance of social conventions. Satire and criticism might be free and pungent, but never to the point of open protest, much less of provocation. Moral preachifying was rife. But even here the moralist, in manner and tone, was the people themselves, impersonal and anonymous. From the viewpoint of modern fiction these sermons may seem singularly mawkish and otiose; but they are far less presumptuously didactic and humourless than the moral treatises of self-assertive individuals, less infuriatingly complacent and hypocritical. References to religion, particularly to Buddhism, also abound; but these too are less offensive and preposterous than in the mouth of a self-obtrusive preacher. These writings seem to be the work of all and sundry and it is this that makes them acceptable to all, if not positively pleasing, and explains their widespread diffusion. It is from them that the people received that spiritual coherence

79

and that faculty of assimilation which for nearly a thousand years resisted the menace of disintegration and preserved the fundamentals of Chinese cultural life.

The Chinese novel and drama, for all their merits and achievements, are of course only two among the many signs of the general cultural trend. Their particular significance resides in their identification, for the safeguard of cultural values, with the common people of China, at a time when, in higher spheres, China was decaying as a political force. Thus the *wen*, that is to say literature, in its grandiose conception as the great mover of human civilization, all-embracing, sustaining, refining, mellowing; the *wen* conceived as the antithesis of the *wu*, that is, militarism, and as transcending law and politics; the *wen* now came to rest, after many vicissitudes, in the common people, and through them, like a spirit through its medium, exercised its potency and virtue.

In this connexion we should like to touch upon a technical aspect of the traditional Chinese novel, all the more worthy of attention as it has been too often overlooked, or noted with derision. The technique in question was so generally employed that to a modern reader, however unsophisticated, it must seem a tedious commonplace. But to practically every popular Chinese novelist it appears to have been of vital importance. While we can find no excuse for its triteness, we continue to believe that a convention which became hackneyed by excess of popular favour may, like the clichés of Chinese poetry, provide very instructive matter for discussion.

This ubiquitous device bears on the manner in which, in those days, every novel must begin. No matter what its subject was—historical events, the rise and fall of a family, great lovers or the adventures of monks and brigands—the novel must always open with a generalization, often naïve, but delivered in the lofty philosophical tone befitting a universal truth. The beginning of the historical novel *The Three Kingdoms* consists of a review of history from the remotest antiquity and an exposition of its "philosophy": "The world situation is always that after long unity there must come division, and after long division there must come unity."

The *Chin Ping Mai*, an extremely licentious and realistic novel about a debauched fop and his relations (predominantly nocturnal) with his concubines, opens with a copious invocation of various immortals and great historical figures anciently famous for their virtues or their vices. The several versions of the *Hsi Yu Chi*, already mentioned, all began with the story of the creation. The last of the few great novels, the *Hung Lou Meng (Dream of the Red Chamber)*, a superb story of family love, is superior to all its predecessors as a work of art. But both in language and in general conception it remained close to popular standards. Its content was readily accessible to the intelligence and imagination of the common people when it was read to them aloud (it was through oral relation that most novels became popular, even among the illiterate). Here too the author began with a long chapter dealing with creation and with historical and religious cycles of retribution, vindication and compensation lasting for thousands of years. After which all the interest is concentrated on the adventures of two young lovers belonging to a great eighteenth-century family, related in over a hundred chapters of minute detail.

Research has brought to light the "pre-existence", so to speak, of most Chinese novels in the narrations of city and country story-tellers ever since the Sung dynasty. In the crude and semi-illiterate synopses of these tales, written down mainly for mnemonic purposes, we find the same grandiose preambles. Elaboration, revision and refinement were assuredly the work of literary men. But they were carried out with deliberate self-effacement. Even the author of the *Red Chamber*, that relatively original and individual work, made it clear that his material was "false words and rustic talk". And he succeeded in preserving his anonymity for nearly two hundred years, until modern research revealed his identity. It was not always possible, however, for the literary man to avoid giving himself away. He was especially liable to do so in the versified passages. But this did not detract from the intelligibility and popularity of these works, when retold to the people. Most of the verses were doggerel. But even when they had a certain polish, there did not necessarily ensue a breach between the author and the people. On the contrary, a certain degree of refinement was calculated not only to raise the artistic standards of the common people, but also to bring among them a feeling for the great classical tradition and thus, in a sense, to unite all classes of society in a common culture.

It is clear that the relationship between men of letters and the people is always a reciprocal one. The mythical, historical and philosophical dissertations traditionally placed at the beginning of the Chinese novel must have been cultivated by the intellectuals since antiquity; but now, having thoroughly permeated all classes of the community, they were to receive, on the level of popular literature, their most forceful expression, less intellectual than hitherto, but all the more susceptible of general acceptance. It was this machinery of the Chinese novel that maintained, for all its apparent absurdity, some kind of philosophy among the people, gave them a cosmogony and a *weltanschauung*, naïve perhaps, but robust, and well calculated to preserve as a living and omnipresent force the humanistic and naturalistic traditions of Chinese culture and to achieve that ideal inherent in the doctrine of the *wen*, a spiritual solidarity transcending all forms of legal, political and military organization. But perhaps the chief merit of this panoramic novel was its gift to the Chinese people of a generous imagination, a means of solace, a cheerful and stoical resignation and a sense of human dignity in the face of the severest sufferings and privations; and this it accomplished thanks to the keen sense it conveyed of the immensity of national historical cycles and of individual experience, however intimate and trivial, as indissolubly bound up with the whole of humanity and the whole of nature.

Having now reached the end of our enquiry we perceive, not without remorse, the multiple aspects and elements of Chinese literature which we have been obliged to pass over in silence. In particular we have scarcely touched upon the evolutionary stages of the novel and drama and the numerous social conventions and customs incident thereto. Least justice of all has been done to drama, which deserved to be treated independently of the novel. Admittedly they had in common the same laxity of panoramic technique and even the same cosmic pompousness and grandiose historicity in pursuance of an identical social and cultural function. But Chinese drama also falls within the tradition of lyric poetry and we should not have neglected to discuss the development of its exquisite verse from common speech and colloquial dialogues, its stage-craft and finally its lapse, through excess of versification, into mere decadent virtuosity and the substitution of a kind of music-hall for lyrical drama. Both the drama and the novel, in effect, passed through various stages of growth and enjoyed various periods of favour. All these we must leave to the judicious imagination of the reader.[1]

On the subject of contemporary Chinese literature we shall be brief. With the birth of the Republic in 1912 China took her place among the nations of the world and her history entered upon a completely new phase in all domains. The first reaction to this new situation culminated in the educational and political movement of 1919. This was called the Fourth of May Movement and was directly provoked by the political stimulus of foreign relations. But its most significant effects were obtained in the literary field. Here its action was closely associated with that of the movement in favour of a vernacular literature, whose aspirations could be more clearly defined than those of a more political nature. Hardly thirty years have passed since then and we cannot yet assess the importance of the results achieved. In the vast scale of Chinese history thirty years are less than a minute. But against the background of the great works of the past the modern literary trend can be seen as a further expansion of those tireless popular energies from which, ever since antiquity, the countless cycles of Chinese creative literature were born and reborn, those same energies thanks to which, in later ages, Chinese culture survived, adapting itself to changing circumstances and developing in spite of numerous foreign invasions.

We are familiar with the fashionable argument according to which the Chinese were able to maintain themselves and assimilate other peoples because, up to the last century, those peoples were their cultural inferiors, but that today, in their contact with modern nations, this situation is reversed. But can we speak of the inferiority of a culture that sets art, literature and philosophy, love of man and of nature, high above militant nationalism, intense political organization and methodical destruction? And what culture can ever be superior that inverts these values? Let us make haste to emphasize that the Chinese are by no means alone in possessing these lofty cultural ideals. It is obvious that they are the common possession of all humanity. We simply mean that in China, for

---

[1] Valuable studies of the cultural significance and merits of the Chinese novel have been made, with deep insight and keen observation, by Pearl S. Buck in *China* (*"U.S. Series"*, pp. 394-405) and in her Nobel Prize Lecture (1938). The best work on the drama is the *History of the Sung Yuan Drama* by the late historian, philosopher and critic Wang Kuo-wei.

innumerable historical and ethnological reasons, these ideals and values have developed over such length of time and such immensities of space, passed through so many trials and errors, survived such repeated assaults of their contraries, as finally to have imposed themselves with incontrovertible authority. It is in the light of these considerations that we grasp the interest to be derived from the study of Chinese culture and of the literature which is its symbolic expression: it does not consist in choosing from among their many qualities those worthy of our emulation, but rather in discerning the vast patterns formed by their protracted development and in understanding them as the expression of the bitter experience of an immense human group striving through its long history to solve its basic problems and survive. Chinese culture may then be seen as a great panel of that historical mirror to which the whole of contemporary humanity may turn, the better to know itself. The cultural history of China thus takes its place, as a functional value, in the enlarged historical consciousness of the modern world. This is the only plane on which Chinese culture may fairly be criticized or defended, no longer in the exclusiveness of its purely national significance, but as an integral part of all human history.

One of the most instructive lessons to be drawn from Chinese cultural values, as developed from the earliest times, has to do with the artificiality and fragility of military nationalism and rival politics, as they existed in China at the time of the ancient warring states and as they continue to exist in our modern world today, and with the possibility of breaking down these factitious barriers and of attaining, in a spirit of universal fellowship, to a conscious and progressive humanism analogous to that which, in a sense, China may be said to have achieved. We may also learn from Chinese history how a culture instinct with the *wen* ideal can, without nationalism or militarism, prevail over racial and national limits, emerge triumphant from armed conquest and preserve its values for the general good.

But our admiration of all these cultural achievements must be tempered with criticism. They are to be judged, like those of any other nation, according to the criteria of modern world history. We shall then realize that something is lacking to them and that they were obtained at perhaps too great a cost.

The spirit of resignation was the fruit of a suffering which must seem extravagant in the light of modern technology. Political apathy facilitated the periodic excesses of tyrants and demagogues, though it implied the comforting assurance that their downfall was a foregone conclusion. Most important of all, these achievements were not the result of any conscious purpose, but rather of a tenacious fidelity to a few great historical and political ideas, known since antiquity and sporadically celebrated, by collective or by individual genius, in verse, drama and the novel. But the full meaning of these great ideas was either imperfectly perceived or else completely obscured. The real agents of their great effects were a robust love of life and the urge to perpetuate it.

In conclusion, if we consider that certain specific characteristics of Chinese culture deserve to be preserved and fostered, in the general interest of our modern world, we must invoke to this end that aid which only science can give, in the form of a *rapprochement* between East and West. When we speak of science we are not thinking merely of the mechanical and technical accomplishments whereby it transforms the material conditions of living. For we believe that science, in the true and original sense of the term "to know", attains its greatest efficacy when it brings to the clear light of human understanding the true meaning of humanity's most cherished values and the means of preserving them in the form of fully rational and ordered states of consciousness, so that human welfare, hitherto rather the effect of hazard than of purpose, may result henceforward from the application of clear and efficient principles capable of ensuring at the least possible cost the greatest possible extent of general good. If the scientific spirit, in a universal synthesis, can render this service to our historical patrimony, then science will no longer be the enemy, but the worthy servitor of humanity.

Essay on the Culture of Japan

by

E. STUART KIRBY

The following study although concerned with Japanese culture in general, gives particular emphasis to the literature of
Japan. Japan's literature exceeds most others in antiquity and
variety. Moreover, its manner is extrovert or self revealing.
The social inhibitions of the Japanese, throughout their
history, have little affected their popular and recreational
literature, which was regarded contemptuously by group and
caste rulers, and has generally been for the Japanese an outlet
for the thoughts and impulses elsewhere repressed. The formal
and learned literature has, on the other hand, been a powerful
preserver of tradition, loyalty and cohesion. Thus the study
of Japanese literature gives a wide and instructive range of
data; and the conflict of motives shows to best advantage in
this connexion.

Regrettably, this literature has not been amply studied in
other countries, owing to the linguistic difficulty, the strange
background and the special character of its relations to other
cultures. The literary factor may nevertheless have been
decisive in the history of the race. The Japanese were tribally
united in primitive times by the respect for legend (the father
of literature). Thereafter, they were first formed and ordered
into a nation by authority wielding not only the sword but
also the magic of the written word. Subsequently, their
peculiar feudal system was founded especially on respect for
the written word. More recently, general literacy and assiduous
textbook work were directly responsible for the success of the
Japanese in mastering Western and capitalistic techniques. At
present, the future of this people depends on its ability and
willingness to know the thoughts and needs of the rest of the
world and to adopt the rules governing international relations
or adapt to the requirements of such relations.

RACIAL ORIGINS AND BASIC PSYCHOLOGY
(PREHISTORIC TIMES)

Ethnology and philology are unable to solve the riddle of Japanese origins; but they show that the islands were originally peopled by diverse strains from different parts of the Asiatic mainland. The order of arrival and commingling is conjectural, but indications support the *a priori* conclusion from the facts of geography—that the north-east Asian strain was qualitatively, if not numerically, predominent. The Aimu (regarded as a Caucasian stock) were at an early stage widespread in all the islands. In neolithic times, Mongolian tribesmen, passing through Korea, made many settlements on the coasts. In the same period there was an accession of features indicating southerly origins (e.g. the wet rice culture associated with south China, and domestic architecture and tribal cults connected with the South Seas). Archaeology shows no palaeolithic culture, but two main types of advanced neolithic development. Apparently, the variety of influences (or local variations) points clearly to a succession of "waves" of cultural impact. These fuse over a very long period (the Stone Age persisting in Japan still as late as the beginning of the Christian era) into a uniform culture. The broad comparison is sometimes made with the prehistory of the British Isles in relation to continental Europe (a similar comparison is made for the Japan of later stages also); within limits, that comparison is not unfruitful, as the interplay of motives of "insularity" and "absorptiveness", is perhaps broadly similar in the two cases.

The above is a very drastic condensation; but it does suggest a starting point, i.e. that the Japanese had from the beginning a mixed culture. From this period already there emerges one trait, throughout very pronounced in the Japanese: an inherent propensity to *eclecticism*. Ethnology shows synthesis; archaelogy shows a range of semantic influences with, nevertheless, a northern predominance. Mythology strongly demonstrates this eclecticism: the northern and central Asian heritages (animism, shamanism, etc.) are happily combined with the southern or Polynesian (cosmogonic myths, tribal cults, etc.). Sociology, at a later period, also shows their eclecticism: the northern and southern affinities (in themselves heterogeneous) are present as a persistent dichotomy, in every sphere of activity. To sum up, the physical types, the peculiarities of custom, religion, way of living, politics, etc. show great heterogeneity, yet great cohesiveness.

The Japanese have always been known as great *imitators;* this characteristic is in fact quite general, and may have been intensified by Japan's particular position in the Far East. European and American nations should recall, however, that most of their own progress was made by imitating each other. It seems unjustified, in fact, to conclude that the Japanese mind has been passive or non-creative, that imitativeness connotes necessarily or exclusively an extrovert turn of mind. Assertiveness, both national and personal, as well as introvert impulses have at various stages of history characterized Japanese behaviour. "Eclecticism" would seem to be a more accurate term to describe their dominant tendency and it has the advantage of stressing the important fact of their consistently active and practical, rather than speculative, character. In selecting their ideas they appear throughout to have done so with the solution to some specific problem in view, and to have been psychologically realistic, in the sense of being little swayed (less than other peoples) by sentimental considerations; their interest has been in doing, rather than in knowing.

For example, the generalization has often been made that the Japanese are mentally a slave race which will instantly and completely change its course of thinking at a word of command or a swing of fashion. At the same time they are described as being peculiarly intransigent in their social loyalty (e.g. the emperor cult) and willing to subordinate themselves to long-term political conceptions (e.g. secular militarism). These two generalizations are scarcely consistent and it is sufficient to recognize that there is doubtless some truth in each of them.

The Japanese have throughout their history been distinguished for their practicality and organizing ability rather than for metaphysics or analysis. Some observers have accordingly stressed the practical bent of the Japanese. "Proof", says a characteristic Japanese proverb, "is better than argument".[1]

---

1 *Ron yori shoko.* Literally: "Demonstration (in practice) is better than discourse (or disputation)."

They tend in this view to conserve what is found "good" (useful or practical), and to select what is "good" in new-found features, for *use* in conjunction. Others see the development of the Japanese as a "dialectical" process. Seemingly, a special law of dichotomy is operative; all through Japanese institutions and actions, there is persistently a juxtaposition of contrast, or mixture of motives, techniques, and stages of development, greater than in any other human group (e.g. the extremes of passion or cruelty alternating with an ultra-stoic self control, the latest technique co-existing with a prehistoric religion, or diverse stages of economic and social development standing side by side). Some observers stress the essential individuality of the Japanese mind. In cultural status and practical competence, the great systems of China and the West, which successively confronted the Japanese, must have seemed absolutely overwhelming to them. Japan adopted each of these systems in turn, but "always there is a hard, non-absorbent core of individual character, which resists and in its turn works upon the invading influence".

These are the words of Sir George Sansom,[1] who goes on to say that this "distinctive temperament" is owing to some dominant characteristic in the racial strain, possibly the warm southern element which is apparent in their imaginative temperament and their primeval myths, though archaeological evidence points to northern origins. This applies particularly to the amoral sensuality exhibited in some of their literature, though repressed or sublimated in their other arts and activities. But there is evidently a good deal of common ground between the several views cited above, and it is over that common ground that the approach to our problem, in my opinion, clearly lies.

Additional allowance should be made for two other characteristics, not peculiar to the Japanese but fully shared by others, especially other Asian peoples. They do not, however, invalidate the main point I have been concerned so far to make. The two characteristics in question are the following:

A native ability (or histrionic talent) for concealing their real intentions, and being careful to present only aspects which may please the auditor. In answer to a question, Oriental

---

1 G. B. Sansom, *Japan, A Short Cultural History*, Appleton, 1945, p. 15.

courtesy demands the answer that will please the questioner, rather than factual accuracy. B. H. Chamberlain observed that, like Talleyrand, the Japanese believe that language was given to man to conceal his thoughts.

The logic of the Japanese (and other Eastern) minds does not insist that any formulation, to be logical, must be monomial. The absolute black or the absolute white are not normal conceptions in this philosophy; there are myriad shades of grey, and it is as foolish to deny blackness or whiteness to any one of them as it is to assert that only one's own variety is the perfect white, while all others are black, and "damned black at that". Thus the exclusiveness and mutual hostility of European religions, politics, or philosophies are more or less incomprehensible to Orientals, whose conception of logic, no less than their usages, permits their simultaneous adherence to more than one of each. The Japanese, with their practical sense and worldliness, while not insisting on a single formula, will insist on a definite solution.

The modern Nazis used the word *Gleichschaltung* (co-ordination) to mean the forcible reduction of all thoughts and tendencies to the common denominator of the party line or dogma. There has been a good deal of that in Japan's history, too. But it is essential to be on guard from the beginning against any confusion between cause and effect. The insistence of the rulers may measure the degree of heterogeneity, or nonconformity, of mind among the ruled. If this were so herd-minded and unindividual a race as is often supposed, there would not be the slightest necessity for *Gleichschaltung;* or if the people were incapable of common-sense criticism of official policies or dogmas, there would similarly be no need for the elaborate indoctrination. As regards temperament and capacity for artistic expression, a similar point should be made: the famous Japanese inscrutability and impassivity are the result of very long training and elaborate codification of conduct which would have been quite unnecessary had not the race been fundamentally imaginative, impulsive, self-willed and sensuous.

This review of Japanese origins and pre-history leads me while advancing these considerations, to stress the necessity for a broadly humanistic and sociologically neutral evaluation. This people of very mixed derivation and varied anthropological heritage consisted originally of small groups, each of which performed great feats of migration and conquest, and must therefore have possessed, above all, adventurousness, self-reliance and determination. This was no collectively planned campaign, but the hardy achievement of small bands of individuals who travelled great oceans in canoes. After settlement in Japan, they lived for centuries as scattered tribes and clans, federating only very gradually into a loosely knit political structure. It is evident that at a later stage there was *Gleichschaltung*, but that this aboriginal individuality and heterogeneity still shows, even at the present day. In later centuries the process of *Gleichschaltung* was modified by other Asian factors and it is likely that the compliance and obedience of the average Japanese, at any stage of history, have not been so sincere and unreserved as they would appear.[1]

THE FORMATION OF THE JAPANESE CULTURE AND THE JAPANESE EMPIRE (FIRST TO EIGHTH CENTURIES A.D.)

Apart from fragmentary Chinese and Korean references, the first written and authentic records date from the sixth century A.D. They relate therefore to a late stage of the process of tribal clan amalgamation, give no direct evidence regarding its earlier course, and are highly rationalized (or selected) to suit an emergent political régime.

Japanese myths and legends represent the Japanese (Yamato) race, not so much as aboriginal but as heaven-descended. Entering into the chosen land, it subdued or eliminated the aborigines, some of whom are represented as subhuman (earth-spiders, etc.); thus the Japanese are not so much the first inhabitants as the first *human* or civilized inhabitants. Collectively, they have divine sanction, being of divine descent; but like the gods themselves, constitute a great hierarchy—the attributes are greatest in the ruler, and diminish rank by rank, the common people being godlike only in comparison with barbarians and animals. This conception was built up by oral tradition. The first historic records show how long established and important, by the sixth century, was

---

[1] See page 90.

the hereditary Corporation of Storytellers (*Kataribe*) as a repository of the national, clan and family annals, and as upholders of the divinity and fame of the rulers.

The topography, with all the islands cut into "pockets" of fertile land, made division into tribes inevitable at the start. Legend and instinct must have worked together for racial solidarity and practical federation. But the patriarchal clan system was locally strong. It appears that there evolved over the centuries a system of "guilds" *(be)* and "corporations" *(tomo)*, ancillary—and distinctly subordinate to the clans. These were groups of persons carrying on the essential professions and occupations. The storytellers were of some importance, though ranking below the priestly and ministerial guilds; and there were three powerful military guilds. The legends relate, in a somewhat confused fashion, how after prolonged strife the local clans became federated under a supreme overlord, the emperor. A main event in this period was the successful invasion from Kyushu which penetrated into the Yamato (Osaka-Kyoto) region; legend puts this in the seventh century B.C., but more probably it took place in the first century A.D. Sociological study reveals that during the same period, the social organization was greatly extended, based on a system of local guilds, corporations or castes, which were gradually linked together on a national basis.

By the seventh century A.D. there was definitely a strong state, under an emperor in Yamato, controlling the whole country as far north and east as Sendai, and having a relatively advanced social culture. Iron and bronze were known, as well as weaving and other social arts; it had an evolved religion (Shinto), and an organized society based on the clan and caste system noted above. Chinese writing was undoubtedly adopted at this time as a means of assuring the cultural and social cohesion of the state. There had in the meantime been considerable cultural influence from China and Korea. In the first century B.C. northern Korea was one of the most prosperous and cultured of the Chinese colonies. Archaeological finds show that southern Korea was strongly permeated with Chinese culture by the end of the first century. Chinese products (as well as Korean imitations thereof, and Japanese imitations of the Korean imitations) are found in western Japan, among the relics of the contemporary indigenous products. Chinese written records of the first four centuries A.D. prove that from A.D. 57 or earlier there were regular relations between China, Korea and Japan, the latter accepting a tributary relationship to China. The Japanese at this period were divided into numerous tribes, each with its chief.

The spread in Japan of knowledge of the Chinese language, literature and methods occurred over the same period, and indeed *pari passu* with the federation of the clans and the development of the social system described above, with its division of labour, caste system, and aristocracy. Presumably the strongest and most advanced chiefs sent emissaries to Han China and Korea, and welcomed instructors from there, for acquiring technical knowledge, and for the prestige of association with them, in order to make themselves still stronger in their own country. Consolidation would inevitably result; in all probability the strongest clans absorbed the weaker, and, as the social system became more complex, the corporations and the castes developed and gradually became linked on a nation-wide basis. Evidence points in this direction.

Literacy (in Chinese) was, then, the original means and symbol of power and advancement. The craft of letters was no less important than the priestcraft in the foundation of the empire. An aura of magical and political power has ever since surrounded the written word, in Japan, more perhaps than in any other country. Literacy was at that time a very difficult accomplishment; there was no question of any commoner aspiring to it. Only the rulers, and those picked by them, could have access to the books and the teachers. Even then, it was a question of learning, not merely new ways of thought, but an entirely new language, utterly different in structure and kind as well as sound, and a script which was very difficult indeed to adapt to the Japanese language. It was no question of simple picture-writing; the Chinese script had already evolved (over some two thousand years) very far from the pictographic into the ideographic and the conventionalized. This was a task for an *élite*, and required a lifetime's apprenticeship. It is simpler to learn to read than to write in Chinese letters.

The results are still discernible: Firstly, the script difficulty imposes a long education, during which speculative or original thinking is inhibited, and the greater party is memorizing.

93

Secondly, veneration for learning is firmly inculcated, but it is not easy to distinguish between the abstract (general) devotion to the superior culture and the personal subordination to its practitioners. The latter are socially the ruling class. In this setting, the difficulty the Japanese have always had in distinguishing between ends and means, is particularly apparent. Thirdly, class or group rule is accordingly facilitated, popular criticism made difficult, and a critical habit of mind cannot be formed.

A special feature is the aesthetic value of the script itself. In China and Japan, calligraphy has always been not only the greatest of the arts but, the *key* to all the other arts from the technical and philosophical points of view. Painting and other arts cannot be practised without a mastery of the calligraphic technique, or understood without an understanding of the values underlying the master-art of calligraphy. There might possibly be an illiterate master-craftsman; but there could not be an uneducated great master.

MASTERY OF CHINESE CULTURE AND RENASCENCE OF JAPANESE CULTURE (EIGHTH TO TENTH CENTURIES)

The first Japanese records are the *Kojiki (Record of Ancient Matters)* and the *Nihonshoki (Chronicle of Japan)*, dated 712 and 716. The latter, written in Chinese not Japanese, is a compendium of historical knowledge, made by order of the ruler (an empress), and is a tendentious work made to justify the dynasty and enhance its prestige. A first version of this, the *Nihongi*, written in Japanese, was rejected. It was not imposing enough as a justification of the ruling house. Other scribes were therefore ordered to write in Chinese.

The *Kojiki* is also a revision of a slightly earlier compilation; its material is largely that of folk verse and legend. But princely experts acted as an editorial board and were charged with sifting "the true from the false".

In the eighth and ninth centuries this procedure was continued and extended, with the compilation of five further works known, together with the *Nihonshoki*, as the "*Six National Histories*". Gazetteers, a form already long used in China, were also compiled *(fudoki)*.

94

Thus Japanese literature was at its inception distinctly an instrument of political and social power. The first men with a full understanding of the Chinese classics, and the ability to expound them, were appointed tutors to the Prince Imperial ' and could have affected only a limited court circle. Some poetry was produced in Japan; most of it is "lyrical". The true picture is evidently that of a long apprenticeship, during which the Japanese seized eagerly on all useful knowledge of a practical sort. They respected the superior culture, but had neither time nor inclination for the higher reaches of its thought; except for the imperial group, which used it to "fix" its own power, and to endow itself with a divine right to rule.

Buddhism reached Japan in the sixth century. Possibly its rapid spread somewhat later connotes, as in the case of China, a state of exhaustion after these initial feats of organization and absorption, and the long warfare; for Buddhism is essentially a mood of disillusionment with the material world. There was in any case a considerable struggle, indeed a civil war, over its acceptance; it was finally installed at the beginning of the seventh century, under the Regent Shotoku who, in the name of Buddhism, put down the clans that opposed him (they happened to be the leading military and sacerdotal groups of the Shinto disposition).

Shotoku promulgated the first written "constitution", based on the Chinese theories of sovereignty, hierarchy, moral force and "rites" (ceremony and propriety). But another century was to pass before the imperial power, as it appears in the official chronicles of 712-16, was fully consolidated. Meanwhile, China had emerged from the troubled period into a period of reorganization under the Sui dynasty (581-618) and had now reached the magnificent culture of the T'ang dynasty (618-906). In addition to several Japanese missions to China, there was a movement of Japanese students to China and of Chinese teachers to Japan. At last a wider and deeper assimilation of Chinese culture began, but the intercourse was still slow, limited, and generally indirect. Only persons specially selected and prepared by the Japanese authorities could participate and only for designated purposes.

To imagine a free cultural intercourse is erroneous; nor is this development to be seen in its true perspective unless it is realized that it proceeded *pari passu* with the consolidation of the Japanese state system. The hierarchical social system was now surmounted by a consolidated, opulent and resplendent imperial and metropolitan court (in which the Buddhist temples and institutions represented a great part of the opulence and splendour). The Taikwa reforms (645–650) establishing a new system of land tenure, local government and taxation, and much centralization of power, mark an important stage in this process. The students of the new learning were given material as well as spiritual privileges, and were bound to the imperial system not only by the ties of intellectual gratification, social status and indoctrination, but also by economic interest. By 710 the reforms were complete, and subsequent law codes, censuses and ordinances carried their work still further. The new capital Nara was being laid out in imitation of the Chinese metropolis Loyang, and the official chronicles were being finally edited.

Clearly, the principal motives for the acquisition of Chinese culture in this period were political and practical. Confucianism was stressed in the form of a doctrine of loyalty. Practical means were studied for the centralization of power. The crafts and arts were pursued for applied rather than abstract purposes; for recreational and self-expressive activities, at this time, only Japanese forms were used, not Chinese ones. The age had a strong instinct for poetry: *tanka* (short songs) and *nagauta* (long songs) having both a lyrical and an epic content, probably developed at the beginning of the eighth century. There was also *uta gaki*, at festivals where folk songs were sung and folk dances performed, when the guests recited traditional poems and songs, and also composed new ones. All the verse forms concerned were purely Japanese; and the practices mentioned have continued in living usage even to the present day. The basic verse forms are quite originally and distinctively Japanese; no parallel to them has yet been found in the literature of any other nation.

As has been rightly said: "In their poetry above all else the Japanese have remained impervious to alien influences."[1] The reason is a technical one; this verse is highly impressionistic, lyrical and pictorial, but it is also highly conventionalized.

No fictional literature appeared in the Nara period (eighth

---

[1] *Encyclopaedia Britannica*, 11th ed., "Japan".

century), but the versification described above was a "mania".[1] Its great anthology *(Manyōshü)* was made at that time; much less esteemed then, and ever since, is a smaller contemporary collection of poems in the Chinese style *(Kwaifüsö)*, which is the only other literary product of the age.

"During the Nara epoch, the aim of instruction was to prepare men for official posts rather than to impart general culture or to encourage scientific research. Students were therefore selected from the aristocrats or the official classes only. There were no printed books; everything had to be laboriously copied by hand, and the difficulties of learning were much enhanced. To be able to adapt the Chinese ideographs skilfully to the purposes of written Japanese was a feat achieved by comparatively few."[2]

The quest for Buddhism appears to have been variously motivated only in minor part by a desire for deeper philosophical satisfactions. Much of it was reduced to the ritual magical copying out of sutras. It is characteristic that such copying of sutras was the standard punishment for members of the upper classes who committed political or social misdemeanours; somewhat, perhaps, as English public schoolboys not long ago were set "lines" of Latin or Greek. Lords or priests who used Buddhism to build up secular power outside the court were ruthlessly put down (e.g. Makibi and Gembö).

The Chinese court at Changan was then entering upon the phase of luxury and epicurism. A large stream of teachers and student envoys went between it and Japan. The Chinese teachers who went to Japan served the court, i.e. the imperial interest, against any opposing factions. The Japanese who went to China were sent primarily for practical studies. But some of them contributed materially to Chinese thought and practice (e.g. Abé Nakamaro, called by the Chinese, Chao Heng, the friend of Li Tai Po, is commemorated by one of the latter's best poems; but in fact he was also a practical man, as is shown by his appointment by the Chinese emperor to a provincial vice-royalty). One, Makibi, attained excellence in history, the classics, jurisprudence, mathematics, and philosophy. Others, on their return to Japan, figure rather in such practical employments as architecture (e.g. Abbot Doji) or

1 Brinkley, op. cit. p. 214.
2 Op. cit., p. 215.

97

as political "trustees" (e.g. Abbot Gombo) than as moralists or metaphysicians.

The Heian epoch (782–1068) witnessed, however, a striking change in the attitude towards Chinese studies. T'ang China was still artistically brilliant, but had fallen into administrative disorder. Japanese students still went to China, but no longer praised or propagated Chinese political or social methods. They took only the art and literature, and the developments of Buddhism, and began to be openly contemptuous of the ability of the Chinese in practical matters.

The appeal of Buddhism was at that time largely aesthetic. "You might be breathless with adoration before a serene and faultless golden Buddha, but you could dislike or criticize the Chinese way of thought and the Chinese principles of government, the more so if they ran counter to your vested interests."[1]

Nevertheless, Buddhism ceased in this period to be regarded in Japan as a matter of incantation, a magic superior to the native Shinto, and proceeded to expand on the philosophical plane. The Tendai sect is a landmark in Japan's cultural history, and an interesting example of Japanese adaptation from Chinese model; it became "a system of Japanese eclecticism, fitting the disciplinary and meditative methods of the Chinese sage to the pre-existing foundations of earlier sects".[2] It took the great step of reconciliation with the native Shinto, which had lapsed into the place of a supplementary religion; appealing mainly to the poorer and lower classes, it offered no attractions to the careerist, and lacked any great protagonists. The new turn in Buddhism admitted the Shinto deities as alternative manifestations of divinity. A wide, though not entire, fusion followed (Ryobu Shinto). This compromise, says Sir Charles Eliot[3] represents a "natural tendency of the Japanese mind, and not the work of one man".

Kōbō Daishi (who studied in China) founded another great sect, the Shingon. But he was equally famous as artist and calligrapher, and invented or perfected a simpler form of writing, the phonetic *hiragana* syllabary which, though it can be only an auxiliary to Chinese writing, greatly simplified the writing of Japanese.

---

[1] Sansom, op. cit., p. 90.
[2] A. Lloyd, *Development of Japanese Buddhism.*
[3] "Japanese Buddhism."

In 894, it was decided to send no more embassies to T'ang. Though Confucian studies were still the main item of the academic curriculum, there was a tendency to go back to earlier commentaries and interpretations (Han, instead of T'ang). Here the Japanese showed that they were still immature and lacking in discrimination in style, for example, an ornate and artificial style of the Six Dynasties was preferred to many better models available. Furthermore they showed not only an innate aversion to abstract speculation, but an interest centred in the political or executive aspects of this learning. Thus we find, for example, the classic on *Filial Piety* universally studied, while the *Analects* are ignored. Japanese scholars began to specialize to an extreme degree in this field, but always in the historical, ritual and juridical aspects *(Books of Rites, Spring and Autumn Annals)*.

At the same time the culture was becoming less academic. Japanese travellers began to bring back from the mainland, not only learned treatises, but some light literature, even pornographic novels. There was a court vogue for Chinese poetry, but this was in a foreign language; at best it was good mimicry. The intellectual life at court, in attempting to adopt a demoded Chinese culture, remained artificial. The middle classes cherished, not brilliance, but competence, orthodoxy and loyalty. Significantly, the greatest stylistic model of the age was a stilted administrative report! As for the people, they took at this stage no interest in the things of the mind. The Buddhist church, more austerely erudite and self-disciplined, began to overshadow the court.

In the tenth century, there was a resurgence of the Japanese values. Practically, the simplification of the language brought about by the introduction of the phonetic syllabary facilitated the development of a spontaneous native literature. Politically, as we have seen, China had come into disfavour; and the Japanese had consolidated their own dynastic, administrative, military and feudal system to the point where they might consider themselves as an independent nation. Socially, also, the time was ripe for such a move. Chinese remained the working medium for historians, jurists and theologians. The Japanese layman began however to figure as l'*homme moyen sensuel*. The Heian period shows them, having set their land and living in order, ready to indulge their aesthetic, sentimental and sensual propensities. A recreational literature arose in the Heian period: "and for this the native language (flexible, colourful and allusive) was supremely well suited. It is the very thing for rambling romances, little love-songs and elegant praise of flowers."[1]

The remarkable *Tale of Genji*, with its easy flow, dexterously portrays the courtly philandering and epicureanism. The *Pillow Book of Shei Shönagon*, combines vivacity with melancholy. Both are available in European translations.

Both are the work of women. The "wits of the men were fuddled with Chinese books and second-hand Chinese ideas" in "a dead language"; but the upper-class women, within the bounds of formal etiquette, "could express what they saw and felt in a living tongue they had spoken from childhood".[2] Male writers, too, poke fun at dry scholars, or transform Chinese demons into amiable grotesque figures, Indian ascetics into nature-lovers; but when they do so (like the author of the *Tosa Diary*) excuse themselves for "writing as a woman writes", i.e. in Japanese.

The Heian culture, aristocratic and metropolitan, did not spread widely in the provinces, or affect the great majority of the population. The dynasty weakened; the emperors became puppets of the Fujiwara family, a regency. The provincial governors rose to the rank of feudal princes, militarist and absolutist in spirit. There was strife in the land. The Buddhist Church gained strength. It offered the main field of work for the creative artist. Evangelistic sects came into prominence, some adhering to asceticism or self-discipline, but most preaching an activist doctrine; certain monasteries were veritable baronies, manned by hordes of armed and rapacious monks.

The middle of the eleventh century saw the end of the first cultural "wave" from China. Until 1367 there was no major political intercourse, and a distinctly diminished cultural intercourse between the two countries. In the intervening period (Kamakura and Ashikaga epochs) Japanese society took on a pattern created by the Japanese themselves, without any fresh adoptions from Chinese or other political models, though there were borrowings in the arts and in certain minor

[1] Sansom, op. cit., p. 237.
[2] ibid.

aspects of practical life. But the language, technically and culturally, was Chinese; the overriding social distinction was the ability to use and quote that language.

THE PERIOD OF FEUDAL MILITARISM (1060–1360)

The Japanese culture became stabilized in this period, and at the same time a new social structure was established. The decline of the imperial power and the struggle among the tribes had resulted in a feudal system dominated by the military class. This system, characterized by its strict hierarchy and based on respect for discipline and the sense of honour, brought about the development of the *Samurai* (those who serve) who had supplied the executive staff of the régime, as well in the military domain as in that of civil administration.

Each new class which comes to power in any society seeks to discover the cultural values best suited to it. On many points the feudalists broke sharply with the tradition inherited from China. As do all ruling classes, however, they knew how to combine the best elements of both traditions and borrowed anew from both China and the West. They always succeeded, however, in adapting these borrowings, old and new, to personal ends more or less foreign to the Chinese. Furthermore Chinese culture was sufficiently rich and varied to satisfy all tastes. It is significant that the purely Chinese elements which have contributed most to the Japanese culture have been in the main adopted from the T'ang period, that is, a period in the history of China, when the soldier was not despised and when the aristocracy itself formed a military caste.

Mostly, however, the Japanese military found the material of their ideology in the antecedents of their own race, and revived and reasserted the national heritage. They developed their own fierce code of honour and, literally as well as metaphorically, a Cult of the Sword. The Heike Monogatari, the great thirteenth-century historical romance, opens with an account of famous swords. The *Samurai* sword was not only the symbol of honour, it was an actual object of ritual worship.

Its rites were, of course, Shinto. Such a cult would seem on the face of it to have practically nothing in common with Chinese civilization. Yet there were devotees who sought to relate even that to Chinese precepts. In short, the letter or the spirit of Chinese heritage was henceforward invoked to justify or explain every kind of Japanese conduct. In a longer treatise, something could have been done to disentangle how much was endogenously Japanese, as material or motives, and how much was Chinese or exogenous as accretion of influence, but in this condensed study it is only possible to point out some of the main lines of this development, with a few examples.

1. By merely using the same terminology, a false identification arises in Japan of "filial piety" with "military discipline".
2. A shift of emphasis thrusts into the foreground the Japanese conception of loyalty to the clan and emperor.
3. An eclectic technique may be used to the same end. For example, the Japanese took those aspects of Zen Buddhism which stressed introspection, and identified them with spiritual intransigence *(fudoshin)*—a quality praised in their own "pre-Chinese" traditions.
4. New institutions or new departures are sanctified by attaching to them old names. For example, "fifth-column" techniques were attributed to Sun Tzu, the Chinese writer of *Art of War* who was certainly an expert on such matters, but lived some twelve hundred years previously.

At this time a new attitude towards China developed. The Chinese military classics were studied, and came to "take the place of the canonical works as the textbooks of the ruling class". The laws of filial piety were not rejected, but duty to an overlord must now come before family ties. The gentle doctrines of Buddhism were not abandoned, but they must be made to square with current practice. So one war-worn general, taking monastic vows at the end of his campaigns, feigns deafness when they read to him the commandment against taking life. Brinkley[1] suggests that this period saw the inculcation of two chronic defects: (a) the indifference of Bushidō, the Japanese warrior code, to any sense of moral responsibility or reciprocity, and also to intellectuality, and (b) the conservatism which killed originality and imposed a rigid and static class system. The first is essentially Japanese, but the second is of Chinese origin.

These remarks are important; nevertheless, due caution

---

[1] Op. cit., pp. 236–7.

should be observed in accepting descriptions of the *Samurai*, which are in the main based on Chinese models.

During this period, Japanese art had separated into two streams. The Kyoto school, that of the court, favoured the rich and the decorative, the graceful and the cursive. Technically, it imitated the Chinese art of the much earlier Sui and T'ang (590 to 907). It developed subsequently into the more popular and "national" school of Japan. The school of Kamakura (the military capital) favoured the more austere, restrained (but forceful), sometimes melancholy modes of the more recent Sung (960–1200), and to a less extent the Yuan (1260–1368); but it joined to these the Japanese cults of nature-worhip and spontaneity, and in general was less formal and abstract than the Kyoto movement. Calligraphy, painting, architecture and landscape gardening (introduced at Kamakura by a Chinese) were developed by both schools, each in its distinctive spirit.

The court conservatively continued its elegant pastimes on refined models from earlier China. It favoured poetry, but showed no great originality, the outstanding product being an anthology *(Hyakunin Isshu)*. At Kamakura, there was little literature but much refined asceticism. The age produced some of the greatest Japanese poets; Chōmei (the Japanese Wordsworth), the ascetic Suigyō, Kenkō (the Japanese Horace, writer of the famous *Tsuredzure Guza*)—all of whom, significantly, were nature-loving hermits averse to both court elegance and military organization and using the poetic forms which were essentially Japanese.

The above may serve to make clear that while the Japanese were still directly imitating the Chinese, their manner of doing so was eclectic. This eclecticism, from this period onwards, characterizes all the cultural importations of the Japanese.

The thirteenth-century development of Buddhism is equally characteristic. The older sects had lost their spiritual power with the decline of the aesthetic and ostentatious court life, and their monasteries became temporal benefices. In the bitter strife and impoverishment of the times, the common people were receptive to the doctrine of the insignificance of worldly suffering. Buddhism revived in various evangelical or "Protestant" forms and became the religion of the people—in that sense, the national religion. Shinran, founder (1224) of the Shin sect, took pride in writing in the Japanese phonetic script, using Japanese grammar and simplifying the precepts for the populace. The Shin was a slightly more optimistic development of the Jodo (pure land) sect (1196), which held this world to be entirely evil; the Shin allowed a possibility of salvation by faith. This development of Amidism was thus carried very far in Japan, more or less independently of contemporary Sino-Indian influences.

A third sect of special importance, better known abroad, is the Zen (from Indian *ahyana*, "meditation".) It was introduced from China in the twelfth century as a contemplative doctrine proclaiming the intuitive transmission of knowledge, and *yoga*. Within two generations it was so developed and changed in Japan as to become a cult which denied the reality of death as well as of life, which was self-reliant and non-intellectual, and prompted the unquestioning obedience of the barrack square—an ideal creed for soldiers.

The fourth sect which emerged in the thirteenth century is named after its founder, Nichiren, a fanatical and intolerant street preacher. His demagogic conduct, and that of other sects, was abnormal in Japan, as in other Oriental communities. This is another measure of the distance the Japanese had moved from the original Chinese standards of civility. Nichiren, with such slogans as "Incantations are futile, the Zen are devils, the Shingon is national disaster, the Ritsu sedition", was the forerunner of the modern Japanese "Ultra-patriotic" agitators.

The older Nara sects were revived at the same time (Kegon and Ritsu) but made little headway against such opponents. All these sects have dominated Japanese Buddhism ever since.

The widespread civil warfare of the fourteenth century, with two rival claimants to the throne, occasioned an interesting work, *The True Genealogy of the Divine Emperor* by Kitabatake. The original Japanese conception of the state and of constitutional law was drawn from Chinese (Confucian) sources in the eighth and ninth centuries, but the Japanese had then been careful to eliminate or modify one of the essential postulates, that the ruler who departed from the ways of virtue and failed to cherish the people had lost the Mandate of Heaven and should be deposed. In subsequent borrowings from China, however, this precept had "crept back"; it appears specifically in the Act of Restoration of the "northern" emperor, Go-Daigo. Kitabatake wrote in support of the rival "southern" emperor, asserting his Divine Right, on the grounds that Japan is the only country founded by the gods themselves, and the emperor is their direct descendant, and sought the elimination of the Chinese qualification. This work did not have any great effect in its own time, but its views were shared by some of his contemporaries, which is at least symptomatic. Three hundred years later (1649) it was printed, and thereafter had great and lasting influence.

RELATIONS WITH CHINA AND THE WEST (1360–1638)

During the reign of Yoshimitsu (1367–1408) and of Yoshimasa (1443–90) a reaction against the spartan and militaristic values of the preceding generations took place. After the dynastic wars morals degenerated and the emperors were indifferent to the people's misery. Loyalty declined and treachery increased in all classes. "The ethical textbooks, which were previously the main part of a literary education, went out of use entirely in this period," notes the standard Japanese history, *Dai Nihon Rekishi*. Greed increased, especially land hunger; vassals, servants, successful administrators, all were rewarded with grants of feudal estates. Thus feudal militarism was completely established. The munificence of the Ashikaga Shōguns undoubtedly encouraged the decorative arts, for example, lacquer. This art, introduced from China, was important in Japan in the eighth century, but under the Ashikagas some new and fine varieties began to be made in Japan. Exported to China, these Japanese examples revived the industry there. Glazed pottery and porcelain also began to be made in Japan, inspired by studies of techniques used in Sung China, but in darker hues, the mood required for the disciplined serenity of the Japanese tea ceremonial. Pictorial art was also revolutionized by Sung influences, both northern and southern, and many private art collections were formed. Literary pursuits were, however, less esteemed than the manual arts, and the great scholars were few, though eminent (e.g. Tchijo Kaneyoshi). Numerous ethical and moral primers appeared at this time.

For the most part the intermediaries with China were the Buddhist priests. Men like the bonze Gen-e made the Sung social philosophy (especially that of Cheng I Chuan and Chu Hsi), and the Buddhist-Confucian eclecticism of the Sung and Yuan in general, the official and accepted tenets in Japan, displacing the hitherto prevailing Han and T'ang derivatives. Their Neo-Confucianism exalted conservatism and imperial loyalty.

Japanese architecture in particular in this period shows strong Chinese (Ming) influence; exteriors were still in Japanese style (unadorned) but interior decoration became a high art. Most characteristic however was the erection of halls for the tea ceremony. This remarkable cult (and pastime) originated in China, but all its developments (owing to the influence of the Zen sect, and dating from this period) are characteristically Japanese, and illustrate the elaboration of Japanese social etiquette to the extreme of ritual for the cultivation of "urbanity, purity, courtesy and serenity". Landscape gardening was developed in this period far beyond its previous (Chinese) conception, and was formalized, with the production of exact textbooks of Japanese rules. Another development far from the spirit of the Chinese original is the making of tiny miniature gardens, with the use of artificially stunted trees. The art of "flower arrangement" also evolved in this period; cultivated mostly by women, but sometimes by men, it developed rapidly towards a strict and sparse symmetry. "Poise" may be a better word, to express the Far Eastern sense of symmetry. In any case "flower arrangement" is a poor translation of the Japanese term, which is literally "flower life", suggesting "significant form"—something more than our "still life".

Innovations, essentially Japanese in character, were introduced in singing and dancing. The plaintive Chinese recitations of blind lutists swiftly developed into the stirring declamation of martial epics. Significantly, the male performers in this genre *(biwa bozu)* affected the garb and tonsure of the Buddhist monks—the warrior monks; the women cultivated especially the variety known as *Joruri*, singing of the sacrifices of love to loyalty. These arts are still popular and flourish vigorously providing the martial music of Japan. The aristocratic equivalent, personally cultivated by the Shōguns, was the famous *Nō*—a solemn mime (with music and a "Greek chorus"), deeply allusive and learned in style, pleasing both Buddhists and military commanders, and interspersed with farcical interludes *(kyōgen)*.

Hence this period is often considered the finest in the whole cultural history of Japan. Meanwhile court life continued on the lines of the older, more sybaritic, or less sincere diversions (versification on the Chinese model, flower-viewing, etc.); its only new departures seem to have been gambling and chess. These court pursuits were derivatively Chinese, and associated especially with the "decadent" periods of Chinese history; the Japanese concluded that such tastes were insincere, effete, and nationally harmful. Such a conclusion was encouraged by the Buddhists, and particularly the Zen priests allied with the military. They selected and stressed these aspects of Chinese learning appropriate and necessary to their social position and interests. They cultivated whatever would develop personality in the officers, yet preserve discipline. On the Chinese basis, they made a number of entirely new constructions, sometimes distorting the Chinese basis. But they drew directly also on their own ancient heritage (Shinto, clan traditions, etc.), for these purposes.

It was in this cultural climate that the new conception of etiquette was elaborated. Japanese social life has ever since been rigidified by a comprehensive and all-pervading code of manners, serving ideally for the transmission of orders and the grading of executive responsibility, but making it practically impossible to know truly what goes on in another's mind; for it imposes a conventional mode of address, a conventional demeanour, even a set phraseology, for every possible personal relationship and every possible set of circumstances.

As this brilliant era of the Ashikaga closed with renewed civil wars, the Japanese began to associate the Chinese cultural values with periods of luxury, decadence, weakness, misery for the people and injustice for the soldier. On the contrary it seemed, the truly Japanese qualities (martial, Shinto, spartan, virile) emerged especially in time of stress or danger. The cultural leaders are no more to blame for this attitude than say Wagner is to blame for Hitler. Certain leaders, however, a century later basing their action on this conclusion were consciously bent on guiding the Japanese mind in an atavistic direction.

The sixteenth century, in particular, has gone down in Japanese history as the age of internecine warfare *(Sengoku Jidai)*, marked by the impoverishment and humiliation of the imperial court, and the transfer of the basis of loyalty from clanship to family relations. The period's three great personages, Nobunaga, Hideyoshi and Ieyasu, were in differing degrees typical. For our present purposes, the important fact of this period is that it marks the beginning of relations between Japan and the West.

In 1549, St.Francis Xavier arrived in Japan at the *personal invitation* of one or more of the Japanese *daimyō* (lords). (Unfortunately, we do not know what their motives were.) But the desire of certain Japanese princes for trade with the Portuguese was a principal factor; the invitation came from the southern region, which naturally desired the economic contact. Xavier's doctrines were well received, until he showed intolerance of accepted Japanese (Buddhist) beliefs; but his gifts of clocks and other Western articles were always welcome. As in China, the Jesuits were patronized for their exotic knowledge, but lost out when they began to denounce fundamental native beliefs. Lords, *Samurai* and others were, however, converted in considerable numbers; a Japanese embassy to Rome returned dazzled by the papal power and wealth.

But the central authorities were alarmed, seeing an alien allegiance arising. Conspiracies were discovered. The rivalry between foreign nations also had a fatal effect; the Spaniards sent missionaries from Manila to compete with the Portuguese Jesuits. The English and Dutch, who had now also established trading posts in Japan, denounced the Catholics with all the venom of commercial rivalry mingled with Protestant antagonism. In 1637 a rising in one of the Christianized fiefs of Kyushu led to the cruel suppression of Christianity. The barbarism and cruelty of the Japanese of this age is demonstrated by the crucifixions, tortures and massacres of the Japanese Christians; conduct in Korea was comparable, the famous memorial to which is the Mound of Ears at Kyoto, made from over 100,000 enemy ears and noses.[1]

A lone Englishman, Will Adams, who arrived as pilot on

---

1 The relation of this conduct to primitive Japanese beliefs is ably traced by A. Morgan Young, *The Rise of a Pagan State.*

a Dutch ship, pleased Ieyasu by his honesty and "sincerity" and was employed by him as shipbuilder and pilot. Ieyasu encouraged competition among the foreigners, particularly among the English and Dutch who did not present the same political and ideological dangers as the Catholics. But the lasting impressions on the Japanese were that the Western barbarians offered advantages on the vulgar plane of commerce, but had no deep philosophic or artistic culture like that originating in China and in their view subsequently perfected in Japan. The West offered mechanical devices, and a religion of day-to-day morality which was not without some merit; but they lacked self-discipline and communal spirit, so that the political complications made Western intercourse hardly worth while. Those impressions have never been entirely effaced. Objectively, envisaging the arrival of these semipirate merchant adventurers many years away from home, of these missionaries and Inquisitors, it may appear that the judgment of the rulers of Japan was not altogether lacking in shrewdness.

JAPAN'S ISOLATION FROM THE WORLD (1638-1867)

During the whole two and a half centuries of Japan's seclusion from the rest of the world, the Tokugawa Shogunate continued to rule the country. Deliberate seclusion dates in effect from about 1670, with an almost complete cessation of cultural importations. In the first four decades of the sixteenth century the foreigners were in Japan, and Christianity was a powerful influence; in the three following decades, Chinese cultural influence was pronounced, and Japan was also more closely involved in Chinese internal affairs than at any previous time. Western accounts have failed to bring out the very interesting point that Japan might easily have become more deeply involved or even united with China at that time. In 1664, when the Mings were making their last stand against the Tartars, they instructed a certain Cheng Chi-lung who had settled in Japan to act as their commander-in-chief and to appeal for Japanese military aid, a full alliance and the dispatch of Japanese forces to the mainland. The Japanese government would almost certainly have agreed had the Mings held out a little longer. Such Japanese intervention might well have led to a condominium, or even a Japanese dynasty, in China. But the offer came too late. Numerous fugitives from China came to Japan at that time, and among them several notable scholars, but this was to be the last influx of the kind.

The Spaniards were expelled from Japan in 1624, the Portuguese in 1638. The Dutch, arriving in 1609, were at first well received, but after 1638, as the only foreigners in Japan, they were increasingly restricted to matters of minor trade, and treated to personal humiliation. The British East India Company's envoys, arriving in 1613, showed extraordinary ineptitude, and withdrew at a loss in 1620. A British attempt to reopen trade relations in 1673 was quite favourably considered by the Japanese, but was finally rejected, possibly at the instigation of the Dutch, because the King of England had married a Portuguese princess. There was of course no question of anything more than a limited trade connexion. Until the mid-nineteenth century, the only fresh foreign contacts were the incursions and reconnaissances of Russian navigators.

This closing of the doors is in startling contrast to the positive and adventurous Japanese activities abroad in the preceding century. The internal change, from the advent of the Tokygawas, was almost as marked. They imposed a despotic and militaristic, but also bureaucratic, régime, and set up a veritable dictatorship in the cultural domain. In 1614, for example, Ieyasu ordered the Toyotomi family to construct a huge Buddhist temple, apparently with the intention of impoverishing them. At the dedication ceremony, Ieyasu picked a quarrel with certain Buddhists alleging that the inscription on the temple bell was disrespectful and treasonable. Further, the dictator did not hesitate to open a political trial at which the matter was learnedly discussed. Scholars, priests and lords were paraded at this grand heresy-hunt, in a manner not dissimilar to that of a modern state trial in a totalitarian country. Ieyasu was, however, in many ways a remarkable man—humane, just, generous, cultivated, zealous, courteous. He encouraged all these virtues; but he exacted the most complete subordination, mental and physical, from all his subjects, and was completely ruthless.[1]

[1] The career and the remarkable character of Ieyasu are authoritatively described in the biography by Professor Sadler, *The Maker of Modern Japan*.

Ieyasu brought all the provincial governors and nobles under his direct control (1611–13). In 1615 he imposed his comprehensive Laws of the Military Houses, which declares: "Literature first, arms next, but concurrently, the rule of the Ancients". Those pursuits were to be followed by archery and horsemanship. Military men were to be in touch with the times, to know the laws, and the will of the dictator. Instructions follow as to discipline, and sumptuary laws. Ieyasu directly and personally promoted a great revival of learning; but regarded it largely as a means of controlling every form of activity, stressing the Neo-Confucian doctrines of allegiance and conservatism.

The new capital (Edo, modern Tokyo) rose to great prosperity as a commercial, literary and artistic metropolis. The easy and luxurious Genroku period (1688–1703) significantly displays a great and sudden progress of popular and recreational forms: *haiku* poems (short, light and epigrammatic), popular drama and melodrama, new dances, *joruri*, and the *ukioye* pictures (wood-block prints). Each of these is essentially "Japanese" in derivation, form and spirit, as distinct from Chinese. They are also in the main sentimental or emotional. The classical Japanese poetry was also much cultivated; most of the standard commentaries on it were made during this period. Performers were admitted to the rank of *Samurai*, while the true spirit of the *Samurai* was declining.

The rise of the merchant class occasioned "social adulteration"; punitive and sumptuary legislation did not suffice to keep the tradesman down as urbanization increased and economic processes became more complicated. By the opening decades of the nineteenth century the social system was thoroughly artificial; the merchant class had widely bought its way into the *Samurai* class, and had intermarried with it. A corresponding social and economic revolution had occurred; the older nomenclature scarcely concealed the fact that a large and powerful middle class had arisen. The older social distinctions represented an arbitrary system which was sustained only by police methods, spies, censors, etc., a travesty of the political formula "encourage the good and discourage the bad".

In philosophy, there were two opposed schools of Confucianism, and a Shinto revival. On the Confucian side, there was

(a) (already noted above) the Neo-Confucianism of Chu Hsi, which is conservative, loyalist and inductive, and (b) the school of the later Wang Yang Ming (Oyōmei: 1472–1529) which was intuitive, conscientious, and deductive. From the first half of the eighteenth century onwards, the former generally prevailed. Though some students would interpret the outcome as another example of the Japanese capacity for synthesis, others say that this was merely a recasting of old materials.

Per contra, the cult of the *Kokugaku* (national learning) represented a powerful revival of Shinto traditions. Associated with extreme nationalism and belief in the divine right of the emperor, this movement was eventually responsible, in face of the social and economic disintegration of the old order and the threat of foreign aggression, for the imperial restoration of 1868 and the end of feudalism. The great protagonists of the new "Nipponism" span the whole epoch: Kada (1668 to 1736), Kamo (1697–1769), Motoori (1730–1801), Hirata (1776–1834).

Meanwhile, the dictators had kept open a narrow window on the outside world: the Dutch trading post at Nagasaki. Up to 1744, the study of all foreign books was prohibited, but thereafter certain Japanese officers were appointed to learn Dutch and report any useful information. The parallel with the first introduction of Chinese knowledge, a thousand years earlier, is striking; practical knowledge was chiefly sought, participation was restricted to nominees of the central government, the results were reserved for the use of rulers and administrators, with no intention of the enlightenment of the whole public, or its literate classes. The first fruits were a development of astronomical knowledge. By the end of the century, the Edo government archives contained what would nowadays be called "foreign-press extracts" and "science-book digests" presenting a fairly wide survey of world events and Western scientific thought. The first foreign arrivals found the high government officials far from ignorant on these matters: though their juniors and the common people had of course no such knowledge, the Japanese rulers knew all that had happened in China, Mexico and elsewhere.

In the first half of the nineteenth century there were occasional visits of foreign ships, and shipwrecked sailors. These were decently though firmly treated, and relations with them kept at a minimum, the ships turned away, the men repatriated.

In 1846, a French vessel touched at the Loochoo Islands. The Dutch had been telling the Japanese that the English and Americans were growing very active and powerful in and around the China Seas, and would certainly be coming to Japan soon. They sent atlases and books explaining the geopolitical situation. The French visitors corroborated these intimations, adding that they had come to invite the Loochooans to place themselves under French protection, in order to forestall the English. It is essential to remember that the Japanese, or at least their rulers, had a clear realization of foreign designs. But they also understood how sharp were the rivalries between the various Western powers.

The story of Commodore Perry's arrival, the opening of the country under the direct threat of his squadron's guns, the impression created by the mechanical devices he presented, and the subsequent victory of the partisans of the imperial restoration, is well known.

The reactions of the Japanese of various classes were exceedingly diverse. They varied according to the political position and self-interest of each individual Japanese and were more directly political than cultural.

The true *Samurai* caste, the traditionalists, swaggered in opposition, and fell on the foreigners with their swords.

Conservatives stressed that exclusion had been proved wise by long experience, that foreign trade was uneconomic merely exchanging precious metals for unnecessary luxuries, and that Japan had the necessary strength to hold her fortress. They quoted the ancient Chinese maxim, "set the far-off barbarian against the near-by barbarian".

Progressives denied the solidity and effectiveness of the contemporary national structure. The Japanese, they urged, must play for time: "Make a show of commerce and intercourse; give little, cede gradually"; "foreign trade can now be profitable, in these changed times", "the essential is that Christianity should not be admitted"; meanwhile, "let the people be economical, save money for building a war fleet and forts on the coasts". All these are the actual words of progressive lords (Ii of Kamon, Toda of Izu, Egawa Torazaemon).

The Shōgunate is believed to have referred to the emperor, in the first place, essentially as a ruse of bureaucratic delay. The loyalists rallied at first under the slogan "Exalt the emperor and expel the barbarians!" The first result was a compromise: the emperor stated that he would refrain for the time being from expelling the barbarians, while the Shōgun stated he would agree temporarily to the opening of trade. Historically, the restoration of the emperor was spontaneously conceived and effected by a narrow circle of leaders, mostly young *Samurai* of low rank. They were men of the middle class, and almost all of them were under the age of 30. The decisive break with the past was carried out without elaborate reverence for old Chinese precepts. At the moment of the revolution, their elders and superiors stood aside and watched. Soon, however, they joined the movement; and the new régime, from its inception, had adherents of every class—princes, *Samurai*, merchants, bureaucrats, students. The last Shōgun himself acceded; for he resigned his autocracy, and became a prince of the new empire. Soon, the elder statesmen, recognized by the new constitution, stood close around the throne; for to the cries of "expel the barbarians" were substituted the sentiments of the imperial rescript: to search the whole world for knowledge, to learn whatever might benefit the nation.

JAPAN BETWEEN CAPITALISM AND FASCISM (1869–1945)

On the many-sided progress of Japan in the modern age, the following cannot be anything more than a marginal comment. Important cultural aspects which have mainly escaped notice are found within the domain of literature. The transformation of Japan into a capitalist country, the organization of a modern nation state, and its growth into a great power, show above all a deeply rooted spirit of realism and a great gift of practical ability. The ninteenth-century Japanese like the earnest young men of other communities during industrialization, looked to schooling and apprenticeship. Working by day in industry, commerce or administration, often under foreign masters or experts, and in the evening at nightschool or in private study, they looked to officialdom for guidance and decisions. Education was deemed equal in importance to national defence. Universal education, including the compulsory study of foreign languages, was imposed in 1874. Modern Japan claims a literacy rate among the highest in the world. The modern Japanese textbooks were imported in millions; and copied in many more millions, with or without the consent of their authors. Japan was, up to the war, actually the principal market in the world, after their own countries, for publishers of all kinds in Britain and the United States.

It is however a mistake to suppose that the Japanese imitated all the practical devices of the West and rejected all the underlying culture or philosophy. They saw that a machine was not to be perfectly imitated unless the mentality of its originator could also be absorbed. They must, as it were, take the abstract, as well as the applied, parts of the curriculum. At the lowest estimate, it was seen that there must be more in the Western system than mere mechanical ingenuity, to account for its energy and its rapid conquest of the world.

By the end of the century every notable European or American work had been translated. Many contemptuously rejected the native heritage. The period was commonly referred to as the era of enlightenment *(Kaika Ki)*. The term would appear to have arisen indigenously, without specific derivation from the European *Aufklärung*. The Japanese of that time wished entirely to conform to the new world standards of capitalism and liberalism. The tremendous intake of Western literature after 1869 was not merely for information; it was made in the definite intention of producing a Japanese literary culture which—though of course in Japanese and inspired by the Japanese heritage—would have the same basis as that of the Western world, and be of the same kind. This is probably the leading instance, in all history, of the direct and complete importation—by enthusiastic acceptance as distinct from imposition—of a foreign culture. The Western knowledge came to Japan very largely by the medium of books. The written word was thus, from a new point of view, again the way to knowledge and advancement. The Japanese of the nineteenth century envied the Westerners, not merely their technical ingenuity, but also their self-possession and their air of complete mastery, in the heyday of expanding capitalism, when the prospects of steady and unlimited progress seemed unquestionable. By hard work and hard study, the Japanese sought to attain the same competence *and the same serenity.*

At the opening of the twentieth century the first new school of independent Japanese literature made its appearance, calling itself naturalism or realism. In form it was mainly a reportage of personal and social life. All recent Western techniques were tried out, with results sometimes faintly reminiscent of James Joyce's *Ulysses.* It also reflected the political setting, it was radical or populist. As a democratic reaction against the feudal conventionality and formalism, which made the language of literature different from that of everyday speech, it strove to develop the colloquial tongue, which it enriched by the adoption of neologisms from other languages. It drew largely therefore on English and American literature; also, for political reasons, on Russian literature (Gogol, later Tolstoy). But it is interesting to note also the strong influence of various French writers. Zola and Maupassant should be placed first; perhaps they were in any case the greatest writers of the moment. Zola was the best teacher of realism; Maupassant's light and cynical worldliness corresponds exactly to something in the Japanese character. Chekhov's influence led in the same direction. Another French writer whom the Japanese acclaimed was Bergson; his *élan vital* was entirely to the liking of their new movement. Partly, however, the French influence was an historical accident, in that French was the foreign language especially used at that time by certain literate classes in Japan; it was the language of diplomacy, the studios, the law (the Japanese were then adopting the *Code Napoléon*), the army (trained by French officers, replaced in 1871 by Germans), the post office and other activities. When one culture is drawing on another, the course of development depends not only on which historical or external models are most to the liking of the borrower, but also on which models happen, owing to immediate circumstances to be most easily accessible to him. The Russian writers, for instance, would surely have had a much greater influence, had the practical difficulty of access to them not deferred their impact till a later stage.

The new Japanese culture represented a remarkable effort to combine Anglo-Saxon activism, German thoroughness, French realism, Japanese responsiveness to nature, and a Russian soulfulness. It made some progress. The original

naturalist school moved gradually from *reportage* into commentary, and thence into analysis. The great plays and novels
of the first decade of the twentieth century are intensely
"psycholgical". The "problem play" was much in vogue. Later,
Ibsen was acclaimed, and imitated. One of the greatest
writers of the time preceding and including the first world war
(Mori Ogai) proclaimed himself a follower of Nietzsche. In the
first decade of the century the main and very general pre-
occupation is with the personal adjustments characteristic of
the times—conflicts of loyalty versus enlightenment, of tradition
versus conscience, of beauty versus lucre. All the varieties of
human relationships were carefully and anxiously examined
by the Japanese writers, who, against the background of these
conflicts, reveal clearly the difficulties of transition from the
ancient to the new values.

In the second decade of the century social change in the
direction of capitalism was marked in Japan. The Japanese
capitalists did very well out of the first world war, supplying
the Allies, developing all sorts of industries, transport and
commerce, at the cost of a useful (but hardly exhausting)
military effort. Japan emerged as a great power. Internally,
there was a corresponding growth of capitalistic or middle-
class motives and standards of judgment. Thus the main successor to the first naturalist-realist movement was a wide school
of "bourgeois romanticism". There were also some strong
strains of idealism. The former element counted a considerable
number of "best sellers" (the sales of books, like those of newspapers, reached figures in Japan that roused the envy of
authors and publishers in other lands). It is not far-fetched to
compare at least one of these (Kikuchi Kan) with Arnold
Bennett or John Galsworthy. These were men who, metaphorically no less than literally, wore foreign clothes and lived
in Western style. More native in garb and mien were the leading idealists. Some were writers of fairy-tales and nature
sketches, who developed a very strong and pleasing current
of impressionism. Others, known as the "Time-to-spare" school,
cultivated a "sauntering" attitude to life, resembling that of
Thoreau; but they did not get the term from him, as it had
long been similarly used in old Japan, and is a main constituent of the spirit of *Haiku* poetry (short, lyrical, and more
or less epigrammatic Japanese verses). The art of the *haiku*

117

was very much cultivated and enriched during this period. The tendency was not however reactionary; it eagerly sought and used new materials and new methods suggested by Western culture. Another very important group (Shirakaba) was composed of Tolstoyan Utopianists and Christian Pacifists (such as Toyohiko Kagawa).

All these tendencies encouraged in the liberal era of the early 1920's, were heavily tinged with eclecticism. A number of other movements had arisen alongside them, mostly representing degenerate forms of romanticism, melodrama and sentimentality—weaknesses into which Japanese emotionalism can swiftly degenerate. One group, called the "decadents", sought romance in the underworld. Another, in the name of "satanism", pursued psychological abnormality. A number went far in the direction of pornography. For this the Japanese have always had a distinct propensity, which could be freely indulged, since their social code allowed much latitude for males in sexual relations. Some romanticists began to "glamourize" the Japanese past, to exalt the picaresque or chivalrous "adventurism" of the old *Samurai* days, in contradistinction to the squalor and the repressions which capitalism or commercialism had brought in its train. It raised the first hankerings for the "good old days" on which Japanese militarism, and later fascist tendencies, were substantially to build.

It was chiefly in opposition to these very tendencies that the communist and working class movement succeeded, in the later 1920's, in attaining remarkable influence in Japan. At that time there was a great militant socialist movement, having a tremendous influence on intellectuals. A group of militants founded, in 1920, "the Sowers", a famous movement of "proletarian literature", including Christian socialists, trade unionists, genuine Marxists, workers and many others. As "positive" theorists, in an age "swamped with mush", they had a great success and enlisted many of the best writers of the time.

The communists, who had started this movement shortly afterwards dropped out for the time being. The parent "Sowers" quickly split up after a series of political convulsions, leaving the movement largely free for "fellow travellers". Almost every notable writer was able to participate in it, or stand close to it, during the mid-1920's.

However, the "true proletarians" had reorganized themselves and reappeared about 1927 as a strong communist caucus. *Flag of Battle*, and other journals, represented a definite communist party organization, not a loose "united front". This movement gained some notable recruits, made a devastating attack on Japanese capitalism and imperialism, and produced a very vigorous and stimulating literature. The latter was of course in line with the contemporary productions of the "proletarian writing" of Russia and Western Europe. The "bourgeois" literature of Japan had reached such a stage of weakness and dilution that it could in no wise stand up to the proletarian onslaught. The proletarian work was of quite high literary quality. Rather poor translations of some of the most notable Japanese proletarian works have been made into European languages (Kobayashi's *Cannery Boat*, Tokunaga's *Sunless Street*). These are perhaps translations at third-hand (from Japanese to Chinese, thence to Russian, thence to English, etc.).

The proletarian movement was in fact eliminated through no efforts of its literary opponents, but through sheer brute force and physical suppression by the police, as part of the general attack on the works and the very lives of the communists and working class organizers. This "police drive" for the liquidation of all "dangerous thoughts" began strongly in 1928, but became much more sweeping after the Manchurian "incident" of 1932. As late as 1936, however, a great national literary contest for the selection of the 20 best writers resulted in 15 being chosen "from the left", only five "rightists". There was a certain aftermath of apostasy, but most of the Marxist leaders literally perished, a few escaped to Russia, and the rest fell silent, or changed their views.

The new orthodoxy praised and embellished the old Japan of pre-capitalist days. Feudal Japan had, at least superficially, "glamour" enough for countless plays, stories, novels, and films. This was poured out in quantity, to the complete debasement of popular taste. The defects of modern life were increasingly blamed on the foreign system, capitalism, on "rotten liberalism and internationalism", "treacherous cosmopolitanism", and other tendencies thus repeatedly denounced by other totalitarian régimes also. Nobility, chivalry, true loyalty, and that "true happiness which lies in service and obedience", were correspondingly indicated to attach especially to the ancient Japanese way of life. Much nihilistic writing stressed the hopelessness of modern civilization and the absence of any solution to modern social problems; this contributed to the same end. The few writers who strove to maintain "detachment" and a "polite" literature could not stand for long against the popular trend.

The beginning of the war (1937 in China) made journalese, "headline writing" and "headline thinking", the order of the day. Yet some writers caught up and developed such contemporary European currents as "imagism" and "symbolism", even though they were forced into an attitude of cultural defeatism, or to apologize for their works as stories which dealt with eccentric or abnormal people. Some of the Japanese public remained politically indifferent, and there were writers who provided for them fiction of a simple, factual and personal nature. The detective story had a vogue quite comparable with that of other countries. Most interesting were the writings from the war fronts; the real soldiers were notably laconic, restrained, objective, factual, and in their writings there was often sarcasm and ridicule of the perfervid enthusiasms of journalists and the catchwords of politicians.[1]

THE PRESENT AND THE FUTURE

The occupation period has seen the reappearance of many of the more serious and reputable works of the pre-war period. There has naturally been a special stress on writings banned by the former régime. But development to date has not been very encouraging. Many qualified observers look with despondency at the large quantities of inferior, even rubbishy, literature of current production which seems to fill the bookstores and stalls of Japan. The cultural situation has however been so confused that it is very difficult—quite apart from the general difficulty of judging a recent or contemporary output —to give even a tentative assessment. The paper shortage was acute—and very uneven in its direct and indirect effects. It is at any rate clear that there has been no great fresh output on

---

1 For a slightly more comprehensive account of modern Japanese literature, see the writer's article in *International Affairs*, April 1948.

the cultural plane. The material difficulties of existence leave the average person no time, energy, or spirit for the extension of his mind.

Ultimately, however, the inquisitive and persistent mentality of the Japanese will lead them again to their own reintegration in a world society. They will certainly use literature, above all as a didactic and formative medium for this purpose.

But how? The question cannot yet be fully answered. No man is culturally or politically "normal" under circumstances of foreign occupation, however truly he may understand its reason, or esteem the occupants. Any programme for the future depends on political decisions which, as no one realizes better than the Japanese, have not yet been made. The Japanese surrender, the more so in that it was unconditional, marked the close of one epoch without yet opening another.

From the above study it is possible to draw the following conclusions which apply to the whole course of Japan's history:

1. The Japanese are eclectic and open-minded, as well as being merely imitative. The necessity or usefulness of learning from others (even if negatively) they have throughout quickly and spontaneously recognized.
2. Such eclecticism is the sign, above all, of their innate realism, pragmatism and aversion to abstraction.
3. Their cultural history has been subordinated to their inner political necessities.
4. There is nevertheless in their character a strong under-current of passion, emotionalism or sentimentality, which requires strict ruling and careful control.

In she formation of recent Western thought on Japan, the anthropological approach has been influential. The peculiar cohesiveness of Japanese society, its subordination of the individual, has been traced back to the very origins of the race, and found to be continuously and consistently a decisive factor. This is very true, and the anthropological analysis has shed much light on the subject. But it is far from the whole truth, and a generalized sociological and cultural approach gives, in my submission, a far more balanced appreciation of the Japanese. It shows them as realists, eclectics with a positive taste for innovation, and pragmatists; but also as a composite society, with class differences and internal social stresses leading to sharp differences of opinion and violent clashes of interest within their community. Their whole history is a series of civil and factional wars, which it is obviously inadequate to regard as merely the expression of a hereditary martial instinct. The "tribal" nationalism is also, in any given period, as much the effect as the cause of this internecine strife.

Once the political decision is known, there should be no greater obstacle to the participation of the Japanese in international culture than there was in the latter part of the nineteenth century. Foreign thought and Western psychology are fairly well known to the Japanese. The general level of knowledge of English and other foreign languages is remarkably high (for reading if not for speaking). The educative process would clearly have to be a literary one. The Japanese are quick and efficient at printing and publishing and are technically well equipped. An extensive (though not materially well endowed) educational apparatus is in being.

All these circumstances are favourable to and augur well for a cultural renaissance in Japan.

Indian Culture
Its Spiritual, Moral and Social Aspects

by

B. L. ATREYA

INTRODUCTION

The United Nations and Unesco are providing common international platforms for discussion of far-reaching and vital problems of humanity. Greater and greater contact between
people of various countries, races and communities, and more
and more knowledge of each other's culture, gradually tend to
evolve a common world culture in which in course of time
the best elements of the various cultures may be incorporated
and synthesized. It is time that this process should be accelerated and consciously planned. Hence the praiseworthy attempt
of Unesco in the form of a cultural enquiry.

LURE OF INDIAN CULTURE

It is a happy sign of the present age that serious thinkers and
mature minds of the West are now realizing the need of graft-
ing the best elements of Indian culture on the tree of Western
civilization. Professor Northrop aptly ends his well-known
work, *The Meeting of the East and the West* (p. 496) with the
following passage: "It should eventually be possible to achieve
a society for mankind generally in which the higher standard
of living of the most scientifically advanced and theoretically
guided Western nations is combined with the compassion, the
universal sensitivity to the beautiful, and the abiding equanim-
ity and the calm joy of the spirit which characterize the sages
and many of the humblest people in the Orient."

This desire to incorporate the best elements of Indian culture in the evolving world-culture is based not only on the
natural fascination of the Western mind and heart for the

distant and unknown. Unfamiliarity and distance often lend charm, but this interest is based also on the sound judgment of those few Western scholars, thinkers and critics who have delved deep into the wisdom of India and have unreservedly expressed their appreciation of Indian culture. Max Müller was one of the earliest European scholars, who made himself acquainted with a few works of Indian religious and philosophical thought. He writes in his *India: What Can It Teach Us?* (p. 6), "If I were asked under what sky the human mind has most fully developed some of its choicest gifts, has most deeply pondered on the greatest problems of life, and has found solutions of some of them which well deserve the attention even of those who have studied Plato and Kant, I should point to India. And if I were to ask myself from what literature we here in Europe—we who have been nurtured almost exclusively on the thought of the Greeks and the Romans, and of one Semitic race, the Jewish—may draw that corrective which is most wanted in order to make our inner life more perfect, more comprehensive, more universal, in fact more truly human, a life not for this life only, but a transfigured and eternal life, again I should point to India."

It is now time that what is best anywhere in the world of knowledge and of wisdom should be brought within the reach of every man and woman living on the earth by those means of quick propagation which modern science has placed in our hands. Every human being has a claim to all that is best in any culture of the world, and particularly the Indian culture, which has never claimed to belong to a particular race, country or colour.

GENERAL CHARACTERISTICS OF INDIAN CULTURE

From time immemorial Indians have called their culture by the name of human culture *(mānava dharma* or *mānava sanskriti)*. It has tried to be so comprehensive as to suit the needs of every human being, irrespective of age, sex, colour or race. As such, it has a universal appeal. Without any attempt at conversion, people are converted to it. Without any state support for the last several hundred years, and in spite of incessant attempts of barbarous foreign invaders to root it out from the soil of India, it has flourished and endured. Although born and developed in India, it spread over almost all parts of the earth. History has not been able to trace its beginning, hence it is taken in India as beginningless *(anādi)*. It has always existed in time and it shows no sign of decay or death; hence it is spoken of as eternal *(sanātana)*. It is called *Vaidic* because the earliest literature in which it found expression is the *Veda*, the oldest books known to the world. It is called Hindu culture, or Indian culture, because it flourished in its earliest stages on this (eastern) side of the river Indus, which is the same as Sindhus or Hindus in various languages.

THE SECRET OF THE LONGEVITY OF INDIAN CULTURE

What is the secret of the longevity and imperishability? In his *Why Religions Die*, a short work but of great worth, Professor J. B. Pratt of America makes a few observations about the Hindu religion, which, according to him, is the only religion which tends to survive the present crisis in the life of all religions. Hinduism, which he calls the "Vedic way" is a "self-perpetuating" religion. "The Vedic way ... the way of constant spiritual reinterpretation ... leads to life—life which is self-perpetuating, self-renewing, and which for the individual and for the world may be eternal." Unlike other religions "not death, but development" has been the fate of Hinduism. "That which in it was vital and true cast off the old shell and clothed itself in more suitable expression, with no break in the continuity of life and no loss in the sanctity and weight of its authority." Generalizing on the secret of longevity of the Vedic religion, Professor Pratt says, "If a religion is to live it must adapt itself to new and changing conditions; it if is to feed the spiritual life of its children, it must have the sensivity and inventiveness that shall enable it to modify their diet as their needs demand."[1] Not only Hindu religion, but the whole culture of the Hindus has been growing, changing and developing in accordance with the needs of time and circumstances, without losing its essential and imperishable spirit. The culture of the Vedic age, of the ages of the *Upanishads*, the philo-

1 Pratt, *Why Religions Die*, p. 122.

sophical systems, the *Mahabharata*, the *Smritis*, the *Puranas*, the commentators, the medieval saints and of the age of the modern reformers, is the same in spirit yet very different in form. It is the same today in spirit as it was in the Vedic times, yet the culture of today is very different from what it was in the age of the Vedas. Another secret of the vitality of Hindu religion, and also of the Indian culture, as pointed out by Pratt, is its catholicity. He says, "Mutually contradictory creeds can and do keep house together without quarrel within the wide and hospitable Hindu family." "Hindu thought ... because of its ingrained conclusiveness, its tolerance, and its indifference to doctrinal divergences, stressed the essential unity of all Indian Dharmas, whether Hindu or Buddhist, and minimized differences." This tolerance of differences of opinion and creed within its own fold and even outside itself is an essential characteristic of Indian culture. This characteristic attitude is expressed in the following statement of the *Yogavāsistha:* "All the diverse doctrines and paths originating at different times and in different countries, however, lead ultimately to the same Supreme Truth, like the many different paths leading travellers from different places to the same city. It is ignorance of the Absolute Truth and misunderstanding of the different doctrines that cause their followers to quarrel in bitter animosity with one another. They consider their own particular dogmas and paths to be the best, as every traveller may think, though wrongly, his own path to be the only and the best path."[1] Every seeker of truth and perfection is allowed in Hindu society to pursue his own method freely, and nobody is expected to interfere or meddle with it. The *Yogavāsistha* says, "The method by which a man makes spiritual progress is the best for him. He should not change it for another, which may not look right to him, nor please him, nor be useful to him."[2]

A typical illustration of liberal adjustment to others' opinion is found in the *Yogavasistha* in connexion with the nature of the ultimate reality, "The ultimate reality is called Sunya (nothing) by the Nihilist, Brahman by the Vedantists, Purusa by the Sankhya philosophers, Ishwara by the followers of the *yoga* school, Shiva by the Shaivas, Time by those who believe

---

[1] *Yogavāsistha*, V. III. 96. 51 52, 53.
[2] Op. cit., VI b. 130. 2.

it to be time, Self by those who take it to be the Self, Not-self by those who do not believe Self to be the ultimately real thing, Something between being and non-being by the Madhyamikas, and the 'All' by those who think so."[1] Every Hindu prays to the ultimate power behind and pervading the universe in the following way. "May the Lord of all the three worlds hear and answer our prayer—the Lord Hari (Vishnu) whom the Shaivites call Shiva, the Vedantists call Brahman, the Buddhists call the Buddha, the Logicians (*Naiyayikas*) call the Creator, the Jains call Arhat, and the Mimamsakas call Karma (the Law of Karma)." In a modern version of the same prayer, a Hindu composer has also included the names of God, Allah, Jehovah and Ahurmazda, as the Christians, Moslems, Jews and Parsis call Him.

This tolerance of Hindu culture has become a philosophy which goes by the name of *Anekānta-vāda* according to which the reality, and as a matter of fact, every expression of it, has innumerable aspects and every thinker views it from one or the other aspect, and, therefore, his view and judgment about the same object are bound to differ from those of others who look upon the object from another angle of vision. A corollary of this doctrine of many-sidedness of reality is found in what is called the doctrine of *Syādvāda*, which means the use of restraint or caution in making judgments. It is a very healthy principle always to remember that our judgments are partial truths and can never be absolutely true. It is on account of this catholicity and this humility which characterize Hindu culture that religious, doctrinal, philosophical and ideological differences among people and communities have not tended to mar the general advancement of the cultural life of the country. All the discordant notes ultimately brought about greater and greater harmony in the culture of the country. Whatever the political, linguistic, racial and religious difference between the various parts of the country, one never fails to find a common culture flourishing in India from Kailash to Kanyākumarī (Cape Comorin) and from Jagannatha Puri to Dwarka. Pratt rightly remarks, "The tendency of Hinduism to absorb its children, and the urge felt by its rebelling children to fall back into the family fold has been

---

[1] *Yogavāsistha*, V. 87. 18–20.

illustrated many times in Indian history. The process is going on today."[1] Because Hindu culture is not averse to foreign elements, it has grown vigorous in every age by absorbing all that was best in the culture with which it came into contact.

In ancient times there was much give and take between the Greeks and the Indians. Within the first century of the birth of Christianity India welcomed it and absorbed its best elements into its own culture. In medieval times it made its own all that was best in Islamic culture, although Islam came to India as a very hostile creed. And now in modern times, slowly and gradually Indian culture is absorbing all that is best in the scientific civilization of the West, without losing any of its vital elements. The Benares Hindu University, the first national attempt in education in India, came into existence with a conscious object of preserving all that is best in Indian religion, philosophy, art and literature and absorbing all that is best in western science. The objects of the university were stated thus, in 1916 when the foundation stone was laid: "To promote the study of the Hindu Shastras and of Sanskrit literature as a means of preserving and popularizing the best thought and culture of the Hindus, and all that was good and great in the ancient civilization of India; to promote learning and research in arts and sciences in all branches; to advance and diffuse such scientific, technical and professional knowledge, combined with the necessary practical training; and to promote the building up of character in youth by making religion and ethics an integral part of education."

THE ESSENTIAL CHARACTERISTIC OF INDIAN CULTURE

The essential characteristic which distinguishes Indian culture from the modern scientific culture of the West, is a thorough understanding of the nature of man and his relations with other beings in the universe and with the universe as a whole. From time immemorial India has tried to build its civilization on the basis of this knowledge. Man being a part and product of nature, India approached nature through man, because it is in himself alone that man can be most aware of reality. There

---

[1] Pratt, *op. cit.*

are many more aspects of reality open to man in himself than those which sense-observation of external nature reveals.

Science cannot give us knowledge of the real nature of man and of the deeper, imperceptible and immeasurable aspects of nature. All the sciences together cannot do this, much less physical and psychological sciences alone. Modern psychology which makes use of the methods of modern science has been running away from the real and inner man and is content to make certain observations, generalizations and correlations of physical, chemical, physiological and biological reactions of the human body. It avoids all reference to soul, mind and consciousness which science cannot observe, measure and record. For it the human personality is nothing more than a "reaction mass", "an individual's total assets and liabilities on the reaction side" (J. B. Watson). Modern science thus leaves out of account all that man considers most important and valuable in himself. It has devised no method yet to understand the real nature of soul, consciousness and mind, not to speak of the nature of God. Although scientific knowledge has proved informative, useful and practical, it has tended to shut our eyes to the deeper nature of man and the universe, and consequently we miss much of what we ought to have known. Ignorance is not so harmful as the denial of the existence of that of which we are ignorant. And there is a tendency on the part of modern man to deny the existence of that of which we are ignorant. He is confined to the outskirts of the universe, lives on the surface of life and is building a civilization which is concerned more with the husk than with the grain of life. Hence the growing dissatisfaction with the modern way of life in the minds of those who are gifted with deeper awareness. Alexis Carrol, the author and eminent scientist, deplores this state of things and suggests that "the only possible remedy for this evil is much more profound knowledge of ourselves" (*Man, the Unknown*). It is this—"profound knowledge of ourselves"— that mainly characterizes Indian culture. All that there is in Indian culture of lasting value, is based on the deeper knowledge of man and the universe. A few of the countless aspects of the culture are selected here for a general and popular treatment.

THE PLACE OF DISCIPLINE IN LIFE

The Indian word for culture is *sanskriti*, from a root which means to purify, to transform, to sublimate, to mould and to perfect. A cultured man is a disciplined man, who has brought his natural propensities under control and has shaped himself in accordance with the ideal placed before him by his ethical consciousness. Manu, one of the earliest leaders of Indian social thought, says that by nature (birth) we are all barbarous, uncultured and uncivilized. It is discipline or *sanskāra* that raises us to a higher status in life. Indian psychologists agree with the modern psychologists that man shares with animals quite a number of natural propensities or instinctive urges which drive him to action. These they call *pravrittis* or drives. They, however, make a distinction between man and animals in the former's being endowed by nature with a power of discrimination and control, called *buddhi* (intelligence).

Buddhi enables man not only to discriminate between the proper and improper exercise of a natural propensity, but also to control all the propensities by weakening some, strengthening others and ordering others to wait for their satisfaction. The man who lives only in accordance with the dictates of his momentary and unorganized animal passions is an animal man *(pashu)*. Man stands between animals and gods. He can by his conduct rise higher to the level of gods or can fall down to the level of animals. If we make a proper use of our power of discriminative control and shape ourselves into the ideal picture which the great seers and leaders of humanity have placed before us, we can become divine and our society heavenly.

Indian thinkers have given us various types of ideals that may suit diverse men and women and have worked out in minutest details the processes through which the ideals are realized in life. Discipline is the key to all greatness, spiritual and moral. The general name for discipline is *yoga*. The *Bhagavadgita* is, in fact, a treatise on all kinds of discipline leading to all kinds of perfection. It is one of the most valuable guides for humanity.

THREE ASPECTS OF HUMAN NATURE AND THE PROCESS
OF PERFECTING THEM

According to Indian psychologists, human consciousness has
three main aspects, viz. awareness *(jnāna)*, desire tinged with
emotions *(ichchhā)* and activity *(kriyā)*. They correspond to
what the modern psychologists call cognition, affection and
conation. Perfection of man should proceed along all these
lines, and the perfected man is conceived as one who is fully
aware of his nature, of his environment and of his relations
with all beings around him; who has a control over his desires
and passions; and who acts rightly under all circumstances
and thus has never to repent what he has done. There is a
definite process of perfecting each of the aspects of man. That
which widens his awareness is called *jnāna yoga* (*yoga* of knowledge), that which brings about control over his desires and
emotions is called *bhakti yoga* (*yoga* of devotion); and that which
trains him in righteousness and disinterested performance of
duty is called *karma yoga* (*yoga* of action).

In addition to these three chief *yogas* there are many other
yogas which aim at the control, training and perfection of one
or the other factors of human personality. *Hatha yoga*, for
example, aims at the control, and perfection of the physical
body. The *kundalini yoga* aims at awakening into operation the
dormant and potential powers of man which are at present
beyond his consciousness and control. The *raja yoga* aims at
the experience of *samādhi* through gradual control and concentration of mind. It makes one aware not only of the unconscious aspects and powers of one's mind but also of many
supernormal aspects and powers of which one is ordinarily
little aware. Cultivation of this and of many other *yogas*
bestows on man unimaginable and innumerable powers of
knowledge and action, some of which have recently been discovered by researches in parapsychology and psychics.

Lest a *yogi* should make an evil use of his powers, as modern
scientists under the control of political leaders of ambitious
communities may do, he is first trained in strict observance
of certain moral principles called *yama* and *niyama* (restraints
and rules), which are considered as the first two stages of the
process of *yoga*. These *yamas*, restraints or controls are:
(a) *Ahimsā*, freedom from ill will against all beings at all times

and in all ways; (b) *Satya*, truthfulness; (c) *Asteya*, abstinence from misappropriation of others' property; (d) *Brahmacharya*, celibacy or sexual purity; and (e) *Aparigraha*, freedom from avarice. And the rules or observances are: (a) *Shaucha*, cleanliness, external as well as internal; (b) *Santosha*, contentment; (c) *Tapas*, austerity or hard life; (d) *Swādhyaya*, study; and (e) *Ishwara-pranidhāna*, surrender to God. Mahatma Gandhi laid great emphasis on these restraints and observances and expected every one of his countrymen to follow at least the first two of them, namely truth and non-violence.

THE SPIRIT OF MAN IS ONE WITH THE SPIRIT IN AND BEHIND THE UNIVERSE

The Indian knowledge of man, and of the universe of which he is a product and a part, has gone too deep to be fathomed by the methods of modern science. By their *yogic* methods, Indian seers discovered that man was a microcosm in which the whole macrocosm is represented. They think that the only way to understand nature generally and in all its aspects is to know man completely through the various processes of *yoga*. They did not depend merely on sensory observation. They refined and perfected the processes of introspection, intuition and *samadhi* (mystic experience) and through them they opened the gates of the vast unconscious and the limitless superconscious strata of being lying within them. They delved much deeper into the nature of man than any kind of external observation can do. They discovered that man is a centre of a circle whose circumference is nowhere, that his dimensions are infinite in extent, and that in his deeper nature he is one and identical with the deepest and ultimate spirit that holds, supports, sustains and pervades the universe. What we ordinarily know and see of man is a very small part of him. In his ultimate essence he is one with the essence of the world.

The *Upanishads* proclaim this truth in unequivocal language. "This Self is the Absolute Reality" *(ayam ātma Brahma)*; "I am the Absolute" *(Aham Brahma asmi)*; "Thou art That" *(Tat twam asi)*; and "Everything is the Absolute" *(sarvan khalu idam Brahma)*, are some of the many "great assertions" *(mahā-*

vākyani) of the *Upanishads*. In one place we read in an *Upanishad*, "The Spirit that is in man and the Spirit that is in the Sun are one and identical" *(sa yascha ayam purushe yascha asau Āditye sa eka)*. The Christ had a glimpse of this truth when he uttered "I and my father are one". According to Indian seers not only man but also all things and creatures in the universe are rooted in one and the same absolute reality which is spiritual in essence. No description of its nature can be given, simply because our terms which are meant to describe this or that object cannot be applicable to that which is the source, ground and goal of all objects. The only things we may say about it is that it is infinite *(ananta)* awareness *(jnānam)* characterized by bliss *(ananda)*. According to the *Yogavāsistha* which deals with the nature of the absolute more exhaustively and satisfactorily than any other work in Sanskrit, the nature of the absolute reality "cannot be satisfactorily talked about or discussed. It can only be experienced within the depth of one's own being".[1] And that which we experience within the innermost and the deepest stratum of our being is what "cannot be expressed in words, what cannot be even indirectly indicated, what cannot be named, and what is not the object of any of our senses."[2] "It is neither a being, nor a non-being, nor anything between the two. It is nothing, yet everything. It cannot be grasped by mind and expressed in words. It is empty of all possible contents, yet is the deepest of all enjoyments."[3]

This limitless and eternal being is perpetually manifest in the world process by its own internal and inherent urge. It expresses itself in the form of the infinite many without losing its basic unity. It allows birth, growth, decay and death to take place by its side without experiencing any one of these changes within itself. The most common word for the absolute in India is Brahman. Search for the nature of Brahman and effort to experience it within ourselves are the main pursuits of Indian philosophy and religion.

---

1 Yogavāsistha, VIb. 31. 37.
2 Op. cit., VIb. 52. 57.
3 Op. cit., III. 119. 23.

INTERCONNECTEDNESS OF ALL BEINGS

Being thus rooted in the same Brahman, all the individuals and beings in the universe are interconnected. Although apparently isolated on the surface, we are like islands in an ocean connected with each other by land at the bottom of the ocean. We are pervaded and permeated by a common self behind us which is Brahman. It is identically the same in all beings, however isolated and different they may appear on the surface. None of us is thus alien to others. This great fact was revealed to Rama by his teacher Vasistha in these words, "How can the thought that some one is one's brother and another is not hold good when there is one and the same all-pervading Self present in all of us? O Ram, beings of all species are your brothers, as there is no being who is unconnected with you."[1] We struggle, hate each other, and quarrel and fight until we realize this spiritual identity and interconnectedness. But when we understand that we are like branches of the same tree or like limbs, organs, and cells of the same body, and are thus interconnected with each other, our attitude in life changes. Fellowship, co-operation, sympathy and goodwill begin to characterize our life. Harmony and happiness characterize those lives which are based on the realization of this principle. The *Isha Upanishad*, one of the oldest of the *Upanishads*, stated this realization in the following words, "Whosoever beholds all beings in the same Self and the same Self in all beings does not hate anybody. When a man knows that all beings are ultimately the Self and realizes this unity in experience, then there remains no delusion or grief for him." The *Bhagavadgītā* and the *Yogavasistha* deal with this idea and base their ethics of universal brotherhood and benevolence on it.

THE NATURE OF MAN AND THE COSMOS

Long ago Indian psychologists discovered that in living his life from day to day, man passes through several types of experiences. Three types of them are known to every one of us

---

[1] Op. cit., V. 20. 4; V. 18. 46.

though not understood properly by most of us—the waking experience, the dream and the deep sleep.

In the waking experience our consciousness works in the physical realm with physical body, physical senses and in relation to physical objects. The world of our waking experience is the world with which our theoretical and practical sciences deal. We do not, however, live in the physical realm for all the time of our life. For some hours at least every day we pass into another realm of existence, namely, the realm of dreams. In dream states of our experience our world of objects, our bodies, and our personalities are more or less the creations of our minds, without relation to the reality of the physical world of our waking experience. Even the time and space of the physical order are not retained in the dream state, where we experience quite a different order of time and space. What is a moment of waking state is sometimes felt as long ages in dream, and while the body of the dreamer continues to lie in his bed he has an experience of travelling far and wide and seeing a vast world with his dream body and senses. The personality of the waking experience does not very often continue to be felt as that of the dreaming subject. An unhealthy, crippled, or miserable man may in his dream feel quite the opposite. Despite all these differences between the two experiences there is something in us which is identically the same between the two states. Otherwise it would be difficult to realize that both the states are our own experiences. We own both as our experiences and remember one in the other. Modern psychology and philosophy have not yet given enough thought to understanding the nature and significance of dream.

Other than and different from both these is a third state of experience which all of us undergo for some time during our existence of twenty-four hours. It is a unique kind of experience which we all like to enjoy and which plays a very important role in our life. It is the state of dreamless sleep in which we are conscious of nothing but the bare existence of ourselves. Mind, senses, body and even personality, with all sorts of mental and physical objects, pass out of our experience in the deep dreamless sleep, and yet there is something in us that keeps awake to know that we know nothing. It is something identical between the three states of waking, dream and sleep, and it is that which remembers the experience of sleep in the waking world. The experience of sleep is objectless, yet it is extremely pleasant and joyful, and every one of us prefers to have it over the other two. We use the help of chemical and mechanical means to go to sleep if we cannot get it ordinarily. So far as the affective aspect of the three states is concerned, it cannot be denied that the deep dreamless sleep is the most pleasant, and the dream state comes next, and the waking one the last.

Occasionally we are lifted into a unique state of forget-fulness of both mental and physical objects, when we are in a momentary contact with the abstract ideas of truth, goodness or beauty. In such rare moments we get so much identified with and merged into the object that we lose all consciousness of time, space and differences. Through the process of *raja yoga*, such momentary experiences of joy and delight can be prolonged and turned into a unique experience of objectless, thoughtless, and differenceless blissful existence, from which no one wishes to return to any of the above mentioned three states of experience. This fourth experience, which is called *samadhi* in India, is a unique state in which there is an extremely delightful awareness of being timeless, limitless, and difference-less, something which cannot be described in words. The only symbol that can very imperfectly indicate the experience is effulgence, illumination or Light. A *yogi*, who could remain in the state of *samadhi* for any length of the time of wakeful world, described his experience as that of "immeasurably de-lightful and cool effulgence of millions of suns in which there is no longing for anything". There is nothing mysterious about it. It is attainable by every man and woman with the help of a teacher who has already experienced it.

Indian thinkers have taken into consideration all types of experience to understand the nature of man. Our modern view of man is based only on the study of our waking ex-perience. It is therefore bound to be incomplete and erroneous. Indian psychologists and philosophers have pondered deeply on all aspects of experience and have tried to understand man in the light of them. They have tried to analyse and synthesize all the states of experience in which man passes and can pass, into one whole concept of man. Through a thorough under-standing of man they have tried to understand the constitution of the cosmos, for whatever is present in man, who is a part of the cosmos, and in whom the entire cosmos is represented, must be correspondingly present in the cosmos. The cosmos is man writ large and man is the cosmos in miniature, in the same way as the atom is now regarded by physical science as a solar system in miniature. It is a common saying in India that whatever is present in man is present in the universe as a whole *(yat pinde tat Brahmande)*. There is a complete correspondence between the two. According to the *Jnana-sankalini Tantra* the human body is the key to all knowledge about the universe *(Dehastha sarva-vidya)*. In the light of the various experiences man passes or can pass through, Indians have come to the conclusion that man is not a physical entity alone. He is mental as well as spiritual at the same time. Correspondingly, nature also has physical, mental and spiritual aspects and realms. *Vedänta-sära,* a small treatise on the Vedanta philosophy, has worked out in detail a comprehensive theory of man and universe on the basis of the various types of human experience. Space does not permit us to go into those details here. It is enough to say that modern philosophy could gain much from a study of Indian anthroposophy.

The most important thing worth knowing about the constitution of man is that he is the spirit manifesting itself through three vehicles or bodies, namely, the causal body, the subtle body, and the physical body. The physical body, the only one of which the modern man is conscious, functions in the waking experience; the subtle body functions in the dream experience; and the causal body in the deep sleep. The physical body is called *annamaya sharira* (body made of what we eat). It is born of the parents' body and dies at what we call death. It is enlivened, moved and controlled by the subtle body *(sukshama sharira)* which is constituted by the vital energies *(pranas)*, sensory and motor powers *(jnanendriyani)* and *karmendriyani)*, subtle elements, mind, intelligence and ego. The subtle body does not get dissolved and pass into nothing at the death of the physical body. It goes out of the latter and lives and moves in the subtle planes of the cosmos which correspond to our dream state for some time, and experiences there the states of heaven or hell spoken of in all religious scriptures. After some time, determined by the desires and acts of the individual, it again returns to the physical plane and enters a newly conceived body, and thus resumes its worldly career. It is really with the subtle body that man knows, feels, thinks and acts in the physical body and on the physical plane. In dream the subtle body becomes isolated from the physical body temporarily and functions more or less independently of the latter.

The causal body is still finer in structure and function. In it are stored in very minute forms all the past experiences of the subtle body. The causal body is the organ of conscience, intuition, telepathy, clairvoyance, psychometry and other remarkable powers of man. It functions on the causal plane of the universe which can be approached by us in sleep, deep trance and mystic experiences. It is the constant basis and support of the subtle and the physical bodies, which function on the mental and physical planes. All the phenomena that take place in the life of an individual for which we cannot account in terms of matter and mind, have their root in the causal body of the individual and in the causal plane of the universe. Through and behind these three bodies functions the spirit *(atman)* of the individual which, in Indian culture, is regarded as identical with the spirit of the whole universe.

REINCARNATION AND THE LAW OF KARMA OR COSMIC JUSTICE

Man, being the spirit functioning through the three bodies, causal, subtle and physical, cannot be said to perish into nothing at the death of the physical body. Physical death affects only the physical body and cannot do harm to the other two bodies. The only way it affects them is that they cease to function on the physical plane of the cosmos. They continue to exist and function on their own planes. Just as when the physical body goes to sleep the mind functions in the dream state, so when the physical body is dead, the subtle body begins to function in the subtle plane of the cosmos and to have various kinds of experiences there. This plane is what is called the spiritual world by spiritualists and psychical researchers. It is on this plane, which corresponds to our dream state, that the dead personalities live until they take their rebirth on the physical plane which corresponds to our waking experience. What death does is to shut off the physical world from the dead by destroying the physical body. It opens, however, a finer subtle world. Modern spiritualistic literature is full of the description of this world and personalities living therein. It is perhaps superior to our physical world in many respects.

Why do we then come back to the physical world when the spiritual world is superior to it? It is because we have entertained many desires connected with this world which still remain to be fulfilled, and because we have incurred here many debts that we have to pay off, and because we have to undergo the consequences of the deeds done in our previous lives on this plane. Desire is the most potent force in our life, and early or late all our desires get fulfilled. But as our desires affect others, and by our acting in accordance with our desires we do good or evil to others, there is a law of retribution that governs the life of all free agents in the universe. It is called the law of *Karmaphala*, or simply as the law of Karma. No one can escape it. "Even the gods have to undergo the good and evil consequences of their acts", says the author of the *Mahābhārata*. It is stated in the *Yogavāsistha*, "There is no place in the Universe—no mountain, no sky, no ocean, no heaven—where one does not undergo the good or evil consequences of the deeds done by one."[1]

For an Indian it is not difficult to understand that the law of Karma operates in the world, but for others it is a concept very difficult to grasp. It is believed unquestionably in India that all our voluntary acts which affect others agreeably or disagreeably, favourably or unfavourably, are rewarded or punished in accordance with the strict law of justice. A Hindu holds that the cosmic order is divine and therefore just and properly maintained. Cosmic justice demands that there should be strict and equitable retribution in nature. There is some arrangement in nature to keep strict balance of action and reaction. Cosmic agencies keep an account of all our deeds and place us in situations under which they can be rightly retributed. Thus no one can escape or evade the good or evil consequences of his deeds accruing to him. If he does not meet the consequences in this life here and now he must do so in some other life, for he does not die completely. The doer of the deeds, the personality of the doer, never dies. There would

---

1 *Yogavāsistha*, III. 95. 33.

be chaos and rule of injustice in the universe if one were to cease to exist without having undergone the consequences of his deeds. Death, being a common experience of every living being at some time, cannot be considered a punishment for any deed. Life here must presuppose a previous life to account for the inequalities of circumstances and life. Death must lead to another life to make the dying person undergo retribution for what he has done in life. Pre-existence and post-existence are implied in the law of justice. Rebirth or reincarnation is thus not only a fact known directly to the seers but also a logical necessity. Reason and justice are both against the conception of life as limited in time. Kant, the great German philosopher, regarded immortality or continuity of life after death as a postulate of moral consciousness. Some of the Western thinkers of modern times who have pondered over the problems of life from this point of view, have appreciated both these doctrines, namely, reincarnation and the law of Karma.

THE FOUR ENDS OF LIFE: WEALTH, ENJOYMENT, RIGHTEOUSNESS AND SPIRITUAL FREEDOM

Life is thus not a meaningless accident. It is a continuous process governed by two principles, desire-fulfilment and law of Karma. Early or late, in this birth or another, we get whatever we desire and work for, but at the same time we have to undergo the good or evil consequences of our deeds in accordance with the strict principle of retribution. As we are free agents we are not being led in any direction by any other force than our own will, working, of course, under the law of Karma. Our own desire and will determine our future. Guided by our desires and controlled by the cosmic law of just retribution, we are afloat on the vast ocean of existence. Desire is the key to our destiny, for we act in accordance with our desires.

Our desires are innumerable and unlimited. Many of them conflict with others. We have to choose some and reject others. As it has already been pointed out, we are endowed with a power of discrimination and control. With the help of this power we should bring about an order in the realm of our desires. We have various kinds of desires. Some of them are for enjoyment of the pleasures of the world and for possessions of the goods of this world while others are for moral perfection and spiritual freedom and peace. Ancient Indians realized that the whole of our life should not be devoted to the pursuit of wealth and pleasure, for the real man, the spirit within us, cannot be satisfied by them alone.

The *Kathopanishad* classified all the desires under two heads, namely, the *preya* (pleasant ones, that is, aiming at pleasures) and the *shreya* (aiming at the good of the soul). The story of the boy Nachiketas emphasized that the latter should be preferred to the former. The Lord of Death offered to the little boy all the wealth, power and enjoyment possible in the world but wanted to keep the secret of life and death to himself. The boy refused to accept them because they did not promise lasting, final and unconditional satisfaction to the soul, for which it yearns. In another illustration, of the *Upanishads*, Maitreyi, the wife of the royal priest, Yājnavalkya, refused to accept the gift of his wealth on the eve of his retirement from the householder's life, simply because wealth gave no promise of immortality for which her soul yearned like that of her retiring husband. The young Gautama left his beautiful wife, newly-born little son, royal palace, and the kingdom to which he was heir, simply because he realized that these objects of pleasure were also the sources of pain and did not ensure lasting happiness. It was enlightenment, Buddhahood, for which he wandered from place to place and which he preferred to kingship.

The tragedy of the modern Western life is that the entire life is spent in the pursuit of those very objects which little Indian boys like Nachiketas and Gautama and a woman like Maitreyi discarded as the unsatisfactory ends of life. The modern man is generally sad, unhappy, discontented and pessimistic. He does not know any higher purpose in life than earning of wealth and enjoyment of sensual and sexual pleasures, which consume all his energies. Indian sages did not altogether despise and hate wealth and enjoyments. They knew that acquisitiveness and sex were very powerful and important drives of man. But they also knew that unprincipled acquisition of wealth and unbridled enjoyment of sensual and sexual pleasures lead to bodily exhaustion, disease and ruin and social disharmony and conflicts. They discovered that acquisition of wealth and enjoyment of pleasures, in order to remain healthy pursuits, have to be guided and controlled by moral principles such as truth, justice, honesty, sincerity, kindness, fellow-feeling, moderation, social propriety, and self-restraint, etc. They realized that observance of moral principles ensures greater individual happiness and social peace than unrestricted and unprincipled pursuit of wealth and pleasure. They knew that there is a deeper joy in life which is more abiding and more native to the soul than that which possessions and enjoyments can yield. They discovered that the source of this unconditional and abiding joy was within ourselves.

To realize this abiding, unconditional and supreme happiness which springs up from within ourselves when we have freed ourselves from the pursuit of pleasures of the outside world, was considered to be the greatest object of human life. Taking into consideration all the needs of life, and so formulating a very comprehensive ideal of life, the Indian thinkers prescribed the following four objects of life to be pursued by every man and woman: (a) *Dharma,* or observance of moral principles which alone ensure individual happiness and social peace; (b) *Artha,* acquisition of wealth or the means that make life comfortable and ensure satisfaction of worldly needs; (c) *Kama,* moderate and controlled enjoyment of sensual and sexual pleasures; and (d) *Moksha,* spiritual freedom and perfection in which an individual rises to the status of divinity here and now. Not one of these ends exclusively but all of them together in life constitute the ideal of Indian culture.

THE ULTIMATE PURPOSE OF LIFE, THE "SUMMUM BONUM"

Spiritual perfection and freedom is the ultimate purpose of our life, without having achieved which we shall not be happy. It is the goal for which consciously or unconsciously we are all striving. It is a long process for most of the souls, but by those who have set their heart on it, it can be achieved more or less quickly. Differences of opinion about the nature of the goal and about the proper methods of reaching it are bound to prevail. Indian culture has a knack of synthesizing differences into a systematic whole. In the *Upanishads, Bhagavad-*

gita and *Yogavāsistha*, which are the most valuable works dealing with the subject of spiritual perfection and methods leading to it, we find very important hints, which no seeker after spiritual perfection can afford to ignore. Spiritual perfection, according to these works, consists in a conscious realization of identity with the Whole in all its aspects. On the physical level the individual has to consciously feel that his body is an organic part of the cosmos. On the mental level, he has to realize that all his thoughts, emotions and actions are interlinked with those of the cosmic mind. On the causal plane, he must feel that he is very intimately connected with all the finer forces of the world, and spiritually he must realize that he is the absolute reality itself and nothing less. This realization of oneness and interconnectedness with everything else is our *summum bonum*.

The essential and common factors in all the methods of attaining this consciousness of identity with the absolute are two: (a) gradual removal of the sense of a false ego which asserts itself to be something separate and independent of the whole, through right thinking, active sympathy and compassion for all beings irrrespective of species, race, colour, creed, community, family or sex, and acts of self-sacrifice in everyday life; (b) expansion of the self on all planes of existence and in all aspects of one's being, by becoming aware of the cosmic influences, forces and realities affecting us every moment and determining what we are, and thereby identifying ourselves with all that determines our being. Through these two simultaneous processes of denying the false little self and affirming the real limitless self in various ways on the physical, mental, causal and spiritual levels, the individual gradually acquires a greater and greater consciousness of his being a centre of the whole, and, in course of time, instead of being conscious at the centre and of the centre alone he becomes conscious of being the whole, loves every one as himself, and acts for the good of everybody. He remains happy under all circumstances for he knows that everything in the whole belongs to him. Nothing is alien to him anywhere and he feels oneness with all. Here and now he is at home with the universe. He is a completely transfigured man, and in place of a selfish seeker of his own happiness, he now seeks for the happiness of all around him, and naturally scatters joy and life around him. He is called a *jivanmukta*, a liberated living man. The *Yogavāsistha* gives a detailed description of the *jivan-mukta*, which is worth knowing. Here is a brief summary of what has been said about such a person in the *Yogavāsistha:*

"Pleasures do not delight him; pains do not distress. There is no feeling of like or dislike produced in his mind even towards serious, violent, and continued states of pleasure or pain. Although externally engaged in wordly actions, he has no attachment in his mind to any object whatsoever. His conduct does not annoy anybody; he behaves like an ideal citizen and is a friend of all. Outwardly he is very busy, but at heart very calm and quiet. He is free from the restrictions of caste, creed, stage of life *(āshrama)*, custom and scriptures. He rests unagitated in the Supreme Bliss. He does not work to get anything for himself. He is always happy, and never hangs his joy on anything else. His face is never without the lustre of cheerfulness on it. He behaves with his fellow beings as the occasion and the status of the person demand, without the least strain on his mind.... In spite of being occupied with actions appropriate to the time, place and circumstances, he is not touched by pleasure or pain arising from them. He never feels despondent, proud, agitated, cast down, troubled or elated. He is full of mercy and magnanimity even when surrounded by enemies.... He works without any anxiety, egoistic feeling, pride or impurity of heart. He does not discard the pleasures that he has got, nor desires the pleasures he has not got. He finds equal pleasure in old age, death, misery, poverty and in ruling over an empire. He keeps his body healthy and does not starve it of its appropriate requirements.... The life of a liberated sage is really the noblest and happiest life. From him goodness is scattered all around. Having seen him, having heard about him, having met him, and having remembered him, all creatures feel delighted."[1]

This ideal can be attained by every man and woman only if he or she works for it. There is no restriction of sex, caste or creed for it. The *Yogavāsistha* quotes an example of Chudala, a ruling queen, who became a *jivanmukta* long before her husband king Shikhidhwaja could become one under her own guidance. Kabir, a Muslim weaver, attained the status of a

---

[1] B. L. Atreya, *Yogavāsistha and Its Philosophy*, pp. 96–100.

jivanmukta. Mahatma Gandhi became one in spite of his intense political activity. King Janaka, in ancient times, was a *jivanmukta*, in spite of his being a ruler. In fact, in India, when it was free and was ruled by its own kings, it was considered desirable that before a prince assumed the responsibilities of kingship, he should have attained the status of a *jivanmukta*. The great Indian king, Rama, after whom an ideal form of government is called "Rama Rajya", a favourite phrase of Mahatma Gandhi, was given practical training in the art of attaining spiritual freedom by his family sage Vasistha. These teachings are recorded in the great spiritual work known as *Yogavasistha*. Plato's idea that philosophers alone should be kings is probably of Indian origin, as we read in Manu's work, "It is only those who are steeped in the wisdom of the Vedas and other Scriptures that deserve to be military generals, kings, magistrates and rulers of men" (*Manusmriti*). India has always been proud of its saints and sages who have in all ages been friends and guides of kings, if not themselves kings.

DHARMA OR ETHICAL PRINCIPLES

Next to *moksha* (spiritual freedom) in importance and value among the four ends of life is *dharma* (moral principles). In fact Brahman and *dharma* are the two most important terms in Indian culture and most of its literature is devoted to the exposition of these two basic ideas. It is very difficult to translate the word *dharma* into English or any other foreign language. It is often wrongly translated as "religion". The nearest word in English to *dharma* is "duty". But it does not convey the full sense in which the Sanskrit word *dharma* is used. Manu, one of the earliest leaders of Indian social thought, derives the word *dharma* from the Sanskrit root *dhri* which means to support, to hold, to maintain, to protect or to keep in balance, and says that *dharma* is what maintains or holds in unity all the creatures of the world. Kanada, another great thinker of India defines *dharma* as that which leads to prosperity and spiritual well-being. Every one of us is advised by the author of the Mahabharata, the great epic of India, to follow *dharma* even at the cost of our individual lives. "Never should one forsake *dharma* for pleasure, for fear, for any wordly gain, or even for life." In Jaina literature *dharma* is defined as that which raises the soul higher in status. In Buddhistic works *dharma* is the very essence of any being.

What then is the concrete nature of *dharma*? Manu defines *dharma* as ten moral principles which every human being should follow in life so that all creatures may live in peace. They are: (1) *Dhriti*, patience and perseverance; (2) *Kshumā*, forgiveness; (3) *Dama*, control of passions and ideas; (4) *Asteyam*, abstinence from misappropriation of other's property; (5) *Shaucha*, cleanliness of body, mind and spirit; (6) *Indriyanigraha*, control of the senses; (7) *Dhi*, cultivation of reasonableness or use of reason; (8) *Vidayā*, acquirement of knowledge; (9) *Satya*, truthfulness; and (10) *Akrodha*, mastery over anger. It is a very comprehensive list of the most general principles which if adhered to in life will certainly not only make an individual life happy and prosperous but will also create a healthy social atmosphere in which everybody will feel secure.

The author of the *Mahabharata* gives a still simpler and briefer concept of *dharma* in the following words: "Do not do to others what you do not wish to be done to you; and wish for others what you desire and long for yourself—this is the essence of *dharma*. Heed it well." This principle is what has been called the golden rule of conduct. It has been preached by almost all the prophets of the world at all times and in all countries. If all of us could follow this principle in our lives— individual, social, communal, and national—there would be no trouble in the world. The world is a hell today because we do not base our conduct on moral principles. We are selfish, greedy and unmindful of others' interests.

NO WORD FOR "RIGHTS" IN INDIAN THOUGHT. DUTIES FOR THE SAKE OF DUTIES

It is remarkable that Indian thought includes no concept of "rights". While there is much talk about duties in its literature, there is nowhere any mention of "rights" which play a leading role in modern social life. Sri Krishna in the *Bhagavadgita*, teaches his friend Arjuna to perform the duties that are demanded by his station in life, without expectation of gain or reward from any quarter. He regards the performance of one's duties without hope of gain or reward as the best worship of God. In the modern age, unfortunately, every one thinks more of his rights than of his duties. What are these rights?[1] "Rights" is simply a glorified word for our individual and selfish interests, sublimated forms of our animal wants. Indian thinkers and writers have said that it is natural for man to demand satisfaction of his natural desires. Why should we emphasize them, glorify them and plead for them? We are naturally prone to assert them. Why should we add to their force by enlisting the power of will on their side? If every one were careful to perform his duties, and were willing to give to others what he expects from them, there would be no need of asserting rights. Assertion of rights, demands of rights and quarrels for rights lead to strife and war. In Indian culture an attempt was made to make men forget them. Good and great men in society never talked of rights but always of duties and others followed them.

People worried more about their debts than their dues. An elaborate theory of man's debts *(rina)* was developed. According to this theory every individual has to pay off the following debts: (a) *Deva-rina*, debt to the forces of nature, for the invaluable gifts of air, fire, water, food, etc. In lieu of those we have to make some offerings of our own to the gods who control nature, as tokens of our gratitude. (b) *Pitri-rina,* debt to parents and to society for having given birth to us and having brought us up. This debt is paid by bringing forth and bringing up children and by contributing to the well-being of the family and society. (c) *Rishi-rina,* debt to the teachers, discoverers and inventors who have brought civilization to this stage and to whom we owe our knowledge. We pay this debt by making some contribution to knowledge, by writing books and by teaching others. A little reflection will convince us that we owe so much to others that it is really difficult to shake off the obligation. To get rid of the obligation to others for our own good we have to do good to others. Keeping this in view Indian culture has prescribed five types of *yajnas* or "sacrifices".

THE FIVE "GREAT SACRIFICES"

Yajna (sacrifice) is another very significant and characteristic term of Indian culture. The Vedas and the later literature based on them, enjoin upon every individual to perform several types of *yajnas*. According to the *Bhagavadgita yajna* is the most essential duty of man. Unfortunately the word *yajna* has been very much misunderstood both in India and by Western scholars. It has been taken to mean only performance of certain rites in which oblations of various kinds are offered to fire. This kind of *yajna* is but a symbol of the offering of what belongs to one to the whole, for the benefit of all beings. In the Vedas, Agni is the name of God who pervades all beings. Every Hindu is expected to give up as much as he can for the good of others. By "others" are not meant only human beings, but all creatures in the world, both visible and invisible. The society to which we belong and for the good of which we should make offerings includes, not only animals of various kinds living in air, water, and on and in the earth, but also spirits and gods who live in the invisible worlds around us. Every man is expected to keep friendly relations with all beings around him, by offering to them what little he can.

Hindu culture has, therefore, worked out a scheme of five kinds of offerings *(yajnas)* to be followed by every man who earns and has something to offer. They are (a) *Deva yajna*, offerings to gods or the powers which control nature and its various phenomena; (b) *Rishi yajna*, offerings to the great seers and sages who have advanced civilization and culture and have given us wisdom; (c) *Pitri yajna*, offerings to our ancestors and parents; (d) *Bhuta yajna*, offerings to the various species of creatures that surround us in this world; and (e) *Nri yajna*, offerings to fellow human beings.

Offerings to gods are made in the form of oblations, prayers and gratitude for the great gifts of nature, such as water, air, fire, electricity, etc. Offerings to the sages and seers consist in imparting knowledge to others and in making discoveries and inventions for the benefit of humanity. Offerings to the ancestors and parents consist in remembering with love and affection the dead ones and in being serviceable to the living parents and grandparents. We should now and then celebrate anniversaries of births or deaths of our ancestors and make offerings of our love, gratitude and good wishes to them on those occasions. All Hindus remember their ancestors in a fortnight of a particular month when they feed poor Brahmans on behalf of their ancestors. Offerings to other creatures than human beings that surround us consist in keeping friendly relations with them, feeding them now and then, and giving them protection and affection whenever they need. Before he takes his lunch every Hindu is expected to keep aside some morsels of his food for birds, dogs and other animals. He is enjoined to feel kinship with every animal and act accordingly. Offerings to fellow human beings consist in doing as much good and service to one's fellows as possible. We must help the needy and should part with an appreciable amount of our income for charitable purposes.

In India almost every rich man thought it his duty and privilege to build public wells, resthouses for travellers, gardens for the use of all, and hospitals not only for men but also for animals. Almost every city in India, and particularly those which are frequently visited by people from outside, has one or more *dharmashalas* (free lodging houses) for travellers. *Dāna*, giving to the poor and needy as much as one can give, is a part of this yajna. On certain occasions kings and rich people are enjoined to give away all they have for the good of their society and service of the poor; and they part with their wealth on such occasions with delight. In fact in the apogee of Hindu culture, rich men and kings vied with one another in giving away and not in accumulating wealth. Greatness in those days was measured by the capacity for giving and not by possessions. The *Bhāgavata Purāna*, one of the most widely read and respected Sanskrit books in India, says that "a man should possess only as much as is necessary for his maintenance. He who accumulates more than he needs for bare living is a thief."[1]

One of the forms of *Nri yajna*, offerings to mankind, is hospitality to a stranger *(atithi-satkara)*. A stranger who happens to visit one or to meet one without any previous acquaintance or notice, is looked upon as a god, and all facilities and services offered to him are regarded as service to God. In

---

[1] *Srimad Bhagawata*, VII. 14. 8.

one of the convocation addresses of ancient India, the teacher exhorts the new graduates to look upon every stranger as a God and to treat him as God (*Taittiriya Upanishad* XI. 2). A Hindu is expected to look upon every human being as his brother or sister, nay, as himself, and upon humanity as his family. A Sanskrit writer says, "It is only petty-minded persons who make a distinction between theirs and others. Those who have great hearts look upon the whole world as their own family". Another writer says, "He who looks upon others as himself really sees."

HINDU SOCIAL ORGANIZATION

It is in this spirit of human solidarity that Hindus organized their social life in the pattern of four vocations (*chatur varna*) and four stages (*ashramas*). *Varna vyavastha* or vocational organization of members of the society, which Hindu culture propagates, is not the present caste system into which it has degenerated as a result of India's having been ruled by foreign powers for centuries. It was not meant to divide society but to bring about its organic unity. It was based on those fundamental psychological and sociological principles, which, according to an Indian thinker well versed in Western and Indian thought, "are fit for use in modern conditions also; and, if properly applied, can solve all problems that are harassing mankind today".[1] The word *varna* comes from a root *vri* which means "to choose". *Varana* or *varna* means choice. *Varna vyvastha* means a social organization based on free choice of vocations in accordance with one's vocational aptitudes determined by heredity and vocational training. Its purpose is not to divide people into castes or classes, as it is generally supposed to be, but to integrate the society into a whole by giving each type of individual a suitable vocational place in it. It aims at efficiency, satisfaction, and co-operation. Modern society in the West is in a chaotic condition. There is a great struggle for existence, power, wealth and superiority. All people seek for one and the same thing, wealth and power. The ancient Indians who planned society on the basis of *varna*

---

1 Bhagavan Das, *World War and its Cure—World Order and World Religion*, p. 480.

understood human nature better and planned a pattern of society in which there would be less chaos, less struggle and less dissatisfaction. They found out that all people fall naturally, into four types. Each of these types has its distinctive vocational aptitude, desires, pleasures, and distinctive ways of living and dressing, etc.

There is a type who seek for knowledge and enlightenment and would be quite happy and contented if society offered them opportunities to pursue knowledge unhampered and to give it to others. These people do not care for power and wealth as long as they are allowed by the society to go on with their own hobby of getting more and more knowledge and spreading it. What they would like to possess are books, laboratories, apparatus of observation, and facilities for investigation and travel. Their main recreation consists in contemplation of God and communion with nature. They hanker more for respect, reverence and public esteem than for anything else. The main end of their life is self-realization and their learning and high character are their only powers over others. They cannot rule, but they can guide the rulers. They cannot be rich and powerful nor do they want to be.

The second type of people are those who love and seek power. They are men of action rather than men of knowledge. By nature and training they are able to administer and execute. Their main livelihood can be in military or executive positions. Their possessions are weapons and articles of pomp and show, and their recreations are various kinds of sports and games. Their main source of strength is military valour. They fail when they wrongly select a teaching profession.

The third type of people are those who neither care for knowledge nor for power but for wealth and property. By temperament they are acquisitive, greedy and commercial. Their main source of income is trade, profit and speculation. Their main craving is for wealth and their main recreation lies in trials of luck and in making plans that will bring more and more money. They excel at counting, calculating and planning. They can very well manage economic affairs and organize industrial, agricultural and other concerns of the state. Their main source of strength is their wealth and capacity to amass wealth.

There is a fourth type of people who are born with a low

intelligence quotient and consequently with little or no interest in science or philosophy, in administration or in economic organization. By temperament they are unambitious lazy and ease-loving, but they are capable of working hard when made to work by others. They exert effort when only they need to in order to earn their livelihood. Their main source of income is wages for their unskilled or a little trained and skilled labour. Their sources of recreation are gross sensual and sexual pleasures, intoxicating drugs, and alcohol. Their main source of strength lies in their capacity to work and in physical endurance. They are incapable of fitting into jobs which require much thinking, executive strength or organizing capacity. They can work only under the guidance, control and command of others. All these types of people are, however, organic parts of society. The *Rig Veda* compared them to the head, hands, abdomen, and legs of the human body.

Indian social thinkers organized an order of society in which each of the types mentioned above could find a suitable vocation and facilities for carrying on the work that is after its own heart, all serving the society in accordance with the best that each can give and getting the delight consequent upon performing its duty in the best way. Heredity, training, personal choice and social selection all played their proper part in assigning a particular profession, which was called a *varna*. The four typical professions, having innumerable varieties within each, were called the learned, executive, commercial and labouring professions, and the four types engaged in them were called Brahmanas, Kshatriyas, Vaishyas and Shudras. Each of them was a complement to the rest. They were organically related to each other as are the various parts of the body. There was no reason for conflict and class war, as each type had to give something to others and also to get from others much of what it needed for its life and health. No professional class was self-sufficient, yet each class was indispensable. Each class had initiative enough to contribute its best to the society as a whole.

Gerald Heard, a great American thinker and writer who has studied the Indian social system has called it "organic democracy", and suggests in his work, *Man the Master*, that it is the type of democracy the world as a whole needs today.

Heard defines "organic democracy" as "the rule of the people who have organized themselves in a living and not a mechanical relationship; where instead of all men being said to be equal, which is a lie, all men are known to be of equal value, could we but find the position in which their potential contribution could be released and their essential growth so pursued".[1] He calls the four *varnas* by the names "seers" (Brahmans), "politicians" (Kshatriyas), "technicians" (Vaishyas) and "coherers". "These four classes are distinguished by unmistakable psychological characteristics which suit them to their particular purpose, function and place."[2] It is this organization that made Indian society stable, efficient and strong. It produced in India great scholars, warriors, administrators, and producers of wealth.

P. D. Ouspensky, a thoughtful Western writer, is of the opinion that "All the most brilliant periods of history, without exception, were periods in which the social order approached the caste system."[3] He thinks that the caste system *(varna vyavastha)* "is a natural division" of society. "Whether people wish it or not, whether they recognize it or not, they are divided into four castes. There are Brahmans, there are Kshatriyas, there are Vaishyas, and there are Sudras. No human legislation, no philosophical intricacies, no pseudosciences and no forms of terror can abolish this fact. And the *normal* functioning and development of human societies are possible only if this fact is recognized and acted on."[4]

DIVISION OF LIFE INTO FOUR DISTINCT PERIODS (ASHRAMA SYSTEM)

Equally important and valuable was the planning of an individual life in four stages or periods called *Ashramas*. This planning was based on a psychological study of the interests, needs, capacities, characteristics and social adjustments of an individual at different stages of life from childhood to old age. Today life is a chaos and a confusion. There is little difference

1 Gerald Heard, *Man, the Master*, p. 129.
2 Op. cit., p. 143.
3 P. D. Ouspensky, *A New Model of the Universe*, p. 447.
4 Op. cit., p. 446.

in the pursuits of man at different ages. From childhood to old age men and women have to earn their living, have to do almost the same kind of work, no matter whether they are fit for it or not. They pursue the same types of pleasure whether they suit them or not. With a great insight into the meaning, purpose and capacities of life, ancient Indians understood the absurdities of such a kind of living, and so mapped life out into four periods of 25 years each, taking the total span of life, when properly lived, to be of a hundred years, and assigned a proper function with its appropriate discipline to each of them.

The first period is meant for building up physical, mental and spiritual health, strength and endurance. It is called the *prahmacharya ashrama* (student life). The second period is called the *grihastha ashram* in which an individual settles down into a family life and performs the duties of a householder. The third period is called the *vanaprastha ashrama* in which an individual retires from the life of a householder and along with his life companion devotes himself to the service of the society in the best way he can without any idea of accumulating anything for his family as he did when he was a householder. And the fourth period was called *sanyasa ashram* in which the individual should give up all worldly pursuits and interests and should devote himself to meditation and *yoga*.

In accordance with the principles of biology, psychology, sociology, economics and politics, the ancient seers like Manu, Yajnvalkya, Atri and Vasistha, determined the function, the discipline, the duties, and the place in society of the individual at each stage of his life. Thus, according to their opinion, a student should do nothing else than that which is conducive to the building up of a strong and healthy body, an alert and penetrating mind, and a pure and noble soul. He has to acquire all the knowledge he can with proficiency in some vocation which he would have to choose as a householder later in life. His living must be in accordance with the requirements of his stage. At a tender age he must leave home and be a member of some educational institution where he has to live a life of mutual helpfulness in the society of other boys of his age. He has not to imitate his parents and other grown up householders in their living a life of comfort and pleasure. His is to be a life of hard work, self-denial, austerity and purity.

Within the time at his disposal he must make himself a full-statured man, ready to undertake the duties of a householder on leaving the educational institution.

The life of a householder is a very responsible life. It has also to be a disciplined life, but the discipline here is of a different kind. He has to acquire wealth, but in accordance with the principles of *dharma*—truth, honesty, justice, kindness and self-control, etc. He can enjoy life, not in an unbridled manner, but with moderation and restraint. He has to bring forth and bring up children without whom a household is not happy, but not without taking sufficient care that they grow into ideal boys and girls. He has to be a productive member of the society by being a thinker or inventor, or an administrator, or an agriculturist, industrialist or financier, or by being a skilful manual labourer, worker or mechanic. His home must be a happy home in which old parents, children, and women must feel happy. A home in which children are not properly taken care of, in which women are not happy, in which old men and women are miserable is, according to Indian sages, like a hell. Prosperity, harmony and sweetness should reign in all homes. Every little home must be a little heaven.

Having lived for twenty-five years or so as a householder, an individual should withdraw his interests from the family and retire to a quiet place where he can think about deeper problems of life and thereby be of some service to the society. He is a fit person to be a legislator, an educator or an adviser to governments. It is such retired people who should take interest in social and political activities of a country and should become ambassadors and high commissioners. Ambitious youths who enter these fields and services with selfish interests and with ambitions to be rich, fail to discharge their public duties properly, and instead of being efficient public servants they make use of the opportunities that come to them for gaining more and more money, power and influence, and often fall a prey to corruption. Indian social thinkers, like Dr. Bhagavan Das, think that only people who have retired from family responsibilities and have no worldly ambitions should be entrusted with great national responsibilities. Most of the great works on philosophy, ethics and sciences have been written by those people who made a proper use of this period of life.

When the individual is no longer physically fit to do strenuous work in the service of society he must make the best use of the rest of his life by settling at some secluded and peaceful place and thinking and meditating on the deeper problems of life and the universe. In this stage he may dictate books, teach those who approach him for enlightenment and guidance. He can also make use of his time by practising some kind of *yoga*. According to Indian culture old age should not be a miserable age. It should indeed be the most peaceful and happy stage of life in which happiness does not depend upon fleeting enjoyments of life but upon the inner light and contentment of the spirit. The Hindu has a strong faith that life does not end in death. Death only opens a gate to another life, the quality and contents of which are determined by our own desires and actions. The last stage of this life is to be devoted to the preparation for the next one. Death is taken to be a welcome change, in which the old and worn out body is to be replaced by a new and better one. A Hindu should always die in peace, because he knows that he has nothing to lose by dying. The later half of his life is called the path of *nivritti* or withdrawal from the attachments to the world, and by the time he dies a normal death he quietly and peacefully leaves this world and gladly awaits entry into another through the gate of death.

REASON AND NOT SCRIPTURE TO GUIDE LIFE

Buddhi, reason or intelligence, is the highest mental principle in man according to Indian culture. It is this principle which determines the truth or falsity of a judgment. On its purity and use depends the happiness and peace of life. It is on its working that there is agreement among all people. Scriptures differ, as do emotions and traditions, but there is always an agreement upon what is reasonable. Hence use of reason is regarded as one of the above-mentioned 10 principles of *dharma* (morality). The greatest prayer in the Vedas asks inspiration for our intelligence. In Hindu culture, therefore, there has always been a great emphasis on being reasonable in all activities of life. The great sage Vasistha advised his pupil Rama, in the *Yogavāsistha*, to be always reasonable and never to accept and do what is unreasonable. We shall close this essay on Indian culture by quoting three passages from the *Yogavāsistha* in which one of the most essential features of Indian culture finds clear expression: "A reasonable statement, even of a child, should be accepted, while the unreasonable ones are to be discarded like straw, even though they are made by the Creator himself. A devotee of reason should value the works even of ordinary persons, provided they advance knowledge and are logical, and should throw away those even of the sages, if they are not such. Such a sentimental person as continues to drink the (filthy) water of a well, simply because it was dug by his dear father, leaving aside the (pure) Ganges water available near at hand, is certainly a slave under others' control."[1] Truth, we must remember, may be supra-rational, but it can never be irrational. Hence an Indian always relies on reason more than on anything else. He closes every activity with the following prayer: "May every being overcome difficulties, may every one look for the good; may every one have a purified reason, and may every one be happy everywhere."

---

1 *Yogavāsistha,* 11. 18. 2-4.

The Basic Unity underlying the Diversity of Culture

The Origins and Meaning of Indian Culture

by

SUNITI KUMAR CHATTERJI

Swami Vivekananda, the great Hindu thinker and champion of the masses, whose brief but dynamic life initiated a revolutionary change among his countrymen in the last decade of the nineteenth century, once observed that different religions were like different languages. The thirteenth century Persian mystic of Islam, Jalaluddin Rumi, had anticipated him in the expression of the same idea by means of a parable in his *Masnavi-i-Ma'navi*, with the moral that men come to peace and harmony when they *understand*. It is the lack of understanding that is at the root of all exclusiveness or intolerance, mistrust or hatred. As the Hindu sages have said, sin is nothing but ignorance. The difference between the various cultures in the world today on reflection is seen to be one of language or expression more than anything else. The whole of mankind forms a single species; and outward diversities of feature and colour, stature and deportment, behaviour and customs notwithstanding, man everywhere is but man, a certain human quality supplying the link of unity in the midst of all diversity. Humanity is one, and human culture as the expression of an aspiration, an endeavour and an achievement, is also one. Human culture does not present any fundamental diversities or divergences in its parts, but is a series of different patterns formed by the permutations and combinations of the same or similar basic elements. The latter are modified by the environment of time and space and by the original racial personality, which itself, however, can be modified through the driving power of a "hero", a leader in thought or action, or through contact with other races and other languages. The physical urge for getting and begetting, for living and propagating, is everywhere present, as also is the desire for a state of permanent happiness for "all this, and heaven too". This desire, which is almost as compelling as the physical urge, is shared by the whole of mankind and has raised men above the level of the merely animal. Religion, with its Janus-face of fear and hope, attempts to unravel the mystery of life and being. These attempts, leading to science and philosophy and cultivation of the emotions (opening up the limitless joys of art and mysticism), are common to mankind in all ages and climes, and they spring everywhere from the pursuit of what the sages of India regarded as the only end for which man is really striving—cessation of suffering and attainment of an ultimate and abiding happiness. And in this common striving, there has never been any isolation of a particular people or group of men from other peoples or groups, whenever contact between them either direct or indirect was made possible. The mainsprings of human culture are thus the same—they are universal; and certain ideals, values, attitudes or behaviours, whether good or bad from absolute or relative points of view, have always been found to be transmissible. These ideals, values, attitudes or behaviours form patterns comparable to languages. All serve to meet the minimum needs of man, but those which express most adequately and most beautifully the aspirations, the endeavours and the achievements of man naturally have a predominant place in the affairs of men. Certain patterns of culture thus stand out pre-eminent; and, becoming feeders and sustainers of weaker or less complete ones, they attain an international and inclusive status.

This play of action and interaction in the cultural sphere is going on for ever. The opposing forces of centrifugence and centripetence are also constantly operating and strife—with occasional violent modification of one pattern by another, or harmony consciously or unconsciously brought about—is also in evidence.

THE IDEAL: A SINGLE WORLD CULTURE

With the hope of one world, one mankind and one well-being for all inspiring our men of learning and wisdom to find a path that can be followed by all, this wistful readiness for a single world culture was never greater than now. We leave aside, of course, men of narrow outlook whose intransigent support of one particular pattern is merely an unconscious expression of a blind egotism which has its roots in both ignorance and a desire for domination. The time is indeed ripe, and the stage is set, for a correct understanding of the various patterns of culture and for exploring the methods for their harmonizing, taking our stand on the fundamentals and not on the accidentals, on the agreements and not on the divergences. When this is achieved, and mankind everywhere is trained to accept the fundamental agreement based on the identity of human aspirations, a new chapter in the history of humanity will begin.

INDIAN CULTURE

The culture of India is extremely complex; in its roots and its implications it is perhaps more complex than any other. And in its complexity, it is like life itself; like life, it is all-inclusive. It is vast as nature herself, nature as she has been manifested in the minor continent of India. In its all-inclusiveness, it may be compared to a tropical forest. Yet it is not so rank and haphazard a growth as to be free from the operation of any law or inner principle, or to have failed to achieve any characteristic or noteworthy expression of itself in ideology and practice.

The geographical boundaries of India (I use "India" to mean the geographical and cultural unit that has always been so known since ancient Greek times, including both India and Pakistan) make the country rather like a pocket, where whatever ethnic stocks arrive stay on to attain a complete development, participating in the life already existing in the country and enriching it with new elements and contributions. This has been a fact of primary importance which we must take into consideration in evaluating the culture of India and in tracing its history.

The Racial and Historical Background of Indian Culture

According to the most recent pronouncement of authorities in the matter, six distinct races with nine sub-types and with their separate speeches belonging to five distinct speech-families have commingled in blood and culture to give rise to the people of India and to its characteristic culture or civilization. The process began at least five thousand years ago, and was accomplished some two thousand years ago, but it continued for some centuries more to function and to spread and consolidate the completed culture of India over the whole of India and over what has been called the lands of Greater India, in south-eastern and in central Asia. After A.D. 700, and particularly after A.D. 1200, it came in contact with Islam—first the Islam of the Arab in Sindh, and afterwards the Islam of the Turk and the Persian in the Punjab. These brought about a profound change in the fortunes of this culture. In the sixteenth to seventeenth centuries, modern European and Christian influences touched the fringe of Indian culture in some coastal areas, when the Portuguese established themselves in Goa and in a few other seaport towns, in western India as well as in Bengal. But Portuguese influences were not deep enough, and the real contact with European culture started after the English became the masters of Bengal in 1757 and subsequently established their empire over the whole of India. From the early part of the nineteenth century, the impact of European culture, through England, became pronounced in Indian civilization, and European influences have been gaining in strength with the passing of years, so much so that the distinctive culture of India is now in danger of losing its personality and character.

Indian Culture: A Combination of Diverse Elements

Indian culture in its broadest connotation would include all that has been achieved in the domain of thought and in the pursuit of the good life by the people of India, as a whole or in groups, ever since the most important component elements of the Indian people (the Austric, the Dravidian and the Aryan-speaking groups) began to form, in the upper Gangetic plains, a single people having a single Aryan speech and sharing the same traditions, the same way of thought, the same attitude and the same life. The culture that grew up in this way about the beginning of the first millennium B.C. (c. 1000 B.C.) took another five hundred years to be fully characterized, and a further five hundred years to expand from the Ganges valley to the whole of India. At the beginning of the Christian era, and perhaps even a few centuries earlier, we have a pan-Indian culture fully established. This culture has been for want of a better term described as ancient Indian, or ancient Hindu, with its three important philosophical and religious expressions, viz., Brahmanical, Buddhist and Jaina. It was not the creation of a single section of the Indian people. It was not an Aryan culture imposed by a superior, civilized, white Aryan or Indo-European-speaking people upon backward or savage, dark-skinned, non-Aryan aboriginals, as was at one time fondly believed. It was in fact the joint creation of the Aryan and non-Aryan. Elements contributed by all were combined into one single type, the combination in some cases being close and intimate, as it were a chemical combination where the component elements were transformed into something new and not easily analysable, and in other cases merely a mechanical mixture, where the components were loosely attached and easily distinguishable. The fissiparous tendencies which are never absent from any human institution have taken advantage of the want of absolute cohesion wherever it was marked.

Diverse Elements Harmonized

The early centuries of the Christian era saw the formulation or systematization of Indian culture and its expansion outside India. The thought-content of Indian culture, which took definite shape in the middle of the first millennium B.C., began to be enriched by the middle of the first millennium A.D. by the development of certain emotional and mystical aspects which were already noticeable in the earlier period. The progress of Indian culture as expressed in formal religion has been like waves succeeding one another in the midst of the sea. The elaborate ritualism of the later Vedic religion of the first half of the first millennium B.C. was accompanied by an intellectual introspection engendered by the commingling of Aryan ideas with those of the Dravidian and Austric worlds. Vedic ritualism centring round the fire-sacrifice was then on the wane, and the non-Aryan ritual and religious practice expressing themselves through worship by means of icons or images and

through *yoga* asserted themselves. Room was found for everything when the fully developed Hindu culture became established during the closing centuries of the first millennium A.D.
Then came the impact of Islam on India; and the direct result
of this was a restatement of both the thought and the emotionalism of ancient and early medieval India—of what has
been called in Indian parlance *jnâna* (knowledge) and *bhakti*
(devotion), the analogous finer elements in Islamic mysticism
and some of its organizational aspects also being accepted to
give new colour and new strength. A common platform between Islam and Indianism was thus evolved by the medieval
sants, bhaktas and *sâdhus,* the saints, devotees and mendicants
of Hindu India and by the *pîrs, darvîshes* and *qalandars,* the
mystical teachers, saints and wanderers of the Indian Islam
on the other. A new phase in the cultural evolution of India
was in this way achieved.

Its Catholicity

To me, the most attractive thing about Indian culture is its
catholicity. Swami Vivekananda was right, at least in spirit,
when he declared before the Congress of Religions at Chicago
in 1893 that the Hindu religion, which is the profoundest
expression of Indian culture, believed not only in universal
toleration but also accepted all religions as true. The Hindu
or Indian mind is all-embracing. It is "totalitarian" in accepting everything through a deep understanding of the fundamentals and of the ultimate reality. Indian culture has room
for all. It does not say, condescendingly, that a particular
point of view or experience may have some truth in it, but it
admits the inevitability and propriety of all points of view and
all experience, and their truth and consequent right to exist,
so long as they help men to realize the best in their *milieu,* and
do not transgress upon the rights of others. It seeks to answer
the question of jesting Pilate, not by reference to mundane
things only, but in the true Indian way.[1] This great hospitable-

---

[1] The following account of an interview between an Indian philosopher and Socrates in Athens
some time in the fifth century B.C. is characteristic and bears the stamp of truth. It is narrated
by the Greek father Eusebins, on the authority of Aristoxenos, the writer on musical theory and
pupil of Aristotle, and is in the direct line of tradition (Socrates, Plato, Aristotle, Aristoxenos).
"Aristoxenos, the musician, tells this story about the Indians. One of these men met Socrates at
Athens, and asked him what was the scope of his philosophy. 'An enquiry into the human

ness of the Indian spirit, as it has been called, its readiness to respect the other man's point of view, and to accept it as true, at least so far as the other man is concerned, comes from a cultured man's recognition that truth is a gem of many facets, and that the anxiety to reduce everything to a particular code or law conceived in our human limitations is but a form of blasphemy. We are like blind people trying to make out the form of an elephant by feeling each a different limb they will be convinced that the elephant is like a pillar, or a snake, or a hard substance, or a wall, or a brush with a flexible handle, according as they respectively touch its leg, or trunk, or tusk, or body, or tail. To know the whole truth is possible for any one in any station, if he is divinely blessed with the gift of perception or realization.

The Obsession of the Historical Sense obstructs Fusion

It has been a blessing for India that until very recently this did not happen to her; the Indians have, in fact, been criticized for their lack of the historical sense. This lack—was it deliberately cultivated?—is the price that was paid for the harmonious combining of the basic Aryan and non-Aryan cultures and traditions into a single Indian culture and tradition. Sober historians may be exasperated at the hopeless intricacies of *purâna*, or ancient Indian traditional chronology, and at the insoluble knots of ethnic admixture, but all that has not been too high a price to pay for the evolution of a composite single ancient Indian culture into which seemingly irreconcilable elements were somehow made to fit and to form a pattern or a design. In those ancient times there could be no modern, scientific attitude towards the problem of races. Diversity of colour in ancient India (e.g. *ârya varna* = "Aryan colour"; *dâsa varna* = "non-Aryan colour") was taken for granted, without fuss or racialism.

---

phenomena,' he said. At this the Indian burst out laughing. 'How can a man enquire into human phenomena,' he exclamed, 'when he is ignorant of divine ones?'" Compare the sentiments expressed by Euripides in one of his choruses (Hippolytus 11.1112 ff.), as paraphrased by Gilbert Murray: "Surely the thought of the Gods hath balm in it alway, to win me far from my griefs; and a thought, deep in the dark of my mind, clings to a great Understanding ...."

"LANGUAGE-CULTURE" ELEMENTS IN THE DEVELOP-
MENT OF INDIAN CULTURE

A study of the racial or rather what may be called the "language-culture" elements in the formation of the ancient
Indian people and its civilization must be the basis for any
understanding of Indian culture.

India was not the home of any autochthonous people. The
materials at present at our disposal yield no evidence of her
having produced any type of anthropoid ape which developed
into man on her soil. All her human inhabitants came from
outside. According to the latest findings of the anthropologists,
as expressed by Dr. B. S. Guha, Director of the Anthropological
Survey of India, no less than six distinct races in nine variations
came from outside and furnished elements in the population
of India, and they spoke languages belonging to five distinct
linguistic families—some kind of primitive African (whether
Proto-Bantu, or Proto-Sudanic, or Proto-Bushman-Hottentot,
we do not know) which is now extinct on the soil of India, and
Austric in its Austro-Asiatic branch, Dravidian, Indo-European, and Sino-Tibetan, which last four still survive or flourish
in India. It is the "language-culture" groups represented by
the speakers of Austric, Dravidian, Sino-Tibetan and Indo-
Aryan [known in ancient India by the names *Nisâda* (Nishâda)
Drâvida, *Kirâta* and *Arya* respectively] that has fused to form
the people and civilization of India, with the language of the
Indo-Europeans or Aryans, profoundly modified in the course
of centuries by the Austric and Dravidian speeches, and giving
its outward *cachet* to this civilization.

The Negroids

The first people to arrive in India were a negrito or negroid
race from Africa, coming at a very early period by way of
Arabia and the coast-lands of Iran; they spread over western
and southern India, and even passed on to the north-eastern
part of the country. A group of them crossed into the Anda-
man Islands (probably from south Burma), where, less than
1,000 in number now, they still preserve their old speech, which
has not yet been properly studied. On the soil of India there
is no trace of their language, and certain wild tribes of south

India, who at the present day are distinctly negroids, speak forms of the Dravidian speech. In Assam, among the Nagas, traces of Negroid elements have been noted. These negroids were very primitive. They belonged to the eolithic stage of culture, and were food-gatherers rather than food-producers. They were either killed off or absorbed by subsequent arrivals, particularly the Austrics. In racial type they were short and black, long-headed and woolly-haired, and had definite negroid traits. Their contribution to Indian culture as it developed later on was nil. A few of their words may have been borrowed by later arrivals and may survive in the present-day languages of India: Aryan, Dravidian, Austric and Sino-Tibetan, but we have no clear evidence. It has been suggested by anthropologists that the cult of the sacred fig tree, and certain ideas regarding the passage of man through the underworld, which we find in modern India, are negroid survivals in the beliefs of the masses. It would be hazardous to suggest a date for the arrival in India of these negroids, but it could well have been before 4000 B.C.

The Nisâdas (Nisâhdas) or Proto-Australoids (Austrics, Austro-Asiatics)

Their physical affinities have led to the next people to come to India being called Proto-Australoids. This term refers to them as they were when they arrived in the country. They were medium-sized, dark and hairy, snub-nosed and long-headed; and before developing further in India, a branch of them passed on through Indo-China and Indonesia into Australia and Tasmania, where they became the primitive peoples of those countries. In India, the Proto-Australoids, who are regarded as a very old off-shoot of the Mediterranean race from Palestine, became established; they spread over the greater part of the country, and here their type was modified into what has been called the Austric. The primitive source-speech of the languages of the Austric speech-family, as postulated by Father W. Schmidt of Vienna (namely, the Austro-Asiatic languages like the Kol or Munda speeches of India, the Mon-Khmer speeches of Burma and Indo-China and Nicobarese, and the Austronesian languages of the Indonesian or Malay, Melanesian and Polynesian groups)

possibly developed in India. The descendants of the Austrics
are found among the lower classes all over India, and the
Austrics have largely entered into the formation of the Hindu
and Moslem people of India today. They were to be found in
the fertile Ganges plain and in the hills and forests of central
India, and even in the north in the Himalayan regions; and
they have kept up their language in the central Indian tracts,
which now form the home of the Kol and Munda forms of
speech. In the riverain plains they gradually accepted Aryan
speech. The bases of Indian village culture were supplied by
this Austric element in the Indian population.

Among the contributions of the Austrics to Indian culture
were, on the material plane, the following: stick and hoe cultivation, fishing, cultivation of rice, cultivation of certain
vegetables and plants like the gourd, the brinjal, the turmeric,
the ginger, and probably some pulses; domestication of the
fowl and taming of the elephant; boats (dug-outs and catama-
rans, and out-rigger canoes) and coastal shipping; and primitive weaving from cotton. On the intellectual and spiritual
plane: counting by twenties as the highest number of com-
putation; some cosmogonic notions, e.g., the universe thought
of as an egg, stages in creation as in the Vedic creation-hymn[1]
and also as in certain medieval vernacular works like the Bengali *sûava-purâna;* possibly the idea of the incarnation of the
divinity in the form of the fish, the tortoise and the boar, which
we find in later Hindu mythology; and the idea of transmigration of the spirit, at least in some of its aspects. The use
of the betel-leaf, the coconut, the turmeric as well as vermilion
in Hindu social life and Hindu ritual is certainly a legacy from
the Austrics. In India they appear to have developed a mentality of "live and let live", a happy-go-lucky attitude to life,
cheerful and sociable, kindly and considerate, which is among
the best cultural and social heritages of the Indian people.
They lacked any deep sense of the mystical, but they appear
to have developed a demonstrative sensitiveness, which has
permeated both life and religion. Their divinities were both
beneficent and malign, the former being more in the background, although generally acknowledged. The profounder
cult of Siva and Uma, the divinity conceived in its dual

---

[1] *Rigvêda*, X. 129.

aspect of father and mother, was to some extent coloured by certain Austric notions, as it was by the Aryan ideas of a sky father *(dyâus pitar)* and an earth mother *(prthivî mâtar)*.

A good many ideas and ways of living, cults and customs, which appear to have characterized the primitive Austrics in India, are still to be found among the Austric peoples outside India, such as the Mons and the Khmers, the Indonesians and Polynesians. Austric elements furnish one of the oldest and broadest bases of Indian civilization; and through these, we have a remote but a very special kinship with the peoples of South-East Asia and Malaya as well as of the islands of Indonesia and beyond. Our relationship with the Mons and the Cambodians, the Vietnamese and the Indonesians, is therefore not merely cultural—it is to some extent genetic also. India and South-East Asia as well as Indonesia at one time formed the same "language-culture" area, the implications of which are no doubt obscured and overlaid by other cultural accretions and developments, but still exist below the surface.

The Dravidians

Probably after the Proto-Australoids or Austrics came, also from "the west", the Dravidian speakers. Among them several slightly different ethnic elements were found—the early Mediterranean, the late Mediterranean, the Oriental and the Armenoid. The main group appears to have been an east Mediterranean people allied to the pre-Hellenic Aegeans (the ancient Cretans and Lycians were both practically the same people on the evidence of Herodotus, the Cretans being known to the Greeks as *Termilai* and the Lycians calling themselves *Trm̂mile)*, and also to the Etruscans or Tuscans of central Italy, who originally migrated from Asia Minor, and certain other Asian or Asia Minor peoples. The Mediterraneans in all likelihood brought the primitive form of speech which subsequently became transformed into the present-day Dravidian languages and dialects of India; and they were the people who introduced towns and civilization, properly so called, into India. The Dravidian speakers had reached quite an advanced stage of culture when the Aryans first came into India during the second half of the second millennium B.C. It is exceedingly likely that the great cities of South Punjab and Sindh (remains

of which we find at Harappa and Mohen-jo-Daro and elsewhere) were the creation of the Dravidian speakers who must
have arrived in India before 3500 B.C., for by 3000 B.C. the
city of Mohen-jo-Daro appears to have been in a flourishing
state. The Dravidian speakers of the Punjab and Sindh were
known by two of their tribal names to the Aryan-speaking invaders—viz., *Dâsa* and *Dasyu* (in later Sanskrit these tribal
names became degraded in meaning, to mean respectively
slave and *robber*)—names which were also known in Iran (as
Daha and *Dahyu*—in Iran *Daha* occurs as a tribal name, and
dahyu became a common noun meaning "the countryside",
originally "the land inhabited by the Dahyu people"). This
shows the prevalence of the same Dravidian groups in Iran
as in north-western India. Later, the name *Dramida* or *Dravida*
(primitive Dravidian—*Dramiza*), which was used in a narrow
sense for the extreme southern group of this people, was extended in a general way to mean all Dravidian-speaking
peoples. The town-dwelling Dravidian speakers of India were
materially far in advance of the nomadic and semi-agricultural
Aryan speakers who later came to India and established themselves as rulers of the land. The Aryans knew of settlements inhabited by a tribe *(grâma)*, with stockades protecting its cattle-
wealth *(gotra)*, or slightly bigger townships similarly stockaded
(pur, puri = Greek *polis*, and *ghrdho* = later Sanskrit *grha*,
Prakrit *gadha*, Hindi *gadh* = "house fort", Slav *gradu*, Ger-
manic *gard)*, but real cities with brick-built houses *(nagara)*
were Dravidian. Towns with paved streets flanked by houses
of brick sometimes more than one story high, and underground
masonry drains, show the cultural superiority (at least on the
material side) of the Dravidian speaker over the Aryan with
his rude hutments of wood and bamboo. The Dravidian
speakers were strong in western and southern India, but they
had spread along the Ganges valley also, sharing the country
with the Austrics when the Aryans came, and probably
dominating the milder and comparatively less organized
Austrics culturally and politically. By far the most significant
elements in the ancient civilization of India as it had evolved
by the middle of the first millennium B.C. were contributed by
the Dravidians. The latter cultivated wheat, and kept cattle,
and seem also to have known the horse. They knew and
practised many arts and crafts. It was their way of life that

was gradually adopted by the Aryans. The organization of society into castes or guilds was perhaps a Dravidian legacy. On the spiritual and religious plane, the Dravidian mind was profoundly moved by faith and a mystical sense, and the ideas of *Yoga* and personal mystical contact with the power behind life were well developed. It was among the Dravidians that the great gods of post-Vedic Hinduism, with both their cosmic and personal significance and appeal, like Siva and Uma, and Vishnu and Sri, had their origin. The ideas of a great mother goddess who was the source of all life, who was both nature and the conscious force behind nature, and of a father god who represented the inactive ultimate reality as a power in repose, appear to have been brought in their germs to India from the original east Mediterranean homeland of the primitive Dravidians and then elaborated in the country, by contact with other races and cultures possessing similar ideologies. The Dravidian ritual of worship by means of flowers and leaves and water has survived as the most characteristic form of Hindu ritual in worship—the *pûjâ*, as opposed to the ritual of the burnt offering of the Aryans—the *hôma*. The deeper elements in Hindu thought and religion were largely the contribution of the Dravidian speakers.

The Indo-Europeans (Aryans)

The Dravidians were better organized than the Austrics, but they could not stand, at least in northern India, before the invasion and infiltration of the still better organized Aryans. The Aryan speakers (who are believed to have represented a cultural union of two distinct racial stocks, the tall, blond, long-headed, straight-nosed Nordics, and the comparatively short and dark and short-headed Alpines) came to India, probably in several successive waves, by way of Iran. The primitive Indo-European people (of whom the Aryans were a branch) are believed to have lived originally in the dry Eurasian grasslands to the south of the Ural mountains. There their language, culture and mentality took its definite form. In material civilization they had not advanced much, as they were a primitive pastoral people depending more on their flocks and herds (the sheep and the horse they already knew, but the cow they obtained from the people of the south, from

Mesopotamia) than on agriculture, though they cultivated barley *(yewa)*. They were still undivided about 2500 B.C., after which they began to spread west and south-west, into Europe, and into northern Mesopotamia and eastern Asia Minor through the Caucasus mountains. In Europe they mingled with the original inhabitants in the various parts of the continent, and ultimately were transformed into the Celts and Italians, Germans, Hellenes, Slavs, Balts and other peoples. In the regions to the south of the Caucasus, they are found in two groups, an earlier one, which became the ruling people of the Hittite kingdom (the Kanisians), and a later one, which formed the Aryan branch of the Indo-Europeans. The Indo-Europeans had tamed the horse in their original homeland, and this was their greatest contribution to human civilization on the material side in their earliest period. But perhaps their greatest gift to humanity was their language, which possessed to a singular degree the power of expression combined with copiousness, and of precision with imaginativeness; while their patriarchal social organization, with the husband and father as the head of the family and the wife also having her recognized status, furnished the pattern to many peoples. They believed in a divinity who was a friend of man, whose abode was in the sky and who was a helper in need; and their notion of the life beyond was of a place where good and brave men were gathered to their fathers. They worshipped the various powers of nature conceived of as forces with certain human qualities, and their ritual was that of the offering or libation put into the sacrificial fire. A sheep or a goat, or an ox or a horse, was killed and its fat and meat, together with barley and milk or butter, was offered to the gods by means of a fire kindled and kept alive on an altar with twigs and wood; a ritual which characterized the religion of the Sumerians and the early Semites also.

The Indo-Europeans who came to northern Mesopotamia during the second half of the third millennium B.C., following the earlier Kanisian tribe which was settled among the Hittite people of Asia Minor, belonged to their *Árya (Ariva)* or Aryan branch. They brought with them the horse, which prior to about 2200 B.C. was not known in the lands of the Near East. The Aryans penetrated into the territories of south-eastern Asia Minor, Assyria and Mesopotamia, as raiders possibly, and as horse-dealers. But they grew numerous, and began to take part in local affairs, and were even successful in establishing themselves as the ruling aristocracy among certain groups of local peoples (as the Harri, the Mitanni, the Kassi, for instance). In their new surroundings, they came to be profoundly influenced in their culture and some of their ways of life, as well as in religion, by the local peoples—notably the Assyrio-Babylonians. The oldest specimens of an Aryan language are found in some Mesopotamian records giving a number of Aryan names and words, and from these, which date from 2200 B.C. to 1300 B.C., we find the presence of a language which in its forms is older than Vedic Sanskrit and is the mother of both old Indo-Aryan (Vedic) and old Iranian (Avestan and old Persian).

The Aryans were prominent in the Near East during the second half of the second millennium B.C. Some of their tribes remained in Asia Minor and Mesopotamia, where they gradually lost their language and their original culture and were absorbed by the surrounding peoples. But other tribes pushed further to the east, into Iran, where they retained their linguistic and cultural characteristics and distinctiveness. After some generations in Iran, a number of Aryan tribes went still further towards the east, and finally reached India. The tribes who remained behind in Iran were the Parsavas, the Madas and the Sakas, among others; and those who came into India formed numerous clans, like the Bharats, the Madras, the Krvis, the Turvasus, the Druhyus, the Bhrgus, etc.

The coming of the Aryan to India—considering Indian history as but a part of world history in general and Near Eastern history in particular—could not have taken place at a period earlier than 1500 B.C. The nomadic Aryans, moving about in their *grâmas* (tribes), pushed from Iran through the passes of Afghanistan into the Punjab. They did not find the country a no-man's land—they had to fight their way and gradually established themselves in north Punjab. We find in the *Rigveda* echoes of these fights and raids and counter-raids among the original *Dâsa* and *Dasyu* inhabitants of the Punjab and the Aryans. In the Punjab, the resistance was not successful, and the Aryans settled in the northern Punjab in large numbers. They then pressed further towards the east—into the land of the Ganges and the Jumna. It is curious to observe

that the Aryans did not venture south, down the course of the
Indus. The reason for this has, finally, been revealed by the
discovery of the ruins of the pre-Aryan towns in the south
Punjab and in Sindh. The presence of well-organized city-
states in this area forced the Aryans to turn their conquering
and colonizing enterprise elsewhere, to the east. Solid blocs
of Dravidians, powerful city-dwellers who inspired fear in the
nomadic Aryans, stood in their way in the south, but in the
east, the Dravidians and Austrics, living side by side and
possibly having no unity of ideal or purpose, afforded an
opportunity to the invaders.

Commingling of Races and Cultures: A Basic Fact of Indian History

By 600 B.C., the Aryan people and their language had spread
over the greater part of north India, from Afghanistan to the
western boundary of Bengal. But in the process of expansion,
which occupied a millennium, great things were happening.
Contacts between Aryans and non-Aryans, at first hostile,
could not but become peaceful when the Aryans settled permanently in the country. *Árya, Drâvida* and *Nisâda* began to
live side by side. The Aryans' language became the binding
element in a new society. A new people came into being,
speaking the Aryan language, and the different groups found
places in the new community according to their cultural
level. There started from the beginning a large-scale mis-
cegenation—mingling in blood as well as mingling of cultures
and religions. The myths and traditions of the Dravidian- and
Austric-speakers were translated into the new Aryan languages,
Sanskrit and the early Prakrits, and later found a place in those
composite works, repositories of the traditions of the ancient
Hindu people in their various origins, which are represented
by the *Purânas* and the *Mahâbhârata*. The *Rigvêda* presents a
purer Aryan world in its early phase in India, but even here
non-Aryan elements are present.

The situation was exactly parallel to what was happening
in contemporary Greece, the Greece of the centuries immediately before and after 1000 B.C. There, too, we have a fusion
of the Aegean and Indo-European peoples and cultures, giving
rise to the ancient Greek or Hellenic people of history, with a
composite culture and the Indo-European Greek language

as its vehicle. In Greece, the process was less complicated and on a much smaller scale than in India, where it involved more than two peoples and culture-types. This fusion of faiths and cultures, and ritual and religious thought, first took place in India in the tract known as the *madhyadêsa* (the midlands), roughly corresponding to the western United Provinces and eastern Punjab of the present day. The non-Aryan (Dravidian, and to some extent Austric) ritual of the *pûjâ* found a place beside the Aryan *hôma* in the later Brahmanical (synthetic) ritual. The priestly classes among the non-Aryans obtained a *locus standi* in the new society with their old vocation; they were transformed into Brahmans in many cases. In this way, by 500 B.C. the new synthesis was more or less completed or, at least, the lines along which it was to develop throughout the rest of Hindu history had been laid down.

The original Austric and Dravidian bases were completed by the newly-arrived Aryan element; and the Aryans' language, which became its official vehicle, gave Indian civilization its special character. The Aryans' discipline and organization, and the accommodating spirit generally shown by the cultural leaders among all the various other sections of Indian society (who, if only outwardly, accepted the Aryan leadership), particularly the Brahman priesthood decided the trend of the Indian mind once for all.

The Kirâtas or Indo-Mongoloids

While *Ârya*, *Drâvida* and *Nisâda* were engaged in building up a composite culture under joint Aryan and Dravidian leadership, another racial element came on the scene—the *Kirâta* or Mongoloid, with its various Sino-Tibetan dialects. The Mongoloid peoples of India now present various dialect-groups. Leaving aside the Chinese and Siamese, who are far away from India, and the Tibetans and Burmese who only touch its frontiers, we have the following groups of Sino-Tibetan-speaking peoples in the country, grouped according to their dialects: (a) the sub-Himalayan peoples of the west, of whom the most important are the Newars; (b) the speakers of sub-Himalayan Sino-Tibetan dialects showing an Austric sub-stratum, like the Kanawaris; (c) the tribes of northern Assam like the Abors and Mishmis; (d) the great Bodo people, who at one time occupied the greater part of north and east Bengal and the entire Brahmaputra valley; (e) the Nagas, in the Naga Hills; (f) the Mikirs, a mixed Naga-Kuki group; (g) the Kuki-Chin tribes, the most advanced of whom are the Meitheis or Manipuris, forming an important Hindu people of eastern India; and finally (h) the Ahoms, late comers in Assam, to which tract they gave their name (Assam = Aham or Ahom), belonging to the Dai or Thai branch of Sino-Tibetan-speaking peoples, and related to the Shan-Siamese-Lao people. The Ahoms, however, have now lost their language and have merged with the Assamese-speaking Hindus of the Brahmaputra valley.

The Mongoloid peoples are known in Sanskrit literature as *Kirâtas*. The first *Kirâtas* with whom the Aryan speakers came in touch appear to have belonged to the central sub-Himalayan region of India. Already in the *Yajurvêda* and the *Atharvavêda* we find mention of the *Kirâtas* as living in caves and hills. Later references to the *Kirâtas* in works like the *Mahâbhârata*, make it clear that by the term *Kirâta* was meant a yellow-skinned people uncouth in their ways of living, inhabiting the Himalayan and eastern regions, who were allied to the Chinese and would be always mentioned with them. The date of the compilation of the four Veda books has quite reasonably been put in the tenth century B.C., and thus from about this period we have evidence of the presence of the Mongoloid *Kirâtas* in India. *Kirâta* tribes, however, were confined only to a part of India—the Himalayan slopes, north Bihar, north and east Bengal, and Assam. Their influence or participation in the evolution of Hindu civilization was thus localized. The Aryan speech was also spreading among them as they were fusing racially with the mixed *Ârya-Drâvida-Nisâda* people. Even when Aryanized in speech, they retained some of their own customs and ideas, particularly in ancient times. Thus the Licchavis of north Bihar, contemporaneous with Buddha, and the tribe of the Sakyas to which Buddha himself belonged would appear to have Tibeto-Burman or Mongoloid or *Kirâta* affinities. Like the present-day Hindu people of Nepal, of Assam and of other places in Eastern India, these ancient tribes might have been of mixed *Kirâta* origin. Buddha thus could be a personality of mixed origin, Aryanized or Hinduized *Kirâta*, like the present-day Gurkhas. In Hindu

175

history and Hindu religion in Nepal, north and east Bengal and Assam, assimilation of *Kirâta* elements is a factor of primary importance. The development of the Tantra school of Brahmanism and Buddhism, with its sublimation of the erotic sentiment and its orgiastic cults, the worship with bloody rites of the Mother Goddess, who was also the Goddess of Destruction, the imperfect Brahmanization of many *Kirâta* cults, combined with certain social usages and ideas (e.g. the independence and initiative of the woman in marital life), and a sense of democracy and equality, are all illustrative of *Kirâta* influence in sub-Himalayan and eastern India.

Attempts to Harmonize and Unify

All the various elements in Hindu or ancient Indian culture were harmonized in an all-embracing whole. This is the special character of Indian civilization. Extreme points of view in many matters and divergent practices are tolerated, out of respect for other peoples' ways of thinking and living, and in a civilized spirit—a spirit of humility which will not arrogate all the truth to itself. The diverse ways of men, and their diverse thoughts, were all present in ancient India, and in sharp contrast; and the persons who were divinely actuated to create a harmony out of this apparent discord in life and thought did not think of suppressing divergent opinions and customs, or worlds of ideas, to impose a single one. They did not think of pressing the superiority of one group over the rest in a spirit of racial jingoism. The fact of different races living side by side within the same country, and gradually approximating to each other's culture and adopting the same language, made narrow nationalism or racialism out of place in ancient India. The sense of people belonging to different *races* was entirely lost at a very early epoch.

Synthesis at the Cost of Historic Memory

History is frequently accompanied by racial or national glorification or chauvinism, particularly when it treats of conflicts with peoples of different backgrounds. There was perhaps in ancient India a deliberate policy of deprecating history as a depository of national or tribal achievements compared with other peoples, as such a glorification of history would act as a deterrent to the fusion of different ideological elements into one single culture-group. The theory of caste, which stressed division of mankind according to their qualities or character *(guna)* and their avocations *(karma)*, and not according to race (a Brahman so born was no Brahman unless he went through certain ceremonies, and certain other ceremonies also exalted people to a higher position), also indirectly helped in this cultural fusion of races.

This basic fact of Hindu history, the presence from the very beginning as "language-culture" groups of different peoples who somehow composed their racial differences and accepted a common cultural environment, brought about the spirit of tolerance and acceptance, which runs, like a thread through the beads of a chaplet, throughout the whole course of Indian culture down the centuries.

Spread of the Basic Indian Ideas within and outside India

As soon as a common Hindu or ancient Indian culture (with its three main philosophico-religious schools of Brahmanism, Jainism and Buddhism) had become crystallized, with Sanskrit and the old Prakrits as its vehicles, and the prestige of the composite Gangetic civilization behind it, it became an irresistible force; and derived as it was from the co-operation or fusion of all sections of the Indian people, it became the universally accepted culture of India. Thus, during the second half of the first millennium B.C. the Dravidian world of the south became inextricably merged with the Austrico-Mongolo-Dravido-Aryan civilization of the north; and later, the Dravidians of the south, by accepting the philosophy and religion of this composite culture, together with the language that was its authoritative repository, viz., Sanskrit, made an outstanding contribution to its development and enrichment. Ideas like *samsâra*, or transmigration, and *karma*, or a man's actions determining his fate, the mysticism of *yoga* with its special discipline and practices, the doctrine of *bhakti* or devotion to God—all these developed in an atmosphere of co-operation between Aryan and non-Aryan. And those who built up the structure of Hindu philosophy in its various schools, the Brahmans and others of north India (of mixed origin themselves), profited by the diversity of points of view presented by the different racial elements. Almost simultaneously with its formation, this civilization was taken by Indian people to contiguous lands—to Ceylon by sea from the Gujarat side, to Burma and Indo-China (Cambodia and Champa), to Malaya and the islands of the Indian archipelago (Sumatra, Java, Borneo, etc.), and to Afghanistan and eastern Iran, central Asia, Tibet, and Sin-Kiang, and then to China, Korea and Japan; and in this way the vast cultural area of a "Greater India" was built up, particularly in Indo-China and Indonesia.

Contact with Foreign Peoples: A Stimulus to Indian Culture

It has been said that national cultures grow out of international conflicts and contacts, and India was no exception to this. A specific Indian culture—the Hindu culture of India—took form with the contact, conflict and fusion of the Austric, Dravidian, Mongoloid and Aryan worlds, as we have seen. Subsequently, contact with other peoples from outside India in ancient and medieval times helped to strengthen the Indian national culture. Thus the contact with the Old Persian people under the Achaemenian emperors, and later with the Iranian Sakas and the Pahlavi-using Persians of the Middle Iranian age, with the Greeks under Alexander the Great and in the following centuries, with the *Hûnas* and the *Turuskas* or pre-Moslem Turks, added new material and intellectual, and even religious and spiritual elements to Indian civilization. All this gave a richer content to this culture without changing its character or impairing the permanent form which it had taken. Architecture and art, policy and the organization of the state, and some aspects of religion like sun-worship were obtained, in a new form, from Iran. From the Greeks came art, probably some indirect impetus in literature, and astronomy. Contact with the Chinese pilgrims, some of the finest representatives of the intellect and culture of China, was similarly responsible for new ideas and attitudes in literature and in art.

The peoples of antiquity and the early Middle Ages who settled in India in large numbers—the Iranians on various occasions (including the Sakas), the Greeks, the Huns, and the various Mongoloid peoples in the east—did not bring a militant and an exclusive faith, with a conviction that they alone were in possession of God's truth and the rest of the world was in error. This attitude of humility facilitated their rapid absorption by the Hindu people.

The Moslem Arabs and Turks: Islam in India

Into this ancient Indian or Hindu world came two disturbing elements with a common ideological background, the second of which profoundly modified Indian life and thought. These were the Arabs, who conquered the Indian province of Sindh early in the eighth century A.D., and the Turks, who started plundering raids from Afghanistan (the first Hindu territory to be lost to India) from the second half of the tenth century. The Turks won for Islam the province of the Punjab early in the eleventh century, and, by the thirteenth century, had conquered north India up to west Bengal and established permanent Islamic rule over this region, with Delhi as its centre. Their empire remained powerful and effective up to the middle of the eighteenth century. The Arabs and the Turks both drew their greatest strength from Islam, and Islam came to India with an uncompromising attitude towards the Hindu spirit and culture, of which it had a very superficial knowledge. Convinced of its great and divinely ordained mission of converting the heathen in India to the true faith as proclaimed by the Prophet, Islam came to India to destroy and to take the place of what it destroyed, and not to fulfil. Its adherents combined mundane advantages, by conquering and plundering the Hindus, with spiritual benefits accruing to them as Knights of God fighting his battles against unbelievers. In the Turkish manner (*Turkâna tarîqä*) they conquered and slew and plundered and converted, and for a time this violent impact with Islam was the greatest calamity for Indian civilization.

Sufiism and Indian Thought

But this militant Islam had another aspect—the higher spiritual thought and mystical experience of Islam as expressed in *Tasawwuf* or Sufiism. In the evolution of Sufiism, primitive Islamic faith in God served as the base, but on it a superstructure was built by later Sufi saints and masters (e.g., Rabi 'a al-Adawwiya, and Muhyiuddin Ibn al-'Arabi) who brought elements of love and beauty, and certain deeper philosophical speculations from Greek Neo-Platonic philosophy (e.g. Dhu al-Nun of Egypt) and that of the Indian Vedanta. An example of the latter form of borrowing is given by Mansur al-Hallaj of Iraq, whose dictum of *ana-l-Haqq*, "I am Truth, i.e. I am God" appears to be based on the Vedantic expression *aham Brahma asmi* "I am the Brahman, i.e. the Supreme Spirit" with which al-Hallaj undoubtedly became familiar during his visit to India about 901 A.D. The gentler "Sufi way" *(Sûfiyânâ tarîqa)* of spreading Islamic ideas was more successful than the Turki way of violence. Gradually, both Islam and Hinduism found a common platform in Sufiism, and an understanding came about, almost from the start, for both the Turki way and the Sufi way began working in India at the same time. With the advent of Islam the uniformity of Indian civilization was broken and a new element (which, at least, in its formal or official attitude was intolerant and not at all inclined to compromise) was established through the development of a body of Indian Moslems, mainly of Indian stock but with a little admixture of foreign blood—Turki, Iranian, Afghan and Arab. But on the whole, this disturbing element was more anxious to retain political power and privilege than to bring about real spiritual conversion. Formal Islam created a great many cultural complications, but brought nothing of value to the civilization of India, except in so far as it created an atmosphere of conservatism and resistance. Sufiism, on the other hand, found an easy way into the heart of Hindu culture, which it enriched both in its social and spiritual outlook and practice, and a number of reformed schools of thought and action developed in India through its direct influence. The line of *sants* or saints, beginning with the great Kabir in the fifteenth century, who stressed the realization of the Deity through love and service to both God and man rather than through religious exercises and ritual is connected with the Indian development of Sufiism. Even the Vaishnava *Bhakti* schools, e.g. that of Chaitanya in sixteenth century Bengal, would appear to have assimilated certain elements from Sufi mysticism and practice. A respectable literature of Sufiism in Persian, the administrative and cultural language of India under the Moslems, was produced by Hindus in northern India; and some radical schools of the Hindu reformation of the nineteenth century were at least indirectly influenced by Islam. In this way Islam, which came to fight and conquer, remained to compromise, and became Indianized—notwithstanding the protests, vocal or otherwise, of the partisans of the Arab script and of literal interpretation of sacred writings.

Résumé: Complex Origin of Indian Culture; Harmonization in its Formulation

Indian civilization is thus, like all other great civilizations, of complex origin, and its bases have been supplied since pre-historic times by the various racial and linguistic-cultural elements which have inhabited the country. The Negroid element is all but eliminated. But the Proto-Australoid or Austric element supplied one of the bases, and the Dravidian another; and on this foundation the Aryans, in co-operation with the others and greatly assisted by their language, built the super-structure, into which were built the traditions and ideologies of the pre-Aryans. The Indo-Mongoloids also added their quota, although within a limited sphere, geographically and in time. In this way, Indian or Hindu civilization became established in something like its specialized form, a form which has endured to our day, some 2,500 years ago. The employment through the successive centuries of the Aryan language as its main vehicle (as Vedic Sanskrit, as classical Sanskrit, as Sauraseni Prakrit and Pali and as the various other Prakrits, as Sauraseni Apabhramsa, and as the various modern Indo-Aryan languages and dialects) has made us too conscious of the importance of the "Aryans" in the evolution of this civilization. Recent investigations prove that over 75 per cent of the various elements in it are of pre-Aryan or non-Aryan origin, although the outward stamp, because of language, is that of the Aryan-speaking people.

A Question of Emphasis

Indian civilization cannot claim to be the sole repository of any particular idea or set of ideas, or behaviour or sets of behaviours, which are not to be found elsewhere. The greatest things thought or said or done by people in India have their echoes or counterparts in other lands. But it is on the *emphasis* that India has given to certain ideas and behaviours, on the approach to the teaching of certain lessons towards the realization of the good life, that the special character of Indian culture lies. Sanskrit literature and its ancillary literatures in the ancient and modern provincial languages of India (including the literatures of old and modern Dravidian languages, and in *Kirâta* languages like Newari of Nepal and Manipuri) give expression to these ideals and these lessons, in part or in whole. The cultural unity of India, with all its diverse elements, is the result of the implicit acceptance of the ideology of Sanskrit literature at its highest and most universal. In the evolution of Sanskrit, however, Dravidian and Austric speakers had a great hand; and classical Sanskrit, and particularly the Prakrits and the modern Aryan languages, have approximated themselves to the spirit of the non-Aryan languages to such an extent that they may be compared to the waters from a different source flowing through the bed of some long-dried river. The cultural history of the various peoples of India in ancient and medieval times is that of their *progressive Sanskritization*, and this Sanskritization is still proceeding. Notwithstanding the advent of a militant Islam and an aggressive Christianity, the leaven has never been inactive. Sufi ideas have, as noted before, supplied a common platform for Indianism and Islam; and the inherent Hellenism or Europeanism of Christianity has made possible an understanding between Indian thought and culture and Christian culture.

The character of Indian culture may be expressed by one phrase: acceptance of unity in diversity, or a harmony of contrasts.[1] Contrasts, and sometimes violent ones, are there, but there is a will to see the harmony, through both ratiocination and intuitive realization.

---

1 The following quotation from a seventeenth-century Hindu writer may be found apposite. Chandar-bhàn (*Candra-bhânu*) was one of the most elegant Persian writers of India. He was a Brahman from Lahore in the Punjab, was a trusted officer of the Mogul Emperor Shah Jahan, and also served the latter's sons Prince Dara Shikoh and Emperor Aurangzeb. His Sufiistic poems composed under the pen-name of *Barahman* (*Brâhmana* or Brahman) are well known. He says: "I have seen with the eye of Unity everything in this world which is full of diversities. Nothing came to my eye which I considered foreign or strange. Excepting the Truth, I have not intimately mingled with anything else."

Indianism: Some Basic Concepts and Practices

This sense of unity and harmony, which represents the most specifically humanistic and human value of Indian culture, has as its basis the following:

1. A sense of the unity of all life and being as the expression of an unseen reality. This unseen reality is both immanent and transcendent. It embraces life and the universe (which are unending through æons) and is the Divine Spirit *(paramât-man)*, or energy *(sakti)* or order *(rta)* working through them.
2. A desire for synthesis in an attempt to combine the apparently disconnected or discordant fragments of life and experience into an essential unity.
3. An urge to realize this ultimate reality in its essential unity, through the path of knowledge, or work, or grace.
4. Harmonization of the emotions, on the higher plane, with rigid adherence to intellect or intelligence.
5. A recognition of the sufferings and sorrows of life, together with an attempt to remove them by going to the root causes and by reaching understanding through knowledge or faith, or both.
6. Feeling for the sacredness of all life which finds its outlet in the negative doctrine of *ahimsâ* (non-injury) and the positive one of *karunâ* (sense of pity) and *mâitrî* (active charity).
7. A great tolerance for all other beliefs, experiences and points of view. Indian culture in its broad and universal aspect, as distinguished from the narrow sectarian points of view, recognizes that the ultimate reality manifests itself in various forms, and that truth is approachable by diverse paths, and as such does not insist upon or inculcate a particular creed which must be accepted by all. It believes that man can attain the supreme good in life if he follows in a spirit of sincerity and charity the best teaching which is available in his environment. The ultimate truth does not pin itself down to the experiences or opinions of any single individual, but it is expressed in the experiences of the sum total of humanity.

Looked at from the philosophical and ethical points of view, the three basic values of Indian culture can be summarized in three concepts—*samanvaya* (synthesis), *satya-jijnâsâ* (desire to know the truth) and *ahimsâ* (non-injury).

The Traditional Arts and their Place in the Culture of India

by

ALAIN DANIELOU

Hindu civilization occupies, at the present time, a very special position. It goes back to the remotest ages of human history. Whatever the over-hasty theories put forward by nineteenth-century historians, no one doubts now that the civilization which flourished on the banks of the Indus in the third millennium B.C. has continued without interruption down to our own day. The early Hindu historians put the beginnings of India's dramatic art and musical system at the sixth millennium B.C., and this date, which was accepted in the ancient world, may well be confirmed by Indian archæology as it develops.

Some of the peoples who created parallel civilizations, like those of ancient Egypt and of the Middle East, made way for different races who developed another culture. Other civilizations like those of Greece and Rome, adapted themselves, through new forms of religion and thinking, to fashion modern civilizations. But Hindu civilization was neither destroyed nor seriously changed by invasions or external influences. It merely gave ground here and there to make room for them, as a mollusc makes room for foreign bodies. Wherever it survived it remained faithful to its own traditions.

The extraordinary longevity of Hindu civilization seems to have no parallel among any people existing today, even including the Chinese. The Sanskrit language, which the children of Brahmans still learn today, often before any other tongue, is the same which the grammarian Pânini studied about 500 B.C. India therefore offers a unique field for the study of the development of civilization and, in particular, of the evolution of art.

In order to give an intelligible picture of the place which art occupies in Hindu civilization, it will be necessary first to show its theoretical importance in the culture of India generally, and the part it has played in its long history, then to refer to present conditions and study the regions of the country and the classes of society where its tradition has been best preserved.

Art, in all its forms, was considered in ancient India as the vehicle or instrument of popular education. Through the theatre, music, dancing, painting and sculpture it was easy to explain to the masses and to enable them to understand without effort, in the form of illustrations and parables, the principles of philosophy, ethics and religion, which dialectical exposition would have brought within the reach of only a cultural minority.

The Hindus have never considered art as essentially different from language. Musical theory was the subject of very deep study by the same scholars who studied philology. Music, like language, is a vehicle for the expression of ideas and sentiments through sounds, and a study of the elements common to these two forms of expression has led to a theory of the grammar of musical language as well as to a theory of the direct evocative value of the sounds of spoken language.

The same profound similarity exists between all the arts. The *Vishnu Dharmottarä*, one of the oldest treatises on æsthetics, emphasizes the strict interrelation between music, dancing and sculpture, which are only differing expressions of the same universal rhythm. The proportions of architectural forms, the canons of sculpture, the concordance of colours form, as do the relations between the intervals of music or of articulate sounds, an aggregate of relationships representing, in the different orders of the sensible world, the same cosmic laws, the same universal ideas of which each of these forms may become the vehicle and the intelligible expression.

The language of colours, the language of sounds and the language of proportions are but equivalent aspects of a single means of expression, instruments which can serve for the representation of ideas. We are, however, more or less familiar with the grammar of one or the other of these languages, and we only really understand the message of the arts to the extent to which we know their grammar—as with the spoken languages—and to which we thus become familiar with the direct expression of the realities which these symbols express. Seen from this angle, art ceases to be a fanciful and instinctive speculation and becomes one of the most important instruments of knowledge, as valid and as logically grounded as geometry or metaphysics. Through art we can attain the highest peaks of knowledge, with all the certainty and logical forms bestowed by the exactest of the exact sciences.

Repeated contact with certain ideas, certain moral and spiritual values, acts on the development of our being as climate acts on the development of vegetation. In the same way, constant contact with certain proportions, with certain relationships of colours and of sounds acts on the development of our individuality and harmonizes our faculties. It is therefore important for man to live surrounded by objects whose influence is favourable, whose forms, proportions and colours set up harmonious subconscious reactions. This has led to the laying down of the various canons which prescribe the proportions of architecture and of sculpture, the relative disposition and proportion of colours in painting, and the use of musical modes in given circumstances to create a particular atmosphere. It might be thought that codes of such elaborate rules would have a paralysing effect on the development of creative genius in the individual artist. The experience of Hindu art has proved the contrary. These rules, since they were not arbitrary but were founded on the general laws which condition the rhythms of life, have given Hindu artists instruments of amazing quality. Just as geometry, complicated as its theorems may be, is no handicap to the architect but the very basis of his creation, so knowledge of proportions and of their symbolic value as well as their psychological effect is no encumbrance but the real foundation of any genuine art. The artist of genius, it is true, may be guided to this knowledge by instinct, but previous acquaintance with the theory of that which he is seeking is of enormous assistance in his work.

Whatever the genius of a sculptor, he is always battling with ignorance. He wants to produce the living form that he sees in inert matter. It is thus most useful for him to know that by lengthening a little the form of a nostril he can infuse life into it, that by placing an ear exactly right he can make it seem to be listening. In the same way it is essential for the musician to know that if he observes subtle interval distinctions, scarcely perceptible to the ear, his song will suddenly shake his audience, will plunge them into melancholy or lead them as he chooses towards joy or sorrow, courage or misgiving.

It was this belief in a cosmic order, whose principles it was the role of art to capture and to make visible, which was at the root of the theory of all the arts in ancient India. And this explains the importance attached to them in Hindu society. The role of art was conceived of as that of a method of universal education. India has preserved down to our day many of the forms of this hieratic and magical art and numerous masterpieces which seem fully to justify its theory.

ART AND YOGA

Artistic creation, like scientific discovery, is looked on in the Hindu system as the revelation of a higher reality, of a principle till then hidden under the appearance of forms. A wax mask, exactly similar to a face we know, is not really a work of art. The work of art must stylize, fasten on characteristic features, not photograph nature but, as Ananda Coomaraswamy explains, imitate nature in the methods by which she creates. The artist must thus seek to perceive the inner reality of things. He sometimes achieves this by intuition, but by methods of mental concentration he can attain it more rapidly and certainly.

It is here that the methods of *yoga* assume a great importance in the arts, and that art itself can be considered one of the essential forms of *yoga:* "mental concentration carried so far as the overlooking of all distinction between the subject and the object of contemplation; a means of achieving harmony or unity of consciousness".[1]

The intensity of concentration of the artisan or artist was given as an example in the *Bhâgavatä Purânä*, where the wise man Dattatreyä, enumerating the 24 masters from whom he learnt wisdom, mentions among them an artisan who was making arrows.

"An artisan who was making arrows was so completely plunged in his work that he never noticed that the royal procession was passing by him with a great din; so he whose thought is totally immersed in the contemplation of the Divine perceives nothing else, neither within himself nor outside."[2]

[1] Ananda Coomaraswamy, *The Dance of Shiva*, p. 43.
[2] Bhâgavatä Purânä, 11, 9, 13.

Shanakarâchâryä makes use of this comparison in his commentaries on the Brahmä Suträs.

Shukrâchâryä, in the fourth chapter of his *Shukräniti-särä*
(before the seventh century) explains the importance of mental concentration. "The artist", he says, "must gain knowledge
of the likeness of the gods exclusively by mental concentration.
Spiritual vision is the best, indeed the true model for him. It
is on the basis of this vision, and not on that of visible objects
perceived by the senses, that he should work. The artist must
strive to paint divine beings. Merely to reproduce human
bodies is bad and even irreligious. It is preferable to represent
a divine being, even though it be ugly, than the most beautiful
of mere human forms."

For the aim of art is not to copy the divine work, an impossible and sacrilegious undertaking, but to reveal its transcendent prototypes, to detach man from the illusions of this world
by giving him a foretaste of the celestial harmony.

"It is through meditating with love on the nature of the
divinity he wants to represent that the sculptor is enabled to
make the images of the temple. To carry out successfully this
form of *yoga*, he must first decide on the general proportions
in accordance with the teachings of the traditional books."[1]

The artist must first prepare a geometrical outline in accordance with the symbolical proportions required for the image
he wants to represent. He must then concentrate his vision and
his thought on this magic diagram, or *yanträ*, till he perceives
through the geometrical lines the form he is to sculpture. This
creative concentration of the artist is one of the highest and
completest forms of concentration: Shukrâchâryä insists on
this point.

"There exists no form of concentration more absolute than
that by which images are created; direct vision of a tangible
object never allows of such an intensity."

The form of concentration practised by the painter or the
sculptor does not differ essentially from religious meditation or
mystical ecstasy. Both lead to the realization of an aspect of the
immanent divinity.

A procedure of mental vision is also sometimes used to realize
the total meaning of the musical modes. The atmosphere of a

---

1 Shukrâchâryä, Chapter IV.

mode is then represented by visual images expressed in short poems. It is only when the musician, meditating on the poem of the chosen mode and on the sounds that correspond to it, has realized within himself the state of soul to be communicated, that he becomes capable of communicating his vision to his audience by the magic intermediary of sounds.

THE ARTIST

The very conception of the role of art and of the nature of creative art necessitates for the artist and the artisan a superior intellectual, moral and spiritual training. According to the *Mânasârâ Shilpä Shâsträ*, one of the principal works on architecture, the artist ought to be "familiar with all the sciences, careful in his work of a character beyond reproach, generous, frank and without enmities or jealousy". And elsewhere:

"The Shilpan should understand the Atharvä Vedä, the thirty-two Shilpa Shastras, and the Vedic Mantras by which the deities are invoked. He should be one who wears a sacred thread, a necklace of holy beads and a ring of *kusha* grass on his finger; delighting in the worship of God, faithful to his wife, avoiding strange women, piously acquiring a knowledge of various sciences, such a one is indeed a craftsman."[1]

The professional artisan and artist enjoyed an assured position under the Hindu system; they were not dependent on the luck of orders or the whims of amateurs for the provision of the conditions necessary for the pursuit of their calling.

"In this connexion it is very important to realize that the artisan or artist possessed an assured status in the form of a life contract, or rather an hereditary office. He was trained from childhood as his father's disciple, and followed his father's calling as a matter of course. He was member of a guild, and the guilds were recognized and protected by the king. The artificer was also protected from competition and undercutting; it is said: 'that any other than a Shilpan should build temples, towns, seaports, tanks or wells is comparable to the sin of murder'. This was guild Socialism in a non-competitive society."[2]

---

1 Kearn, *Indian Antiquary*, Vol. V, 1876.
2 Ananda Coomaraswamy, *The Dance of Shiva*, p. 47.

The case was somewhat different for the individual who did not belong to the guild of artists but who wished to exercise the calling of painter or of architect. His position was that of an amateur indulging in art for his pleasure, as was often done, and even making money out of it; but his official profession continued to be that of his caste. If he wanted to make an exclusive profession of his art, he could only count on his talent and on the patronage that talent might win him, for he had little chance of acquiring certain professional secrets only revealed to members of the guild. Such cases must have been rare and the advantage of having a profession, an assured source of a living, was too great to be light-heartedly jettisoned. Even if his amateur craft took all his time, that was no reason for the self-taught artisan to abandon his caste and the system of security which it represented.

THE THEATRE AND DANCING

The *Nâtyä Shastra* explains that when, after the end of the Golden Age, the intellectual capacity of man became smaller, the wise men met together and appealed to Brahmâ the Creator, asking him for a method of teaching that would be less abstract and within the reach of all. The god then taught the wise man Bharatä the arts of the stage: music, mime, the dance and dramatic art. Taken together they were called the fifth Vedä, because by their means all knowledge useful to man can easily be imparted to him. This method of teaching does not call for previous technical studies; it is therefore readily intelligible and open to men and women of all castes and all callings alike.

This legend shows clearly the exceptional place which the arts have always occupied in Hindu civilization and the respect and honour in which artists were held since art was one of the essential methods in the teaching and intellectual training of the people.

Even down to our days, in some parts of India where the old theatre and the old form of architecture have survived, the ballet master, the teacher of elocution and the master architect are still scholars who wear the sacred cord and have the rank of priest and who see to it that technique does not degenerate and that vulgarity, so-called popular taste, finds no place on the stage or in the decoration of monuments.

When the Moslem invasions disorganized the Hindu kingdoms of the twelfth to the sixteenth centuries, the importance of the arts of the theatre diminished rapidly. What this importance in the life of the people amounted to can be judged from the fact that, when Malik Kabir conquered southern India in the thirteenth century, he carried off as hostages ten thousand musicians and dancers with the Brahmans who were their masters. Firoz Shah, when he defeated the king of Vijayanagar in the fifteenth century, demanded the delivery to him of two thousand male and female dancers and musicians. A little later, Ala-ud-din carried off a thousand singers from a southern Indian temple. All the northern Indian troops had been massacred during the first invasions.

Dancing and music have been the subject of an extensive technical literature in every period for more than two thousand years, and it is thus easy for us to follow their development. Legend depicts the universe itself as having been created by the dancing of Shivä, and when this god descended on earth he danced naked in the forests the male dance of *tandavä*. It was Pârvatî, Shivä's wife, who taught the shepherdesses of the primal age the female dance, or *lasyä*. And it was the god Krishnä, playing his magic flute, who revealed to men the sixteen thousand principal musical modes and the sixteen thousand different rhythms. Arjunä, the hero of the *Mahâbharatä*, was dancing master to the daughters of a king.

The Purânäs explain that the god Shivä taught music and dancing to the inhabitants of India eight thousand years ago. Alexander's historians, who came to India about 326 B.C., give the same date for the period when Dionysos (Shivä) taught the Indians music and dancing.

The amplest work which we possess on the techniques of the dance, prior to the Middle Ages, is the *Nâtyä Shâsträ*, whose present version probably dates from just before the Christian era. It is a practical manual for the use of musicians, mimes and dancers, composed of extracts from older works. The schools of traditional dancing in southern India today still follow exactly the technique described in the *Nâtyä Shâsträ*. Certain works, such as the *Abhinayä Darpanä* of Nandikeshvarä on dancing and those of Kohalä and Anjaneyä on music, are probably much older.

The Popular Theatre

Despite the fact that the Moslem emperors were hostile to the theatre and that the British Government did nothing to support or preserve traditional art, the theatre still plays a large part in popular life in India. Besides the little theatres run by strolling comedians who travel from fair to fair, regular representations of legends chosen from the great epic poems are an important feature of life in every region of India, and the tradition survives in the former Hindu colonies such as Bali and Java, in spite of Islamic influence.

In most towns and villages, nearly every evening for two months, amateur or professional companies perform episodes from the *Râmâyanä* and the *Mahâbhâratä*. These performances are called *râmä-lîlä* and *krishnä-lîlä*. Every evening the stage is set up in a different place in the village, which represents a new scene of the adventures of the heroes. Platforms, pavilions and stairways are built for these performances and remain in place from one year to the next. The public wanders around between the platforms, and gods and heroes exchange their memorable words over the heads of this moving and attentive crowd. Between the acts, singers and musicians play interludes. In the north of India the performance is often resplendent, with elephants covered with brocades, glittering costumes and numerous acolytes.

Generally speaking, the playing of the actors has nowadays become mediocre. But the structure of the traditional theatre remains intact, with its public, its funds and its organization; it would suffice to re-establish the theatrical schools to train the actors anew. This would be all the easier since the old schools have survived in certain provinces and afford an example of a technique of acting, miming and dancing which in our time has no equal in any other country.

The Schools

The schools of miming and dancing which still exist today are situated in the areas which were furthest removed from the

192

invasion routes, particularly in the small states of the province of Orissa, in the Andhra country, in the Madras region and on the Malabar coast.

At Tanjore are to be found the great masters of the *bharatä nâtyam*, the ancient dance of the *deva-dâsîs*, the women dancers dedicated to the service of the temple. The institution of the *deva-dâsîs* was officially abolished several decades ago, but many of the best masters are still alive and teach the dance to amateurs and a few professionals. The *bharatä nâtyam* today still represents the great tradition of the Hindu classical dance in all its purity.

The technique of the *bharatä nâtyam* was laid down with a view to its being danced by women only. It takes the form of variations either on pure dance, putting the accent on the rhythmic element (as in the Spanish dance) or on expression-istic dance, illustrating a subject or a story with the aid of mime and of symbolic gestures, called *mudrâs*. There are also dances arranged for ensembles, but these are rarely performed since the temple companies have ceased to exist and no one has been able to meet the expense of reconstituting private companies on a comparable scale.

In the province of Andhra there still exist a few male schools of theatrical dancing, which similarly follow the ancient defini-tions of the *nâtya shâsträ* and have *mudrâs* resembling those of the *bharatä nâtyam*, though they differ from this considerably in style and composition. These schools are among the most interesting in India, but their dancers have never yet given performances outside their native province.

In Orissa, the dancers wear masks. Many of the little local kingdoms till recent years had excellent schools, of which the best known is that of Seraikalla. At Seraikalla, the princes of the reigning family are themselves dancers and take part in public performances. Apart from these theatrical companies, the former *deva dâsî* school at Puri has still a few representa-tives, though it is gradually disappearing. On the other hand, certain traditions of popular dancing remain very lively throughout Orissa.

The mimed drama of Malabar, the *kathâkali*, is now famous. In its schools future dancers receive an intensive training, with massages and special exercises, for more than ten years before appearing on the stage. The *mudrâs*, or symbolic gestures, which are very numerous and are different from those of the *bharatä nâtyam*, constitute a dumb language by means of which the dancer can relate no matter what story. Through muscular control, facial movements and astonishing expressions are achieved while special make-ups form a living and multi-coloured mask. The *kathâkali* performance generally lasts all night, and at certain seasons there are performances almost every night in the villages.

The undiscriminating interest which amateurs of the dance have displayed in the *kathâkali* over the two last decades has, unfortunately, done it considerable harm, because all the modern hybrid Indian ballet companies have tried to snap up the young artists when they came out of the school and have been using them in quite another type of dance, more in harmony with contemporary tastes. As the number of *kathâkali* schools is very small and they can only train a few pupils, they are now without staff and there is a grave danger of the tradition being interrupted, for it needs years of experience on the stage after leaving school to train a new master.

Kathâkali performances always take place in the open air on a ground reserved for entertainments at some distance from the village. The theatre consists of a little stage under a pavilion supported on four columns and set in the middle of the ground. Four alleys radiate from it in the four directions. The public sits on the ground all round, only leaving the four alleys free, since the various characters use them to approach the stage. In the centre of the theatre is a large oil lamp with a number of wicks, so that the actors are more or less well lighted according to their distance from the centre and their brilliant masks suddenly appear or fade into the night. As in the Japanese *nô*, the actors wait in the alleys for their turn to mount on the stage, thus giving an advance indication of the way in which the plot is going to evolve.

Popular Dancing

Apart from theatrical dancing, various forms of popular and sacred dance play an important part in the life of the peoples of India. Among the ordinary people dancing is still an essential part of every rejoicing, and the figure dances for men and women in the villages are remarkable for the technical ability of the dancers and the variety of the figures.

There are also numerous castes or sects which have dances peculiar to themselves, but these can generally only be seen in public on certain days of the year on the occasion of special feasts. Certain nomadic tribes, analogous to the gypsies who emigrated to Europe, and certain minor religious orders, also have extremely lively and technically remarkable dances.

The primitive tribes of central India, Bengal and Assam provide an extraordinary variety of ritual, warlike, erotic and symbolic dances. Even a brief account of the chief kinds of dance would be a substantial work, of the highest artistic and ethnographical interest.

Wedding Dances

The old Hindu marriage ritual calls for the presence of professional dancing girls. This custom is still very generally observed in most of the regions of India, so there is not a town without its dancing girls. The technical quality of these dances has unfortunately deteriorated recently on account of prejudice, which now causes professional dancing and singing girls—whose status was once similar to that of the Japanese geisha—to be classed with prostitutes. There are, however, among them artists of the first rank and of irreproachable conduct.

Among the masses, wedding dances are generally executed by young people, sometimes semi-professionals. These dances often have a marked erotic character. The young boys' dances of the province of Orissa are famous.

Devotional Dances

Dancing is looked on as one of the forms of veneration of the divinity. There are thus devotional dances, which are executed in the temples and before images of the gods. Almost all the great mystic poets of India sang and danced their works in the temples. Even today there are parts of India, Bengal in particular, where numerous groups—sometimes the entire village—meet together for a *kîrtanä*, in which a soloist sings long poems of mystical love of which each verse is repeated in chorus by the crowd, while part of the "worshippers" dance, accompanying themselves with wooden castanets. The *kîrtanä* plays a considerable role in social and cultural life. It brings together the rich and the poor, the university man and the peasant, in these celebrations which, apart from their religious meaning, have a considerable artistic value. Many of the *kîrtanäs* are the work of the great poets and musicians who have flourished in the Vishnuite school of Bengal since the sixteenth century and whose compositions have earned themselves a high place among the musical works of India.

Other Schools of Dancing

The *bharatä nâtyam* has been really preserved only in southern India. In the north, several important schools of dancing have been formed, based upon regional popular dances. The chief of these are the *kathak*, a men's dance of the Lucknow region, and the dances of Manipur, a small state on the Burmese frontier.

The *kathak* is a static dance bringing out, by movements of the feet, the complex rhythms of drums. It is an old popular dance of which variants are found throughout the area stretching from Turkestan to Afghanistan, in the north of India and in Rajputana. From this dance, elaborated by celebrated dancers from the court of Lucknow, has sprung the *kathak* school. Many woman amateurs have studied the *kathak* for some fifteen years and have debased its style and its sobriety. All the same, excellent performers are still to be found in Lucknow, at Jaipur and in central India.

All the modern attempts to create a sort of Hindu ballet have been the result of hybrid mixtures taking their elements from the *bharatä nâtyam*, the *kathâkali*, the *manipuri*, the *kathak* and the various popular dances, without preserving their technique or style. The result of these efforts has been in general prejudicial to the preservation of the classical art, as well as to the reputation of Hindu art abroad.

MUSIC

Hindu music represents the furthest evolved and the most complete form of modal music, the musical system adopted by more than one-third of mankind. From remotest times, India has been the source of musical inspiration and technique, from

Greece to Indonesia. Of all the classical arts, it is music which has best resisted the disorganizing factors which have been making attacks on Hindu civilization for several centuries. Despite all the social and political changes, classical Hindu music has retained its greatness and its popularity right down to our own day.

The music of the musicians is naturally distinct from popular music, but this distinction is less marked in India than in most other countries and takes the form of a difference in technical perfection rather than in the nature of the music. In certain branches, that of rhythm in particular, the semi-professional village musician is no less finished than the great executants of the towns. And the technique of rhythm here concerned is exceedingly difficult; it has no equivalent in Western music.

Music plays an important part in Hindu life, in all the feasts and religious or social ceremonies. Concerts given by celebrated performers may draw audiences of thousands who pay very high prices for their seats. But musical education is not limited to certain social classes. A Ganges waterman, who often himself sings and plays the flute and the *tablâ* (double drum), will appreciate to the full the execution of the most difficult classical music he may hear at public concerts, religious festivals or even on the radio.

On the other hand, ritual liturgical intoning and traditional Veda music represents a very simplified form of music, whose artistic, if not its historic, interest is comparatively limited. The Vedic chant should not, however, be confused with the classical music sometimes played in the temples, nor with the mystical chants that can often be heard in temples and holy places and which are sometimes of a very high musical quality.

Music has always been honoured and performed in every class of society. One of the most famous sages of ancient India, Nâradä, was a musician and wandered over the world with his *vinâ* (a plucked stringed instrument). Kings and queens have been famous singers. We often see in the Sanskrit theatre a king himself playing the stringed instruments. A great number of the works on musical theory have been produced by sovereigns. Even up to a comparatively recent period, we find a good number of technical works written by royal authors. Such are the *Mânü Kautuhalä* of Râjâ Mânä Simhâ of Gwalior (beginning of sixteenth century), the *Sangîtä Sudhâ* of Raghun-

âthä of Tanjore (1614), the *Sangîtä Sârä Sangrahä* of Jagajyo-
tirmalla, king of Nepal (*c.* 1650), the *Shivä Tattvä Ratnâkarä*
of Basavä, king of Keladi (*c.* 1700) and the *Sangîtä Sârä* of
Maharâjâ Pratâp Simhä of Jaipur (*c.* 1790).

Swati Tirumal, who was king of Travancore from 1813 to
1847, composed a great number of melodies which have
remained famous throughout southern India and which have
been published thanks to the assistance of the Travancore
Government.

India is an agglomeration of differing races and cultures.
Although the unification of the contributions of the various
ethnic and linguistic groups has produced a common civilization, each of these groups has retained its personality and
certain characteristics of its original culture. It is thus that
Hindu music, though theoretically unified, possesses distinct
schools, which are descendants of the ancient systems, or
matäs. The two principal groups today are those of the north
and south of India which are supposed to be the representatives
respectively of Aryan and of Dravidian music. But there exist
many other schools which differ widely both in style and in
form and are probably related to very ancient civilizations.
Thus certain peoples of the Himalayas have retained to our
own day a musical system based on descending scales, as was
archaic Greek music—a system which has gone out of use in
the rest of India since probably the fifth century B.C.

Modal music, as we have seen, is constructed like language.
The relationships of sounds, the harmony, are presented in
succession and not simultaneously, and memory creates the
link between them exactly as it does for the words of spoken
language, which we must recall in order finally to understand
the total meaning of a phrase. Until we have assimilated this
mental procedure, Hindu music will have no meaning for us
and will appear as monotonous as the sound of a voice reciting
a poem in a language we do not know.

One of the advantages of modal music is obviously that a
sole musician, or one accompanied by a drum, can execute
the greatest musical works. Indeed, the orchestra in India is
only used for the most inferior sorts of music—what we might
call fairground music—great music always taking the form of
a solo, as does the rhetorical art. Thus the belief held by many
Europeans and modernized Indians, according to which the

extension of certain forms of harmony represents progress, is based on a complete misunderstanding of the system.

Classical Hindu music takes the form of fundamental themes on which improvisations are developed according to strict and detailed rules. In certain cases, notably with vocal music, the theme is very important and the improvisation chiefly ornamental, particularly in the music of the south. These themes are real compositions and are often the work of famous masters. Each generation has thus its musicians, its composers, who give new forms to the eternal roles of music. Many works going back to the sixteenth century are still currently executed today. It must however be remembered that the greatest music is that which has the least fixed elements and which cannot therefore be handed down in the form of compositions. For it should be emphasized that every time we comply with Western prejudice by speaking of compositions and composers, these terms bear no relation to anything comparable with the meaning they have in polyphonic music and refer always to a semi-popular form of music.

The romantic personality of Mirâ-bâï (1499–1570) stands out among the great creators of mystical chants. Springing from one of the warrior clans of Rajputana and married to the brother of the ruler of Mewar, Vikramâjitä, she fled from the fortress of Shitor and abandoned family and fortune to live as a beggar-woman at Brindâvanä, the holy city of Krishnä. She spent the rest of her life there singing and dancing in the temples. Her admirable melodies are still very popular in our day, and there is rarely a musical evening where some of the songs of Mirâ-bâï are not heard.

The most recent of the great creators of melodies was Rabindranâth Tagore. For all the emotions which stir or torment men from childhood to old age, he created melodies whose words and music he composed simultaneously and in which he expressed with unrivalled grace sentiments of a complexity which few are capable of analysing. In his native Bengal there is no one, from the shepherd to the most exalted official, who does not find for each new emotion a fragment of the work of Tagore which explains to him his own feelings. It is astonishing to see the sensibility of an entire people awakening and developing under the stimulus of the melodies of a musician of genius.

It has always been so in India, and musicians, by their mystical or warlike, their sensual or sentimental outlook, have played a considerable role in guiding its civilization at different periods of its history.

ARCHITECTURE AND THE VISUAL ARTS

The setting for the life of the individual is provided by the community, whose structure is reflected in the layout of the town and the village. Any harmonious social life depends to a large extent on this setting. By its form, its planning and its æsthetics a town exerts a profound influence on the character of its population. The planning and decoration of a town should therefore be decided with due regard to the purpose and working of the human community. They are determined by considerations of a symbolic as well as of an utilitarian kind, which find expression in the actual layout of the plan, in the architecture and the siting of the monuments, the decoration of the dwelling-houses and even the design of the most everyday objects. The aim is to make everything that surrounds life the image of a certain fundamental harmony, a representation of the cosmic order which becomes a means of constant communion with a higher order of things, with the harmony of the transcendent worlds. This conception of the symbolic value of forms and of the influence which they necessarily exert on human development led to the emergence of a society where the arts assumed great importance and played an essential moral role, and where an ill-proportioned door or an ill-balanced façade were considered as anomalies as regrettable, and susceptible of producing physical or psychological reactions as serious, as the fact of a man's being hump-backed or club-footed.

Today a very special type of modern education, in which artistic values have no place, has deprived the ruling classes of India of any artistic training, whether Hindu or Western. The traditional artisans have, however, preserved a conception of the sacred value of forms and proportions which makes the humblest object a potential work of art, and the old canons are still systematically applied in every form of popular art and handicraft.

The "*Shilpä Shâsträ*"

The artistic theories relating to architecture, sculpture and painting are set out in the *Shilpä Shâsträ*, a body of works which explain the relationship of forms and colours with cosmological theories and define the principles and the utility of the arts as well as their exact correspondence with the principles of logic, metaphysics and mysticism. Many of the theoretical works of the *Shilpä Shâsträ* seem today to be lost. It is however probable that systematic research in the enormous libraries of manuscripts in India—of which the greater part have never been catalogued, nor even classified—would result in the rediscovery of a good part of them.

In the theory of the visual arts and architecture, form is presented as a mode of expression, a language which is not essentially different from spoken language and which we can easily understand once we have comprehended and assimilated the symbolic value of the elements of proportions and colours used, just as we should do for the words of a new language.

The *Shilpä Shâsträ* begins by explaining the nature and lie of the land on which a house or a city is to be built and sets forth the omens which will enable its qualities to be known.

It goes on to the layout of the town, which, with a few variations of detail, is always the ancient plan of Hindu towns, forming a square or rectangle with wide avenues crossing each other at right angles and dividing it into districts allocated to the various guilds. Thus there will be the scholars' district, the soldiers', the smiths', the cobblers', the shopkeepers', the dancers', the musicians' district, and so forth, arranged in a prescribed order taking account of concentric circles and of the symbolism of the various directions in relation to the symbolism of the various trades.

Nowadays the town of Jaipur, in Rajputana, is the only one existing which has been built on a plan of this kind, though the distribution of the inhabitants in accordance with their calling is no longer strictly adhered to.

In the town, the temples in honour of the different aspects of the divinity should be located at the four cardinal points, each one in the middle of one of the sides of the external square. In the centre of the town will be the public square, the market, the palace of the king or of the local chief, the administrative offices, and the tree of the elders (replaced in larger towns by an assembly hall) under which the representatives of the various guilds meet to discuss matters of general interest.

Large artificial ponds, with stone steps leading down to them, serve as public baths. For those whose calling is a dirty one, such as tanners and refuse collectors, there are special districts outside the walls, and no person belonging to their community should himself draw water from the wells of other citizens (a custom which has given birth to the misconceptions concerning untouchability).

Similar rules to those which govern the plan of the town prescribe the plan of the house, with its inner courtyard, its reception room, its storerooms, its kitchens and bathrooms, its men's and its women's part with their various rooms.

The plan of the house is looked on as a living entity, represented by a being of human form, the *purushä*. The plan has thus its head, its eyes, its ears, its arms, its legs, its stomach and its sexual organs, and the disposition of the various units of the house—kitchen, storerooms, bathrooms, reception rooms, the chapel and so on—depends on the position of the various organs of the *purushä*. Very interesting diagrams representing the relationship of the *purushä* and the plan are to be found in works on architecture, and such diagrams, printed in colours, are to be bought in every bazaar in India.

After the study of the plan comes that of the proportions of the different rooms of the house and of their apertures; then the question of their decoration, with sculptured ornaments outside and frescoes inside. Almost the only place in northern India where it is still possible to see beautiful stone-built homes of this type, covered with sculptures and ornaments as they used to be built before the Moslem invasion, is the ancient city of Jaisalmer, in Rajputana. But despite the confusion to be seen in the layout of modern towns and the obvious foreign influence in the style of their buildings, it must not be believed that the principles of the *Shilpä Shâsträ* have been completely forgotten. The builder and the contractor still take great pains to follow the traditional rules in deciding the proportions of the rooms and the positions of their doors or windows, and the "Western-style" façade is very often merely a façade laid on to cover a very conservative plan.

In areas where the ruin of the peasantry in the nineteenth century did not produce too great a deterioration, the architecture of the village still follows the old canons and offers a remarkable variety of plans and styles. Certain villages in central India might be villages from an exhibition with their neatly dressed verandahs under thatched roofs, their heavy doors of sculptured woods and their walls gaily decorated with multi-coloured designs.

The Temple

The centre of the Hindu town, as of Hindu life, is still the temple. It is there that—as in the cathedrals of the Western world in the Middle Ages—the entire people has poured out all the treasures of its genius and its wealth. The central temple occupies the place of honour in the town, while the smaller temples, dedicated to secondary divinities, mount guard round its circumference. The temple is built in accordance with the same rules which express the harmony of things, the mark of the divine rhythm in the world of forms. Rising from an elevated platform, its tower dominates the town and can be seen from a long way off. The interior of the temple is dark and bare. Oil lamps shed a feeble light on the image to which the faithful bring offerings of flowers and of fruit. Their visits are short, for the temple is not a public place of assembly or of prayer but the abode of a god, where priests busy themselves about his service. Pilgrims only make short visits there, as they would to the court of a king. The outside of the temple is as rich in decoration as its inside is bare. The temple portrays the entire history of the cosmos and the hierarchy of the celestial worlds. It is covered with symbols and images and the sculptor can here give free rein to this inspiration.

In southern India, and even in Rajputana, the tradition of the temple-builders has not yet been completely lost and it is still possible to see an occasional temple being built according to the classical method.

Sculpture

Hindu sculpture makes use of a theory of plastic expression based on correspondence between certain proportions and

203

certain sentiments or qualities, just as the relationships of sounds determine the sentiments and ideas evoked by musical harmony. Codes of symbolic proportions, which analyse the smallest details of the human anatomy, down to the form of the nostrils and the nails, the breadth of the navel and the relative position of the toes, enable the apprentice sculptor to study the character of a person through his external form. However, the types generally chosen to be sculptured should not be living beings, with their mixture of qualities and defects, but purified, ideal types, representing sensual perfection intellectual perfection, grace, beauty, courage and serenity. Hindu sculpture always seeks to create types and not to represent individuals. Character is portrayed not through an effort at expressionism, but through a knowledge of the types among whom the qualities in question predominate and by a systematic use of the physical characteristics which correspond to these. This science of the relationships between physical and mental qualities in the human form has produced a sculpture which, stylized though it may be, is prodigiously alive, with a grace and an intensity of expression probably never approached by the sculpture of any other country. This art, of which numerous specimens are still to be found on the walls of medieval temples, was in great part swept away by the first waves of the Moslem invasions, since Islam forbids the representation of the human form. The only temples which have survived are those of deserted towns, where the solitude of the jungle acted as a protection against human vandalism. There are, fortunately, enough of these temples to enable us to follow the development of this magnificent art. But from the invasions onward, the walls of the temples could no longer be covered with processions of gods in human form or of men and women in divine form.

"The general ban on the fine arts was not removed even by the Mogul emperors, and it continued to have full effect so far as religious art was concerned. ... Not even Akbar, who took a most liberal and enlightened view of art, permitted the representation of a human being, or of the Deity, in a mosque or building consecrated to religion, nor did he attempt to revive a school of religious painting."[1]

---

[1] E. B. Havell, *Indian Sculpture and Painting*, p. 191.

The work of the sculptor was thus from then on limited to decorative work and to consecrated images intended for the insides of temples or for household gods. Sculptors' studios are however still numerous in India, but nobody seems to have worried about developing their productions, which are often excellent, nor of utilizing for educational purposes the last surviving heirs of traditional Hindu sculpture.

There is today no contact between the traditional artisan and the modern sculptor who has learned nothing in the official art schools but the elements of contemporary Western art. The part played by the Westernized sculptor is, moreover, very slight. The vast majority of Indians only deal with the traditional artisan, who provides them with the ritual images, the only pieces of sculpture to be found in their houses.

Apart from sculpture proper there is also to be found, particularly in southern India, a terracotta art which turns out votive images representing men, horses, elephants, often of very large size and of the most studied workmanship. The art of working in bronze, once so widespread, is now practically extinct.

In Bengal there are artisans who make nothing but temporary clay images which are honoured on the occasion of certain festivals and then destroyed. These images, generally large in size, are sometimes wonderfully done and the making of them provides the artisan with a regular living. On the occasion of the Puja, great statues are to be seen, covered with jewels and ornaments, carried in solemn processions from every village, from every quarter of the towns, preceded by dancers and singers, to be cast into the waters of the Ganges or of some other sacred river once the worship is over. The love which the Hindu lavishes on these statues and the indifference with which he gets rid of them are characteristic of the age-old psychology of devotion and detachment which is so profoundly rooted in the Indian soul and is sometimes so difficult to understand from the point of view of Western positivism.

Erotic Sculpture

It would be impossible to discuss Hindu sculpture without mentioning one of its outstanding forms, erotic sculpture, for many of the masterpieces of medieval art are of this type and there is not an important temple which has not a great number of them.

The act of love has always been looked on in India as the accomplishment of physical destiny, the highest form of bodily activity, that by which man burns himself up in the gift he makes of himself. It is the tangible image of the spiritual union by which man on the mental plane dissolves himself in joy. Before the arrival of foreign moralists, the idea that sexual pleasure could not be considered as a gift of the gods, in the same way as riches, the harvest and the fruits of the earth, would rarely have entered the mind of a Hindu. Even the strict ascetics of the Jain religion decorated their temples with intertwined couples as much as they did with flowers or with mythical animals. Just as the merits of fasting have nothing to do with those of cookery, so the virtue of chastity does not acquire a jot more value if the beauties of eroticism are condemned: on the contrary.

Erotic symbols therefore occupy a central place in the sculpture of the temples. Ananda Coomaraswamy explains that: "In an anthropocentric European view of life, the nude human form has always seemed to be peculiarly significant, but in Asia, where human life has been thought of as differing from that of other creatures, or even from that of the 'inanimate' creation, only in degree, not in kind, this has never been the case.

"On the other hand in India the conditions of human love from the first meeting of the eyes to ultimate self-oblivion have seemed spiritually significant, and there has always been a free and direct use of sexual imagery in religious symbolism. Physical union has seemed to present a self-evident image of spiritual unity; at the same time operative forces, as in modern scientific method, are conceived as male and female—positive and negative. It was therefore natural enough that later Vaishnava mysticism speaking always of devotion *(bhakti)* should do so in the same terms; the true and timeless relation of the soul to God could now only be expressed in impassioned epithalamia celebrating the nuptials of Râdhâ and Krishnä, milkmaid and herdsman, earthly bride and heavenly bridegroom. So there came into being songs and dances in which at one and the same time sensuality has spiritual significance and spirituality physical substance, and painting that depicts a transfigured world where all men are heroic, all women beautiful and passionate and shy."[1]

Painting

In Sanskrit literature, painting is considered an occupation not unworthy of princes. In a play attributed to King Harshä of Kanauj (606–647), the *Nâgânandä*, a prince spends his time painting from memory the portrait of his beloved Malayâvati. He calls for a piece of red arsenic to draw and uses blue, yellow, red, brown and grey. Malayâvati looks on at the work of her lover without being seen, but the portrait is so little of a likeness that she thinks it is that of another young woman and faints away with jealousy.

In *Shakuntalâ*, the king himself works at the portrait of his lost wife. In another play, attributed to Kalidâsâ, the beautiful musician and dancing girl Mâlavikâ is an attendant of Queen Dharinî, who takes great care to prevent her appearing before the king. However, without thinking about it, the queen uses her attendant as model for a fresco in her apartments. The inevitable happens, and the king falls in love with the portrait.

The fresco was an important element in the decoration of homes. At certain periods the walls of nearly all the rooms of palaces and the houses of the rich were covered with decorations and paintings representing mythological, everyday or erotic subjects.

"A *chiträ shâlâ*, or gallery of mural paintings, was an indispensable annex to an Indian palace till quite modern times, or until Indian art fell into disrepute and it became fashionable for Indian princes to import inferior European oil paintings and European furniture."[2]

"The palatial *chiträ shâlâs* were quadrangular cloisters surrounding one of the palace gardens or pavilions, sometimes reserved for the ladies of the *zanana* and sometimes apparently a public resort. There are many allusions to them in Sanskrit literature. The Râmâyanä describes Râvanä's palace in Ceylon, where:

---

1 Ananda Coomaraswamy, *Transformation of Nature in Art*, p. 44.
2 Havell, *Indian Sculpture and Painting*, p. 156.

"Gay blooming creepers clothed the walls,
Green bowers were there and picture halls
And chambers made for soft delight." [1]

"The process employed was usually that which is known in Italy as *fresco buono*, in which colours mixed with lime-water are applied to a prepared surface of the finest plaster while it is still wet, so that they are chemically united with the ground. Indian *fresco buono*, when the wall is a suitable one, is an exceedingly permanent process for interior decoration and much more durable in a tropical climate than oil painting. But as it was largely used in exposed situations, or in buildings which were not 'themselves of a permanent kind, very few of the early Indian fresco paintings have survived." [2]

The most beautiful specimens which have been preserved are those of the Ajantâ caves, which date from the second century B.C. to the sixth century A.D.; after which come those of Badâmi (sixth century), of Bâgh (*c.* 500) and of Sittanâvasal (sixth century). Frescoes dating from the tenth to the seventeenth century are to be found in various big temples in the south of India, and others of the seventeenth and eighteenth centuries in the palaces of the kings of Travancore and of Cochin. Here and there it is still possible to see fragments of mural paintings of every period, but the embellishment of palaces and princely houses has tended increasingly towards purely decorative themes. The artisans of Rajputana are today the most noted for their skill as decorators and the quality of the materials they use.

The ancient custom which lays down that houses must be redecorated when a marriage takes place is still observed and now takes the form of somewhat primitive paintings on the outer walls which depict highly-coloured hunting and war scenes, animals and gods. These paintings are sometimes charming and are the work of specialized artists who are also decorators of pottery.

In certain regions, particularly Orissa, all the village cottages have their walls painstakingly decorated with patterns in white or in colours.

Formerly every house had its love chamber, the *rangä mahal*, which was set aside for the pleasures of the master. These

---

1 *Sundara Khanda*, Book V, cant VI, p. 297, Griffith translation; E. B. Havell, op. cit., p. 156.
2 E. B. Havell, op. cit.

rooms were decorated with frescoes illustrating the principles of the *Kâmä Suträ*. Many houses still have such rooms, but the paintings have generally been covered over with plaster or with whitewash.

"In the *Sârattha Pakasini* . . . allusion is made to a class of Brahmans known by the name of Nakhä, who wandered about with pictures mounted on a portable frame showing 'scenes of good and evil destinies, of fortunes and misfortunes, and pointing out that by doing this one attains this, by doing that one attains that'.

"The moral and religious teaching of the great Hindu epics was, and still is to a certain extent, popularized in a similar way by minstrel-painters wandering from village to village, but the scheme of modern progress elaborated by the educated townsman has no use for this traditional method of popular culture, so the Indian villager desirous of recreation or edification must wait patiently until the cinema points the modern way to enlightenment."[1]

The Symbolism of Colours

The same cosmic laws which architecture seeks to express by proportions find their expression in painting through the relation of colours. These correspondences according to the Hindu theory are not arbitrary, but represent a reality which explains the effect of colours on our moods.

The three fundamental tendencies which condition all existence have each their equivalent in terms of colours. *Sattvä*, the ascending or centripetal tendency, expressed in the force of cohesion and of aspiration towards unity, virtue and salvation, is represented by the colour white. *Tamas*, the descending or centrifugal tendency, the force which is behind decomposition and annihilation, but also behind detachment and liberation, is black or midnight blue. *Rajas*, the tendency to circular movement, the resultant of the equilibrium of the other two, and which expresses itself in all creative force, passion, action and procreation, is red.

According to the *Vishnu Dharmottarä*, the most ancient treatise on æsthetics,[2] the colour of the objects painted should imitate

---

1 E. B. Havell, op. cit., p. 182.
2 See Kramrisch translation, pp. 16–17.

nature, but the whole aspect of painting which seeks to express emotions and sentiments should follow the rules of correspondences between emotions and colours. Thus love is dark blue, laughter is white, compassion is grey, anger is red, heroism is a gilded white, fear is black, astonishment or perception of the supernatural is yellow, and disgust is indigo.

Miniature Painting

Like sculpture, the art of the fresco had to be abandoned wherever the sway of Islam extended, but it was immediately replaced by miniature painting. From the fifteenth century to the present day, a great number of schools have produced works of considerable interest. Series of miniatures, generally on paper and surrounded by illuminations, represent the stories of myth, or of history, as the frescoes used to do, but with this difference, that the miniatures could easily be slipped into a book or an album and evade the eagle eye of the inquisition.

The rulers of many Indian states were patrons of painting and maintained the great artists of bygone centuries. Apart from the so-called Mogul school, consisting of painters protected by the emperors of Delhi and Agra, the principal schools were those of Rajputana, the Deccan, Kangra (in the Himalayas) and Basoli. The last representatives of these traditional schools have for the most part recently lost both their patrons and their work, and the artists turned out by the Anglo-Bengali school, founded at the end of the nineteenth century, have begun to flood India with the products of an affected art, imitated from the English pre-Raphaelites, which is rampant in almost every art school now existing. A few attempts, like that of Jamini Bey, to seek inspiration again in popular art have, however, met with considerable success.

"Alpona"

Alpona is a temporary decoration of the earth by means of colours dissolved in rice-water. When any important ceremony is to take place, the women lay out a fairy carpet of geometrical patterns, flowers and birds, which only lasts a few hours, before the entrance to the house and in the principal rooms. In certain regions of India, the outer walls of the village cottages are also decorated in this way. The art of *alpona* is one of those in which the young Hindu girl can exercise her talents, and it attains a particular delicacy in Bengal.

PUJA

In a discussion of the arts in India it is difficult to pass over an art which is a very peculiar one but which is, in a sense, the most important of all, because it is probably at the root of all the others. This is *puja*, the "ritual of adoration", which is a very important element in Indian life and occupies part of the day of many Hindus, both men and women.

The Hindu does not go to temples or public places to pray; he recollects himself and meditates in solitude, on the banks of rivers or in gardens, and he personally honours the gods in the sanctuary of his house with flowers, incense and offerings.

These rituals, whose technical accuracy must be without a slip, call for long practice before they can be carried out correctly. They make use of many symbolic gestures which are common to them and the dance, and others which are peculiar to them. The decoration of the image, the arrangement of the flowers, the rhythmic circles which the worshipper traces in the air with the flames of lamps, make *puja*, altogether apart from its spiritual meaning, an activity all of whose elements are essentially æsthetic and which should therefore be classified among the arts.

After a ritual bath which purifies him of all stain, the worshipper, clad in a newly washed robe of rose-coloured or yellow silk, enters the sanctuary where the silver vessels, the flowers, the incense, the holy water and the offerings are prepared. The worship can be that of an image or of a symbol.

Here is how the *Ganeshä Purânâ* described the preparation of one of these rituals in honour of the elephant-headed god Ganeshä, who symbolizes the union of the macrocosm and the microcosm.

"Thou shalt rise at daybreak and after a ritual bath, clad in clean raiment, shalt sit on a new mat and concentrate thy thoughts as thou dost every day.

"Take then clean and pure clay, without grit or insects, mix it with water and fashion of it a beautiful image of

Ganeshä, complete with all his members, his four hands holding an axe and all his appurtenances. Place the image on a pedestal, then wash thy hands and go seek water.

"Gather round thee then all thou canst of the holy things of the rituals: the eight sorts of perfume, the rice, the red flowers, the odorous resins, one hundred and eight white and blue sprigs of the Durvâ herb, each with three, five or seven shoots, a clarified butter lamp and an oil lamp, all sorts of offerings pleasant to the taste, sweetmeats, pastries of milk and of sugar, rice in small grains, cooked meats, camphor, betel nuts, aromatic powders, cashew nuts, cardamons, cloves, saffron, mangoes, breadfruit, grapes, bamboos, seasonable fruits, coconuts and offerings and gold that thou mayest give to the priests.

"When thou hast gathered together all these things, sit down in a solitary place on dry grass or on the skin of a buck."

The worshipper then endows the image with life by invoking the name of the god in sacred formulas *(manträs)*.

"Then there should be made the different gestures, such as that of 'approach', which have been learnt from a Master. When thou pronouncest the secret *manträs*, the six centres of the body (heart, forehead, crown of the head, arms, eyes and palms of the hands) should be consecrated to the god.

"The holy things and the offerings of the ritual must be purified also and the worshipper must concentrate his mind on the image of him who has the face of an elephant. He has but one tusk, his ears are like a winnower's fan, and he has four arms whose hands carry a lasso, a hook and things good to eat. Garlands of red flowers are round his neck.

"He who grants the wishes of his faithful is served by Intelligence and by Success, who are his two wives. For it is he who gives man the intelligence and success that enable him to accomplish the four aims of life, that is to say virtue, prosperity, pleasure and final liberation."[1]

After having invoked the god, the worshipper bathes his image; he decorates it and venerates it with lights, flowers, incense, offerings and water, representing the five elements (flowers: ether; lights: fire; incense: air; water: water; food offerings: earth). He lays before it the gold and the stuffs

---

[1] *Ganeshä Purânâ*, 34, 39.

which will be given to the priests. Then, the ritual finished, he withdraws its life from the image by new *manträs*.

THE MINOR ARTS

Music, painting, sculpture and architecture were considered by the ancient Hindus as sciences *(vidyâ)* on the same footing as geometry, grammar or logic. The term art *(kalâ)* was reserved for the minor arts and handicrafts. There were many of these arts: there were reckoned to be 32 sciences, 18 professional arts and 64 minor arts which are spoken of in detail in the great medieval encyclopædias, in the *Shukrä-niti-särä* and even in Jajämangalä's commentary on the *Kâmä-suträ*.

Most of these minor arts were fostered by the Mogul emperors, who were all interested in handicrafts. They were, however, often discouraged under the British occupation and made way for imported products. It was chiefly in the princely states that the minor arts were able to stand their ground: carving and miniature painting on ivory, wood-carving, copper, enamel and cloisonné work, carpet making and the weaving of textiles with elaborate patterns, earthenware, the making of musical instruments, gold and silverwork and the setting and cutting of precious stones, in a word a whole gamut of techniques which formerly surrounded the life of the Indian people with a mass of attractive objects.

Hindu society, with its guild system, was planned so as to make the village a self-sufficient and independent unit. This feature has to a great extent survived, and, in principle, each region of India produces everything it needs. That is why the products of local handicrafts travel so little. Each region has its own forms of pottery, copperwork and textiles, which preserve the traditional forms in great variety and wealth.

Pottery

Pottery plays a key part in the life of the village community. Every Indian village has its potter and every region has its style. Today it is generally only a question of terracotta: the former potteries, such as those which produced the famous blue Delhi ware, stopped working in the course of the last century.

213

Such of them as have been reorganized, like that of Gwalior, have concentrated on imitating English products and have completely abandoned the traditional techniques and patterns.

There are, however, to be found here and there ancient techniques, like that of the black and silver pottery of the Benares area, whose production, though now much diminished, could be started up again.

Copperwork

Together with pottery, copper objects form the kernel of the necessary implements of village life. Copper utensils of every shape and size, generally superb in their form and decoration, and the product of local handicrafts, are on sale at most fairs. Luxury copperwork, which was the former trade of Benares, with its inlaying of metals of various shades, has practically ceased to exist today.

Ancient Lists of the Minor Arts

The lists of minor arts given by the ancient Sanskrit authors are chiefly interesting for the light they shed on ancient civilization. Most of these techniques have lasted down to our own days. It will be interesting to examine two of these lists, that of Jayämangalä and that of Shukrâchâryä.

In his commentary (prior to the twelfth century) on Vatsyâyanä's *Kâmä Suträ* (art of love), Jayämangalä enumerates the ornamental arts which were current in palace life. He reckons up 64 of them: (1) singing; (2) musical instruments; (3) dancing; (4) painting; (5) engraving on wood in order to print on materials; (6) the cutting of paper stencils in order to draw patterns on the forehead with sandalwood paste; (7) carpets of flowers; (8) staining of the teeth, the clothes and various parts of the body; (9) decoration of the earth; (10) arrangement of day-beds; (11) the art of playing music on bowls filled with water; (12) the art of water-fights; (13) the casting of spells and magic; (14) the art of twining flower-garlands; (15) headdresses of flowers; (16) dress (decking out the body in clothes, jewels and flowers); (17) ear-rings; (18) perfumes and incense; (19) jewellery; (20) conjuring; (21) aphrodisiacs; (22) manual dexterity; (23) cooking; (24) drinks; (25) sewing, knitting and making fringes; (26) puppet theatre; (27) the art of lute and drum playing; (28) riddles; (29) diction; (30) recitation of sentences whose meaning and pronunciation are difficult; (31) reading aloud; (32) charades; (33) rhyming games; (34) basketwork; (35) engraving and sculpture; (36) joinery; (37) study of the form and proportion of objects; (38) appraisement of coins; (39) alloys of metals; (40) appraisement and knowledge of the origin of precious stones; (41) medicinal herbs; (42) cock-fighting, frog and partridge-fighting; (43) the art of teaching birds (parrots, mynas) to speak; (44) massage; (45) secret language; (46) cheating the barbarians (writing in hieroglyphics or in code); (47) foreign languages; (48) chariots of flowers; (49) interpretation of omens; (50) construction of machines; (51) exercise of the memory (learning by heart); (52) group reading; (53) improvised poems; (54) use of the dictionary; (55) knowledge of the metres of poetry; (56) metaphors and other flowers of language; (57) disguises; (58) cutting clothes; (59) games of chance; (60) game of dominoes; (61) children's games; (62) etiquette and good manners; (63) the art of conquests; (64) physical culture.

Shukrâchâryä, in his great work (prior to seventh century) on the art of governing, enumerates the principal forms of professional handicrafts. After saying that the number of possible trades is unlimited, he describes a certain number and recalls that the castes who practise them are generally known by the name of their trade.

The seven primary arts are related to the celestial pleasures described in the Gandharvä Vedä and are: (1) dancing (pure and descriptive); (2) instrumental music (string, wind and percussion instruments and drums); (3) dress (embellishment of the body with clothes, flowers and jewels); (4) disguises (taking on the appearance of a given person); (5) arrangement of day-beds (with cushions and flowers); (6) games of chance; (7) the erotic art (positions, etc.).

The 10 following arts are related to medical science, the art of long life *(ayurvedä)*. They are: (8) preparation of wines, liqueurs and drinks; (9) elementary surgery (lancing abscesses and removing splinters); (10) cookery and use of spices; (11) horticulture (trees, medicinal and decorative plants); (12) metallurgy and mines (extraction of minerals and metals and their working); (13) pastry and jam-making; (14) medical use of metallic products; (15) refining of metals; (16) alloys; (17) extraction of salt (from the sea or from mountains).

Next come the arts which form part of the military art *(dhanurvedä)*: (18) archery; (19 wrestling; (20) boxing and other forms of violent fighting; (21) warlike engines (Manu forbade such engines to be of too great a size); (22) utilization in war of elephants, chariots and horses.

The remaining arts have to do with the sciences of nature *(tanträs)*: (23) the art of postures *(âsanä)*, which forms part of the science of *yogä;* (24) horsemanship and the driving of wagons and elephants; (25) pottery, ceramics and copper-work; (26) painting and its six elements (form, proportions, expression, likeness, relation of colours, composition); (27) architecture (construction of wells, tanks and monuments) and surveying; (28) mechanics (manufacture of machines to measure the time, the movements of the stars, etc.); (29) dyeing; (30) steam engines (use of water, fire and steam for various tasks); (31) means of transport, construction of boats, carts, etc.; (32) rope-making; (33) dressmaking and cutting, (34) study of precious stones and their influence; (35) refining of gold and of silver; (36) imitation jewellery (diamonds made from sugar crystals deceive even experts); (37) Goldsmith's work (the art of making gold and silver ornaments and of gilding and enamelling); (38) Leather work (the skinning of dead animals and cleaning and dressing of skins for making leather); (39) Fancy leather work (softening and dyeing leather and making useful articles from it); (40) dairywork (butter, cheeses, etc.); (41) sewing, knitting, etc.; (42) swimming; (43) domestic sciences; (44) laundrywork; (45) hairdressing; (46) pressing of oil; (47) agriculture; (48) the art of climbing trees; (49) the art of serving gracefully; (50) basketwork; (51) glass-making; (52) irrigation; (53) canal-building; (54) forges (ironwork); (55) saddlery (saddles for elephants, horses, camels); (56) child welfare; (57) children's food; (58) children's games; (59) the art of punishing (suiting of the punishment to the offence); (60) calligraphy; (61) preparation of the betel nut. There are two further forms of art which are the foundation and the secret of all the others. They are: (62) manual dexterity; (63) patience. Without these two arts, none of the others can yield satisfactory results.

Manuals of the Minor Arts

Certain works written in Sanskrit or other Indian languages give detailed instructions on the form, proportions and material to be used for everyday objects. One of the principal works of this kind is the *Tanträ Särä*, a very large volume which contains descriptions of innumerable objects and lays down the form and the proportions they should have as well as the material of which they should be made according to the kind of person who is going to use them.

Many Hindus even today will never order a ring, a piece of jewellery or an object of everyday use without having looked up the instructions given in the *Tanträ Särä* or some similar work.

Modern Handicraft Schools

The ravages of the modern handicraft schools have been widespread. Generally organized either by second-class technicians or by amateurs imported from overseas, they have introduced new forms, methods, techniques and materials haphazard without taking sufficient account of the knowledge and originality of the local artisans.

In the textile industry in particular, the last 30 years have seen the disappearance of some of the most beautiful of the old techniques, patterns and colours in favour of adaptations of modern European designs, which, it was thought, would have more commercial value.

A few rare attempts have been made to stem the tide, for instance by the Kalâ Ksheträ of Madras, which has tried out with great success the experiment of resurrecting the old-time colours and patterns.

The great centres of hand-loom weaving, like Benares, although they generally bow to the prevailing taste, still produce silk and gold thread materials, amazing in their quality and the beauty of their patterns. On the other hand, the enormous weaving business organized by the Indian National Congress under the name of the Gandhi Ashram, though it has certainly played a considerable economic and political role, has scattered broadcast throughout India the most inexcusable patterns and colours and has done immense harm to high-quality craftmanship and to the public taste.

THE CRISIS OF MODERN ART

This brings us to the wider problem of the crisis of modern art in India, which corresponds moreover with a crisis in Indian civilization generally.

When India was under British administration, education, as is usually the case in colonial countries, was organized with the principal aim of training civil servants. It was therefore an utilitarian education, foreign to the country in its curricula and its principles, and leaving on one side as useless all that could properly be called cultural values.

This education was inculcated into several successive generations, and shaped the administrative class and the *bourgeoisie* of present-day India—a class which seems as incapable of appreciating Western music as Indian music, the philosophy of Plato as that of the *Upanishads*, Italian painting as Mogul painting. There is probably no place in the world today more empty of any æsthetic value than the home of the Indian of the ruling class, where the intellectual horizon barely extends beyond the newspapers and the cinema.

While this was happening, the whole life and cultural tradition of the people withdrew into the non-anglicized elements of the population: the orthodox Brahmans, certain princely families and the people. The people, who have remained Hindu in their dress as in their thinking, seem almost a different race from this westernized class. They have nothing further in common with it: they do not speak the same language, they do not hold the same beliefs, nor do they share the same conception of the aim of human life.

The result is that almost everything that has stood its ground of the ancient traditional civilization can be made to appear to a superficial observer as something in the line of folklore, of mere popular forms of art and thinking. Yet it is only by studying the scholarly counterpart of this popular art that we can understand its history and measure its real importance.

The contacts of most foreign visitors to India are naturally limited to the part of the population which speaks English. For this very reason they are immediately drawn into surface movements which do not represent the inner life of the country and can give no idea whatever of the magnificent contribution that India could still make to the culture of the nations.

The problem of Indian civilization today is that of the re-education of the ruling classes. It is a difficult and hazardous task, but it is one that must be undertaken if we are to preserve and make available to the outer world all the wealth that India still possesses in almost every branch of intellectual and artistic activity. The statements that Havell made nearly half a century ago are as applicable now as they were then:

"Even in our day, the Indian craftsman, deeply versed in his *Shilpä Shâsträ*, learned in folklore and in national epic literature, though excluded from Indian universities—or rather, on that account—is often more highly cultured intellectually and spiritually than the average Indian graduate. In medieval times, the craftsman's intellectual influence, being creative and not merely assimilative, was at least as great as that of the priest and the bookman."[1]

"The endowment of chairs of Fine Art in Indian universities, after the fashion of Oxford and Cambridge, the establishment of schools of art and architecture in which Indian students can learn the theory and practice of the fine arts, as taught in London or Paris, and the patronage of Indian artists by sympathetic Governors and high officials, do nothing to alter the system which is destroying root and branch the tradition of art in India. They only tend to obscure the vital issues and to create an atmosphere of make-believe which is more harmful in its influence than a policy of *laisser-faire*."[2]

An effort on the part of foreign countries to appreciate and honour the representatives of the old traditional Hindu culture might have a salutary effect and also open up for Western thinking and art priceless sources of inspiration.

BIBLIOGRAPHY

Works in Western languages dealing with the theory of Hindu art are extremely few and unrepresentative. The following books may, however, be referred to; they are almost alone in offering an authentic and adequate documentation.

Nâtyä Shâsträ, English translation by Manomohan Ghosh, Calcutta, 1951.

_____
[1] E. B. Havell, *Indian Sculpture and Painting*, p. 186.
[2] Op. cit., p. 251.

Vishnu Dharmottarä, English translation by Stella Kramrisch, Calcutta, 1928.

Mânasärä Shilpä Shâsträ, English translation by P. Acharya, Oxford University Press.

Transformation of Nature in Art, by Ananda Coomaraswamy, Harvard University, 1935.

The Hindu Temple, by Stella Kramrisch, Calcutta University, 1946.

Canons of Orissan Architecture, by Nirmal Kumar Bose, Calcutta, 1932.

Northern Indian Music, by Alain Danielou, London, 1950.

Remarks on Diversity of Cultures and on the General Characteristics of American Culture

by

EDGAR SHEFFIELD BRIGHTMAN

What an absolute uniformity of culture would be is difficult to imagine, although approximations to it in totalitarian states offer vivid suggestions. In a uniform culture there would be everywhere the same ideas, and the same expression of ideas, in institutions, art, philosophy, science, and religion. In order to be maintained, such cultures would have to be regimented; all newspapers and books would present the same point of view and a complete spiritual monotony would obtain. Merely to state the conception of a uniform culture is to condemn it in the eyes of everyone who values freedom and creativity. Hence, in principle, diversity of cultures is to be welcomed.

On the positive side, one may specify the advantages of cultural diversity in various fields. Perhaps we may best express these advantages by noting the operation of diversity in four specific fields.

1. In the intellectual life variety of opinion stimulates thought and is a source of new and fruitful hypotheses to members of various cultures, as they learn of each other. Further, when thinkers discover that they can arrive at common truths, despite cultural differences, confidence in truth and the value of co-operation is enhanced.

2. In the æsthetic field national and regional and religious varieties of art have always delighted observers and have enriched æsthetic experience. In fact, the artist by his very nature insists on the creation of diversity.

3. In the moral field the advantages are doubtless more questionable. It is here that cultural relativity seems to be most devastating in its effects, and conflicting cultural standards of right and wrong lead both to tragic conflicts and to a general weakening of confidence in objective standards. On the other hand, there is at least one moral advantage in

this situation. It cultivates the need for a tolerant and sympathetic understanding of differences, and a determination to overcome oppositions.

4. A final advantage might be called the evolutionary. Diversity of cultures might be regarded as nature's rich production of variations, followed by a struggle for survival which need not be military or destructive, but on the spiritual and cultural level. In other words, the variety of cultures constitutes a vast system of experiments. The human race is so direly in need of improvement that any experiment in cultural variety which has the slightest promise of offering something better may well be tried and may well contribute to the eventual bettering of mankind.

INCONVENIENCES WHICH MAY RESULT FROM THE DIVERSITY

We need to consider what the chief inconveniences are. In my opinion they may be reduced largely to two. First, there is the danger that each variety of culture may become a static tradition. We see this in fixed class distinctions, unchanging religious traditions, rigid moral codes which take no cognizance of the advance of science, and so forth. If each cultural stratum has a fixed form, the advantages of variety are largely cancelled. The second main disadvantage is that cultural diversity often breeds a sense of superiority and of intolerance toward other cultures, leading sometimes to extremes of non-co-operation. These evils are seen at their worst in certain forms of economic and religious culture.

The main question is how to remedy these inconveniences. In general I think that the remedy is best found in an appeal to the forward-looking elements in each culture, rather than by any attempt to impose improvements from outside. For example, when the Nazi movement was developing in Germany, the American Friends Service Commission printed a series of leaflets with extensive extracts from the most liberal and democratic of German writers. This method—though in fact it did not succeed—was a better one than circulating in Germany excerpts from the best French, Swedish, British, or American writers. The conflict between Moslem and Hindu culture in India is best assuaged by showing each group that it is disloyal to the highest ideals of its own religion when it assumes an intransigent attitude. In general, also, information and travel tend to lessen the conflicts. Prejudice is largely based on ignorance and fear, and when a good representative of any culture interprets his culture, the general result is a heightened appreciation, even if a full agreement is rarely reached. Friendly personal contacts and discussion, and international correspondence, as well as wide reading, all contribute to the desired end of world co-operation.

It seems to be going too far to say that mere variety would contain its own remedy. In fact if variety were the last word, and cultural relativity were absolute relativity, I do not see that there would be any hope at all. Absolute diversity would be as incurable as is the unity of absolute monolithic totalitarianism. It is not the diversity as such which contains the cure, but rather the fact that beneath all diversity there are certain common traits of humanity and of reason which are to be found everywhere. Absolute diversity would mean absolute unintelligibility. No communication would be possible and no acts other than acts of violence could be performed between such cultures. But, given a common humanity, the diversity of cultures may tend to heighten the appreciation of that humanity, as well as to enlarge tolerance.

ABOUT THE AMERICAN CULTURE

Any such characterization as the questionnaire desires is necessarily coloured to some extent by the subjective convictions and the necessarily limited information of the reporter. The following remarks, therefore, must be taken *cum grano salis:*

Philosophic Culture of the United States

In general it may be said that until recently the American philosophic tradition was almost entirely a continuation of European philosophy. It is true that Ralph Waldo Emerson spoke for "the American scholar", and that Walt Whitman wrote of "democratic vistas". Nevertheless Emerson especially drew his inspiration from European (and Oriental) sources.

223

Whitman, who called himself a personalist, was a more authentic voice. In general, the nineteenth century was dominated by philosophical idealism, with the Hegelian influence more prominent, although accompanied by a marked stream of Lotzean thought. Herbert Spencer was widely read, but attacked; and Comte was not taken seriously in very wide circles. It was believed that there was a fundamental harmony between idealism and ethical democracy. In the twentieth century, especially from 1910 on, there has been a revolt against idealism, starting with James and Dewey as pragmatists, and continuing as a broad stream of naturalism. Analytic realism, as exemplified in Perry, and logical positivism have contributed to the attack on idealism. On the whole, except for one or two brilliant thinkers (such as Blanshard), absolute idealism has passed out of the picture, but a more empirical and pluralistic personalism and panpsychism are prominent and influential. There are some signs of *rapprochement* between some of the neo-scholastics and some of the personalists. In general, then, the temper of American philosophy is toward the empirical and the personal, the social and the ethical, rather than toward *a priori* and logically necessary systems. However, the very wide interest in symbolic logic is a strong movement in a contrary direction. The American public is not sufficiently alert intellectually to be aware of the cultural crisis involved in the conflict between naturalism and idealism.

Artistic Culture of the United States

There is a widespread and increasing interest in the fine arts all over the country, expecially in music and painting. Departments of the fine arts in colleges and universities are flourishing and cultivation of the drama in little theatres is a national phenomenon, especially in summer. Viewing the field as a whole, it may be said that widespread experimentation is characteristic; there is no form of novelty or of abstract art which is not undertaken with enthusiasm somewhere. But on the whole the national taste remains conservative. Many of the new forms are regarded by the great majority of the educated public as both unintelligible and ridiculous. And the desire to see the best of the classics far surpasses interest in quaint novelty. This is illustrated by the universal response to excellent productions of Shakespeare in the motion picture, and also by the vast crowds which have recently thronged the museums of our chief cities when a display was made of the great paintings of Germany which had been rescued by our forces and then loaned to the United States. It is true that there is an enormous amount of bad taste and of passionate admiration for the cheap and tawdry in music, the motion picture, and the "comics", but in spite of the avalanche of uncultured and worthless artistic expression, it is my conviction that sound æsthetic taste is considerably on the increase in the United States. The radio has contributed much for improvement.

Scientific Culture in the United States

It must be said that the development of science at the present time is positively astounding and almost without limits. American industry needs physicists and chemists in practically every field, and there is also an immense demand for psychologists. In fact, industry rewards scientists with salaries so high that it is difficult for universities to retain on their faculties the best teachers of science, since business can pay three or four times as much as any university can afford. Since World War I, the importance of science for government, especially for the military arm, has been greatly magnified, and researches on atomic fission have occupied a large amount of the time of scientists. The government, furthermore, has enlisted the aid of universities for research that is deemed to be socially valuable, and the sciences have received financial aid from the government on a scale hitherto unimaginable. There is a wide popular interest in science: boys know more about science than their parents ever knew. Men of science are listened to with a respect that is very rarely accorded to philosophers. At the same time, it must be noted that the responsibility for the atomic bomb and the dreadful prospects for the future which confronts humanity if the bomb is used extensively, have produced in many of the most thoughtful scientists a new sense of ethical and social responsibility. They have become aware that science alone cannot control the powers which it can produce. Scientific leaders are very active in urging a more ethical attitude among nations, and the development of a world government which will make the use of the atomic bomb impossible and will turn the energies of science toward constructive ends for the benefit of mankind. But it must be admitted that the political thought of the nation is not yet fully aroused to the world crisis which follows on the scientific advances of the present.

The Ethnic Culture of the United States

As is well known, America is a melting pot. Although the Anglo-Saxon stock was in the majority for a long time, yet from the very earliest days there were mingled with it, in various parts of America, the Dutch, Pennsylvania Germans, the French and Spanish groups of the south, the Irish, Jews, Swedes, and many others. More recently, Italians and eastern Europeans, especially Poles and Bohemians, have appeared in large numbers. For a long time immigration was unrestricted, save for the exclusion of Orientals, and even that came to be modified; but of late, the government has questioned the unlimited capacity of America to assimilate, and immigration has been notably restricted. There has been a remarkable combination of the preservation of ethnic traditions and customs with an equally remarkable mingling of the races on a common democratic and friendly basis. In almost every university classroom students of most varied ethnic origin sit together and work together with the utmost goodwill. It would, of course, be absurd to say that ethnic problems have been solved in the United States. The government has no reason to be proud of its treatment of the American Indian. The Negro problem is even more acute now than it has been in recent years, since the southern states have resented President Truman's insistence on civil rights for all. In fact, it is chiefly on this issue that the new States' Rights Party was organized, as a defection from the Democratic Party; the real purpose of the new party not being any ideal of states' rights in the abstract, but simply and solely the maintenance of white supremacy by segregation of the races. The problem of the treatment of Negroes in the armed forces is also a festering sore which not only produces deep resentment among Negroes, but also friction between the whites of the north and the south. On the other hand, there is much genuine goodwill in the south and in many communities racial relations are bettering. And it must be granted that even in the north, Negroes are on the whole treated as social inferiors. Speaking broadly, however, and for all races including the Negro, it may be said that members of any ethnic stock think of themselves first and foremost as Americans, rather than as Poles or Italians, etc.

Notes on the Culture of the U.S.A.

by

JOHN SOMERVILLE

ORIGINS

If ever there were a clear case of direct cultural influence and borrowing, it is in the relations between Europe and the U.S.A. Perhaps the most accurate expression for the relations in question is the word transplantation. Culture patterns were brought from Europe and set in the new soil, very much as living plants were. The cultural survivals of the Indian tribes which inhabited our territory at the time Europeans discovered, explored and began to settle it, are negligible so far as any significant role or effect in the national life of our people today is concerned. The general public still sees a few Indians (mainly in and around the "reservations"), and there is a certain consciousness of Indian life which still exists, mainly in our literature and in our popular arts, but there is little that is deep or vital about it. There may be unconscious effects of the early confrontation of races; however, the discussion of such possibilities would be speculative and of little value to the present purpose.

Our vast land, with its exceptionally rich resources, its high degree of fertility, its favourable climate and geographical situation (all of which proved of great influence in the development of our culture) was not given to us by Europeans, but practically everything else was—at least, at the beginning of the period of white settlement. The cultural transplantation from England, France, Spain, Holland, Portugal, Italy, Scandinavian and other countries began in the sixteenth century and continued on a "colonial" basis until late in the eighteenth century. The main influence came from England. This country had gained a dominant position among the colonial powers, supplying the new land with its settlers, and the new state with its language. Our revolutionary war was, in one sense, a family quarrel among Englishmen.

No American is unconscious of the European background and influence, and, in most of us, it is a deep-seated fact in our lives. We are all immigrants, and we know it even when we do not acknowledge it. Of course, it might be said that most other peoples are immigrants too, but many of them, as peoples, have forgotten the experience. The facts are remote, and obscured in the mists of time. To them, it is not a matter of living memory, and it seems of little concern at present. But to the vast majority of Americans, the emergence from immigrant status is a matter of only a few generations or less. It is a living fact, always to be reckoned with in one way or another. Just as our country is commonly called "the New World" by Europeans, "the Old Country"—meaning some European land—is a household expression among Americans.

In fact, it is hardly too much to say that most Americans lead what might be called a double life on the plane of national consciousness. This peculiar fact has a thousand ramifications in our culture. Every American is conscious of his own non-American ancestry, and feels it natural to inquire about the national ancestry of other Americans with whom he deals. In his mind, this is a fact, like occupation or place of residence, which helps to distinguish one American in the eyes of another. Sometimes the distinctions are discriminations in the bad sense (colour and race barriers of various sorts are backward tendencies in our culture), but even where the distinction has no invidious character, it is likely to be made. Manifold problems of education, occupation, politics, and social life revolve around differences of European ancestry, especially among more recent immigrants, and those who have been less thoroughly "assimilated" in the new environment.

We thus feel European origins at the roots of our being, and in the context of our values, although the feeling is not, in all instances, favourable. For example, there always has been, and still is, a certain amount of American "isolationism". But even this is not an indifference to Europe so much as a conscious reaction against it—a desire to be quit of its conflicts, and rid of its problems. However, most Americans have a great spiritual respect for Europe as a seat and source of culture in its higher manifestations. This is seldom directly expressed, and the "average" American often appears to be either unduly dazzled by, or unduly indifferent to, direct confrontation of a serious cultural character. Cultured Europeans of goodwill would do best in their relations with Americans if they yielded neither to the temptation to condescend nor to castigate. Underneath a surface of over-smart superficiality or apparent indifference, a real hunger for culture can be found among Americans, as witness the mass and volume of our educational facilities, unequalled by any country in proportion to population. However, we have often been (or thought ourselves) victimized by polished Europeans, which is one of the reasons why we have a certain national suspicion of elaborate manners, manifested, for instance, in the fact that a stereotyped villain in our popular arts has for long been the suave and condescending European whose pretentions to culture are seen in the end to be but an instrument of guile in the service of duplicity. Indeed, this sort of fear of being imposed upon has been carried to the point where even Americans of exceptionally cultured speech or manners may be met with suspicion by their compatriots.

My fellow-countrymen, on their part, would do well, in approaching Europeans, to avoid extremes of either boastfulness or abasement. It would be best neither to flaunt nor be apologetic about our national accomplishments, the differences of which from those of Europe are at present largely matters of degree, and therefore supplementary rather than contradictory. Our importance can be taken for granted; there is no longer any need to assert it. We would do well to go about the business of learning what we have to learn as quietly as possible.

ASPIRATIONS AND IDEALS

I take the liberty of setting forth here what I have written in another connexion, as part of a recently published book entitled *The Philosophy of Peace*,[1] a study of ideological aspects of contemporary cultures in terms of strengthening, wherever possible, the basis of peaceful co-existence.

---

[1] New York. Gaer Associates.

No one ever voiced the spirit of America as superbly as Walt Whitman. He gave expression, as no one has done before or since, to our strength, to the forces of life in America, to America's faith in itself (which is also mankind's faith in itself—that is why he is significant to other peoples), to the limitless, new, emancipating affirmation of life we represented, to the sense that things were now possible, in America, that were never possible anywhere before; while at the same time he saw more fully, and pointed out with more cheerful honesty than anyone else the immense road we have still to travel before we shall have fulfilled our aspirations, and spelled out in reality the meaning of America.

But that is not all. It is not only the magnitude of our moral aspirations measured over against the relative littleness of our accomplishment so far. That might have been nothing more than the familiar call to duty, to sacrifice something for the sake of our ideals, to share something with those less well off. That was not the nature of his vision. What he saw was that the actual realization of democracy in its fullness in America would raise everyone to a level incomparably higher, and to a mode of life incomparably fuller in every sense, including the material sense, than any small circle of aristocrats ever enjoyed in any aristocratic society, however splendid, in the past.

There was the combination marvellous: the sense of heroic opportunities, the pettiness of present fulfilments, and the sure faith in the unprecedented magnificence of what could be done. He gave to all this the rich, sensuous expression of a poet, but even here, complete American that he was, he pioneered, and not just for the sake of pioneering. He broke through the narrow, restricted forms of the aristocratic inheritance, and uncovered a wealth of democratic creativity which suggested the immensity of untapped Niagaras.

Whitman was certainly no conventional poet. However, it is not only with a poet, conventional or otherwise, that we have to deal. To say that Whitman was the great poet of democracy, while true, might even give a false impression, as if it were merely a matter of hymns and pæans. He is also a surpassing philosopher of democracy. In my judgment, we have had none greater since the Civil War. His prose work, *Democratic Vistas*, is, and should be recognized as, a very bible of American democracy.

For us, today, Whitman is perhaps even a better man to look to than Jefferson, because he went on, so to say, where Jefferson left off. The name of Jefferson means the priceless political victory that gave American democracy birth. The name of Whitman means the social fulfilment through which alone it can grow up. The mortal danger of democracy in America is that it will stop growing. Here the situation is precisely like that of a living child. It either grows or dies. There is no such thing as just remaining the same.

Whitman never "glorified" America in the sense of proclaiming that everything is grand and wonderful as it is. He does take this attitude towards nature, but he also takes it for granted that the nature of man, as an intelligent, culture-building animal, is to enrich his mode of life, and raise its level. To him, America meant always an opportunity, not yet a *fait accompli*. We are great, not in that we have already created a full, living democracy, but in that we have created the opportunity to create it. "To commence, or have the road cleared to commence, *the grand experiment of development* . . .",[1] he wrote. Was there ever a better characterization of democracy?

Whitman thought historically about democracy, that is to say he saw the problem in its living depth, its time perspective. He understood from the start that the problem was not just to maintain the *status quo*, any more than the life problem of a child is to maintain its *status quo*. He saw that the issue was growth or death.

More than that. He saw that the need was not just growth as such. Here he is, I think, greater in his vision than my great teacher, John Dewey. Whitman saw and named what it was we have to grow out of, and that gave him a grasp of what it is we have to grow into in order to fulfil ourselves. Not only a grasp, but a creative grasp. One of the most interesting things in his description is his very appropriate selection of the word "gorgeous".

When a nation like ours (and this is true, *a fortiori*, of other nations) starts to build democracy, it does not start with a clean slate. Democracy is a new way of social life, and there is an old way of social life already there. The old way of life is not only in politics. It is in the psychology of the people, in their race relations, their attitude toward the female half of

---

[1] W. Whitman, *Democratic Vistas*.

the human race, in their religious ideas, in their literature and art, in their manners—as Whitman puts it, "in all public and private life, and in the Army and Navy".[1]

"For not only is it not enough", he says, "that the new blood, new frame of democracy shall be vivified and held together merely by political means, superficial suffrage, legislation, etc., but it is clear to me that, unless it goes deeper, gets at least as firm and as warm a hold in men's hearts, emotions and belief, as, in their days, feudalism or ecclesiasticism, and inaugurates its own perennial sources, welling from the centre forever, its strength will be defective, its growth doubtful, and its main charm wanting."[1]

He did not forget the charm. In his view, to build democracy does not signify an act of charity in the gloomy spirit of Puritan self-abnegation. The real flowering of a *people* will make all the gorgeous pageantry of the Middle Ages seem like a mere turn of preliminary vaudeville before the feature attraction on the programme of history. We have never yet seen, nor really tried to bring about, any such flowering.

The results of the way we have done things so far are only too well summed up in Gray's "Elegy in a Country Churchyard":

> *Full many a gem of purest ray serene*
> *The dark, unfathomed caves of ocean bear.*
> *Full many a flower is born to blush unseen,*
> *And waste its sweetness on the desert air.*

Nine-tenths of all the potential talent, creativeness, inventiveness and genius of humanity since the dawn of history have been buried alive in what Gray called "the short and simple annals of the poor".

Discouragement does not go with democracy. What goes with democracy is the natural confidence of Whitman, unafraid of what might be found on the "Open Road":

> *I think heroic deeds were all conceived in the open air...*
> *I think I could stop here myself and do miracles,*
> *I think whatever I shall meet on the road I shall like,*
> *and whoever beholds me shall like me!*

There is the aspiring accent of our American culture.

---

[1] W. Whitman, op. cit.

ACHIEVEMENTS

It is not necessary to say a great deal about the technological and industrial aspects of our civilization. The unprecedented accumulation of material power is well known throughout the world, and is indeed, historically speaking, a breath-taking phenomenon. From the status of a colonial rebel assuming, by force of arms, a precarious independence in 1776, to the status of the richest and most powerful state in the world one hundred and seventy years later—but two long lifetimes—is something quite unique in world history. The development of our country as a whole thus follows the exact pattern of what has been for millions of individuals, "the American dream".

However numerous the problems that were created in the process, and whatever crudity, vulgarity, exaggeration and distortion were involved, this whole development confirmed and immensely increased man's confidence in himself. It is these facts in their panoramic unfolding which are the source both of Whitman's vital enthusiasm and his candid realism. In the sense of formal cultural accomplishment, there are numerous subjects deserving of mention, but they cannot be explored in detail within the limits of this paper. There is a fruitful and brilliant cultivation of natural science, of which technology and large scale industrial production are applications. There are bold new developments, like "modern" architecture, especially in the larger scale of business and public buildings, which represent a kind of union of art and science, new developments in the fine arts, and even more in the immensely influential popular arts, now sometimes called "mass media", such as the screen, radio, press and advertising. Among the more serious fields, contemporary American literature is especially strong, and it is interesting to note that one of the sources of its strength is precisely the work of Whitman, who pointed out our artistic deficiencies with such forceful genius that he created, in the process, a good deal of what was lacking.

Philosophy in its strict or technical sense has never assumed a prominent part in the building of our culture, except indeed the political philosophy which helped inspire our very birth as a nation. This was, of course, the philosophy of the democratic enlightenment coming from seventeenth-century England and eighteenth-century France, Locke and Rousseau, Jefferson and Paine. There were also the various theologies of religious dissent and there is still a Puritan strain of some strength, especially in New England. However, the writings of professional philosophers, and the content of courses called philosophy in our colleges and universities contain or reflect little that has been of decisive influence in our actual history. Probably most Americans consider that church is the place for spiritual nourishment, even when they are not churchgoers, and they almost never think of philosophy as a guide to or a reflection of the activity of the American nation as a whole, of its dynamic, living culture. William James and John Dewey are the only American philosophers in whose work one can find an approximation to such a relationship on any considerable scale. But the generality of educated Americans are content to leave the works of philosophers to specialized students and teachers of philosophy, whose number and influence are quite small.

In our American culture, there are many tendencies, many currents, and many cross-currents. There are marked differences of temper at different stages of our brief history, and there are at present evident sectional differences within our large territorial expanse. What spirit, in actual fact, dominates the whole? Perhaps it might be called scientific effectiveness. We respect other spiritual attainments, such as aesthetic creativity, religious dedication, and philosophic speculation, but as a rule we respect them from a distance, and in that distance between them and us there is a certain gulf which relatively few of us have bridged. What we intimately admire is scientific effectiveness. We know that this is at the basis of our prolific productivity, and in it we sense the source of our strength as a national state. In our folk-mind, a politician is a genial fraud, a professor is an absent-minded character, an artist is a queer fellow, a clergyman is a spiritual luxury, and all of them are for special occasions—elections, college days, vacation trips, Sundays. But a scientist is someone to be reckoned with every day. The sort of thing he does has a vital relationship to productive work and good health; it would obviously be folly to ignore it. Among adjectives like artistic, religious, philosophic, and scientific, the prestige attaching to the last is incomparably the greatest. Thus the practice of medicine probably commands more genuinely unreserved respect among us than any other profession, and by far the most effective advertising appeal consists in some supposed judgment pronounced by science, or, more particularly, by physicians.

The hopes and dreams of Americans, often fulfilled to a remarkable degree, are usually centred around the raising of living standards, including the improvement of educational opportunities. We like to feel we are building "bigger and better", and it would be difficult for us to admit that anyone else could really get better results. We are open and friendly, we are hard and disciplined workers, accustomed to planning, but on an individual and competitive more than a collective basis. We are cheerful rather than gay, quick rather than deep, intelligently ingenious rather than emotionally imaginative. Most of us have an ingrained and powerful feeling that every person should have his rights and his chance in life. To admit that the contrary is the case in our country makes us so uncomfortable that we have sometimes preferred to deceive ourselves on this score.

I find it difficult to sketch the American character without suggesting, so to speak, that everyone is a potential American. And indeed, if this were not true, in a sense, there probably would be no America, considering our origin. I hasten to add that I see no reason why everyone should actually become an American, but there is, I think, a peculiarly American manifestation of universalism in the fact that there is, among most of us, no consciousness of any barrier in principle to anyone else in the world becoming one of us.

The Place of Spanish Culture

by

FRANCISCO AYALA

DEFINITION OF SPANISH CULTURE

In Western Christian civilization a body of culture has existed with characteristics of its own, since the period of the Spanish Empire's political expansion in the sixteenth century and covers still all those territories in which the Spanish language is still predominant.

Within that body of culture, there are cultural divergencies resulting both from the original autonomy of the territories which were culturally assimilated, and from their later independent development along different lines, owing to their special historical circumstances.

The various cultural soils on which the Spanish branch of Western culture was implanted gave it several different local characters, evidenced not so much in institutions and forms of intellectual expression, as in customs, outlook and mentality. There must also be taken into account the different lines of development of the various states after the rupture of their original political unity, particularly from the beginning of the nineteenth century onwards, and the different ways in which they adapted the nationalist ideology of the period. At times, in their strivings after nationhood, certain states reverted to their ancestral cultures, which had survived only in the individual stamp they had impressed upon the common culture over the centuries, being reduced in other respects to mere vestiges bereft of dynamic power. Yet the results of this process of differentiation, though perhaps not illusory, were certainly superficial, and were happily counteracted by the simultaneous cultural unification owing to social change and technical progress, whereby oral and traditional culture were gradually squeezed out by urban culture, with its greater power to influence the masses through newspapers and books, radio, films, etc.

Thus, despite the internal differences in Spanish culture, it undoubtedly exists as an independent and objective reality. The living fact of a persisting and clearly-defined cultural community, based principally on identity of language, is evident wherever the Spaniard—whether from the Peninsula or the Americas—carries his language. Just as the North American refers to us all as "Spanish", so we all, whether we be in the United States of America, in France or elsewhere, have a sense of brotherhood.

For us, our language is not only an instrument of spontaneous and immediate communication; it is also the only generally recognized symbol of our collective unity, which *ipso facto* gives it a positive emotional value.

CHARACTERISTICS OF SPANISH CULTURE

It would not be quite accurate, however, to say that our language is the sole instrument of communication shared by us all, since sharing a language also means sharing its fundamental images and cultural outlook, which are deeply embedded in the subconscious. While the Spanish-speaking world is internally divided over cultural problems and has often been rent by terrible civil wars, yet underneath there is a remarkable unity, a definite way of life, to be seen in its reactions, character and, most obviously, in the very nature of its strife and discord. However varied its forms of expression, that character is still recognizable throughout the area covered by our culture. And it is its different aspects which, when seen through foreign eyes, constitute the well-known conventional picture of the Spaniard, in some ways perhaps a caricature, but none the less genuine enough. From that over-simplified conjunction of characteristics—arrogance, pride, a lively sense of personal dignity, an unpractical turn of mind, indolence, and artistic taste—let us single out the particular trait, individualism, which both our own people and foreigners so frequently tend to consider specially representative of our character, and let us try briefly to analyse it.

Anyone who looks mainly at our public life, which leaves

so little scope for liberal practices, or our social life, which is but rarely distinguished by respect for other people's privacy, may wonder wherein lies this individualism, which is as often vaunted as it is condemned. There is no doubt that, generally speaking, we do not consider our neighbour as an individual who, *as such*, is *a priori* possessed of the same rights and obligations as anyone else. Nor do we consider a member of the community to be entitled to our respect solely *because* he is a member of it. We see him as a given individual, Mr. So-and-So, that is to say, as one particular person and no one else. The often tiresome and exhausting activity of our social intercourse is due to this continual obtrusion of the individual, of the over-developed ego. For it is clear that, with this basic attitude, each man's ego is the central and supreme point of reference, the measure of every value. This means that we are governed by personal sentiment, which affects us both for good and ill. Hence that lack of a sense of social unity, which accounts for the rarity in our countries, in contrast to the Anglo-Saxon world, of charitable foundations, benevolent institutions or privately organized public charity. We are more inclined to conceive and practise charity from man to man, which is of little use in modern, industrialized society, with its mass populations and its giant cities.

It is for the same reason that we have so little respect for public institutions. The state is merely a fictitious person, not considered as deserving of the probity of dealing which would be demanded in relations between individuals, so that our people refuse to admit that it has any moral claims. Financial dishonesty, nepotism or similar vices may sometimes be more common in other countries, but are rarely viewed with the approval characteristic of peoples for whom personal friendship stands above everything. Phrases such as "As it's for you", or "Since he is recommended by so-and-so", are not only invariably used, with real effect, throughout the Spanish world, but are also courtesy forms used even in cases where no such consideration is actually involved. All this is no doubt wrong and distressing, but it is characteristic of that type of individualism which values the particular individual above everything, and therefore refuses to respect impersonal values. It is in fact the concomitant of the rule of personal sentiment.

Yet this type of radical individualism, which is not an ideology but an attitude to life, has, along with its defects, great virtues. The most important of these is that it tends always to treat the individual as a human being, endowed with moral responsibility, and not as a means or tool to allegedly higher ends. Even in dealing with an enemy, the man-to-man relationship is close, direct, and strong, so that while anger or bitterness may rage, we do at least avoid that cold inhumanity which has in recent years been such a horrible feature of some forms of social technique.

ORIGIN AND SURVIVAL OF THE INDIVIDUALITY OF SPANISH CULTURE

Spanish civilization first spread during the Spanish Empire's political expansion in the sixteenth century, and today, after the breaking-up of that empire, is to be found wherever Spanish is spoken. Basically, the distinctive characteristics which differentiated it even then from the remainder of the Christian West, have persisted, with no sign of any real internal development. On the contrary, it seems to have remained stationary, despite its assimilation of the successive advances of technical civilization. And it is this spiritual quiescence which lends it that old-world air so attractive to the traveller.

This aspect of Spanish culture can be traced to the Protestant Reformation, from which Spain cut herself off in implacable opposition. Technical progress in the last few centuries has been bound up with the new mentality of the Reformation—freedom of thought, individualism, activism. Max Weber, for instance, in what have already become classical studies, has demonstrated its influence on capitalism, the driving force behind that progress. But since Spain not only remained Catholic, but adopted a violently reactionary attitude towards the Reformation, it is not surprising that, instead of keeping in step with the march of modern civilization, with the moderation and balance that other countries where the Church was more tolerant achieved by timely compromises, Spain, while accepting some of the fruits of technical progress and even making some distinguished contributions of her own to such progress, in no way altered her basic cultural concepts. Each new attempt at spiritual adaptation to modern life, or modernization, led straight back, after fierce civil strife, to counter-reformation.

Here we have the cause of those picturesque incongruities and archaisms of ours which entertain the foreigner and divide us among ourselves. The industrialization of life implies the adoption, in every sphere, of the criterion of efficiency, and in society, efficiency is the counterpart of the lust for power. To make use of the hundred and one tools and implements designed to satisfy that criterion and still to guide our conduct by æsthetic or moral considerations or by individual whim, is bound to result in flagrant absurdities which modern man in the strict sense of the term, that is, man conditioned to the functional relationships of technological civilization, will greet either with laughter or indignation, but in any case with surprise.

Even after three—or, more accurately, four—centuries, the form impressed on our culture in the sixteenth century has persisted in its essential character of humanistic Christianity. However much it may have deteriorated, this is still a potential resource at this critical moment in the history of mankind, when the forces which have brought us through modern times to our present situation are not merely useless, but actually dangerous. The world needs to be given a new spiritual trend in keeping with the new conditions.

What are those conditions? One factor is the really extraordinary efficiency which has enabled the West (directed since the Reformation by nations freed from the narrow dogmatism in which Spain has continued to live) to develop technology and to use it to spread its power. There is no longer any *terra incognita* in our planet, which has been rigorously reduced to a single technical unity, which has in other words been conquered by Western man. The very magnitude of the political forces now dominant makes the possibility of armed conflict between them disastrous—possibly it would mean the end of all our civilization. If we rule out that one disastrous possibility of war, the ambition and competition for power which have hitherto constituted the driving force of technical progress lose all meaning. Technology will then have to be adjusted to a world no longer governed by functionalism under the impulse of the will to power, but directed by spiritual values capable of giving a new meaning to human life. We shall have to renounce that unbridled activism from which both the positive and the negative results of progress derive, that is to say a rise in the general standard of living combined with appalling destruction and oppression.

At the point we have reached—and man's present general bewilderment shows clearly that we stand at the cross-roads —the archaistic Spanish culture offers, in its pure tradition, inestimable resources capable of rendering invaluable services to a world in the throes of spiritual reorganization.

PRESENT POSITION OF SPANISH CULTURE

In the first place, Spanish culture represents a community of culture rather than a political organization or power structure. Indeed, while it is true that Spanish civilization spread across the world under the dominating influence of the Spanish Empire, that empire very soon lost its energy (the defeat of the invincible Armada in 1588 marks the date on which it ceased embarking on large-scale undertakings and entered upon its decline). From the beginning of the nineteenth century onwards—in the violent civil strife between the European and traditionalist trends which lent an appearance of political life to a power which was in reality dying—the Empire finally split up into a number of independent states, in each of which, whether in Europe or America, the tragic process continued. As a result, none of those states has any great power in the international sphere. No one could reasonably fear that their activities, even in the improbable event of their being closely co-ordinated, might have a dangerous or disturbing effect. Being divided politically and technically dependent on the centre of world power in the West, any such tendency on their part would be not only vain but practically inconceivable.

On the other hand, Spanish culture, while it may appear an "anachronistic" form of Western civilization, is not a closed, impenetrable enclave with rigid bounds. From the beginning of the eighteenth century, cracks and fissures began to appear in the walls of the counter-reformation. A century later, the civil conflicts known as the Wars of Independence brought about its complete collapse in some countries, its partial collapse in others; the Inquisition disappeared; and the struggle between the European and traditionalist trends continued throughout the nineteenth century to the present day. The more influential *élites*, and on occasion even governments, tried in various ways to equip their countries for "progress", which meant accepting and introducing, not only the material elements of technological civilization, but also the corresponding political institutions, philosophical concepts and ways of life. The success of these "civilizing" influences varied from one region to another in the Spanish world. In general, however, even where the original stamp of Spanish culture survived in strength, it was the individual's character, his fundamental reactions and his attitude to life, which remained peculiarly Spanish, but rarely his ideology. Against the background of our cultural tradition, the most contradictory ideological beliefs exist side by side (one need only note the variety in the local politics of any of our countries), and the philosophical, scientific, literary and artistic concepts prevalent elsewhere in the West are known, shared and discussed.

It is evident, as indeed the works of many Spanish-speaking writers and thinkers testify, that we are at least as keenly interested in clarifying the meaning of this world we live in and in discovering the requisites of healthy future development as are the most active and fertile intellectual centres of Western civilization. A catalogue of all the excellent publications in Spanish on the subject of the historic crisis now confronting us would, in fact, be impressive.

SPANISH CULTURE IN THE PRESENT HISTORIC CRISIS

The success of the West in extending its dominion and its civilizing influence throughout the world has, in reaching its apogee, rendered harmful those very cultural trends which have led not only to brilliant achievements, but also to the horrors of total war, to the destruction of Hiroshima. Unconditional admiration for technical progress and the cultural principles on which it is based has cooled.

The whole world is in doubt about the future of mankind, which today is more or less directly controlled by the West.

The mighty technical system which constitutes its civilization, built on the ethics and mentality of conquest, no longer has anything to conquer. The problem now is to maintain its existing level, while adapting itself to a less dynamic form of life in which the interest of society must be centred no longer on external action, but on the deeper cultivation of the human personality.

For that purpose, and this explains the reigning confusion, the predominantly activist cultural attitudes which have hitherto constituted the driving force of modern history are valueless; indeed, they are obstructive. Our own peoples and others have long abandoned the contempt in which they formerly held those values which make Spanish culture appear somewhat old-fashioned when contrasted with that of the "modern nations", and they have done so for a very profound reason. Owing to the cultural "backwardness" we are the representatives of a particular fundamental outlook, once considered a hindrance but which, in the new circumstances, may become useful. This outlook is a part of that basic humanism of which we have already spoken—a great resource in a civilization where purely "technical" relationships are tending to oust "human" relationships.

Because we are members of Western civilization and also because we have been untouched by the ravages of its later development, we peoples of Spanish culture can act as mediators, as a link between the other great cultures which must co-ordinate their action in this new era if mankind is to become one. We can contribute points of view and conceptions which, without renouncing the benefits of technical civilization, may make it possible to adapt them to a mode of life guided by the highest spiritual values—values which are, perhaps, more easily understood by the peoples of age-old cultures, than is the frantic activism which has conquered the West.

Similarly, our relative lack of political power, presumed to mark "inferiority", is now proving to be a point in our favour, since it precludes any possibility of our being feared. So, in a different way, is our natural tendency to consider the individual as a particular human being. A vital and intuitive appreciation of the importance of our fellowmen keeps issues from becoming confused or obscured by racial considerations. Representatives of Spanish culture should be given an opportunity of contributing to the common cause, so far as possible without political commitments. Psychologically their experience of their own cultural community, which includes a number of medium-sized and small states, fits them to make such a contribution.

It would also be highly advisable to provide for wider dissemination of the ideas of writers in the Spanish language (not only on purely social and political questions, but in every sphere), if they are to exercise their best influence. It is with great difficulty that Spanish literature can cross the linguistic barriers. Whereas, until the seventeenth century, any Spanish book had immediate repercussions throughout the world, books written in Spanish since then have usually—in contrast to books in English or French—either been permanently restricted to a local audience or have won a belated and precarious place in international thought.

The Contact of Cultures in Mexican History[1]

by
SILVIO ZAVALA

GENERAL REMARKS

The discovery of the New World put an end to one of the most spectacular divisions in the history of mankind. It also marked the beginning of an exceedingly important stage in American history, when Europeans began to live side by side with Indians.

From the point of view of this study, the period of separation is no less interesting than the period in which the Old and the New World were united following Columbus's discovery: indeed, chronologically it was far longer. Estimates of the existence of man in America vary between twenty and twenty-five thousand years, that is to say, some two hundred centuries from the time when the first Asiatic immigrants crossed what is now called the Bering Strait.[2]

What is the significance, compared with that tremendous era of separation, of the four hurried centuries during which the lands of America have been opened to the influence of immigrants from Europe, Africa, Asia and elsewhere, who arrived so much later in the wake of Christopher Columbus's ships?

It would seem as though fate had purposely fashioned their history round one of the greatest new ventures ever undertaken by mankind, followed by a rapid process of amalgamation

---

1 This study was prepared at the invitation of Unesco, as part of an inquiry into the relations of cultures.

2 There might of course have been later immigrations via Asia or across the oceans. But neither the peoples of America, nor those of Asia or other regions of origin, can now throw any light on the chronological order in which these further contacts took place between the New World and other parts of the earth, a fact which in itself confirms the hypothesis of the very early date of such transmigrations. Consequently, the area which today we know as America began to extend its influence over the rest of the world only after the discoveries made at the end of the fifteenth century of the Christian era.

246

which may even now be considered as recent, incomplete and fraught with difficulty.

A significant factor in this part of American history, besides the lack of balance in its chronology, to which we have already alluded, is the cultural content of the stages preceding and following Columbus.

For during the long ages of that separation, patterns of life and culture were gradually evolving, both in Europe and America. Herein lies the originality of the situation with which we are concerned, for in each continent mankind was advancing in strength and knowledge, but in total ignorance of developments on the other side of the ocean. That is also why, when the meeting at last took place, the interchange of commodities and culture was so great and so rapid. For instance: (a) the Europeans discovered and adopted the use of maize, kidney beans, cocoa, pea-nuts, Mexican tomatoes, chillies, potatoes, tobacco, chewing-gum, gum, turkeys, llamas from the Indians;[1] (b) the Indians received wheat, rice, barley, sugar, horses, oxen, ploughs, letters and gun-powder.[2]

---

[1] In this connexion, see the well-documented study by A. Caso, "Contribución de las culturas indígenas de México, a la cultura mundial", in *México y la Cultura*, Mexico, 1946, pp. 51–80, in which he concludes "that at no time in its colonial life, nor in the short years of its independence, has Mexico contributed to universal culture inventions or discoveries even remotely comparable in quantity or quality with those contributed by pre-Hispanic Mexico".

[2] This aspect was duly emphasized by the first Spanish chroniclers of the new continent. In a chapter on "Things they (the Indians) particularly lack", Gómara lists: weighing instruments, metal money, iron utensils, candles, ships, wine, animals for draught purposes and for milking, letters, silk, sugar, linen, hemp. On this he comments: "They (the Spaniards) gave them (the Indians) draught-animals so that they need not themselves carry great weights, wool to clothe themselves... and meat, that they might eat, for they had none. They showed them how to use iron and oil-lamps, and thus to improve their living conditions. They gave them money, that they might know what they were buying and selling, what they owed and what they had. They taught them Latin and Science, and this was worth more than all the silver and gold they took from them; for letters conferred upon them the real dignity of Man, whilst silver was of little use to them. So that to be conquered was almost the best thing that could have happened to them, and to become Christians the best of all." Politically, Gómara remarks on the change from native tyranny to a free and Christian form of government.

Bernal Díaz argues that the Indians practised the rite of sacrifice, and that cannibalism, polygamy and various shameful practices were common. From these, the *conquistadores* freed them, implanting in them the saving truths of the Christian doctrine. He speaks of their conversion to the true Faith, of how they were baptized, and were taught the skills common in Castile (the working of silver and precious stones, painting, carving in wood and stone, silk-making and weaving, hat-making, soap-making, etc.), how to keep law and order (annual municipal elections) and letters (Latin, reading and writing). He refers to the introduction of domestic animals, the plough, wheat, trees and fruits from Spain, the use of horses, equestrian games, bull-fighting, the use of domestic animals for draught purposes, and the drovers' cries used in Castile. Similarly, he mentions the founding of cities, towns and places inhabited by the Spaniards, of bishoprics, archbishoprics, law-courts, monasteries, hospitals, churches and schools for all, in which teaching was given in grammar, theology, rhetoric, logic, philosophy and other arts and studies; and lastly, the introduction of type and of master printers to print books in Latin and in the Romance languages.

This theme was developed understandably enough by the Spanish historians of the new

247

These are but examples; to compile a full list we should have to review the entire history of the cultural standards attained by Europeans and Indians respectively during the many centuries of separation.

This competition between cultural elements has given rise to the endless dispute between the partisans of Indians and Spaniards, since it is just as possible to emphasize the abundant benefits bestowed by one culture whilst ignoring the contribution made by the other, as to compare the two contributions and demonstrate that the advantages conferred by one far outweigh those conferred by the other.

But this meeting of two cultures has also been interpreted more in the spirit of harmony: "Every individual should understand and know that in every latitude and longitude, there are other human beings—his brothers, whatever the colour of their skin—who have played their part in making his own life easier or pleasanter."[1]

The meeting of cultures which followed the discovery of America provides instances both of such fraternal interchanges of human labour, invention and achievements, and of other less happy relationships due to the release of the forces of conquest, disease, pillage, oppression and ruin. Every culture has its good and bad aspects, and cultural interchange embraces both. The philosopher-historians of the eighteenth century saw this clearly; they even attempted a critical evaluation of gains and losses. For one thing is certain, if smallpox and syphilis can be passed on, so can the art of building arches or preparing chocolate.

America is so vast a continent that account must be taken of the special characteristics of its various regions (e.g. Mexico, Canada and Brazil). Variations in the human and temporal aspects of the historical development of each region must also be considered. That is to say, among the many factors which have undoubtedly influenced the nature of American society, allowance must be made for the influence of the Spaniards, the Portuguese, the French and the English, the absence or presence of Indians and Negroes, and the actual date of colonization.

After these preliminary remarks, we can proceed to examine

---

continent (Solórzano Pereyra and Antonio de Solís in the seventeenth century, the Abbé Nuix in the eighteenth, and many authors in the nineteenth and twentieth centuries).

[1] P. Rivet, *Los orígenes del hombre americano*, Mexico, 1943, p. 83.

the significance of Mexican history in relation to the contact
of cultures.

INFLUENCE OF THE NATIVE ELEMENT

The repercussions of a meeting between different cultures
naturally depend on the strength and degree of development
of the peoples who are joining their destinies.

The European colonizers who settled in uninhabited or
sparsely populated lands with rudimentary cultures were in
a different position from those who came into contact with
large groups of culturally advanced Indians. This is in part
the cause of the profound difference between the colonization
of the half-empty territory which now constitutes the United
States, or the large plain of the Rio de la Plata, and the
occupation of the well-populated lands of Mexico and Peru.
Again, in the Antilles and in Brazil respectively, the Spanish
and Portuguese colonists failed in their attempts at permanent
amalgamation with the Indians. For once they had broken
up the weak organizations which they found on arrival, the
colonizers drew on African labour, and the societies they
instituted were therefore ethnically and culturally very different from the Amerindian societies. So that the very non-
existence or weakness, or alternatively, the prevalence in large
numbers of a native population, greatly influenced the composition of the new society which grew out of contact with
the whites; it was also partly responsible for the differences in
the types of cultural exchange.

The most successful and interesting cases of fusion have
proved to be those in which the constituent elements were large
and heterogeneous, that is to say, where the representatives of
different cultures really lived together, giving and taking values,
so that they either produced an important Mestizo population
or exchanged inventions and compared experiences.

Mexico provides a happy example of this type of co-existence.
In the valleys of its high tableland, large Indian groups had
congregated for economic, climatic and cultural reasons, and
there, especially between the fourth and fifteenth centuries of
the Christian era, they evolved complex and interesting ways
of life.

No uniformity of culture can be claimed for the various native peoples of Mexico. Although certain general traces of affinity are recognizable among the various communities covered by the term "Indians", this does not preclude considerable differences between them, both in the field of strictly physical anthropology, and as regards their material life, customs, language, political organization, religion and other cultural characteristics. Nor, apparently, were all these groups living at the same "historical time", since there are divergencies between the past experience which each had accumulated through its civilization and historic consciousness. In the north of Mexico, for instance, there were nomadic tribes, such as the so-called Chichimecas, who lived by fruit-gathering and hunting, while in the central regions there had evolved more settled ways of life, based on agriculture.

Today, archaeologists can distinguish between the different kinds of ceramics, discover the differences and similarities of their architectures, the comparative ages of the various strata, and the greater or lesser development of the various groups.

In short, the pre-Columbian panorama offers a vast field for a study of the variety and interaction of Indian cultures.

The kind of relationship varied according to circumstance. There were irruptions, frontier defence, wars, alliances, periodical raids to capture prisoners for sacrifice, trade agreements, slavery, tributary servitude, the acceptance of foreign gods, the barter of women, and imitation of arts and occupations.

These influences, and the varieties of resistance offered by different groups, gradually made history, which is recorded quite differently in the annals of the Tenochcan, Tlatelolcan, Texcocan, Tlaxcaltecan, Huejotzingan or other tribes.

Moreover, these differences were later to be reflected in the type of contact between them and their European conquerors and colonists, for clearly relations with the nomadic tribes of the north could not be the same as with the sedentary groups of the central tableland. In the one case, the Spanish armies had to deal with an elusive, fleet-footed enemy who could not be attacked in pitched battle, so that hostilities dragged on and colonization was difficult. In the second case, they could expect a decisive victory on the battlefield, followed by a process of feudal domination. That was, in fact, what happened in the more important conquests of Mexico and Peru, where the social process culminated in the apportionment of land under grant from the Spanish kings.

Well-disciplined Indian armies were here to be found fighting as allies of the Spanish army, having joined it without resistance or opposed it without success. That was the case of the Tlaxcaltecans and Mexicans, and it enabled the skill and military customs of certain pre-Columbian peoples to survive even after they had ceased to be independent.

Among the Indian population, it was perhaps the priests who suffered most from the arrival of the Europeans. The change from the native polytheist religions to the monotheism of Christianity deprived them of their duties and status. They gave ground, only after a covert struggle. Idolatry persisted and fought for survival within the new forms of Christian society, but that was not enough to compensate the former pagan priests for the loss, through the Conquest, of their prestige and office.

In the political sphere, the great leaders, Montezuma, Cuauhtémoc and Atahualpa, lost their lives together with their dominions. The native aristocracy, however, met with a more varied fate. Some upper-class Indians intermarried with Spaniards of the Conquest, for example, Doña Marina, and Doña Isabel, the daughter of Montezuma. A few overlords *(caciques)* broadly speaking kept their lands and authority. They had of course occasionally to bear with plunder or with high-handed action on the part of the Spaniards, but they themselves seized lands which had formerly belonged to the headman, to the religion, or to the Indian communities *(calpiscas)*. It was, moreover, not unusual to find the Indian overlord rearing goats or pigs, that is to say, making use of European innovations to improve his own economic position. On the other hand, we read of Indian noblemen, completely ruined, hoeing the land and working with the *macehuales* (ordinary Indians). The Spaniards did not abolish the overlords as an institution. They turned them into instruments for their own purpose, which was the domination of the natives and their possessions. The overlord was sometimes able to make ingenious use of his position has a mediator, to ensure his own survival and prosperity, despite the serious threat to his authority and well-being entailed by the tremendous political changes resulting from European domination. There were also *macehuales*, who rose to positions of authority in their villages, despite the protests of the former overlords, as a result of the changes introduced by Spanish colonization.

The economic life of the Indian community had a considerable influence on the type of relationship established with the Europeans. Thus we see the Michoacan Indians, who were acquainted with metals, moving with the Spanish colonists to the mines in Zacatecas, while the Tlaxcalan farmers helped to settle and colonize the Saltillo region. The agricultural produce of the pre-Hispanic Indians was of vital importance in feeding the Europeans until the latter had established themselves. Later, Indians recruited by forced labour did whatever work was required in the fields. The Indians paid tribute to the agents in money and kind. And ultimately the workers, who were legally free, but whose movements were hampered by debts, populated the great estates which the settlers of European origin had acquired at the expense of native owners.

The Indian craftsmen, who were adepts in various forms of manual work that could be used in the new forms of social life, undoubtedly made a great effort to adapt their tools, their economic habits and even their artistic notions to the new demands created by colonization, whilst maintaining their status as skilled workers. Despite occasional competition from European craftsmen and administrative measures aimed at preventing their access to the higher guilds, they were able to continue exercising their craft, so that even the most magnificent temples erected by the invading culture bear the mark of their skill and artistry.

Thus, notwithstanding the strength and cultural prestige enjoyed by the European conquerors in the lands where highly-developed Indian civilizations were flourishing at the time of the invasion, the latter civilizations did not die out. Indeed, from a purely demographic point of view, it was not possible for a few thousand Europeans to cause more than two million Indians to disappear. There were, of course, great changes in religious, military, political, economic and artistic forms; but, with or without the knowledge and consent of the new masters, the pre-Columbian cultural forms survived to some extent.

One proof of this is furnished by the language. The Indian

inhabitants of Mexico continue to speak Nahuatl, Otomí, Tarascan, Maya, etc. They learn Spanish slowly, as a second language, and it is only in the towns inhabited by Europeans or their descendants, and among the growing Mestizo population, that Spanish predominates and the native languages are gradually being forgotten.

The situation is similar with regard to the preservation or modification of dress, customs and the indigenous arts, indeed everything connected with folklore. For folklore is usually endangered by contacts between cultures, even when it is simultaneously enriched by contributions from without. Instances of this are the Moorish and Christian festivals which have taken such firm root even in Mexico, or the art of *charrería*, using imported horses and bulls, which has become typical of the new society.

The process of fusion was by no means identical in methods, intensity, or even speed in all parts of the country. An analysis of the social situation at any given moment gives quite different results according to whether we are dealing with the capital of a province, with a near or remote village, or with a tribe, as was shown by Redfield in Yucatan. For the same pattern of culture does not apply to the whole country. We have, on the contrary, a society with considerable internal gradations and differences, developing from its original constitution, and not determined solely by economic factors. There are people, for example, who go unshod and sleep on the floor, not because they are too poor to buy shoes or beds, but because their cultural traditions allow them to forego those amenities without discomfort. Here we see the influence of this people's peculiar historical formation, which is also responsible for that striking contrast between primitive and modern conditions, a matter of astonishment even to the most unthinking traveller in Mexico.

The number of Indians in Mexico and the quality of their deeply-rooted, pre-Columbian traditional cultures readily explain the survivals to which we have alluded, and the way in which the Indian cultures resisted the imported European culture, became amalgamated with it or completely disappeared.

A study of the process over a period of time and a comparison of successive stages show that ethnic and cultural

253

intermingling has been increasing from century to century. Thus, Mexico was less markedly Indian in the eighteenth than in the sixteenth century. Later, the elements of modern culture—easier communications, greater economic activity, schools and medical squads—gradually displaced the native traditions and survivals, despite certain lapses that occurred, especially in the interior of the country.

Moreover, notwithstanding outbursts of intense Indian propaganda, the Mexican state has always been a major influence for unification, through important factors such as the "national language", namely Spanish. The Western alphabet was adopted for writing, and the pictography of the old native manuscripts is no longer used.

One might justifiably mention native religious survivals, but churches of Western type have now replaced the pyramids, and the Latin mass has taken the place of the old rites, including human sacrifice.

Travel today is usually by horse, donkey, cart, train or motor-car. On the roads, the Indians still tramp on foot, carrying their heavy loads. Yet as soon as higher wages permit, they make use of "trucks", piling them high with hen-coops, baskets and vegetables, and lending a highly primitive touch to local forms of transport. And among the bare feet may be seen an occasional pair of shoes, indicating that their owner is approaching Mestizo culture, which is in turn accepted increasingly freely and naturally.

Thus, in a population which, fundamentally, has retained the racial and cultural characteristics of peoples who were evolving in the New World long before its discovery at the end of the fifteenth century, we find a process of constant and increasing change resulting from inevitable contact with the world of European origin.

THE COLONIZERS

The Spaniard of the Conquest had had no lack of earlier cultural contacts. He had a complex historical tradition, to which Iberians, Celts, Tartessians, Mycenaeans, Phoenicians, Greeks, Carthaginians, Romans, Visigoths and Arabs had all contributed. In his own peninsula, in the neighbouring islands and along the African coast, he had lived together with Moors, Jews, Canary Islanders and Africans.

He had fought with those peoples, had experienced strife between religions and also their co-existence, had looted and been looted, and had occasioned and suffered the abduction of women and the enslavement of men.

In regard to ideas, letters and the arts, he had been influenced by both Western tradition and Arabic civilization.

The lands he had won in the slow process of eight centuries of reconquest had once again to be brought under the plough, and laboriously colonized. New towns were founded, the villages wrested from the enemy were divided up, and in the more densely populated provinces the former inhabitants were generally left where they were, so that Christians and conquered lived together. Inevitably, religious, linguistic, legal and social problems arose, such as always accompany the violent union of peoples with different cultural and historic antecedents.

Relations were not always governed by the same criteria. There were times when patience and understanding prevailed, others when violence and rancour were rife.

Christianity's constant tendency to encroach on Moslem culture meant that Spanish history in the Middle Ages was the history of an era of religious and military crusades which inevitably extended to the conquest of America. It was not without significance that that event took place at the end of the fifteenth and the beginning of the sixteenth centuries—a period very different from that of the English emigration which founded the North American colonies in the seventeenth century, when life in Europe, especially outside Spain, was already reflecting the transformation due to the growth of the middle classes.

This explains why the missionaries were in the vanguard of Spanish exploration and colonization in America, gaining a pre-eminence for the Church which lasted for centuries. For the same reason, instead of groups of burghers interested in industry and trade, there came hosts of warriors intent on propagating the "True Faith" and imbued with feudal ideas about seizing land and subjecting the natives to slavery.

To the astonished native peoples of America, therefore, Spanish culture was at first associated with violence and warlike might, with the greed of soldiers anxious to lord it over others, with the domineering presence of the new Faith, and with the economic aspects of an advanced way of life that could only be maintained by unremitting labour on the part of the vanquished.

Such methods of penetration and their abuse were appropriately and firmly denounced by a few vigilant spirits who retained the capacity for self-criticism, itself a fine characteristic of Spanish civilization. In such matters, the freedom of expression allowed them was in marked contrast to the inquisitorial dogmatism which prevailed in religious affairs.

Upon this scene of power or debasement—depending on whether we consider it from the angle of the victors or the vanquished—and resulting from the sharp clash between two unknown worlds, the first bridges of understanding were built: the union of the Spanish men with native women, sometimes resulting in the birth of Mestizo children; converse between the Spanish or Indian interpreters as they learnt a foreign tongue; the alliance of Spanish soldiers with Indian warriors to combat other enemy Indians; the first baptisms with Spanish godfathers, whereby religion bridged the gulf between races and cultures; and the missionaries' inevitable study of Indian language and culture, as a result of which many of them conceived a genuine admiration for the beauty of the Indian language or esteem for material or moral culture of another kind (Sahagún, Molina and, two centuries later, Clavijero).

In the various tasks of colonization which followed the first episodes of the conquest, Europeans and Indians were obliged to work together in building cities, churches and palaces; in exploiting mineral resources; in tilling the soil and rearing flocks; in the gloomy mills; in the craftsmen's workshops; in the hostelries and behind the droves of beasts along the roads; in unloading the ships in port—in short, in all the many aspects of economic life in which the manual labourer works along with his overseer and serves the interests of the colonizing group. For not everything was done by the soldiers of the conquest. There were also founders of cities, missionaries, miners, architects and artists. And the presence of all these types of men with their various activities created a more broadly based and diversified society and new kinds of relationships. Moreover, European emigration to the colonies was spread over three centuries; it was not the work of a moment.

As a result of these contacts, new social classes were formed within the structure derived from the conquest. The commoner from Europe often rose to lordly heights or great wealth, while the Indian nobleman might easily fall from his previous position, or at best retain it in changed form. The Creoles or descendants of Europeans born in America were different from the Peninsular Europeans, and were often in conflict with them. In the early stages, many Indians were enslaved according to traditional European law. Other half-free workers completed the variegated social pattern.

On occasion, that pattern was further complicated by the presence of African Negroes. Yet, as Gamio has shown, their case was always different from that of the Indians. For the Negro was torn away from his homeland and transported in heterogeneous groups which were then sold into slavery and dispersed; he forgot his own language and was more violently uprooted from his culture than the Indian, who merely received the European in his own environment. Naturally, the Negro did not immediately forget his religious beliefs, songs and dances or his memories of Africa,[1] but the culture he carried with him was less firmly based and less complete than were the highly-developed Indian cultures which mingled with European culture on the lines already described.

Moreover, the New World's racial and cultural contacts with Asia should not be overlooked, for voyages were soon undertaken from the coasts of New Spain towards the Far East, and the Spanish advance to the Philippines opened the door to oriental influences in America. There was slave traffic from the Far East through Manila, to feed the mills of Mexico, Puebla and other cities. Oriental arts and luxury left their mark on the life of the upper classes, with the periodical arrival of Pacific galleons, carrying procelain, lacquers, silks, etc.

The history of Spanish-native relations is closely bound up with the possession of land, water, minerals—in short, of all the country's great natural wealth. The native owners might be simply despoiled or thrown out, or enterprises dating from

---

[1] See the study by Roger Bastide, "Dans les Amériques Noires: Afrique ou Europe?", *Annales, Economies, Sociétés, Civilisations,* Third Year, Oct.-Dec. 1948, No. 4, pp. 409-26.

prehistoric times might be extended, or again, European technicians might succeed in opening up new sources of wealth as yet untouched by native culture: for instance, the great cattle prairies in the north, mining centres such as Zacatecas, or great ports for trading with Europe, such as Veracruz.

There were notable regional differences between the urban and rural communities, between the ports and the interior of the country, between the mining areas and the agricultural or cattle-breeding centres and the sugar plantations.

So that, whereas the initial wars of conquest, the widespread activities of the missionaries and the exploitation of natural resources inevitably brought Europeans and natives together, the union was by no means always harmonious. For contact does not in itself imply harmony. Indeed, the violent combination of contrasting elements may well lead to human suffering, enmity, and the oppression of one class by another.

The colonial life established by the Spaniards among the Mexican Indians was not exempt from such friction, as was to be expected in view of its warlike beginning and the subsequent social domination. Into the hierarchical system of the state and society, there even crept something akin to a legal caste system. There were free men and bondsmen; men who paid tribute and men who were exempt; men with full legal rights and men who had none; men who had access to civil and religious office, and men who had not; and men who had, or who were deprived of certain prerogatives. There were special laws for each group of the population—Spaniards, Creoles, Mestizos, Indians, Negroes and all the other castes.

Yet within this combination of circumstances which appeared to convert this great meeting of European and Indian cultures into a breeding ground of acerbity and maladjustment, there were certain elements of fundamental amalgamation. There were certain general ideas germane to the Spanish people; there was racial cross-breeding, and there was the fusion and exchange of cultural values whose intrinsic merits were such as to benefit both the victors and the vanquished.

Let us consider in some detail those forces which were finally to enable Mexico to become almost a model Mestizo country.

The sixteenth-century Spaniards were Christians who believed in the descent of the entire human race from the same parents, as a result of which all men were brothers in the eyes of God, whatever their colour, beliefs or customs. Being a creature of God, every man had natural reason and the ability to know his Creator and to save his own soul. Man in his natural state was free. But, through sin, he fell from that state, was obliged to divide up wealth, to defend himself with arms against injury, to reduce his enemies to slavery and to accept the burden of political inequality.

Many Spanish thinkers defended the application of those principles to the conquest and colonization of the New World, thus forging a doctrine in defence of the Indian's person.

Not only were there several Spanish Government laws which protected the Crown's new vassals, recognizing their right to liberty and the possession of property, and to such of their customs as were compatible with Christian rules, but the Church admitted them to the fold as believers. Thus the bonds of religion came to exercise a more powerful hold than the temporal differences which separated the victors from the vanquished. The Christian conception of man, and the admission of the Indians into the fellowship of the Universal Church, forged the first links between two worlds socially still so far apart.

Naturally, the oecumenical doctrine of the Christian faith could not admit the survival of idolatry. The heathen was converted with some show of impatience, and the pressure brought to bear on the neophyte tended to endanger his free will. Yet all this was partly outweighed by the virtue implicit in bringing the true faith to the heathen for the salvation of his soul.

Once converted, the Indians were persecuted if they abandoned the Christian religion. Ultimately, however, they were granted the privilege of exemption from the jurisdiction of the Inquisition, "for they are but rude and ignorant men, many of whom have not yet been properly initiated into the beliefs of our Holy Catholic Church".

Moreover, the intolerance of certain aspects of official Christianity was compensated by the wonderful generosity of Christ's teaching, which was able to encompass the peoples of the Old World and the New. For had the sixteenth-century Europeans come to America with temporal and spiritual principles incapable of crossing the frontiers of Western peoples and Western culture, they would have lacked those universal values which could be extended to other peoples, and it would not then have been possible to unite the two worlds.

The secular breach between Americans and Europeans could not be healed by a close union of men and cultures unless both peoples and cultures adopted broad principles which would embrace both their own and a foreign entity. And that was the noble task which fell to Christian doctrine after the European discovery of the New World. It was not really Columbus's ships which bridged the two worlds, but the universal concept of man with which the discoverers were imbued.

Thus, Las Casas described the function of the Christian religion in the critical situation engendered by the discovery of the New World: "Our religion is uniform and is suited to every nation in the world; it accepts all equally and deprives none of its liberty or authority, neither does it hold any man in subjection on the grounds of colour or on the pretext that some are by nature slaves and some free."

According to a number of eminent Spanish theologians, barbarism was the result of a wrong upbringing rather than of a natural lack of ability, and could be corrected by teaching the right habits and the Christian religion. Thus the racial factor could more easily be subordinated in importance to education, economic well-being and cultural adaptation. The subjection of the untutored should not resemble slavery, but rather the guardianship of minors, redounding to their advantage by raising them to the level of human dignity and of religion.[1]

All this, of course, was mere theorizing about colonization. The philosophers' ideals had to stand the test of reality and of the appetites of those who had been given the task of colonizing. Thus was born the conflict between rights and facts, between written law and actual practice in the provinces. The Indian might be free under Spanish thought and law, but in practice there were powerful social obstacles to his freedom. That was an inevitable consequence of the conquerors' mili-

---

[1] A synthesis of these ideas may be found in *Filosofía de la Conquista*, Mexico, Fondo de Cultura Económica, 1947.

tary power and the secular work of colonization. Yet throughout the process which resulted in the exploitation of native labour, the belief in the natives' right to freedom and protection was continually fighting for predominance among the Spaniards in America.

Naturally, not every churchman, official or colonial was an apostle ready to sacrifice himself for the Indians' conversion and well-being. There was plenty of exploitation and excess in the lands dominated by Spain. But perhaps for that very reason, liberal ideas played a more important part in the colony, for they were more than mere academic show or legal ornamentation; they laid the spiritual foundations of an administrative régime whose successes and failures were daily put to the test of hard fact.

Since Spanish-American colonial institutions had free and noble ideals, they were infused with a spirit of reform. Even that acquisitive society, therefore, was subject to the influence of the finer human values.

The ideas we are discussing not only brought about a more generous attitude towards the Indian, they also affected another problem with which modern colonial policy has been concerned.

Insufficient attention has been paid to the early appearance of petitions for Negro liberty. The Archbishop of Mexico, Friar Alonso de Montúfar, of the Dominican Order, exclaimed in 1560: "I pray the Lord that there may be an end to the captivity of and traffic in the bodies (of the African Negroes), and that more thought be given to bringing them the teaching of the Holy Gospel, that they may be free in their own lands in body, and even more in mind, and to teaching them the true knowledge of Jesus Christ." That is to say, in place of the slave trade, he envisaged an African continent apostolically receiving the Christian Faith, without infringement of Negro liberty.

To some extent, the Spanish slave traders accepted this attitude, but it was not embodied in the same laws and practices as in relation to the Indians. Negro slavery was still accepted, and in those days both kings and subjects in most European countries took advantage of it.

The influence of the foregoing ideas should not be overestimated; their principal aim was transcendental and they were only incidentally concerned with the social order. We have already pointed out, and would repeat, that those ideas could not of themselves solve the secular problems arising out of the clash between Europeans and Americans. Yet they undoubtedly helped to bring those peoples closer together and to enable them to live in harmony. For in the midst of war and slavery, this message of brotherhood and fellowship in God smoothed over many differences and made possible gradual progress towards ultimate reconciliation. At the very least, it was the forerunner of the theory of religious and civil equality which later facts and beliefs converted into something more tangible.

As far as institutions are concerned, the attitude of the Spanish Government towards the survival of Indian culture was, in some respects, fairly flexible. For example, when it was proposed to Philip II that Spanish be made obligatory and the native languages suppressed, he restricted himself to ordering: "It would seem improper to compel (the Indians) to abandon their natural language; teachers may be provided for those who voluntarily wish to learn Spanish, but let order be given that this be done by entrusting the office to no one who does not know the language of the Indians."[1]

This attitude, as well as other practical reasons, permitted the survival of the Indian *caciques* (overlords) and nobles, "since it was only fair that they should retain their rights". Similarly, existing forms of litigation were tolerated, provided they were not obviously unfair; and so were the ancient laws and customs introduced by the Indians in the cause of good government and sound policy, again so long as they did not conflict with Christian religion or with the Spanish laws relating to the New World, as laid down in the collection known as the *Recopilación de Indias*.

Besides the ideological and institutional foundations of the new Spanish-native population, there was another, flesh and blood, basis. I mean racial cross-breeding.

So long as the European and native races remained different in origin, it was of course hardly to be expected that the two groups, or "republics", as they were called in the sixteenth century, would maintain friendly relations. Indeed, we know

---

[1] I have developed this theme in my study "Sobre la política linguistica del Imperio Español en América", *Cuadernos Americanos*, Year V, Vol. XXVII, No. 3, May-June 1946, pp. 152–66.

that in many respects they did not. Generally speaking, however, the Spanish Government adopted a generous policy in the matter of the composition of its possessions, which extended equally to the government of Spanish cities and Indian villages. We have already seen how the Church was able to help in enabling the two races to live side by side.

Racial union, however, went much further than mere harmony between different entities, since it finally merged them into a single entity, changing the characteristics of both. That was the result of cross-breeding.

It started with a purely biological urge. The conquering Spanish groups brought a few women with them, but not enough to render relations between the soldiers and the native women superfluous.

Spanish society placed no institutional or religious obstacles in the way, but racial differences were gradually converted into social differences, which explains why Europeans rarely married native women. But extra-marital unions were frequent, and, where it seemed desirable from the point of view of both parties, marriage could be formalized without any ban by Church or state.

In the earlier stages, the emergence of a group of Spanish-native half-castes or Mestizos solved no problems, for there were neither enough Mestizos, nor was their position sufficiently strong, to have a sudden effect on the dualism of a hybrid society. The Europeans and the native peoples continued to predominate over the half-castes.

It was in fact the turn of the Mestizos to feel out of place among the other two groups, failing to adhere completely to either. This tragedy, which is inherent in an unstable and insecure position, is clearly reflected in the writings of a few Mestizos who achieved brilliant success in literature. Among some, their native ancestry predominates, while others show a tendency, more apparent than real, to assimilate with the conquering group. Inca Garcilaso is a case in point.

Yet it was the suffering and inner drama of this group created in no-man's land that was to provide the most promising solution. For as the Mestizo population increased, so the groups which had engendered it gradually diminished. And once the process of ethnic union had begun, it increased continuously, until Mestizo offspring outnumbered the original groups. At that stage, the overwhelming numbers of the third element finally determined the country's social composition and gave that element a definite status in the public consciousness.

To appreciate the importance of this process, we need only think of the regions opened up by missionaries, in which the absence of any secular Spanish element impeded or delayed cross-breeding. In such countries, the celibate missionaries lived in the villages among the Indians, who continued to intermarry, maintaining their original purity of race. There was no opportunity for Mestizos to be bred to any appreciable extent.

It may be, as was claimed in apologetic missionary literature, that relationships were peaceful between the groups of European missionaries and the native neophyte communities. But the secular element which watched the evolution of these societies from without, forcefully asserted that no hybrid society could be forged under such conditions, nor could there result from them the union of Spaniards and Indians which was supposed to be one of the ultimate objectives of Spanish colonization in America.

The churchmen naturally replied that such union was prejudicial to the Indians, since they were exploited by the colonials. This attitude was borne out by certain laws of the Spanish monarchy, which aimed at segregating the Europeans and the natives, using much caution in regulating their relationships.

It was colonial life rather than the beliefs or laws of metropolitan Spain which finally made for greater interpenetration, reflected chiefly in the increase in the number of Mestizos.

It is curious to note that friction also arose between the Mestizos and the Indians, for the former naturally sought assimilation with the dominating social group, and it was even necessary to issue laws to prevent oppression of Mestizos by Indians and vice versa.

The Spaniards in turn tended to have certain doubts about the human qualities of their Mestizo descendants, although they generally ended by recognizing them and accepting them without excessive social restrictions.

Thus the Spaniard's natural propensity to biological union with the Indian woman, the absence of institutional hindrance where marriage was considered advisable, the presence of a continually growing Mestizo group and its own covert but constant struggle against social prejudice, all contributed to the strengthening of this sector of American society.

At one time that society was considered to be the final and most perfect fruit of the union between Europeans and Indians that could have resulted from the Discovery. Its very existence provided the most direct and plausible evidence that the many centuries that had separated the two races and cultural worlds had come to an end. And since they existed biologically, the Mestizos would develop their own conscience and philosophy, which would ultimately make one of the most original contributions to the history of the New World.

This idea was first propounded in Mexico, in the eighteenth century, by the Abbé Clavijero, who maintained that the Spaniards would have been wiser to follow a policy of intermarriage such as would forge a single nation out of the Mexicans and themselves. To him, the advantages of such a policy to both nations were as evident as the disadvantages of the contrary policy.

Something of the kind—as Gilberto Freyre has brilliantly shown in our day—occurred in the cross-breeding of whites and Negroes in Brazil, in the face of more active racial and social opposition.

In considering the emergence of the Ibero-American Mestizo world, it is essential to take the European factor into account as we have done, yet it should not be forgotten that neither the Mexican Indians nor the Brazilian Negroes resisted the Europeans as did other cultures that were subjected in comparable circumstances. I am thinking, for instance, of the relationship between French Christians and Arab Mohammedans in North Africa. In such cases, the obstacle is not racial, but predominantly religious and cultural, because the subordinate community has beliefs and institutions which constitute obstacles to marriage with Christians.

In other parts of the world, on the other hand, where Europeans live together with natives, it is Western culture which offers resistance, in the form of segregation laws for Negroes or the prohibition of matrimony. In short, separation is fostered by racial prejudice.

Cross-breeding prospers only where the obstacles raised by both parties no longer operate with sufficient force. The countries with which this study is concerned fall into that category. But even where the biological phenomenon exists, there remains the grave problem of assessing it, of deciding whether or not it holds out promise for the future. And, as there were difficulties in the way of the emergence of a Mestizo ethnical group, so there are difficulties in the way of reaching a positive assessment of that group.

It is in this respect that the combination of the ideological with the social process becomes important, for it is one of the most influential factors in the formation of the Mexican people. Indeed, apart from its physical existence, it is essential that a nation should acquire a set of moral ideas in keeping with its biological constitution, and it will acquire such ideas only if the formative cultural elements are propitious and liberal. That has, I believe, been the case in Mexican history.

Racial cross-breeding may occur before institutional forms of segregation or hierarchy are broken down, in which case events will have outstripped the evolution of the moral prejudices governing cross-breeding. Or again, as in the case of Christianity introduced by the Europeans, the idea of cross-breeding anticipates and opposes the social hierarchy and segregation established by conquest, which means that cross-breeding and confraternity may be possible ideologically before they are possible in practice.

In either case, what matters is not whether the idea or the practice of cross-breeding came first, but whether both evolve in the same direction.

The new country thus has ideological and social foundations. We must now consider its cultural foundation. By this I do not mean the exercise of the intellect, or literature, that is to say culture in the narrow sense, but the exchange of all those values which are the fruit of human invention and through which the peoples are enabled to live and develop in the light of accumulated experience.

We already know that the American peoples received a valuable dual legacy from native and European stock. That, at least, is a point on which most people agree, for everyone is ready to concede that foreign cultural experience has something of value to offer.

It did not take the Indian long to appreciate the usefulness of the domestic animals brought by the European. Similarly, he soon realized the advantage of iron axes for cutting down trees, and of iron hooks for fishing. As Métraux has shrewdly observed, the missionaries drew the men of the South American forests not with sermons alone but also with iron implements, which the savages could not resist. Spiritual goods followed in the track of material wares, and the alert missionary took as much trouble in preparing his forge as in translating his catechism into the native languages.

At tragic times of native rebellion, such as occurred in New Mexico around 1680, the groups which had succeeded in temporarily freeing themselves from European domination attempted to restore pre-Spanish customs. They reverted to polygamy, abjured baptism, abandoned the use of the foreign tongue. And in this they encountered no difficulty. When, however, a priest with extreme ideas of idolatry suggested sacrificing all the oxen, breaking up the ploughs and reverting to traditional methods of cultivation in place of those imported by the Europeans, the natives were not prepared to accept those impassioned proposals, claiming that the benefits brought to them unconsciously by their masters, that is to say, imported by them as part and parcel of Spanish culture, were "close to their hearts".

Thus the exchange of material culture is one of the first and most firmly rooted characteristics of a meeting between human communities with different traditions. But we must not forget that its effects are limited. Malinowski has given important examples of exchanges of this type in parts of Africa where human contacts—that is, contacts between spiritual cultures— have resulted in sharp disagreements.

As for the inventions and commodities imported from Europe, they were not all of Spanish origin. Despite the commercial and political restrictions imposed by Spain on her Indian provinces for the purpose of enforcing her rule, there was continuous infiltration from other parts of Europe, for instance printing, invented in Germany; the process of amalgamating silver with mercury for mining purposes, which Bartolomé de Medina confessed he had learnt from a German miner; or vaccination against smallpox, carried out under Charles IV's orders in his distant colonies.

Once the Spanish barriers to America's communication with the rest of the world had been removed with the acquisition

267

of independence in the first decades of the nineteenth century, culture was imported more openly and more rapidly. An English professor, R. A. Humphreys, has recently pointed out that the history of the movement of people and capital from Europe to America in the nineteenth century is also the history of a closer union between the two continents.

The Spanish Americans then began to adopt an eclectic attitude, which left its mark on their literature and which presented a certain advantage in that it was highly receptive to cosmopolitan ideas. That attitude may be interpreted as an inevitable phenomenon of colonial culture, characteristic of an area that is incompletely developed, *vis-à-vis* the exigencies of contemporary civilization. At the same time, this habit of accepting progress from whatever quarter and of judging it impartially, the capacity to appreciate the contributions made to culture by other nations, and the absence of that nationalistic pride often found among the great leading peoples, were of course signs of a healthy mentality.

Thus a number of favourable elements contributed to the formation of Mexico. Its vast territory was won by the endeavours first of the Indians and later of the Spaniards. Indian villages exist side by side with Spanish cities; the vocabulary of the country recalls its two-fold origin; the techniques and arts reflect both influences; Indian and Spanish traditions are inextricably linked in political thought and action; and in the people's mentality Christian understanding has its place beside intolerance and prejudice.

By the end of the Spanish period, however, neither the Christian doctrine nor cross-breeding, nor the combination of cultural elements, had succeeded in overcoming the social differences, the hierarchical inequalities, the class divisions, the lack of economic balance, in short, the country's underlying heterogeneity.

Many endeavours had been made to build up and unify the country since the first clash between two strange worlds, but the process was slow. It was shortly to undergo other profound changes in a new historical phase, the phase of Mexican independence.

POLITICAL INDEPENDENCE

With the advent of political independence, a change occurred in the country's relations with Europe. Dependence on a single nation of that continent disappeared, to be replaced by the first commercial and cultural contacts with other countries which previously had only been able to exercise an influence either illicitly or through the official Spanish channels.

On the American continent, Mexico began to establish itself as a nation and to enter into closer relations with the United States, as was indeed necessary between neighbouring countries. These political changes brought in their wake a number of cultural changes, a different economic life, other techniques, new tastes.

Within the country, the disappearance of the Spanish Government, and the introduction in the eighteenth century of equalitarian notions derived from the Age of Enlightenment and the French Revolution, precipitated political reforms as a result of which the process of social unification initiated during the Spanish period was considerably speeded up.

One of the great military leaders of the Independence, Morelos, opposed the social divisions inherited from the colonial days, proclaiming that the "kaleidoscope of Indians, Mulattos, Mestizos and their offspring" must disappear, "and only regional characteristics remain, all being known simply as Americans".

The first draft Constitution of 1814 incorporated the doctrine of political equality for all Mexican citizens: "The happiness of the people and of every citizen lies in the enjoyment of equality, security, ownership and liberty. It is the aim of government as an institution and the sole objective of political association to preserve those rights."

This declaration, of which the tone was dictated by the new political doctrine inspired by the North American and French revolutions, was straight forward both in inspiration and objective. In the case of Mexican society at the beginning of the nineteenth century, however, it was not possible to dissociate this equalitarian theory and legislation, under which every Mexican was supposed to be a full citizen, from the social organism which had evolved during the centuries of colonization and which was ultimately most affected by the new doctrine. For in regard neither to economic position, nor to cultural development nor to effective social prerogatives, could such equality be expected among the races and classes which formed the complex of Mexican peoples.

One result of this situation was the lamentable failure of the optimistically constructed legal edifice. Political equality remained on paper, but it was far from existing in reality. Yet, just as during the centuries of colonization, Christian doctrine had persistently opposed the oppression engendered by the clash between Europeans and Indians, so, in the new phase of Mexico's existence, the equalitarian principles of modern revolution represented objectives which were in theory unquestionable and must therefore be pursued. Thus, the new ideology gave strong legal and practical support to the age-old Christian principles of harmony which the Europeans had imported at the time of the discovery.

This considerably strengthened the "concept of the Mexican", a concept which, as we have seen, had a rather limited historical influence, but was none the less important, inasmuch as it laid the foundations for the gradual achievement of the Mexican people's equality and cultural unification.

The proclamation of the sovereignty of the people and of political equality did not immediately result in the abolition of racial and social distinctions. The cultural gaps between the various members of the Mexican body politic were not filled, neither were slavery and peon labour abolished nor the mill workers saved from their economic plight. In fact, it provided no antidote to misery in lands which were badly irrigated, wrongfully distributed and inadequately exploited. The citizens of the Constitution continued to be badly-paid labourers, oppressed by debt and enjoying but scanty personal liberty or legal rights. Similarly, constitutional theory was incapable of defending the country or its working classes from the effects of economic colonialism due to the large-scale influx of foreign capital, which seized the mines, the communications and the budding industries; in short, all the resources which represented greater wealth (although, admittedly, it also brought with it tools and technical knowledge).

Once the structure of the colonial state had been destroyed, the country became a prey to anarchy, insurrections and disturbances. It was also invaded by foreign armies and suffered territorial losses.

All these troubles brought together Mexicans from different parts of the country. Members of the subject classes, who would otherwise have remained unknown, came to the fore; hereditary distinctions were abolished; opportunities occurred for marriage between people of different classes who, but for these struggles, would have remained among their own people; and even in drawing rooms the traditional ruling class with their fine manners rubbed shoulders with the new leaders of more common habits.

The seizure of power, the sudden acquisition of wealth, and opportunis took the place held during the last years of colonial society by family privilege, succession, army promotion, ecclesiastical appointment, positions purchased from the king by the great commercial monopolies, the old landed estates and the fortunes derived from mining.

Yet such sporadic movements lacked the constructive virtues of a genuine, properly directed social revolution. They broke down a few obstacles, they created a few openings, but they did not solve the problem of entire classes. Only much later, during the period of reform half-way through the nineteenth century, did the middle classes begin to expand at the expense of the clergy.

From time to time, an individual would make a spectacular rise to the top of the social ladder. For let us remember that it was nineteenth-century Mexico which made possible the career of Benito Juárez, the humble Indian who laboriously forged his own culture—having inherited the traditions of his race—until he reached the highest position in his country and, indeed, in the history of the American continent. Striking proof of the progress made in the formation of the Mexican people is furnished by the fact that Benito Juárez, in writing to Maximilian, the Habsburg, about the situation created by the French invasion, was able to say that he, who had "risen from the humble masses" to be entrusted with the Presidency of the Republic, would fall, if Providence so decreed, but with honour. It was as though the ancient dialogue between Charles V's European soldiers and those of the native empire were being revived, but under new circumstances and with different results.

The arrival of the Imperial Court, of the European armies and of new customs and tastes, inevitably left its mark on society in the recipient country, thus continuing the influences —especially French and English—which had begun in 1821 with the arrival of diplomats, engineers, dressmakers, pastry-cooks, theatrical people and other immigrants.

Two strongly contrasting periods succeeded each other in Mexico's history, the period of "Porfirismo" and that initiated by the 1910 Revolution. In a work of this kind, we can only briefly explain the significance of both periods in regard to the general evolution of Mexican society.

During the long period of General Porfirio Diaz's government, the influx of foreign capital and technicians brought Mexico into direct contact with the outer world. Commercial, shipping and diplomatic relations multiplied. Railways linked the ports directly to the capital, and the capital to the frontiers in the north and south. The telegraph cut the distances between inhabited parts of the country and made correspondence easier with the rest of the world. Consequently, Mexico strengthened her ties with European and American culture, and even with the Far East. For instance, Mexican literature of the period contains interesting references to Japan. The process of bringing town and country, different regions and cities, closer together was speeded up. In the words of Cosío Villegas: "As roads and means of communication in general improved, so the country's wealth, ideas and feelings, as well as the Mexicans themselves, circulated more freely." It should not be forgotten that this period was also the apogee of material progress in many parts of the world.

Mexico's economy became increasingly colonial, however, owing to the growing importance of foreign capital. In the countryside there were still the big estates, and the peons continued to be oppressed by debt and other hardships. The newly developing industries had government support in rejecting the workers' demands. In matters of culture and taste, European models prevailed and were slavishly imitated. Those who derived profit from bureaucratic influence—the landowners, the banks, the army and the representatives of foreign capitalism—surrounded the dictator.

This political combination gave the Mexican people 30 years of peace such as it had not enjoyed since the end of the

Spanish régime. The ennoblement of the ruling classes who gave their children a European education, the problems raised by absenteeism of landlords, and admiration of foreign countries, to some extent distracted attention from Mexico's own problems.

Not that the study of the native peoples was abandoned, or the cult of native-born heroes, or the teaching of Mexican history. But many educated people were in a way inwardly ashamed that the country should be what it was. Hispanophobia persisted, and the problem of Indian culture was felt as a "burden", a "drag" on progress, which distinguished Mexico from the countries with an entirely white population. The Indian was regarded as "debased". Thoughts turned to European immigration, to making a white race. Cross-breeding was sociologically condemned as a source of unrest and frustration. The concept of the struggle for existence, the theories of Darwin and Spencer, were borrowed to support a philosophy derogatory to Mexican life.

The solution adopted was both illusory and deceitful, namely to conceal the real facts of the situation in Mexico by preventing the poor from entering the urban districts where the *fiestas* were held to impress the foreign diplomats. The impossible was attempted—an imitation of what the country neither was nor could be.

Perhaps the concept of Mexico had never been further from the facts or in greater contrast to them than it was then, even though the attempted imitation of other countries implied a cosmopolitan attitude very different from the type of nationalism which excludes all other values. But its defect lay not in its openness to foreign influences—in itself usually salutary and fruitful—but in the fact that it was founded on the shameful rejection or dissimulation of the Mexican personality, of the country's real essence, thereby concealing the one thing which would enable the people to create forcefully and authentically. Mexico could not come into being by a vain attempt to imitate Europe or the United States, except by deviation from its historical evolution. Its contact with those foreign cultures enriched and invigorated the country, but only where it accepted instead of evading the ethnic and cultural personality forged by its own history.

The revolution which started in 1910 violently corrected

this trend of ideas and facts. Once again, the country experienced a stirring conflict which broke down the barriers of class built up during the peaceful years of the dictatorship.

For a brief moment, Villa sat in the presidential chair, to the consternation of the urban population. Zapata proclaimed the agrarian revolution. And the leaders were in turn Creoles, Mestizos, townsmen and country folk, men of every kind of culture.

This time, the revolutionary programme and ideal was the economic and educational advance of the masses. Yet another step was to be taken towards social democracy, though its progress was still unrelated to political democracy. In rebuilding the country, account was to be taken of the outcasts of fortune, who were to be given, economically and culturally, an opportunity of living fuller lives, both as citizens and as human beings.

At long last, race was no longer an obstacle. The Indians were, after all, but the first immigrants to reach this country, which was a meeting place of cultures. The archaeologists found traces of their past greatness. Artists sought inspiration from their age-old creations. The state arranged to provide funds and education for the Indians, launching a vast campaign, the ideological culmination of Christian and political doctrines which had long exercised a favourable influence on the internal harmony of the Mexican people.

But this time, as before, there was no magic solution. Contemporary social ideas, the economic endowment implicit in the redistribution of the land, the growing vitality of industry due to the nearness of the United States or to national initiative, and the instruments of educational propaganda, all acted powerfully in the direction we have indicated. But neither irrigation, nor communications, nor teaching, nor welfare progressed with the speed or force needed to close the gaps in Mexico's cultural composition. There still remained abysses of misery, ignorance and primitive existence.

This was the tense, unfinished Mexico which was visited by the delegates to the Unesco Conference at the end of 1947.

Even on the aerodrome, one of them, Lucien Febvre, noted that white, copper-coloured, black and brown human beings mingled without hindrance or mistrust. And later he commented in an article: "Mexico is a fortunate country. In 1948, the word 'racial hatred' has no meaning for it." His reflection was engendered by comparison with war-scarred Europe, which had just been suffering the mad fury unleashed by the Nazi theory of race.

The healthy moral position reached by Mexico at the end of the historical process we have just surveyed was obvious not only to any thinking European who carried in his heart the memory of the ominous experiences of the Old World during the second world war, but to any impartial observer who wanted to compare the solution reached by Mexico with that reached in other parts of the world where there have been contacts between different cultures.

One has only to think of the differences in ideology, institutions and sensibility between the white and Negro elements of the southern United States, or between the British and the descendants of the Dutch, Africans and Hindus in South Africa, to realize that men of different races and cultures can by no means always be successfully united by a programme of Christian, democratic and social unity of the kind tried out, albeit imperfectly, at the various stages of Mexican history.

The thoughtful traveller may pause to reflect on our people and on the way it has achieved this deep-seated unity and solidarity between men originally of quite different cultures. There has been no lack of mistakes or suffering in the process. But the advance continues, backed by the strength and optimism which will enable it to succeed; and the ultimate aim is basically right even though public opinion and the social conscience may on occasion lag behind, or even deviate from, the fundamental concepts apparent in Mexican history.

The Arcana of Spanish-American Culture

by

Leopoldo Zea

Few cultures show clearly such great inner dissensions as does the Spanish-American culture. The reason is that the Spanish-American culture contains within itself a diversity of cultures which appear to have been imposed in layers, as it were, but which in fact were inextricably linked with and determined by the particular history of Spanish America. Cases of serious inadaptability, resulting from a certain attitude to life, give the foreigner the impression of superficiality, of lack of sincerity, and even of a lack of creative ability. Yet that very inadaptability and its outward manifestations are associated with problems which have perhaps never been discussed before in the whole cultural history of the world, or at least not as violently as they are discussed in Spanish America.

From the beginning, Spanish America was divided into two parts, indeed into two worlds. The division was assisted, although not necessarily determined, by a combination of historical and geographical circumstances. In the last resort it was the people who inhabited and still do inhabit this America who gave to its culture the Spanish-American stamp. The cultural dissensions of which we have spoken simply reflect the conflict which has marked the whole of Spanish-American history, a conflict all the more pathetic because it has been an internal one.

Spanish-American culture consists of a number of cultural forms assumed gradually under the influence of the peoples with whom it was brought into contact by historical circumstance. These cultural forms are, in turn, the expression of human situations and attitudes in themselves so divergent that when compared with one another they may even seem contradictory. These contradictions went side by side with the "superposing" of cultures, which would appear to be one of the main cultural characteristics of this part of America. We use the term *superposing* because it is the opposite of cultural *assimilation*. Superposing means placing one thing on top of or next to another, without changing either, even where the things are divergent or contradictory; whereas assimilating means merging, i.e. making a single thing out of two different things. Superposition keeps alive such conflicts as already exist between the various things superposed, while assimilation eliminates those conflicts.

To revert to the various cultures which have formed or stimulated the formation of Spanish-American culture, the most important are the following:

1. *Native culture*, characteristic of this part of America when the European discovered it. It is a culture rich and powerful in the tablelands, e.g. of Mexico and Peru, but weak in the plains, in the Argentine Pampa, throughout the territory which was later to become the vice-royalty of Rio de la Plata, and in the Antilles.
2. *Spanish culture*, the culture of the men who discovered, conquered and colonized this part of America.
3. *European culture*, which was used from the eighteenth century onwards by the Spanish Americans to justify the wresting of their political independence from Spain, and to establish a new political and spiritual order to replace the order imposed on the former colony.
4. *North American* culture, whose political and technical forms provide the Spanish American with a model of what he aspires to be, he himself being affected, inevitably, by the tremendous development of the North American peoples.

CONTACT WITH NATIVE CULTURE

When he discovered America, the European found himself face to face with men and peoples who shared little of his concept of the world and therefore of his concept of culture. Emerging as victor in the fight, he tried not so much to understand them as to absorb them by subjecting them. Admittedly, the Christian missionaries studied the life, customs and culture of the natives, and many books were written on the subject. Yet their sole aim and object was to proselytize. Native life, customs and culture were studied only so that they might the more easily be changed and replaced by the conquering Christian's attitude to life. All that was sought was sufficient knowledge to make possible the conversion to Christianity of a culture which could only have been inspired by the "Devil". From time to time, an attempt was made to assess how far Christianity, in some form or other, had penetrated this culture. Whatever did not belong to the Christian attitude to life had to be destroyed and eradicated; so the idols and temples of the Aztecs and the Incas were destroyed and eradicated, the images of the saints and the Christian churches being *superposed* on them. Thus one culture was buried beneath the other. A Christian church rose up above every Aztec Teocalli. As may be seen at Cuzco in Peru, new towns grew up on the foundations of the old. The new houses of the Christian lords arose above the stones of the Inca palaces, and these two "superposed" cultural worlds still exist, side by side, on the Mexican and Peruvian plateaux.

To the Christian, American native culture was, and could not be other than, the work of the "Devil". These peoples were "in a state of sin", abandoned by the hand of God. In the eyes of her European discoverers and conquerers, America appeared "guilty" before God;[1] in other words, "guilty" according to the Christian or European concept of the world and of life.

There was no appeal against that judgment. The Indian was given no opportunity to speak for himself; at best, he could speak only through the European's incomplete interpretation of him, or through spiritual laws that were not his own. The significance of native history was subordinated to a general interpretation of the history of Western culture, and native culture became a mere appendix to European culture. The history of native culture prior to the Discovery and the Conquest was merely "exotic", with no meaning for its Western interpreters. Analysed according to laws quite unrelated to it, it lost the force of its expression becoming silent and muted, yet formidably active. Indeed, beneath the thick layers of Western culture which was intended to cover it, its power could be felt by the Spanish Americans, especially those of the tablelands.

---

1 An excellent study on this subject is contained in Luis Villoro's book *Los grandes momentos del indigenismo en México*, published by El Colegio de México.

The European interpretation of native culture was used to justify the second great step taken after the Discovery, namely the Conquest. The Discovery had been "providential"; that is to say, according to the ideas of the time, it had been made possible by Providence. All these peoples with whom the Europeans were suddenly confronted had remained hidden and been kept apart from Western culture for a good reason. Their discovery proved that that reason had disappeared. Europe's mission was to subject them, to convert them to Christianity, and to bring them into the fold of universal culture. America's history really began with its discovery. The first step in the Conquest had to be a judicial inquiry. Who were these men who had remained ignorant of universal culture? Were they men or beasts? And if they were men, what sort of men were they? Thus arose the great polemic about the nature of the native. He emerged from it absolved, provided that his past, i.e. his culture, was condemned absolutely. On no other condition could he be saved. His past was the sin which must be wiped out, and his present and future must be governed by the culture of his conquerors.

The native, however, continued his activity underground. His culture remained alive underneath the new world which was coming into being. Even his conquerors began to realize that their position was precarious, and to lose the assurance they had felt as the heirs of an oecumenical culture.

Something they could not express bound them to the conquered country. Thus began the struggle which was to become typical of the Spanish-American way of life. The Spanish Americans were no longer Europeans, yet they rejected any tendency to confuse them with the inhabitants of the American towns. Outwardly, they had conquered those peoples by imposing on them their language, their religion and their culture. Inwardly, however, they felt that everything was different, that it was no longer at all like the world they had left behind. Whatever was imported was marked by something that was American. Outwardly, the result always looked like the European model; but its content was different.

The European who had conquered America and imposed his customs and habits on its natives realized that it was but a "superposition". These were men of whom he both knew and felt that they differed from him. They remained silent and sullen in his presence. When they spoke, they did so in the language he had imposed on them, but the words took on another meaning. These men had been given a religion to replace their own pagan religions, but its rites and devotions belonged to a different world. It was difficult for the Christian to recognize their new religion as authentically his own. Moreover, the idols which had been buried with their temples reappeared as ornaments in the new Christian churches. Their diabolical faces showed in friezes, columns and cornices. They even climbed the altars, and were to be seen among the angelic figures which decorated the cupolas, the Christs and the saints which were the objects of devotion. The cultural world condemned by the Europeans reappeared at religious festivals. Even death had assumed a new character; it was no longer the death of the Christian, for which he must prepare all through his life. Death now took on forms, for example among the Mexicans, which the European could not understand. It seemed that it was death that had been conquered; it had become an everyday thing, like the games played by children.

The European conqueror of the New World was well aware of all this. He felt himself drawn to this world, enveloped and almost hypnotized by it. But he also felt that, were he to let himself go, it would mean renouncing the "universal culture" to which he belonged. Thus began the frenzied struggle which his sons and grandsons were to inherit. The Spanish American began to feel inferior—different, that is, from the European world in which he had been cast—inferior because he was afraid to remain outside the world which had proclaimed itself universal. But instead of trying to understand the underlying causes of this difference, he judged it as his European ancestors had judged that other culture which was foreign to them, by standards which were no longer his own. And in the light of that judgment, the culture which was to be that of the Spanish American emerged reduced in so far as it failed to resemble its model.

CULTURAL CONTACT WITH THE SPANISH WORLD

Spain was the European country to whose lot it fell to colonize this part of America; but at the very moment when she succeeded in this colonization, she lost her sway in Europe. In the old continent, she represented a cultural force which had been conquered in the fight between the Christian and the modern spirit, between the Middle Ages and the New European Age. Spain had at her disposal a huge new world to colonize, but she had lost the battle of Europe. Another nation, England, was to symbolize the ideal of modern man. New forms of life and a new outlook were making their appearance on the horizon of Western culture. Within the bounds of that horizon, Spain clung to the world of which she had once been the paladin. Unable to win Europe over to the Catholic cause, she closed her cultural frontiers, enclosing within them that part of America with whose colonization fate had entrusted her.

Thus Spanish America was converted into one of the bastions of a declining world, a bastion well sealed and well defended to prevent the intrusion of the destructive seed of modernism which was invading and corrupting the Old World. It was the task of the colony to construct that bastion. The Spanish Empire established a social and political barrier, the Catholic Church a spiritual barrier. Their connexion was logical. Both Spain and the Catholic Church knew that whatever happened, the social order established in America would depend on the mentality of the individuals of which its society was composed. If a social and political order were to be stable, the individual must, in the first place, be educated to respect that order; it would, in the colony, depend above all on the appropriate attitude being established beforehand.

In the field of culture, Spain imposed on this part of America the philosophy and the outlook of Christianity, which was at that time passing through a crisis in Europe. This philosophy was scholasticism; but it was no longer the creative scholasticism of a Thomas Aquinas in the thirteenth century, or even the revitalized philosophy of a Suarez in the sixteenth century. The philosophy which was imposed on these countries, as it had been imposed on metropolitan Spain, was already stiff-jointed and toughened by its efforts to defend the aims and interests of the medieval world, then battling against modernism. It was no longer the creative philosophy of an oecumenical order, but the champion of an order which was crumbling on every side.

The idea of a medieval order created by scholasticism was

imposed on the Spanish-American mind together with a sense of respect for, and submission to, the theocratic order represented by Spain. A system of pedagogics was created with a view to training men faithful to Spanish theocracy, and believers no less faithful to the creed which justified it. The Holy See watched carefully to ensure that no change was made in the intellectual order thus imposed, and it was this enforced "protection" which gave rise to many of the complexes from which the Spanish American was later to suffer.

Socially, the colonial institutions derived largely from the contact between conquerors and conquered. The conquerors of North America, like those of the South American plains, encountered nomadic native tribes; and consequently rudimentary forms of culture. The Spaniards, on the other hand, who conquered the American tableland where countries like Mexico, Peru, Colombia, Equador and Bolivia have become established, encountered powerful native cultural groups, whose social organization was so advanced that it was a cause of considerable surprise to the conquerors.

That is why, while the conquerors of the plains—territories which now form the United States, part of Argentina, and Uruguay—had relentlessly to pursue and exterminate the inhabitants, the conquerors of the tableland merely adapted their domination to the cultural and social forms they found there. Only the outward signs were changed; the cultures themselves were allowed to persist. The native masters were replaced by white masters, the gods by Christian images; the result was the "superposing" of which we have already spoken. Where the native had lived, the Spaniard appeared, bringing with him serfdom. Under this process of superposition, a people was converted into an instrument for exploitation.

Matters were different in the plains, where the European, in his struggle with his environment, had to rely solely upon himself. In the uplands, material, i.e. manual, labour was assigned to the servants—in other words, to the natives. In the plains, however, the conqueror was forced, in the absence of foreign hands, to use his own. Thus, in the one case such work became a degrading thing, reserved for the "Indians"; while in the other it became a source of pride, ultimately producing the "self-made man" of North America and the proud "forgers" of the Argentine nation—those who, in the name of "civilization", opposed the "barbarism" of the conquerors of the American tablelands.

As a result, the creative energies of the Spanish Americans remained unproductive, subordinated to the cultural interests defended by metropolitan Spain and to the personal interests which had grown up in the colony. The spiritual barrier established to defend the Catholic outlook (represented by Spain) frustrated every creative effort made at the higher cultural levels, and brought to naught every bold attempt to escape from the orthodoxy laid down by the Church. That orthodoxy prescribed the limits for all painting, poetry, literature, fine art, and philosophy; no new ground could be broken. Baroque became the outlet for Spanish America's creative genius enabling it to escape from the reality imposed on it; for Baroque allowed it to deny that reality, scorn it, and treat it with contempt. Baroque created by denying, by evading; it could not "affirm", since any affirmation was immediately subjected to the test of orthodoxy. Scholasticism again, prevented the Spanish American from seeking an outlet for his creative genius in the field of experimental science. Science, as it was understood in Europe at that time, remained foreign, because it contradicted religion. Revelation took precedence over explanation.

Social conditions in the colony, moreover, rendered science unnecessary. There, man did not have to wrest secrets from nature; he needed no special techniques to make his labour more productive. Labour—manual work—was provided by the native, whose lord and master he was. To live as a lord, all that was needed was the fruit of the earth and the gold and silver that the native, by his labours, could produce. To have any other ambition was to fall into that incoercible and satanic pride which was contaminating the European peoples who had been corrupted by the new philosophy. Thus, the Spanish American brought up in this environment was provided with a solution for every problem—religion, politics, society, art, philosophy, etc.—his creative impulses had to be divorced from reality and confine themselves to the realms of imagination, dreams and Utopias. The future, the morrow would provide him with the means of escape from a reality with which he had no concern. The cultural world in which he found himself struck him as *superposed*, as a crust which one day would have to be broken, a wall that would have to be pierced. The future would doubtless indicate the moment. Though he was a Spaniard to the core, Spanish culture was to become foreign to him; he would seek opportunities for rejecting it. He was to come to feel that which was most profoundly himself as the thing most foreign to him, as something accidental, and therefore useless and devoid of substance.

CONTACT WITH THE MODERN SPIRIT

Despite all precautions, however, the modern spirit in all its forms was to infiltrate into Spanish America. Overcoming or evading every obstacle, the new ideas gradually made their appearance in the colonial world which had apparently been so well defended. Modern philosophical ideas were even found in the Church which was supposed to be responsible for keeping them out. For the Church, which had been entrusted in Spain and America with the task of ensuring that those countries were not contaminated by the new ideas, was itself affected by them. It is a remarkable fact that most of the great men associated with Spanish America's independence were ecclesiastics. Some of them prepared the minds of the Spanish Americans for the claiming of their independence; others even took up arms and died for it. This fact can be explained if we remember that the Church was the only real cultural entity in Spain and Spanish America. It was the Church which decided on the orientation of culture, the Church which stated what might or might not be done. Those most closely connected with the world of ideas, therefore, were the members of the Church; and they were thus the most exposed to contagion from the new ideas that were rapidly evolving.[1]

Confronted with a mode of thought that was no longer creative but mere wellworn formulae which had become meaningless in a changing world, the churchmen themselves began to doubt. Without ceasing to be believers or good Catholics, their mentality began to evolve in the same way as Europe's had evolved as a result of the appearance of modernism. They doubted neither God nor His works, but they did

---

[1] See Olga Victoria Quiroz-Martinez, *La Introduccion de la filosofia moderna en España*, El Colegio de México, 1945.

begin to doubt whether the social and political order preached by the Church and by metropolitan Spain was really the order established by God—whether, in fact, it was His work. They began to distinguish between the human and the Divine, between that which was of the Church and that which was purely political. Reason—that same reason which had become the new God of the new European philosophy—was, after all, also a Divine creation. It was an instrument given to man by God, that he might put it to the best possible use. After all, the two fields—the human and the Divine—should not be confused. Each had its own science. For the Divine, not all the knowledge in the world could suffice, for it must be based on Faith. It was for the human that God had given us reason. Thus faith was confirmed, while at the same time human capacity for action in this world was strengthened.

Once the distinction had been drawn between human and Divine, the teachings of Descartes, Bacon, Locke and Gassendi became the pivot of educational reform in the New World. It was the Church which protested most loudly against scholasticism and its disastrous results. It was the Church which was to plead for the study of the experimental science. Even the Inquisition began to mitigate its action.[1] The polemics between the partisans of the new philosophy and those of scholasticism were to shake the entire American world. Condillac and Newton added their influence to what had gone before. By the end of the eighteenth century, the Spanish state itself was to patronize those doctrines.[2] In the most important cultural centres of Spanish America, the virtues of modernism came to be discussed and proclaimed. In Mexico City, Bogota, Lima, Caracas and Cordoba, minds were to be found which the new philosophy had inspired with a new desire—the desire to know their own world, to feel and make known its greatness and beauty and, at the same time, its capacity for self-sufficiency.

The viceroys of the Spanish colonies, who welcomed this new trend sponsored by the Spanish Bourbon dynasty, could never have supposed that it would result in the struggle which finally gave those countries their independence. Newton had

1 See Monelisa Lina Perez Marchand, *Dos etapas ideologicas del siglo XVIII en México, a través de los papeles de la Inquisicion*, El Colegio de México, 1945.

2 See Bernabé Navarro, *Introduccion de la filosofia moderna en México*, El Colegio de Mexico, 1948; Pablo Gonzalez Casanova, *El masoneismo y la Modernidad cristiana en el siglo XVIII*, El Colegio de México, 1948.

penetrated the universities and, with him, experimental science. From it sprang the desire to know and experiment with America's soil. Scientific work of major importance was carried out. Observatories were built: and expeditions were organized to obtain knowledge of American soil, flora and fauna. The first treatises on these subjects appeared, and a rational study was undertaken of the American past. In all studies of this kind, as we have already indicated, the churchmen occupied a privileged position. The Spanish-American Jesuits, exiled in Italy, revealed a world which had hitherto been hidden. And all the work showed America to be a land of vast promise.

For Spanish Americans, these experiments made America the centre of their lives. For this America, which they were learning to love, they would be ready to give their lives. A land so rich in promise was surely worth all the lives offered for its freedom. Suddenly, to the intense surprise of metropolitan Spain, the telescopes were transformed into guns and rifles, the scientific treatises into declarations of liberty, and the scientists into warriors. Spanish America was taking the first great step towards her independence, which in the first place was to be political independence.

An era of optimism preceded and followed the movement for the political independence of Spanish America. The philosophy of the encylopaedists provided the Spanish Americans with the arguments justifying their country's new claims. Spanish America was at last to make its own history and its own culture—a universal history and culture, like that which France had begun to build with the Revolution. Spanish America, freed from its colonial chains, was to set the feet of its culture on the path of progress. Now it was the Spanish world which was to be judged by standards similar to those it had itself used to judge the native world. In the light of the new philosophy, the colonial world represented the last stronghold of reaction. The colony was a world in a state of sin, opposed by *progress*—an obscure, shadowy and negative world, the last refuge of the reactionary forces which had sought in vain to stand fast in Europe. The revolution of American Independence completed the work of the French Revolution. A new kind of man, freed from his whole past, was entering on his own history. America's dreams were coming true at last, and Utopia was becoming a reality. The imposed Spanish culture was broken; a new kind of man was about to emerge, and with him a new culture, rational and universal.

Yet the Spanish American quickly realized that all his enthusiasm was woven around an illusion; for Spain clung to him most tenaciously. The political ties between Spain and ourselves had been severed, but the inner ties held fast and could not be loosened, even with all the philosophy at our command. Spain was present in spirit, the customs and the habits of the Spanish Americans, and her mark was visible everywhere. Political independence was not enough; a deeper, more radical and more personal emancipation had to be achieved.

SPANISH AMERICA'S STRUGGLE FOR INTELLECTUAL EMANCIPATION

Far from feeling independent, the Spanish American was more aware than ever of his bonds with the Spanish world, from which he thought he had freed himself. This being so, the whole cultural complex he had built up in order to achieve and justify his political independence became a mere useless instrument. The theory of universal man proved false; universal man, whose rights had been proclaimed by the French Revolution, simply did not exist. There existed only individuals, each of whom was unique, with his own faults and limitations; and the Spanish American was but one of these individuals.

Political independence had not been followed by the arrival of that world which had been promised by the new philosophy to every human being simply because he was a man. Except for the political change, everything remained the same. The Spanish American peoples had not achieved their freedom; they had merely changed their masters. The Revolution of Independence had shown that those peoples were incapable of liberty. Not all human beings were entitled to liberty merely because they were human beings. There were those who were born with such a right, and others who were congenitally deprived of it.

Once political freedom had been achieved, the Spanish Americans faced a distressing and sorrowful spectacle—the spectacle of countries decimated by long and interminable

287

revolutions. Anarchy and despotism alternated with one another in a vicious circle. Revolutions became the inevitable consequence of tyranny, and tyranny the consequence of revolutions. Violence was met by violence. Order was essential, but only as a means to survival; government was necessary, but only with a view to subsisting. Spanish America was divided and subdivided, not into nations, but into little political chieftainships *(cacicazgos)*. The War of Independence had been succeeded by a war of vested interests. The battles were now fought for the interests of the clergy, the militia or the military leaders *(caudillos)*. Each group sought to concentrate in its hands the greatest measure of power.

The whole Spanish-American scene, in the nineteenth century, was one of oscillation between two extremes—anarchy and dictatorship. There were dictatorships of every kind— conservative, constitutional, liberal, or personal. There were dictatorships to maintain an order similar to that of Spain, or to establish liberty; dictatorships expressive of "reaction", and dictatorships expressive of "progress". No one cared about the people; no one cared about the liberty of the individuals who only yesterday had set out to conquer that liberty. Modern culture was a something "superposed", which had allowed the Spanish American to cherish the illusion that he could change.

The Spanish American carried the evil in his blood, his mind, his habits and his customs. Only by changing these could he become different. It was then that there arose in Spanish America a Pleiad of men whose object it was to achieve an authentic and sure emancipation from Spain— Sarmiento, Alberdi and Echevarria in the Argentine; Varela and Luz y Caballero in Cuba, Bilbao and Lastarria in Chile, Montalvo in Ecuador, Rodriguez in Venezuela, Mora, Altamirano and Ramirez in Mexico, and many others in all the new countries of Spanish America.

The Revolution of Independence, they said, had been inspired not so much by a spirit of liberty as by the Spanish love of domination present in the blood of all of us. Hence it was only a political, not a social revolution. We wrested Spain's sceptre from her, but we kept her spirit. The struggle had taken place between two Spains; and when it ended, nothing had changed. The same privileges remained, but new privileges had been added to them. The liberators themselves maintained this *status quo*. Spanish America was still the spiritual colony of a living past.

Realizing this, Latin America's spiritual emancipators embarked upon the strange and difficult task of plucking out a part of themselves, their past and their history. With the verve, courage and obstinacy they had themselves inherited from Spain, they set about eradicating Spain from their very being, wherever it appeared, even if in the process they had to leave behind pieces of their own flesh and bones.

The past or the future? That was the question. The choice had to be made and there was no escape. "Republicanism or Catholicism!" cried the Chilean, Francisco Bilbao. "Democracy or Absolutism!", "Civilization or Barbarism!" was the choice offered by the Argentinian, Sermiento. "Progress or Reaction!" demanded the Mexican, José Maria Luis Mora. Liberalism or Tyranny! No compromise solution was possible. The choice was between the absolute predominance of the colony and that of the new ideas. Compromise was ruled out, because the one was in absolute conflict with the other. And in the pursuit of their ideals, one-half of Spanish America set out to exterminate the other, and vice versa; that was the scene in the second half of the nineteenth century. New and bloody revolutions stained the soil of this part of America, to end with the victory of the emancipators.

Yet within himself the Spanish American still carried his past, Spain, just as he carried that obscure and silent world which Spain had fought so fiercely to suppress or at least to cloak, the world of the native. The future—at least, the emancipators' dream of an ideal future, uncontaminated by a rejected past—could not come into being. Despite all their efforts, the Spanish Americans remained Spanish Americans, sons of both Spain and America. The forces that had formed them and that they had not learned to dominate persisted in them, alive and troubling. It was in vain that they had tried to hide them under superposed layers borrowed from other cultures; those layers always cracked, revealing the hidden reality.[1]

---

[1] See the writer's book entitled *Dos Etapas del Pensamiento en Hispano-américa*, El Colegio de México, 1949.

NORTH AMERICA IN THE SPANISH-AMERICAN
CONSCIENCE

Never, surely, has any people been so acutely aware of the existence of another people as the Spanish Americans are, and always have been, of the United States of America. Long before they had achieved their own political emancipation, and throughout the period of their independence, they were aware of North America. At times, it represented their highest ideals; at others, their supreme negation, and a disappointment. Among other things, North America has been largely responsible for the Spanish American's feeling of inferiority. North America has been the ideal never attained by Spanish America.

In the Spanish American's conflict between what he is and what he would like to be, North America symbolizes the latter, just as Spain symbolizes the former. North America was the yardstick for measuring the results of our emancipation. Unfortunately, the results were always negative. "Owing to the fatal sequence of events at the time," said the Argentinian Echeverria, "our revolution began as it should have ended, and worked in a direction contrary to revolutions in other countries. Look at the United States; when colonial power crumbled, democracy was ready, beautifully and well organized, radiant with intelligence and youth, springing from the head of the people as Minerva sprang from the head of Jupiter." The Chilean Francisco Bilbao compared the two Americas and drew negative conclusions from his comparison. "The origin and development of United States society," says Bilbao, "is marked by freedom of thought as an inborn right, the first of all rights; whereas the mutilated freedom proclaimed by the revolutionaries of the South was *subservient* freedom of thought, free research *restricted* to externals, to politics, administration, etc." Why? Because the North was Protestant and the South was Catholic. Because the one believed in freedom to search its conscience, while the other was the mere recipient of dogmas. "Whoever is free when it comes to accepting dogmas must be free when it comes to making laws." That (according to another Chilean, José Victorino Lastarria) is why "in the North the people was sovereign *de facto* and *de jure*. The people made the law and administered all its interests through its own representatives. In Spanish America, the people did not exist; society was uneducated and lived only for the glory and profit of its sovereign, an absolute and natural lord."

The Argentinian, Juan Bautista Alberdi, exclaimed: "The North Americans do not make a song and dance about freedom, they practice it in silence. For them, freedom is not a divinity; it is an ordinary tool, like a pickaxe or a hammer. Washington and his contemporaries fought even more for their individual rights and freedoms than for their country's independence. But in obtaining those rights and freedoms, they simultaneously achieved independence—unlike the South American countries, which obtained political independence, but not individual freedom." Another Argentinian, Domingo Faustino Sarmiento, cried with his usual violence: "Let us recognize the tree by its fruits. They are bad, sometimes bitter, always rare. South America will remain backward, and will renounce its ordained mission as a 'branch' of modern civilization. Let us not stop the United States in their forward march as some have proposed, but rather catch up with them. Let us be America, as the sea is the ocean. Let us be the United States."

But fear was added to admiration. In a country like Mexico, which had felt the impact of North American power in its most wounding form through the loss of more than half the territory of Mexico in the 1847 war, admiration was mingled with the fear of a new attack. "We need colonization," said Justo Sierra, "and manpower wherewith to exploit our wealth. We must pass from the military to the industrial age. And it must be a quick transition because, if we are weak, the giant who is growing next door and coming ever closer . . . will absorb and disband us." And elsewhere he added: "Mexico is destroying itself, while beside us there lives a wonderful collective animal whose huge vitals can never be sated. He is armed to devour, whereas we become daily more fit to be devoured. Faced with this colossus, we are likely to provide evidence for Darwin's theory; in the struggle for existence, chance is altogether against us."

The combined admiration and fear of the United States felt by the Spanish American, together with his desire for emancipation from the habits and customs inherited from the colony, engendered a new philosophy in all these countries, *positivism*. Poor education had made the Spanish Americans what they were; and if what they were was to be changed, their education must be changed. If so, on what model? On the best model of the time—the Anglo-Saxon. The nineteenth century was the Anglo-Saxon century. The British Empire was at the height of its power on the European Continent; in America, too, the Anglo-Saxons set the standards of progress. How, then, was the level of progress attained by those peoples to be reached? By a form of education which would endow a Latin people like the Spanish Americans with the qualities of the Anglo-Saxons. We Latins, said the Spanish-American reformers, are by nature dreamy and deeply mystical, with the absurd result that, instead of disciplining our knowledge by strictly scientific methods, we cultivate our imagination and our taste for dreaming. If we are to change, we must become eminently *practical*, and cultivate experimentation and research. We must be *positivist*, like great peoples—the British and the North Americans who are now setting the standard of progress.

Thus positivism, initially in the French and finally in the English sense, became the official doctrine of all Spanish America; positivism took the place that scholasticism had occupied in the colony. It became the instrument wherewith to establish a new intellectual order, to replace the order imposed by the conquerors. Educational reforms in keeping with the principles of the new philosophy were introduced in all the countries. A new generation, as it were, made its appearance in Spanish America between 1880 and 1900. A new order was established in every country, claiming to be based on the principles of positive science—an order designed to ensure great material comfort for the people. Railways were built, and industries multiplied. An age of progress and great optimism was born. In politics, the words freedom, progress, democracy and order became, virtually speaking, new "programmes". Large-scale immigration into the various Spanish-American countries justified the belief that the long-sought ideal was at last being achieved; for it would give these countries what it had given North America. Spanish America seemed to be approaching nearer and nearer to its model. Other United States were formed south of the Rio Bravo. Yet there were sounds of discontent from certain strata of society; there was talk of "materialism" and "egoism". Despite the various proclamations, education failed to reach all classes. Comfort was not within the reach of all citizens. It was easy to see that there were great social inequalities. In every Spanish-American country oligarchies appeared which seized the reins of power in order to advance their own personal interests. New tyrannies, too, arose, like that of Porfirio Diaz in Mexico. The new railway industries had appeared, but none of them was in the hands of Spanish Americans. Spanish America was but a colony, and a new one at that, the colony of the great European and North American *bourgeoisie*.

The liberalism and democracy of which so much had been heard were still quite unlike their models. At bottom, they were merely words, under whose cloak the old forms of government persisted. All the innovations were simply "superposed". Underneath were the live facts which it had been vainly sought to conceal. The permanent colonial "forces" continued to exercise their sway, although disguised in new raiment. This setback, and North America's intrusion into the Spanish-American countries to protect her own interests, converted admiration into repulsion; not everything was positive in this America which had been taken as a model. Its people, the paragon of freedom, did not act in a spirit of freedom when it came to dealing with other races and peoples. Francisco Bilbao wrote: "They did not abolish slavery in their states, they proved unable to preserve their heroic Indian races. They rose up as champions, not of a universal cause, but of American interests . . . and Anglo-Saxon individualism. . . . That is why they flung themselves upon the South."

Confronted with this negative North America, qualities of which the Spanish Americans had previously been unaware were thrown into relief. "The North has liberty," said Francisco Bilbao, "while the South has theocratic slavery. Yet words and light have sprung from the womb of suffering; we have rolled back the stone from the sepulchre, and buried those past centuries in the tomb of the centuries that were to have been ours." Unlike the United States, we Spanish Americans have had to "organize everything at one stroke. We have had to set the seal on people's sovereignty from out the very midst of our theocratic education. . . . We who are poor have

293

banished slavery from all the southern republics; yet you, who are happy and rich, have not done so." "We have assimilated the primitive races and will continue to do so, because we consider them our own flesh and blood; while you Jesuitically exterminate them." "We do not believe that the earth or the enjoyment thereof is man's supreme aim; we accord to the Negro, the Indian, the disinherited, the unhappy and the weak the respect due to the title and dignity of a human being."

Thus, in the Spanish-American conscience there was born another North America, one which, by contrast, showed up the value of the Spanish American's hidden qualities. In his *Ariel*, José Enrique Rodo, the great Uruguayan master, underlines these differences, noting the points in our favour. "One imitates those," he says, "in whose superiority and prestige one believes.... But I see neither glory nor usefulness in perverting a people's character—that which constitutes its particular genius—in order to compel it to identify itself with a foreign model to which ... it would have to sacrifice the irreplaceable originality of its own spirit.... That amounts to the absorption of a dead thing by a living organism, simply by adding them together." Here, again, we have the idea of superposition. All that education, all those attempts to turn us into Anglo-Saxons by a positivist education, have merely succeeded in giving us a character to which things have been "added", and which is consequently false.

Speaking of North America, Rodo says: "Its prosperity is as great as its inability to satisfy any normal concept of human life.... This people, lacking the deep-seated traditions needed for its own guidance, has proved incapable of replacing the inspiring idealism of the past by a lofty and disinterested concept of the future. It lives for the immediate present, and therefore subordinates its entire activity to the egoism of personal and collective well-being." Other Spanish-American thinkers have the same opinion of this North America which used to be their model. The Mexican José Vasconcelos, setting out his theory on the *Cosmic Race*, says: "How these strong empire-builders must laugh at our provocations and our Latin vanity! Their minds have not the ballast of Ciceronian phraseology, nor has their blood the contradictory instincts which result from the mingling of "subject" races. But they have committed the sin of destroying those races, whereas we assimilate them; and it is that which gives us new rights and the belief in an unprecedented historical mission.... The Latins did what no one in the Anglo-Saxon continent thought of doing." And Antonio Caso, who is fighting positivism in Mexico in order to direct education into other channels, says of the United States: "There are people in the world who have achievements to their credit, but achievements lacking in moral stature. That is why the United States has become and remains dominant. But it should be remembered that, sooner or later, the lofty spirit and the great ideals inherent in the peoples of Latin America will rise above every form of imperialism."

Are we dealing merely with contradictory points of view? Why should there be one outlook which *admires* and another which *rejects*? There is in fact no such contradiction. Each people has a number of facets which are displayed in turn according to its attitude towards other peoples. Spanish America has felt, and continues to feel, admiration for the North America symbolized by Washington asserting the Rights of Man, by Lincoln abolishing slavery, or by Roosevelt interpreting democracy in its universal aspects. But there is also another North America, symbolized by its territorial ambitions, the North America that speaks of "manifest destiny", the America of racial differences and of imperialism. The former, as we have seen, made apparent the defects of Spanish America; the latter showed up its good points. The Spanish Americans had no difficulty in noting that the second North America entered into an alliance with the negative forces of Spanish America, thus perpetuating the colonial spirit against which the latter was vainly battling.[1]

---

[1] On this point, see the writer's works: *El positivismo en México*, El Colegio de México, 1943; *Apogeo decadencia del positivismo en México*, El Colegio de México, 1944; also the previously-mentioned work: *Dos Etapas del Pensamiento en Hispanoamérica*; and the essay entitled "Norte-América en la conciencia hispanoaméricana", published in *Cuadernos Americanos*, in the May and June 1948 issues, as well as the Report presented to the Second Panamerican Philosophical Congress held in New York in 1947 and entitled "The Interpenetration of the Ibero-American and North American Cultures", published by the review *Philosophy and Phenomenological Research*, Vol. IX, No. 3, March 1949.

THE PRESENT CULTURAL CONSCIENCE OF SPANISH
AMERICA

Spanish America is at present fully conscious of the series of
historical vicissitudes of which we have been speaking. The
growing awareness of this historical development has gradually
eliminated the collection of complexes which formerly restricted its creative genius. The underlying cultures which
formed it are now clearly evident, and Spanish America is
now more or less precisely aware of its debt to each, while at
the same time distinguishing its own contribution, i.e. the
characteristics of its own culture. Now, by way of preparation
for fully creative activity, it is concentrating on what we have
here called "self-knowledge", or an understanding of its own
identity. The past—that past which used to be denied in
vain—is now *denied* in the only possible way, namely, by
relegation to history. In every Spanish-American country
there have arisen historians of essentially Spanish-American
ideas, thought, philosophy and culture.

The history they are writing, which is growing steadily in
volume and accuracy, is revealing many facts of importance
for the understanding of Spanish-American culture and of its
relationship to the other cultures with which it has come into
contact. As a result, the feeling of inferiority which seemed to
stamp Spanish-American culture is gradually disappearing,
for its own output is appreciated at its proper value. Its ties
with other cultures are recognized, but according to a more
balanced scheme of values.

As regards European culture, Spanish America knows itself
to be its most direct heir; it knows that it is now becoming
responsible for that inheritance. Inheriting means not imitating, but assuming certain powers. That explains why Spanish
America is concerned at Europe's crises just as if they were its
own. It is no longer content to live in Europe's shadow, but is
genuinely anxious to occupy a responsible position in regard
to Europe.

The Spanish American has now also come to understand
a number of feelings which he formerly did not grasp. He
knows that it is precisely the most American aspects of his
character which drew him towards Europe while simultaneously making him resist complete Europeanization. Ame-

rica felt drawn to Europe as a child towards its father, but at the same time it refused to become the image of its father. That is why, despite all its efforts, its imitations were generally speaking never perfect, but merely "poor copies". It was what made the copies "poor" that was American. Actually, however, the judgments were false, and things were apt to be called "poor copies" that were, in fact, merely "different". The history of our ideas has revealed this error. In the course of his history, the Spanish American has made use of a certain number of ideas imported from Europe; but these were transformed as soon as they came into contact with our world, so much so that it would be difficult for a European to recognize them as his own, even though they have retained their original name. Not so long ago, a well-known French sociologist was horrified at the interpretation given by Spanish America to Auguste Comte's positivism, and regarded it as falsified. Today, we realize that, whereas Europe was creating and recreating its classical writers, we Spanish Americans remained ignorant of ours. And we were ignorant because we based ourselves on a false assumption, insisting that we had no classical writers, because we wanted them to be like those of Europe. We complained that the work of our thinkers, artists and politicians was *different* from the model instead of being *like* it. In other words, we deplored the fact that they had a personality of their own, for in reality that was what made the difference. Today, however, these works are being analysed in a different spirit. From now on we can see what is really ours, what is personal, in the work of Spanish-American writers.

This new Spanish-American attitude to Europe now permits of genuine co-operation. There is no longer any question of denying, just as there had been no question of imitating. Denial would mean adopting a position as false as the earlier one. Whether we like it or not, we are the descendants of European culture. It is from Europe that we have received our general culture and framework—our language, our religion and our customs. Our outlook on life is European in origin. To abandon it would mean abandoning the innermost substance of our being, of our own personality. We can no more deny that culture than we can deny our parents. But just as, without denying his parents, the individual acquires a personality which no one will confuse with theirs, so Spanish

297

America must have a cultural personality which has no reason to be confused with the culture it has inherited. Realizing this, it now demands a place of its own side by side with, or even as part of that culture; and, what is more, a place involving responsibility. It wants to be a collaborator, not an imitator. But what that place shall be will depend on what Spanish America itself can offer.

To us, this dual cultural past of Spanish and native culture is our most intimate substance, the very basis of our existence. Our main task now is to accomplish a process of conscious assimilation, amounting to rehabilitation, of the past. Thereon depends the attainment of a future which hitherto has been built only on dreams.

Many aspects of Spanish-American history have as yet been only imperfectly assimilated. There are still many old grudges, rooted in a past which should already be far away; but at least we realize they are there. In many Spanish-American towns there are still partisans of "native policy" *(indigenismo)* ranged against partisans of "Spanish policy" *(hispanismo)*; many of the problems raised by the original meeting between Spanish and native culture are still matters of dispute. Discussion also centres round the colony and liberalism; but people are beginning to realize that the best way of ending such discussions is to embody them in history. Spanish America will attain cultural maturity only when it has clearly grasped the relationship between the two halves of its being. Once the problems of "Spanish" and "native" policy are no longer subjects of discussion, Spanish America will really become what its name implies—a fusion of the American and the Spanish world within this particular continent.

As for North America, the desire for understanding is mutual. Until quite recently, and apart from exceptional cases, North America's interest in the Spanish-American countries was confined to the economic sphere—at the most, a trader's interest in Latin America as an easy outlet for his goods, or a financier's interest in land for purposes of speculation. That type of interest was only too obvious to the Spanish Americans themselves, and the result was the reaction of men like Rodo, Vasconcelos or Caso. For it meant that North American interest was inevitably confined to a Latin America beset with revolutions, a country of half-savage, turbulent peoples who deserved only despotic governments headed by men who had the approval of the civilized world.

This attitude has changed, and with it that of the Spanish Americans. North America is now interested in Spanish America for other than purely economic reasons; the emphasis is no longer on markets, raw materials or finance. Today, mind is interested in mind; and to this attitude Spanish America responds. One part of America no longer denies the cultural and spiritual gifts of the other. All that is required is continually increasing knowledge, so that there may be a greater measure of understanding.

Conversely, Spanish America no longer aspires to be a second North America, though there is no contempt of the latter implicit in this attitude. Nor does it mean that there is no intention of assimilating a certain number of North American ideas and processes basic to contemporary civilization. We want to adopt from Anglo-Saxon America only those things which we consider essential to Spanish America's development and, for us, the practical spirit characteristic of the North Americans is desirable only in so far as it meets our own particular needs.

SUMMARY BIBLIOGRAPHY

The following works may be consulted in addition to those already mentioned:

CRAWFORD, William Rex. *A Century of Latin-American Thought.* Cambridge, Mass., Harvard University Press, 1944.

FRONDIZI, Rivieri. *Panorama de la filosofia latinoamericana contemporanea.* Buenos Aires, 1944.

GAOS, José. *Antologia del pensamiento de lengua espanola en la edad contemporanea.* Mexico, Seneca, 1945.

———. *Pensamiento de lengua espanola.* Mexico, Stylo, 1948.

HENRIQUEZ URENA, Pedro. *Las corrientes literarias en la América Hispana.* Mexico, Fondo de Cultura Economica 1949.

———. *Historia de la Cultura en la América Hispana,* Mexico, 1947.

INSUA RODRIGUEZ, Ramon. *Historia de la Filosofia en Hispanoamérica.* Guayaquil, 1945.

Spanish Problems through the Ages

Notes on antecedents intended to facilitate the comprehension of certain aspects of Latin America

by

P. BOSCH-GIMPERA

It is difficult to grasp what is really meant by Spain; too often we take a part for the whole. We must also take into account the historical circumstances which have strengthened certain of its tendencies to the detriment of others, as well as certain abnormal internal developments, which, though they took place long ago, still make themselves felt today. A distinction should be made between what may allow the spirit of Spain to become a healthy factor of civilization, and what will lead it into dangerous courses.

An understanding of the civilization and problems of Spain is essential also to an understanding of those of the Americas. This complex world, made up of the evolution, in a propitious environment, of a number of European elements mingled with the indigenous races, can be explained to a large extent only in the light of Spanish influences, often decisive. In order to discover the essence of the American tradition and study its problems, its values and its conflicts, it is therefore first necessary to understand Spain.

THE PROBLEMS OF SPAIN

The first problem—still obscure—is that of the very formation of Spain. Strictly its formation is still incomplete, for the Spaniards do not form one coherent people, conscious of its community of interests and imbued with the same ideas. A territory of diverse topography, climate and resources necessarily involves—and still more so in the past—the existence of fundamentally different ways of life; difficulties of communication further reinforce individual and regional peculiarities.

A second problem arises from the constant failure of endeavours to create a durable cohesive organization. All attempts at political unification have been inspired by foreign models, and have failed to reduce the diversity of the Spanish people. Even those solutions which lasted longest and appeared the most stable, failing to understand the depth of this diversity, based themselves upon the superficial strata of the various ethnic groups of Spain, or only upon some of them at the expense of the others; thus they resulted in building a superstructure without deep roots. The Spanish peoples preserved their personalities; for only from a synthesis which respected their differences could a vigorous and healthy Spain take lasting shape.

A third problem arises from the conflict between survivals from the past—from which Spain is never freed—and new trends. The result is a lag in the evolution of Spain, compared with other countries; new problems are added to old ones which have not yet been solved.

Prevented by the obstacles of history from developing normally, the Spanish temperament, potentially an inexhaustible source of constructive energy, aggravates conflicts and puts new difficulties in the way of the stabilization of the country and the efficient discharge of its undertakings.

DIFFICULTIES RELATING TO A SYNTHESIS OF SPANISH CULTURE

The lack of integration of the elements of the Spanish world into a coherent synthesis, the mere transplanting there of political machinery, and the embarking upon courses foreign to its logical development, have led on numerous occasions to disaster from both the political and cultural points of view. This land of extraordinary vitality and creative fertility sometimes does not advance beyond the institutions of the precursors or the first endeavours to develop them; the effort stops there, stagnation follows creative periods, revivals setting in amidst upheavals are stifled by the violence and by the dead weight of a blind and clogging tradition. And, in spite of all, the Spanish spirit and Spanish culture are a living force, which, although revealing itself intermittently, has from its beginnings risen again and again phoenix-like from the ashes of its seeming annihilation.

The splendid dawn of Spanish culture should not be sought in the Spain of the sixteenth century. Its roots are deeper, and the political course followed since the Renaissance constitutes one of the great deviations in the history of Spain.

It is the same with peoples and cultures as with geography. We see in Spain a world in itself, a world of great and ever-changing variety which takes its form and shape very slowly.

The Spain of old, paralysed in its growth by the Roman Empire, took on new life; we meet it again under the apparent political unification of the Visigoths as under Moorish domination; this Spain it was which led to the formation of the peoples and States of the Middle Ages. The civilization of Rome itself could only establish itself durably in Spain—especially in the east and south—by building upon the Mediterranean links created a thousand years before by Greek and Phoenician settlers. While Romanization and Christianity constitute attempts to absorb the country within Western civilization, Islam, by bringing new values and erecting a new superstructure, stirred up fresh strife, to be sure, but contributed no less towards the cultural growth of the Spanish peoples. Moslem culture itself benefited from the Spanish inheritance, and threw out highly original offshoots. It deeply influenced the peoples who had escaped conquest by the Arabs; France in particular, by its geographical position, came quickly within its orbit, but the whole of Europe was introduced through Spain, to those elements of Greek philosophy and Oriental learning preserved in the lands of Islam which from the eleventh century onwards formed the foundations of European civilization.

Spain might then have known a normal evolution. The Spanish Moslems, acclimatized to the country, nursed no implacable hatred towards the Christian peoples; the germs of the medieval Spanish states existed in the very heart of Moslem regions; as a result, natural affinities led to the formation of groups. Besides the two large inland masses—Leon and Castile—which were in the fighting line, as it were, Galicia maintained contact with Europe and formed a beacon of culture, with its religious centre of Compostella, the goal of pilgrimages from Cluny. In the east, Catalonia, with its Carolingian traditions and its contacts with France and Italy, developed in the direction of industry and shipping and tended to become an organized state in which feudal particularism was balanced by a flexible central organization seated in Barcelona. Catalonia also formed an important centre of culture and served as a link between north and south. The Moslem kingdom of Seville was the natural nucleus of a large Andalusian population distinguished for their art, their literature, their philosophy and their science.

It was on the periphery that, in contrast to the backward "centre", the most important nuclei of culture were situated.

The rise of the military power of Castile and Leon after Alfonso VI marks the first great deviation of the history of Spain in the Middle Ages. The despotic character of that monarch provoked political conflicts bringing him into conflict with the Moslems of Andalusia. As a result of this quarrel, there were renewed invasions by African peoples—the Almoravides and the Almohades—which aroused, by reaction, a crusading spirit. It should be noted that this spirit had just appeared in Europe as a result of the conflicts which had broken out in the Orient between Byzantines and Seljuks. Kept alive by the monks of Cluny in Castilian Spain, which they helped to rally to the purified religious discipline of the West, it brought about a permanent state of war for several centuries, and accentuated the bellicose character of the Castilian Church and aristocracy, while worsening the already unbalanced territorial and economic situation of the Christian states. Beside Portugal and Catalonia, stabilized and directing their energies towards the exterior, the kingdom of Castile was a growing and unbalanced power, perpetually at war either on its frontiers or within them. It was a land of agriculture and of cattle-breeding, which left industries and commerce to the Moslems under its rule and to the non-absorbed Jews. This was a new source of unbalance with regard to the periphery of the Mediterranean (Catalonia) or the Atlantic (Portugal and, rather later, the Basque country).

During the last centuries of the Middle Ages, the culture of all the Spanish peoples revived. And it was again in Catalonia that it was most developed—Catalonia, now become the nucleus of a confederation comprising Aragon, the province of Valencia and the Balearic Islands, and maintaining relations with Sicily and Italy, and having wide commercial relations in the Mediterranean, Africa and the East. We may observe in Catalonia and the confederate countries a democratic evolution in advance, in some respects, of that of other peoples of the peninsula and even of the rest of Europe—with a parliamentary system imposed on the princes, and an executive based on popular representation. We may also find there an entirely successful attempt to maintain cohesion among political groups of different natures and cultures. From a cultural point of view we might point to the philosophy of Lully and of Sebonde, and the political science of Eiximenis; as well as to an art and literature in close contact with France and Italy. The Renaissance was felt very early in Catalonia, and from there spread to the other Spanish peoples. Castile—heir to the traditions of Compostella, and of Jewish and Islamic learning spread by the translators of Toledo and by Alfonso X—created an original literature. Although the monarchy remained authoritarian and militarist—the heritage of the Visigoth traditions of the state of Leon—the Castilian people grouped themselves into *comunidades* (species of autonomous republics under the sovereignty of the king) and struggled to preserve the democratic spirit which was still alive in the municipal organizations, even though it had failed in the Cortès.

There existed at all times a certain peninsular solidarity, with tendencies towards political co-ordination, side by side with the organization of a cultural community and the establishment of relations between the peoples; neither the diversity of languages nor the particularism of institutions were obstacles in this respect.

The personal union of the kingdoms, heralded for some time, was hastened by the extinction of the Catalan dynasty, and by the tenacity and skill of John II (Trastamara) of Aragon, who brought about the union of the thrones by the marriage of Ferdinand and Isabella. It was perfectly natural that the Spanish world should seek a greater measure of co-ordination at a time when vast territorial units were being formed in Europe. The marriage of the Catholic kings was not the first manifestation of this trend; it was the outcome of a historical process. Neither was it an attempt at true unification; it was a personal union between crowns, for the separate organizations in each country remained almost intact until 1714, when the first Bourbon introduced a form of centralization modelled on the France of Louis XIV. A first attempt, made under Philip IV by Olivarez, who was obsessed by the example of Richelieu, came to nothing and helped to provoke the Wars of Secession, during which the union with Portugal achieved by Philip II collapsed and separatist movements arose, not only in Catalonia but also in Aragon, and even in Andalusia.

It will be said that it was Spanish particularism which prevented the formation of a coherent whole. The failure was due rather to attempts at union made by methods contrary to the character of the peoples. The growth of absolutism—the result of the general tendencies in monarchies at the end of the Middle Ages, reinforced by Roman Law—conflicted with the tradition of political freedom; this tradition first succumbed in Castile, especially under Charles V. Castile, which was "nearer" the kings (whose aristocracy was used by the kings themselves and whose people found a distraction in the glories of foreign wars and in the American enterprise), was the first to fall asleep. Portugal, on the other hand, having lived through its great age of discovery, would not resign itself to the role of a satellite, and gained its independence, which it fortified by the alliance with England. As for the kingdoms of the eastern periphery—far removed as they were from the enterprises of the crown, and treated as rebels when they sought to fight to maintain their ancient liberty—they remained true to their traditions and characters.

The forcible unification brought about by Philip V seemed definitive because the peoples (weary of the struggle) submitted to it, in the same way and for the same reasons as they had bowed to the absolute rule of the Catholic kings and Charles V. In the nineteenth century the problem of the peoples arose once again; there was a linguistic and cultural revival, followed by "regionalist" and "nationalist" tendencies which some politicians and thinkers thought they could co-ordinate into a federalist system. There is every reason to suppose that the new venture of achieving unity by violence will leave the problem still unsolved.

THE DEVIATION OF SPANISH HISTORY FROM ITS NORMAL COURSE

The end of the fifteenth century and the reign of the Catholic kings mark a crucial period. It is the beginning of the political and cultural greatness of Castile, now tending to occupy first place in the Spanish world, and taking the imperial road; but the empire was ephemeral; it ruined Spain and brought about its decadence, entailing tragic consequences whose effects are felt even today. The formation of the empire was, moreover, due to chance; it was the outcome of the convergence of numerous factors which were all present at the time and caused a considerable deviation in the history of Spain, similar to that of the eleventh century.

At the moment when the reconquest was about to come to an end, a first stroke of chance opened the New World to the Spaniards. The Portuguese had systematically engaged in exploration and discovery, the most brilliant period being that of Manuel I and the Infante Henry the "Navigator". Spain had not the same tradition, except for the exploration attempted by the Catalans in Africa (where they preceded the Portuguese and organized a large-scale policy of intervention in Algeria and Tunisia), their commercial relations with Egypt and the East, and the conquest of the Canaries by Castile, which later attempted expansion in North Africa. Failing to find support from the King of Portugal for his project to discover the route to India via the West, Columbus turned to Castile, which—after much hesitation—decided to aid him. Originally, indeed, the project aroused little interest, and even after the discovery there was some disappointment until territories richer than the West Indies had been conquered.

America was enough to absorb the energies of Spain, released at the end of the internal wars; and the riches of America could have helped to create a prosperous country, just as overseas power made England and the Netherlands prosperous, had Spain confined its foreign policy within the limits which its peripheral position seemed to dictate. For her prestige in Europe she could have been content with her Italian policy, which was then following the line of the Catalan expansion in the Mediterranean during the Middle Ages. Even if they had given rise to conflicts, in particular with France, the Italian wars would not have been catastrophic for the future of Spain. But chance was to intervene a second time, in the form of the marriage of Juana and Philip of Hapsburg. Regarded as an alliance with a dynasty personifying the Holy Roman Empire, and consequently as a means of giving the kings of Spain fresh prestige and reinforcing the balance of power in Europe, this marriage put the Spanish Crown into the hands of Charles V, Emperor of Germany, and plunged Spain into the whirlpool of the politics and problems of the Empire.

At that moment the destiny of Spain was changed; until the Peace of Westphalia, and even up to the establishment of the new dynasty at the beginning of the seventeenth century, she was to bear the consequences of Charles V's European policy, and finally become a satellite of the Holy Roman Empire. The Wars of Religion, in which Spain championed the impossible ideal of Catholic unity, exhausted her and caused her to lose her privileged position in Europe. In the times of Charles V and Philip II, Spain maintained her supremacy only at the cost of the blood of her sons, and by wasting the substance of her American treasure in the payment of her armies and the maintenance of their prestige.

It was chance once more which put an end to the conflict between Spain and Europe; the degeneration and sterility of the last Spanish Hapsburg made Spain a satellite of France, which installed a French prince on the throne. Henceforth Spain had no weight in the destinies of Europe, where her former power was recalled only as one recalls a nightmare of the past.

The internal consequences were no less disastrous for the Spanish Empire. At the beginning of the modern period, when the wars against the Moors and the state of internal anarchy overcome by the Catholic kings had ended, it was a natural sequence that the authority of the state should be reinforced and its structure organized, the work undertaken by Ferdinand and Isabella, and continued by Charles V and Philip II, being developed. The liaison with the empire, and the religious mission assumed by Spain, led Spanish absolutism into excesses quite foreign to the other monarchies of Europe; Philip II instituted a régime which would today be called totalitarian, concerning himself with everything, and using for his own political ends an Inquisition which became a monstrous system of espionage, a menace overhanging every country. Only those with "pure" Christian blood escaped the purges; all Jewish "contamination" was tracked down, and was enough to serve as a bar to the holding of certain honours and certain posts; scientific books were subject to a censorship which examined every word in them; it was forbidden to study abroad, except in certain specified universities. Thus a government, which should have set up a well-ordered and efficient system for making the best of the country's natural resources and organizing economic life, degenerated into a captious bureaucracy.

The new difficulties proved too much for the country's economy. Elements which could have played an important part were eliminated; the balancing factor which Catalonia might have represented was disregarded, and Catalonia itself declined. Yet its long commercial, industrial and maritime tradition might have proved most useful for the American ventures. The installation of the Turks at Constantinople had put an end to trade with the East, but Catalonia would have found in the American trade a compensating factor profitable, at the same time, to Spain as a whole. Yet the Catalans, and with them the subjects of the other Catalano-Aragonese kingdoms, were pushed aside because they were "foreigners" in Castile, for whom the benefits of the Discovery were reserved. The expulsion of the Jews and the Moors—the best business men, and the most skilled farmers—did great harm to the rich parts of Spain; it was fatal to agriculture (still in a primitive stage) and cattle-breeding, on both of which the economy of Castile was based. Castile was to become almost deserted by the end of the seventeenth century; moreover, it had to bear the sole burden of the taxes which the other kingdoms, virtually excluded from European enterprises, refused to pay.

The result was a deviation in cultural development, and a decadence arising from a state of unbalance and internal unhealthiness, from which Spain has never recovered.

In order to strengthen their authority and eliminate any factors making for decomposition, the Catholic kings decided to achieve religious unity by every means that lay to hand—if necessary, by violence—by seeking their strongest support in the Church: a recourse to the tradition of the medieval "political and military" Church in Castile.

The objects were clear—to fortify authority by eliminating all political or religious dissent, and to give the royal authority the "transcendent" character of a religious mission, in accordance with that crusading outlook, conducive to fanaticism, which certain sectors of the political Spanish Church had infused into the reconquest.

The result was a feverish combination of spiritual disunity and ossification, of formal orthodoxy and scepticism. Moreover, with the passing of the scholastic revival, which bore so original, deep and detailed an imprint at the time of Arias Montano, Lainez and Suárez, there set in a period of philosophical and religious sterility.

The spirit of the Renaissance, to which Spain seemed to have given so marked an impulse, was eclipsed. There was no longer any following for the ideas of the great pioneers of modern thought—for the generous humanism of Vives and Valdès, or for the courageous outlook of Vitoria, who challenged the ethics of the wars and conquests of Charles V or for those who, like Las Casas, took up the defence of the American Indians, while postulating the bases of international law and so aiding the work of Grotius. Nor was there any fertile soil for the democratic trends in the political science of Fox Morcillo, Suárez and Mariana, who tried to prescribe limits for absolutism and to make the royal will subject to a rule of law stemming from collaboration with the people, and who upheld the theory of "power derived from the community". Vives lived abroad; Valdès, too, left Spain, and Vitoria's book had to await its author's death before it could find a publisher at Lyons.

As for inventions and the natural sciences, the medieval heritage of Arab and Jewish science was lost; and the revival, though productive of remarkable results, did not proceed beyond the pioneering stage, the pioneers often lapsing into obscurity, as in the case of Servet's discovery of arterial circulation. In the arts, the Golden Century placed its last creations at the service of the Church, the kings and the aristocracy, whose wealth contrasted sharply with the desperate poverty of the masses.

It was the swan song of a world that was disintegrating.

None of his contemporaries, and only a mere handful of minds that came after, grasped the underlying message in the life of Cervantes and his Don Quixote—a symbol of the bitterness bred of failure in an enterprise enthusiastically begun by a young, vigorous and exceptionally gifted people, but a people made to strive towards unattainable ends and forgetful of essential tasks. Like Don Quixote attacking the windmills, the Spain of Philip II—who failed to exploit the victory of Lepanto, and turned a deaf ear to Cervantes' appeals that the slaves in the prisons of Africa should be succoured—persisted in its hostility to the Netherlands and England and sent its armada on its voyage of defeat. These are the reasons, among others, that make Don Quixote a masterpiece of Castilian genius; brought forth in sorrow by Cervantes, it is, in the guise of an "adventure" novel, a symbol of the virtues and defects of the Spain in which he lived.

THE CONSEQUENCES OF THE DEVIATION

While, in Europe, the Renaissance led to the philosophic and scientific expansion of the seventeenth century, Spain wilfully remained, right up to the eighteenth century, in ignorance of everything that was taking place abroad; even under the Bourbon dynasty she shunned all "dangerous" French innovations, and persisted in the most arid and obscurantist medieval tradition, clinging to decadent scholasticism and formal Aristotelianism. Thus the University of Salamanca refused to establish a chair in the new science of mathematics, and Madrid resisted all plans for the dredging of rivers because "it would be contrary to the plans of God, who would have made them navigable had He judged fit to do so".

It is hardly surprising that a spiritual rift took place between Spain and Europe, who were already, owing to Spain's connexion with the Hapsburgs, in opposite political camps. Europe regarded Spain as a fanatical and backward country, opposed to all progress—forgetting what was owed to Spain, and the tremendous influence it had exercised at the time of its greatness. The "black legend" arose; created by William of Orange's propaganda pamphlet, it culminated in Masson's article on Spain in the Encyclopaedia. The legend disturbed the Count de Floridablanca, Charles III's minister, and he issued replies to it; but they achieved no publicity, and were without effect. Moreover, they announced Spain's pride that it had neither a Descartes nor a Newton but that it had nevertheless produced philosophers and legislators who "preferred to work for the good of humanity, rather than create imaginary worlds (!) in the solitude of a dusty study".

Spain, then, persisted in its errors; and though it began to cast off its old skin, thanks to certain leaders of thought who approved new trends and supported the enlightened ministers of Ferdinand VI and Charles III, it remained fettered to its obscurantist tradition, hostile to all change and regarding every novelty as a form of decadence. It dreamed of a return to the glories of the sixteenth century, a "paradise" that had been "lost" through the fault of those countries which had become contaminated by modern heresies, had woven a hateful conspiracy against the "champion of the faith", and had sought, by their intrigues, to annihilate the power of Spain.

The fragile nature of the vaunted "spiritual unity" was soon revealed. In a Spain divided in two, the rift widened daily and gave rise to ideological struggles and irreconcilable political hatreds; there being no possibility of compromise, periods of progress alternated with periods of reaction, in a welter of internal disorder and savage repression. To Europe and America, from time to time, came masses of refugees, including, often, the intellectual leaders. It was only to be expected that no progressive solutions or moderate opinions could make themselves felt and that extreme views, on either side, held the field. Isolation was no longer possible for Spain, and the country was drawn into European currents; but their influence came too late, and failed to result in the establishment of stable institutions. Even when, in apparently normal periods, a constitutional régime seemed on the point of taking shape, something always happened to interfere with the process.

The traditions of the older Spain still lingered on, clogging progress and often definitely preventing it. It was impossible to operate, on a regular basis, institutions that were attacked from all sides; the oligarchies were in command, and changes in either direction took place, not by legal and peaceful evolution, but by a process of revolutions and "pronunciamentos", which often involved fearful civil war. This was the scene in

Spain in the nineteenth and even the twentieth century. During the Napoleonic Wars, the principles of the 1789 French Constitution were adopted there; but the Cadiz Constitution of 1812 was in effect set aside by Ferdinand VII on his return, and, though reinstated by the Revolution of 1820, it turned out to be short-lived. After the new period of reaction, and amid the upheavals of the Carlist War, a Charter similar to that of Louis XVIII was issued by the Regent Maria Cristina—the *Estatuto Real*—and under Isabella Spain adopted a new "Orleanist" constitution supported by military reactionaries who prevented the '48 revolution from having any repercussions in Spain. Of that revolution the revolution of '68 may be regarded as the delayed equivalent, just as the First Republic of '70 may be considered the equivalent of the Second French Republic. For long the Restoration remained an "Orleanist" régime, only becoming democratically-inclined and constitutional at a much later stage; especially in the country districts, various cliques maintained a real dictatorship *vis-à-vis* the local authorities who were protected by the oligarchy. Militarism still held on to its political influence, even though it had failed in its wars against the last of the subject peoples overseas, on whom a colonial system was still imposed although the rest of the American continent had shaken it off in the time of Ferdinand VII. King Alfonso XIII, who aimed at exercising personal authority, set up, in agreement with the army, Primo de Rivera's dictatorship. The 1931 Republic might be compared, allowances being made for the interval, with the Third French Republic of 1870; it came to grief, after trying to deal with all the unsolved problems left over from previous centuries, as well as the more current ones—the co-ordination of the various peoples, the religious, agrarian and military problems, education and social questions. Once more civil war broke out.

It is a constant proof of the Spanish people's great vitality that the slightest period of peace or normal internal conditions is followed by a cultural revival, or by economic reconstruction, often taking place apart from the state or in despite of it. The state is nearly always something artificially superimposed upon the country. As the bases of its constitution are nearly always in process of discussion, the state, instead of inspiring and organizing the forces of the people, holds them back and paralyzes them. There are many examples of this. Though the economic and cultural revival of the eighteenth century was supported by the ministers of Ferdinand VI and Charles III, the state on the whole had little part in the industrialization of Catalonia and the Basque country in the nineteenth century, the hard-won participation of the intellectual leaders in the philosophical and scientific movements throughout Europe, the revival of the universities and the new output in art and literature which have gained, for Spanish writers, artists and scientists, new prestige and new respect abroad.

This Spanish world—so varying in aspect, never settled, perpetually in search of balance and stability—develops and flowers throughout history with its complex and strongly marked characteristics, amid a series of struggles and inner contradictions. It is hampered by century-old obstacles, and weighed down by a superstructure which it never succeeds in regarding as its own. Often deflected from its normal course, it advances by jerks. Its scene is dominated by contrasts—the contrast between the imposing but grim and austere Castilian landscape and the gay attraction of Andalusia and the Mediterranean littoral, matched by the contrast in the character of the people, who may be either gay or preoccupied, leading their strenuous lives, impetuous and passionate, in perpetual "agony", as Unamuno says, and, to use his expression again, imbued with the "tragic nature of life".

In the extension of the Spanish world to America, we find the same conflicts and complexities, heightened by the surroundings of another continent. On the one hand, we have the continuation of purely Spanish development; on the other, its adaptation to the lands of the immense New World and a mixing or clashing with the latter's races, resulting in the formation of new nations with new characteristics. Here, conquest and the settlement of masses of immigrants do not partake of pure "colonialism". The tendency is to create new "Spains"—organized as new kingdoms—to which the Creoles feel themselves at once attached, though often struggling against the structure imposed by the mother country. The lines on which these Spanish peoples have evolved and the varying nature of their contacts with the native races explain the differences between them; but that does not mean that, once freed from the mother country's control, they escape from the complications, from the "agony" of Spain. In the synthesis effected between its old cultures (whether developed or still in the primitive stage) and the culture of Spain, Spanish America, though embarking on a new history, bears the clear imprint of the Spanish heritage, with all its virtues and defects.

BIBLIOGRAPHY

BOSCH-GIMPERA, P. "España, un mundo en formación", *Mundo Libre*. Mexico, 1943. No. 19–20.

———. "España", *Anales de la Universidad de Valencia*. 1937.

———. "Factores progresistas y retardatarios en la historia de España", *Revista de Indias*. Bogota, 1946.

———. *El poblamiento y la formación de los pueblos de España*. Mexico, Universidad Nacional, 1945.

———. "Cervantes y un momento crucial de la historia de España", *Cuadernos Americanos*. Mexico, July-August 1938.

———. "El problema religioso en Espana", *Espana Nueva*, Mexico, 1947. No. 105–106.

GRANADOS, M. *España y las Españas*, Mexico, 1950.

DE ALBORNOZ, A. "España, haz de pueblos", *España libre*. New York, 23 April 1953, p. 3

CALMETTE, J. *La formation de l'unité espagnole*. Paris, Flammarion, 1946.

CASTRO, Americo. *España en su historia; Cristianos, moros, judíos*. Buenos Aires, Losada, 1948.

SÁNCHEZ-ALBORNOZ, C. *España y el Islam*, Buenos Aires, Editorial Sudamericana, 1943.

———. *La España musulmana*, Buenos Aires, 1945.

———. "Sensibilidad política del pueblo castellano en la Edad Media", *Revista de la Universidad de Buenos Aires*. 1948, No. 5, p. 77 ff.

MENÉNDEZ PIDAL, R. *La España del Cid*. Madrid, 1929.

———. *El imperio hispánico y los cinco reinos; dos épocas de la estructura política de España*. Madrid, 1950.

———. *Introduction to Vol. I of Historia de España*. Madrid, Espasa-Calpe, 1947.

GIBERT, R. "Observaciones a la tesis del imperio hispánico y los cinco reinos", *Arbor*, Madrid, March 1951. XVIII, No. 43.

CARRETERO NIEVA, L. *Las nacionalidades españolas*. Mexico City, 1948. Supplements to *Las Españas*.

SOLDEVILA, F., and BOSCH-GIMPERA, P. *Historia de Catalunya*, Mexico, 1946.

NICOLAU D'OLWER, L. *Del patriotismo i la democracia en el procés institucional de la Catalunya antiga*. Barcelona, 1933.

DE FIGUEIREDO, F. *Las dos Españas.* Mexico City, 1944. Re-publication.

MARAÑON, G. *El conde-duque de Olivares.* Madrid, 1936.

AZAÑA, M. *Una política.* Madrid, 1932, p. 432 ff.

DE UNAMUNO, M. *Vida de Don Quijote y Sancho, "Collección Austral".* Buenos Aires, Espasa-Calpe.

MACKAY, J. A. *The Other Spanish Christ; A Study in the Spiritual History of Spain and South America.* New York, Macmillan, 1932.

DE MADARIAGA, S. *Ingleses, franceses, españoles, "Collección Austral".* Buenos Aires, Espasa-Calpe.

ZAVALA, S. "El contacto de culturas en la historia de México", *Cuadernos americanos.* Mexico, 1949, No. 4. (Unesco enquiry on the relations between cultures.)

ARCINIEGAS, G. *Este pueblo de América.* Mexico, Fondo de Cultura Económica, 1945.

PICÓN SALES, M. *De la conquista a la independencia.* Mexico, Fondo de Cultura Económica, 1950. 2nd ed.

The African Negroes
and the Arts of Carving and Sculpture

by

MICHEL LEIRIS

The year 1920—which may be regarded as typical of the period following the first world war—seems to be an important date in the history of European interest not only in what was then almost always known as "Negro art"—a slightly condescending term, however full of admiration its users may have been—but, more generally, in the artistic products of the Negro peoples. Gobineau himself, that propounder of racial theories, had acknowledged as early as 1854 that those peoples possessed "in the highest degree the sensuous faculty without which no form of art is possible".[1] In 1920, the year after Devambez, the Parisian picture dealer, had arranged the first African and Oceanian exhibition ever to be held in an art gallery, we find various indications that there were already quite a number of people, at least in France and Germany, interested in African native art and literature. In Munich, for instance, a new edition of Carl Einstein's *Negerplastik*, first published in Leipzig in 1915, was brought out by Kurt Wolff; that work, by a poet and art historian, was the first important study of African and Oceanian sculpture, considering it from the Cubist point of view. The same year, Hermann Bahr's *Expressionismus* was published by the Dolphin-Verlag, also of Munich; this contained three reproductions of Negro sculptures, which were included for the purpose of comparison with the works of European artists belonging, or regarded as belonging, to the expressionist movement. In Paris—where jazz had made its appearance even before the end of the 1914–18 war, and was quickly to arouse enthusiasm among many musicians, some of whom in fact drew inspiration from it—the Editions de la Sirène published a selection from the oral literature of

---

1 *Essai sur l'Inégalité des Races Humaines*, Book II, Chapter VII.

the African Negroes, compiled by the traveller and writer, Blaise Cendrars, under the title of *Anthologie Nègre*. In its third issue, published in April, *Action*, a literary and modern art review, edited by Florent Fols, printed an article entitled "Opinions sur l'Art Nègre", containing a number of critical comments on African statues, masks and other objects. This was a public recognition of the growing vogue among cultivated Frenchmen for these works, which were from then on to be found in many private collections; previously, only a few individuals, apart from one or two colonial officials and specialized ethnographers, had been interested in them.

Among the prominent people in various walks of life whose opinions were briefly set forth in *Action* were the Orientalist, Victor Goloubeff, the art-dealer and collector, Paul Guillaume, the Fauve painter, Maurice de Vlaminck, and three cubist artists—the sculptor Jacques Lipchitz, and the painters Juan Gris and Pablo Picasso.[1] Side by side with these artists, all four of whom belonged to what was then generally known as the *avant-garde*, and poets like André Salmon, Jean Pellerin and Jean Cocteau, stood the illustrious name of the late Guillaume Apollinaire, whose death had occurred less than 18 months before, but whose renown had already spread far beyond professional literary circles. His interest in Negro art had been shown in many ways: in one of his most famous lyrics, the opening poem in the collection entitled *Alcools*, he had called upon the "fetishes of Guinea and the South Seas" which he had then had in his room; in his "Soupirs du Servant de Dakar", a poem written in the firing-line during the war he was not to survive, he had conjured up the life of Africa; exotic images like *lacs nègres, câpresses vagabondes*, and *chabines marronnes* abounded in his work, while the "surrealist drama" *Les Mamelles de Tirésias* was set in a Zanzibar of his own imagining. To represent his views, *Action* chose a prose extract from "La Vie Anecdotique", a regular feature in the *Mercure de France*, in which he had for several years written not only as a student of folklore but also as a commentator on current events. On more than one occasion, the subjects he chose for

---

1 Picasso was certainly one of those whose attention was very early attracted to so-called "native" objects, but the person who collected the opinions set out in this article contented himself with attributing to him—possibly not altogether without spitefulness—the sweeping sally: "Negro art? Never heard of it!"

his articles and the ideas he expressed in them were deliberate departures from strict anecdotage, as witness the two pages, from which *Action* reproduced its extracts, written in April 1917 on what (without going too closely into the accuracy or otherwise of terms which no one had at that time considered critically) he calls "the fetishistic sculpture of the Negroes".

Although the comments included were generally favourable, since the editors had obviously planned to pay a tribute rather than to conduct an impartial inquiry, they were not all equally enthusiastic. It is to be noted, for instance, that Paul Guillaume—who was the most appreciative of all—has no hesitation in describing African sculpture as "the fertilizing sperm of twentieth-century intellectual life", whereas Jean Cocteau—less partisan but certainly no less dogmatic in his assertions—seems to be concerned with nothing more than the fashion in art when he says, summing up his views (at least as presented in *Action*), that "the artistic crisis about Negro art has become as tiresome as Mallarmé's Japanism". But, though opinions varied, one point emerges clearly—there must be a similarity between trends of African sculpture, at least in some of its features, and certain aspects of recent Western art, since several distinguished representatives of the latter are explicit in their praise of the former, or, at least, record the fact that it is viewed with sympathy in the circle to which they belong. The question is, therefore, whether to admit at once that an exotic form of art—long regarded as, at best, a curiosity—has exercised a decisive influence on the Western world, or whether to say simply that there has been a convergence—in the history of taste rather than in the history of art properly speaking—similar to that which accounted for the impressionist painters' and the symbolist writers' infatuation with the Far East.

It is common, in books on the history of the great new movements, such as fauvism and cubism, which developed in the arts in the early years of the twentieth century, to find Vlaminck credited with the "discovery" of Negro art. This is regarded as extremely important, since the growing gulf which gradually became apparent between the plastic experiments of Vlaminck's contemporaries and the various methods previously used by painters to represent creatures and things on canvas is largely attributed to it. Firmly established as this legend is, and Vlaminck himself did more than a little to spread it, it is however by no means true that Vlaminck was the only one of the fauves and cubists to be struck, at a very early date, by the remarkable quality of Negro sculpture, which led some people, including Guillaume Apollinaire, to compare it with the art of the ancient Egyptians. But, while it is equally untrue to say that "Negro" works—a term long applied indiscriminately, in these circles, to sculptures from Africa and the South Sea Islands—were the most important factor in the development of cubism, it cannot be denied that they were of inestimable help to artists like Picasso and Georges Braque, even if only as possible witnesses for the prosecution in the case which these two painters and theirs fellows were making out against Western naturalistic art.

As early as 1908, a collection of some twenty "Negro" works, in the sense in which the term was then used, had been assembled by Henri Matisse, while André Dorain owned a mask from the Congo and Braque another African mask. In 1907, Picasso—one of whose studios was to be symbolically transformed by Apollinaire into that of "l'Oiseau du Bénin", Croniamantal's painter friend in *Le poète assassiné*—already had a statue from the Marquesas, among other exotic works, in his house. While the idea of a revelation entirely attributable either to Vlaminck or to any other contemporary artist is therefore untenable, it is true not only that there was something in the air which aroused the interest of all these painters in the arts of the so-called "primitive" peoples, but also that those, at least, who were labelled cubists had quite consciously borrowed some specific features from Negro sculpture.

Academic art, as a result of its rigid training in the use of outworn formulas, was steadily losing vigour. Impressionism, which had undoubtedly once marked a needed effort to get back to essentials by painting direct from the subject and seeking to reproduce sensation in its pristine freshness, had ended, in consequence of its excessive emphasis on light and light's ephemeral play on the surface of objects, by producing canvases in which everything appeared to merge into a coloured mist, and in which material things were treated not as permanent but in their most fugitive guise, as the light fell on them at a particular season or a particular time of day. Breaking away from the withered formalism of academic art,

319

and reacting against impressionism, the cubists returned to a form of painting in which outlines were sharper, and which aimed at depicting something more than the immediate outward semblance of objects, and tried instead to penetrate to the very essence of their material being. Old resources like perspective and chiaroscuro were rejected as mere tricks to secure an easy effect. Painters now sought to grasp the inner reality of things they painted, not merely as they appeared to the eye, but by grappling directly with their subjects in a way which completely revolutionized their work. When we consider the state of mind in which these artists were, and the need they felt to develop a new artistic alphabet, less staled by use than the old—whose symbols were to be grouped on the canvas as it were organically, instead of simply decoratively or as a means of filling up space without any great significance—we can understand why they were so interested in forms of art which seemed like new languages to those who sought a new and more vigorous mode of expression in painting. But, just as the impressionists had turned to the art of the Far East because of certain affinities they found in it—the love of nature, the concentration on detail rather than the whole, the taste for decorative composition—it is a legitimate supposition that there were certain positive affinities which led the cubists to turn to the art forms of the so-called "primitive" peoples and, particularly, to those of the Africans. This is attested, for instance, by some of Picasso's works even prior to his usually recognized "Negro period" (1907–09)—a designation based admittedly, on somewhat superficial and accidental similarities. There is other evidence of it in the borrowing of techniques to which we referred above, such as Picasso's use—in the works he did in 1913, where a cylinder (or cone) in relief represents the hole in a guitar—of the process employed on the lower Ivory Coast to represent the eyes in many types of *wobé* and *dan* masks, as well as in those from the Sassandra region.[1]

As Eckart von Sydow suggests,[2] the reason for the sympathy

---

[1] In a study of "L'Art Nègre et le Cubisme" in *Présence Africaine*, No. 3, pp. 367–77, Paris, March to April 1948, Daniel-Henry Kahnweiler, who was a close friend of the main protagonists of the movement throughout, draws attention to the extreme importance of such borrowing, describing it as a "decisive discovery... which made it possible for painting to coin symbols, freed sculpture from the tyranny of the block and gave it transparency".

[2] "African Sculpture", in *Africa*, Vol. I, p. 210 ff.

of movements like cubism in France and expressionism in Germany towards African Negro art is to be found, in the first case, in the "architectural character" of African works, which was bound to appeal to artists who were mainly concerned with plastic problems, and, in the second, more romantically, in what Sydow calls their "mystic emotional content". The study of the form and significance of this sculpture—which has such deep affinities with Western works and which may be said to have brought about an upheaval by which all contemporary art, and even our conception of the world, has been affected—is thus of very real and practical interest; it is not simply inspired by the curiosity of scholars or dilettantes in search of some new thing, which too often accounts for the attraction exercised by what is distant in space or time. Apart from the fact that such a study will help us to define the nature and limitations of the convergence we have mentioned, it is not unreasonable to suppose that it will also, incidentally, supply a means of assessing what the civilizations of Africa might contribute, more generally, to world civilization.

Far from being evenly distributed throughout what, in France, is usually called *l'Afrique Noire* (equatorial Africa) in contrast to *l'Afrique Blanche* or North Africa, African Negro sculpture is, broadly speaking, confined to an area comprising the forest belt and part of the savannah lands. According to Mr. James Johnson Sweeney,[1] "the northern boundary of this region might be drawn from the mouth of the Senegal River on the Atlantic coast in the west, running east across the top of the great bend of the Niger and along the shores of Lake Chad, and then south-east along the northern shores of Lake Victoria Nyanza and the northern border of Tanganyika to the coast. The southern boundary may be regarded as following that of Tanganyika to the Belgian Congo and then running westwards through south Angola to the Atlantic."[2]

In the forest region, the main centres of creative art are generally to be found, not in the heart of the jungle, but on the edges of the savannah and along the coastal strip, or in clear-

---

1 *African Negro Art*, The Museum of Modern Art, New York, 1935, p. 17.
2 The translation of this and other passages from works written in English is provisional, as the originals are not readily available.

ings and higher parts of the country as, for instance, in the Cameroons—in other words, in the districts offering most scope for the development of social life or in those, marked by deforestation, where men have established permanent settlements in the more or less distant past.[1]

Throughout the area defined above, it is in the more or less sedentary agricultural societies that we find people practising the art of sculpture, i.e. the carving, fashioning or casting of three-dimensional representations of objects. Among the Negrillos or pygmies of equatorial Africa, who live by hunting and food-gathering, and whose material civilization is still extremely rudimentary, the visual or plastic arts, as understood by Westerners, are almost unknown. Nor are there sculptors among the hunting and food-gathering bushmen of South Africa, though they have left behind impressive evidence of their artistic ability, in the form of cave paintings.[2] The peoples whose main means of livelihood is stock-rearing—more or less nomadic pastoral tribes who, irrespective of their standard of living, are no better equipped than hunters or food-gatherers to carry much paraphernalia about with them in their wanderings—do not appear to have produced any noteworthy works of art, apart from ornaments and a few of their arms and utensils. Moreover, as Professor D. Westermann[3] points out, "In the course of their many migrations from north to south along the east coast, they often mutilated and destroyed the surviving remnants of African art. Livingstone realized this, and indeed found a direct relation between the presence of artistic works and the distribution of the tsetse fly, which makes cattle-rearing impossible." It should also be noted that where social and political bonds are fairly strong, and, above all, where large states have been built up and have endured for any considerable period, among certain sedentary peoples in both the savannah and the forest areas, circumstances are most favourable to the development of the arts. It is obvious

---

1 Georges Hardy, *L'Art Nègre—L'Art Animiste des Noirs d'Afrique*, Paris, Henri Laurens, 1927, pp. 134–35.
2 Apart from the cave paintings of the bushmen and a few other peoples, almost the only form of paintings found in equatorial Africa is decorative, e.g. for the ornamentation of hut walls. In Ethiopia, a country which has been profoundly affected by Hamitic-Semitic influences, and which has been Christianized since the fourth century A.D., we find some religious painting (often reminiscent of Coptic painting) and secular painting of more recent development.
3 *Noirs et Blancs en Afrique*, translated by Dr. George Montandon, Paris, published by Payet, 1937, p. 87.

that, in societies which have reached this stage, there is, on the one hand, greater division of labour so that producers are more highly specialized, while, on the other, the demands of a more complicated form of religion, or even of court life centred around a king or chief, tend to produce a wider and more varied market.

With very few exceptions (such as the sophisticated art represented by the bronzes and ivories from the old kingdom of the Benin, which may without exaggeration be said to have known a "golden age" in the sixteenth and seventeenth centuries), African sculpture is an art practised by agricultural peoples or by craftsmen living among them. It may therefore be described as "rustic" in the sense that, generally speaking, all its constituents (materials, technique and inspiration) seem to be directly determined by local conditions which are always, in greater or less degree, those of a small rural community; and that even its most striking achievements owe nothing to virtuosity—a quality of little value in itself, which develops only when there is a large and varied public before whom the artist delights to display his talents for their own sake.

In all the agricultural societies of equatorial Africa where the art of sculpture is known, it is practised by men who may or may not be specialists. Generally speaking, statuary is the province of professionals, such as smiths—who, in many communities, are specialists in the skills of wood-working as well as in metal-working—or people holding some recognized position in the community. This is the case, generally speaking, with objects used in magic and religious rites among the Baluba of the Belgian Congo. Masks are however very often made by non-professionals, as, for instance, by young men undergoing initiation, under the direction of their elders. "Professional" art, which, at least in the towns, where the craftsmen specialize most, might be said to be "conscious" art, may therefore sometimes be contrasted with the art of the common people, which may possibly, in certain instances, represent real "popular" art. This may account for a phenomenon found among the Dogons of the French Sudan, a people which has been studied in many books on ethnography: there is, in all probability, a far greater variety of style in their masks—which are made by male initiates and neophytes for the funeral ceremonies of important men of the tribe—than in

323

statues and other pieces of sculpture manufactured by professional metal-workers. The influence of the local type may well be greater in respect of these masks, which are made by all men in a given region than in respect of the works of the smiths, who, among the Dogons, as everywhere else in equatorial Africa, are a distinct caste with their own special secrets and, to some extent, stand apart from the communal life of the village.

While the women do no sculpture, properly speaking, comparable with that produced by the men, a reference must be made to the dolls which, among many of these peoples, are made by little girls or by their mothers or elder sisters. These little figures are often remarkable for their delicacy and grace; the best-made ones have the heads, and sometimes the whole body, modelled in wax, while the simplest of them may be made from some natural object which is merely touched up—in the Mandingo country for instance, a peeled corn-cob may sometimes be used, the "beard" or husks surrounding the fruit being twisted to imitate plaits.[1] Such objects may be regarded as corresponding, in fact if not in intention, to the "ready-made" found, in the very forefront of the *avant-garde* of modern European art, in certain of the works of Marcel Duchamp and the surrealists.

It is to be noted that the arts of statuary and the fabrication of masks have most vitality among the peoples who have remained faithful, in religion, to what Maurice Delafosse called "animism".

Delafosse pointed out that the term "fetishism" which, as we have seen, was used by Apollinaire, and which is still the term most commonly employed, is incorrect because, although there is indeed an element of fetishism in the religious life of the Negros, the same element occurs in Western religions and particularly in Roman Catholicism, where it is represented by the veneration accorded to relics and objects of piety. Delafosse, who had a deep practical understanding of African life, preferred to use the word "animism" to characterize the common features generally to be found in the religions of the

---

1 Eric Lutten, "Poupées d'Afrique Occidentale", in *Bulletin du Musée d'Ethnographie du Trocadéro*, No. 5, Paris, January 1933, pp. 8–9.

black-skinned peoples.[1] "Animism" might be very summarily defined as the belief, not only in the existence of one or more principles which survive the body, but in the inhabitation of every distinct element in the countryside—every plot of ground or natural feature such as stream, tree or rock, which can be separately distinguished—by a simple or complex spirit which is peculiarly its own and which has to be reckoned with in the same way as the souls of the dead; these latter are able either to enhance the faculties of the living or to do them harm, depending on whether or not they have been propitiated by sacrifices or other offerings. Such a belief in the existence of a multitude of powers or spirits, which does not necessarily exclude a belief in higher deities such as the sky-god who sends the rain, is a constant feature in all the religions of the African peoples. Almost all their rites and religious concepts are bound up with the family and the locality in which they live, as the spirits which are the primary objects of their veneration are the ancestors of the group—the guarantors of its vitality—or the powers inhabiting the particular portion of space where the tribe has settled, often to some extent identified with the ancestors themselves. Statues or other objects serving as mediators between man and these invisible beings in the rites designed to propitiate the latter are dedicated to the various types of supernatural beings whose protection must be secured if the group is not to perish.

It is, therefore, for the worship of these local and relatively clearly visualized divinities, and more especially for ancestor worship, rather than for the worship of the great god who is generally too distant and too little particularized, that we find these peoples producing figures or objects which, by their more or less definite form or their constituent materials, maintain a symbolic connexion with the powers in question. In these circumstances, it is not surprising that, when a group is converted to one of the great monotheistic religions, the effect on its art may, without exaggeration, be said for the time being to be completely sterilizing. Although we do find sculpture representing subjects drawn from Christianity in more than one group converted to monotheism by Christian missionaries, the aesthetic quality of that sculpture is generally much

---

[1] *Civilisations Négro-Africaines*, Paris, Stock, 1925.

debased, while, in groups converted to Islam there is often no sculpture at all, as the Mohammedan religion traditionally proscribes all images. The custom of making and wearing masks sometimes survives for entertainment rather than ritual purposes, but sculpture properly speaking is scarcely found except in the applied arts, in such things as chairs, doors, and instruments like locks or pulleys for looms, etc.

When European art historians and ethnologists began to study African Negro sculpture, one of their first concerns was to classify the different styles found in it. It is, no doubt, possible, with Carl Einstein,[1] to make a general distinction between African and Oceanian sculpture—the former being mainly concerned with solving "the problems of concentration and association in space", and the latter seeking rather "the decorative compositions achieved by discontinuity" and being skilled in "infinite variation in the use of intervals and spaces", not to mention the greater richness of its symbolization, which accounts for the interest which the surrealists were later to take in it. Nevertheless, this distinction certainly does not hold in all cases[2] and, as Einstein in fact perceived, does not exclude very great diversity in the works produced by African Negroes.

Mr. Georges Hardy, who, as he has shown in his *Vue Générale de l'Histoire de l'Afrique*,[3] attaches the greatest importance to the influence of climate, has sought to classify the various styles of sculpture according to the main climatic and ecological zones. According to this writer, whose *Géographie Psychologique* is an introduction to a science which he regards as the "essential final stage in the study of human geography", a distinction is to be made, in equatorial Africa, between the "symbolism of the savannah" and the "realism of the forest".[4] A more austere form of art, with a more marked tendency towards stylization, is said, in contrast, to be characteristic of the borderland between desert and forest, an area in which two factors have contributed to this trend in sculpture, namely

---

1 *La Sculpture Africaine*, translated by Thérèse and Raymond Burgard, Paris, Crès, 1922.
2 In the French Sudan and the Upper Volta, for instance, the masks and head-dresses of dancers are often complicated, open-work structures. On the other hand, statues from the South Sea Islands, such as the *Tiki* of the Marquesas, show no "discontinuity".
3 Paris, Armand Colin, 1923.
4 *L'Art Nègre*, p. 118ff.

the "wide horizon of the savannah", where the eye can rove across vast empty spaces and objects stand out in their simplest lines in the dazzling light, and the indirect influence of Islam, which entails a departure from anthropomorphism. In the wet forest belt, where the light is softer and where the inhabitants, living in scattered, self-contained groups, differ in temperament from the peoples of the savannah, who are generally less apprehensive and more inclined to gaiety, "everything—the narrowness of the social community, the circumscription of religious vision, the lack of imaginative vigour and the necessity of crystallizing in concrete form the idea of supernatural power, the way in which the group is thrown back upon itself, and the very special importance it attributes to ancestor-worship—all tends to make the craftsman concentrate more exclusively upon the material he has to work". With certain exceptions such as the funeral *byori* of the Ogooué region— almost flat wooden figures, covered with sheets of copper, which obviously come under the heading of "symbolic" art— the sculpture of the forests is said to show a distinct tendency towards realism; and it is in this region, according to the former Vice-Chancellor of the University of Algiers, that we find the local human type reflected in statues and, in many of the masks, simple representations of the human countenance.

This classification, with its great emphasis on the influence of environment, is probably not so satisfactory as the less cut-and-dried distinction made by Eckart von Sydow, who begins by distinguishing between "simple art" and "elaborate art" and goes on to investigate the geographical distribution of each type. As he says, "Taking African sculpture as a whole, we find that the elaborate formal type predominates in a wide belt stretching from the northern end of Lake Tanganyika and from Lake Bangwoulu (in Northern Rhodesia) and running roughly westwards, with branches stretching to the south, to the Atlantic, then running up in a narrow strip to the Cameroons and round the Gulf of Guinea to Sierra Leone, and finally sweeping in an enormous curve through the western part of the west Sudan. In this great curve of country, stretching from French Guinea to the country of the Habe (or Dogons) and the Mossi, a distinguishing feature of the art is a very strong tendency towards ornamentation, whereas, in the rest of west Africa, there is a perfect balance between naturalistic

327

and decorative styles. Enclosed between the southern and the northern and north-western branches of the elaborate style, there is a continuous region in the northern Congo and the east and central Sudan where we find an extremely simple style of art, which also occurs in east Africa, in some places in South Africa and in Madagascar."[1]

As we study further and learn more about the morphological characteristics of specimens of African sculpture now assembled in museums or private collections, and as new examples of the art are collected, we find it harder to accept such broad and general classifications. We find increasingly that there is far too much variation in style and that the distribution of the different styles is, owing to the frequent and extensive migrations which have occurred in the history of Africa, far too complicated for us to make profitable use of such summary distinctions as "the art of the savannah" and "the art of the forest", or "simple art" and "elaborate art". At the very most, we can only distinguish certain influences or certain similarities between different regions. Examples are: the influence of ancient Ifa art (noted for the classic—in European eyes—terracotta heads dug up by Leo Frobenius during archaeological research in western Nigeria) and the influence of Ancient Egypt, which, according to Mr. Henri Lavachery, was felt at both ends of the Belgian Congo;[2] the similarity which was noted long ago between the extreme purity of geometric form, nevertheless not excluding an element of naturalism, in the sculpture of the Baoules of the middle Ivory Coast and that of the Fangs (or "Pahouins") of the Gaboon; the influence of the Yoruba art of western Nigeria to be discerned in Dahomey and Togoland; and the resemblance between certain softstone figurines produced by the Kissis (French Guinea) and bronzes from the old Kingdom of the Benin. There can no longer be any question of other than empirical classifications, and the most recent writers on the subject—such as Professor Melville J. Herskevits[3]—confine themselves to studying one area after another and seeking to define broadly the style or styles to be found in each of them.

---

1 Op. cit., pp. 224–25. It should be noted that ethnologists generally consider Madagascar as belonging, from the cultural point of view, to the South Sea Island group rather than to the African Negro group.

2 "Essay on Styles in the Statuary of the Congo", in *Negro*, by Nancy Cunard, London, 1934, p. 687 ff.

3 *Backgrounds of African Art*, "*Cooke-Daniels Lecture Series*", Denver Art Museum, 1945.

It may be asked whether, in the circumstances, there is any point in trying to discuss the arts of sculpture and carving among the African Negroes as if those arts represented a single whole capable of isolation from the same arts as practised among the various other peoples of the present-day world. We should probably be inclined to laugh at any African Negro who might attempt, in an essay as short as this, to deal with the whole of European sculpture, as if certain common characteristics could be objectively defined through all the differences of detail. It would, however, be true that, for a Negro, there would indeed be some common characteristics, even if only to the extent that our art-forms contrast with the forms to which he is accustomed.

Mutatis mutandis, and subject to the same reservations, it is not altogether ridiculous for a European to attempt to define the respects in which the works of African sculpture, as a whole, differ in form and significance from works of European sculpture. There is admittedly a danger that we may underestimate the variety of African sculpture; as we are less able to appreciate the respects in which creatures or things unfamiliar to us differ from one another than the respects in which they differ from those to which we are used, we tend to see a certain resemblance between them, which lies, in point of fact, merely in their common "differentness". The general features of African Negro sculpture to which I now propose to draw attention will therefore be, so to speak, negative features, since to some extent I shall have to shut my eyes to the rich diversity actually to be found in this sculpture in order to concentrate on the respects in which it *is not* what our own sculpture generally is. Such a study will, nevertheless, help to define, from one point of view, what may—in spite, again, of a multitude of subdivisions—be regarded as the civilization common to the African Negroes, considered not so much for itself as for the things in which it may differ from, and complement our own civilization.

In Europe and Asia, stone has been much used in sculpture, but in Africa wood is the material most frequently employed, both in the savannah regions where trees suitable for carving are comparatively rare, and in the forest country where there are plenty of good quality hardwoods. Even without violent destruction in the course of military operations (wars, forays and conquests) or in connexion with religion (as in the *autos-da-fé* too often celebrated by missionaries), wooden carvings are bound to perish in a relatively short time, as the material is easily damaged by insects and the climate of both tropical and equatorial Africa is bad for it. Specimens going back to archaeological times are therefore very rarely found, and then only when they are made in some more durable material. This has detracted considerably from the prestige of the African Negro civilizations, which did, in point of fact, give birth to great empires but which have left behind none, or very few, of those monuments which might have borne lasting witness to their greatness.

Wood may admittedly be used in conjunction with other materials, as it is, particularly, in masks—disguises which may, for instance, have a back-piece made of basket-work, or be lined with fibre and sometimes also decorated with currency-shells, tufts of hair, European glass beads, copper nails, etc.—and in certain statues, which may have ornaments added or have inlays of some other material to represent the eyes and so forth. It may sometimes be simply a support, covered, for instance, with antelope-skin, as it is in the Cross River masks; it may be painted different colours, or covered with a thick crust of flour-paste or coagulated blood left behind from sacrificial rites, or almost hidden by the nails driven into it for the purposes of magic, as it is in the *kondé* from the French and Belgian Congo, made in the shape of men or animals. But, for practical purposes, leaving aside all the magical and religious associations of the trees, wood is, for the African Negro, both the easiest raw material to obtain and the simplest to work. Generally speaking, throughout Africa, the carving is done with the simplest tools; axe, adze or machete is used to fell the tree, to cut out the block and carve it, a knife sometimes being also employed for certain finer details. The use of hardwoods for sculpture and carving is obviously becoming daily more rare. Even where hardwoods are easily obtainable, they always have the disadvantage of being more difficult to work. This did not matter in the days when economic factors exercised less influence, but it has to be reckoned with more and more as the new opportunities opened up by European colonization, the new obligations imposed, such as the payment of taxes, and the demands of an increasingly complicated system, which have to be coped with in every sphere of activity, leave the craftsman neither the leisure nor the independence to do his work at his own pace. Forced to adapt himself to the quicker tempo which, even at a distance, European influence imposes in every department of life, the native craftsman quickly comes to prefer the woods which are easiest and quickest to work to the finer and more durable varieties. This tendency is accentuated by the decline of old beliefs and loss of respect for old customs, resulting from the new outlook of the people.

Though wood is by far the most common material employed by Negro sculptors, stone, clay and terracotta, metals, ivory and wax have also been used. Incidentally, the art of metalworking has been known to the Negroes from very early times; they extracted their own iron before the arrival of the Europeans and, until the discovery of America, were the main suppliers of our gold. Instances of the use of these other materials are to be seen in the softstone birds found in the ruins of the medieval city of Zimbabwé (Northern Rhodesia) and in certain ritual objects still employed, such as the stones carved in the shape of people used by the Kissis of French Guinea, or the similar statuettes from Sherboro Island off the coast of Sierra Leone; in the busts of ancestors and other terracotta figures left behind by the Saos, whose civilization flourished around Lake Chad between the tenth and fifteenth centuries; in the terracotta funerary figures from the region of Assinia on the border between the Ivory Coast and the Gold Coast; in the terracotta heads discovered in the tin mines of northern Nigeria, described by Mr. Bernard Fagg; in the sun-baked clay animals, horsemen and other miniatures of everyday objects made as playthings by children in many parts of the country; in the bronzes from the Benin, where the lost-wax process of casting was used to produce very fine works, which were indeed the first specimens of African Negro art to arouse European admiration and whose perfection was at first attributed, though it is now believed erroneously, to the contacts which the kingdom of the Benin had had with Portuguese traders; in the "proverb weights" of the Agni and Ashanti on the Ivory Coast and the Gold Coast, small bronzes used for weighing gold, decorated with geometrical or symbolic designs or depicting a great variety of subjects usually bearing some relation to proverbs or popular sayings; in the copper figurines sold by Hausa pedlars, amusing curios for Europeans, whose subjects are generally drawn from everyday life; in the golden ornaments, sometimes made in the form of masks, from the lagoons of the lower Ivory Coast and the Baoulé country; in the figurines, pendants, head-rests and other objects from the Congo—products of an art found mainly in the forest regions, where ivory is abundant, and which has become an industry in many places, so that anyone can now pick up specimens designed for the market in the form of chimney-ornaments, chess-men, and various table utensils and desk requisites. These are all forms of carving or sculpture using something other than wood as the raw material, and some of them, at least, are made by processes calling for quite a high level of technical skill among the people who produce them.

Whatever the material of which they are made, from the humblest to the most precious, and whatever the use for which they are intended, the thing which strikes the Western eye first, in the form of most of these sculptures, is the absence of *naturalism*. This is the only reason why they were for a long time considered ugly—and still are by many people. Before we were prepared to admit that they had any artistic value, certain naturalistic conventions had to be flouted by those of our own artists who were determined not to accept the restrictions imposed by such prejudices on free creative art. Thus we find the cubist sculptor, Jacques Lipchitz, referring, in the issue of *Action* we have already mentioned, to the African Negroes' "true understanding of proportion", "sense of design", and "acute perception of reality", but he obviously means by "proportion" something different from what we regard as the natural proportions of the human body (proportions which are of importance only from the point of view of anatomical science and do not matter at all with respect to the impression of harmony conveyed), and by the "reality" so acutely perceived something other than a model for the manufacture of pedestrian imitations of the "plaster-cast" variety. Similarly, it was Juan Gris, one of the greatest of the cubist painters and one of the artists who have thought most clearly about the contemporary problems of painting, who recognized the essential dignity of "Negro art" and sought to relate it to classical Greek art in these few phrases, which sum up his "opinion" as set forth in *Action:* "Negro sculpture gives us clear proof of the possibility of an *anti-idealistic* art. These sculptures, imbued with religious spirit, are diverse and particular embodiments of great principles and general ideas. How can we fail to recognize the virtue of an art which, proceeding thus, succeeds in individualizing the general in such a multitude of different ways? It is the very opposite of Greek art, which took the individual as the basis in an *attempt to suggest* an ideal type." Lastly, Tristan Tzara, one of the founders of the Dada movement, in a poetic note published in 1917, had been one of the first to pay tribute to the native artists of Africa whom he describes as being able to "construct a balanced hierarchy"; he pointed out that the African artist, "concentrating his eyes upon the head . . . loses the conventional relationship between that and the rest of the body", and also emphasized the importance these same artists attach to the vertical and the symmetrical.[1]

Thus the writings of European intellectuals, who did not pride themselves on their learning or scholarship but were sympathetic towards a form of art in which they saw, above all, something consistent which was completely divorced from the dusty official academic art of the West, delineate clearly enough, in spite of certain inaccuracies, some of the most characteristic features of African Negro statuary as it appears to our eyes.

The most striking and constant features of this art are the importance of proportion and mass in the statues, which are always monumental in feeling although generally small in actual size; the immobility of the figures represented, immutably fixed in a stylized posture (generally standing upright and, as it were, "at attention") and seemingly transmuted into terms of the eternal, without the inevitable touch of the fugitive which must always be associated with any expression of the psychological; and the observance of the law demanding that the median bisecting the body lengthwise, through the nose, sternum and navel, shall remain vertical, whatever the attitude

[1] "Note 6 sur l'art nègre", in *Sic*, No. 21-2, Paris, September-October 1917.

of the figure. All these features help to produce the "divine moderation" which, according to Sydow, seems to inform Negro statuary. As he puts it somewhat pompously in another context, Negro statues are alive with a "strength full of intense, concentrated and serene energy" and imbued with a "natural stability which has in it something mature and permanent".[1]

As any visual art, irrespective of period and civilization, is, by definition, linked with a certain conception of the world, it is only to be expected that there should be some connexion between the outward semblance of African sculpture and carving and the ideas prevailing in the societies in which such works are produced. Now that we have considered the material structure of African Negro sculpture and its relation to our own aesthetic standards, we must go on to consider it from the point of view of the function it fulfils in the societies which have given birth to it. If we have been correct in what we have said above, there should be no discrepancy between the form and the significance of these works. If we had time to undertake a more thorough study, we should have also to examine the works concerned from the point of view of the exact intention of the various artists who produced them, but in this essay we are confining ourselves to broad generalities. In any case, it is only right to acknowledge that, even it we wished to go into the question more thoroughly, we should be brought to a halt at the very outset, with regard to this last question, for want of even a minimum of material on which to work.[2]

Writing about the religious function of sculpture among the ancient Egyptians, Alexandre Moret says: "Priestly learning and the sculptor's art are combined to create images which may 'satisfy the hearts of the gods'; in particular, the characteristic attributes of the god must appear in his image. . . . Crowns, sceptres and ornaments must all be reproduced with the most scrupulous accuracy as, otherwise, the god would fail to recognize his image and take up his abode in it. . . ."[3] These

---

[1] Op. cit., p. 214.
[2] The study of African Negro aesthetics considered as a distinct entity has not yet been begun. It would be necessary to obtain information, in each group considered, not only about the personal history of the artists (vocation, training, etc.), but about the taste of the public (what statues or masks, for instance, are considered to be better than others? What is the basis for this opinion?).
[3] *Le Nil et la Civilisation Égyptienne*, Renaissance du Livre, Paris, 1926, p. 422.

remarks on one of the most wonderful civilizations of the ancient world—and, moreover, an African civilization—might be applied, almost as they stand, to Negro sculpture in general.

With certain exceptions, such as the bas-reliefs decorating the walls of the royal palaces of Abomey, or the bronze plaques which used to adorn pillars in the main street of the city of Benin (commemorative sculpture or simply examples of what Mr. Georges Hardy calls "court and domestic art"), or such again as the modern copper statuettes of everyday things, the weights used for weighing gold, and various other specimens of applied art, African Negro sculpture may be said to be, in the main, sacred sculpture. As in ancient Egypt, we constantly find ritual magic and the visual arts associated among the present-day peoples of equatorial Africa.

Religions like those of the agricultural societies of equatorial Africa, whose main purpose is to guarantee the survival of a community by the continual sequence of reproduction and harvest, rather than to enable the individual to secure his own salvation (as is the case in our religions), are generally found matched with forms of art displaying very obvious collectivist characteristics and closely related to some practical end.

The African artist, with his deep respect for the customs of the group to which he belongs and for the tradition he has inherited from his ancestors (whose living representatives are the heads of families), will not strive, as the best of our artists do, to create something essentially personal; in the emblematic representation of beings which, in the nature of things, are not of this physical world, and whose features are defined by the beliefs of the community, the native artist always has to apply formulae leaving only a very small degree of individual freedom, handed down from generation to generation and imposed by the elders of the group. Thus, the religious, archaistic and inevitably stereotyped traditionalism of African Negro sculpture helps to convey that impression of rigid stylization which strikes Westerners, accustomed to some degree of naturalism in the visual arts, with such force.

Whereas, in Europe, the main aim of statuary has gradually come to be the production of things to be looked at (either purely for pleasure, in secular art, or to represent objects of veneration or execration, in religious art), the situation in Africa is entirely different. There, works of statuary are not

335

mere effigies, directly or indirectly associated, for purposes of ornament, with architecture, but are instruments in the fullest sense, made for practical purposes and standing, to some extent, by themselves, since (apart from such things as the bas-reliefs and plaques mentioned above) they are not intended to be parts of a whole—of a building which it is one of their purposes to adorn, or simply of a room or other place in which they are displayed. Leaving out of account such rare exceptions as the famous royal statues of the *Bakuba* brought back from the Belgian Congo by Torday and Joyce, the oldest of which probably dates back to about 1600, the statues of spirits or deities, ancestors or kings (who are also sacred beings, with some attributes of divinity) are not intended to be portraits faithfully reproducing the features of king, ancestor, spirit or deity for the veneration of the group; they are works of sculpture to be used rather than to be looked at. During the ceremonies in honour of the beings whose material emblems they are, these statues temporarily become containers or dwelling-places for the spirits in question; through the accomplishment of the necessary rites, the beings they represent at least in part enter into and animate them. There is no need for the exact features of these beings to be reproduced; they must be depicted symbolically. This accounts for the special importance attributed to certain details, such as distinctive physical features, tattoo marks and other signs, insignia of honour, etc. In many instances, these statues are indeed touched and handled by the officiants as if they were tools of a special type; they are regarded with a mixture of emotions, compounded of fear and respect, and anointed with blood or other sacrificial substances.

While this is pure supposition, indicating a possible line of research rather than representing even the rudiments of a theory, it is legitimate to enquire whether some such instrumental function may not, at least in part, account for such characteristics as the extraordinary power which African Negro sculptors can give to their "volumes", which are almost always so full and so resolutely established—as many writers, including Carl Einstein, have already noted.

African Negro sculpture—unlike our sculpture in-the-round, derived from Greco-Roman sculpture—is not concerned with the production of figures which may be viewed from every angle without losing their harmony of form, and which are created mainly to be looked at. When we examine African statuary, we are more likely to find figures displaying what we might describe as "selected aspects", not intended to satisfy the real or imaginary viewer regarding them from every angle, but constructed, simply and solely, with a front, a back and a side view. These figures not merely serve as a means of localizing spiritual forces instead of being simply effigies, but, being sacred objects, must be kept hidden, at least in ordinary times, from the eyes of the public. They appear to represent, in actual fact, the "anti-idealistic" art mentioned by Juan Gris, which was his guide in his own efforts to make each of his works embody, in concrete everyday form, the abstraction from which it was derived. With regard to the strict function they are intended to fulfil, these figures are indeed a practical means of crystallizing the immaterial, localizing it, at least in part and for a time, in an object fashioned in its image (a necessary condition to enable the object to serve as a container or recipient) and which, for this reason, will in very truth represent an "incarnate idea". I venture to use in this context, with only a very slight stretch of interpretation, an expression which I heard employed a few years ago by Leopold Sedar Senghor, the Senegalese poet, in giving a summary and general definition of what distinguishes the Negro civilizations— "civilizations of the incarnate idea", or in other words, civilizations in which the perceptible form has an immediate virtue of its own—from the civilizations developed by the white and yellow races. This technique, aiming at an "incarnation" in the fullest sense of the term, is obviously in sharp contrast with that employed in classical Greek art, which was idealistic in that its statues aimed not at embodying the immaterial but at idealizing individual reality—in other words, at generalizing the particular in order to exalt it into a type, which the sculptor merely "sought to suggest" (in Gris' words) to the eyes of those intended to contemplate the work. The statues employed in Negro ritual are particular "concretizations" of personages standing apart from ordinary mortals, representing natural spirits or the souls of the dead, sometimes associated with "great principles"; in any of these cases all the sculptor has to do is to indicate the significant features of his subject—the only similitude necessary to create the link between the statue and the

337

spirit. These statues have not an illustrative but a technical function to fulfil; and it would seem that their utilitarian function, as things to be handled no less than viewed, gives them the amazing solidity and vitality which they are now recognized to possess, at least by those of us whom the development of art in the West has freed from the conventional idea that natural proportions must be preserved. Imbued with a harmony achieved by the craftsman all the more easily because he is not distracted by ideas of naturalism, with a balanced rhythm of their own, created in conformity with immutable standards instead of in the pursuit of personal caprice, these statues also display a seeming solidarity of structure, which is no doubt connected with the fact that they have been constructed like tools to satisfy certain definite needs, without any of the mannerisms inevitably introduced into his work by an artist whose main object is to produce something deliberately beautiful. We should still have to establish, however, why African sculpture in general is so different from that of the South Sea Islanders, for instance, which may also be said to have an instrumental function but in which, according to Mr. Maurice Leonhard;[1] there is to be seen a tendency "to slide from realism to the geometrical style", only rarely found in Africa. It must be acknowledged that we have no solution to suggest for this problem. The answer might perhaps be found by relating it to a psychological problem involving far more than aesthetics; this is the question of the capacity which the African Negroes seem to possess, in the words of the Senegalese essayist, Alieune Diep,[2] "for the concrete and immediate enjoyment of life", a capacity whose possible relationship with the rhythmic genius which seems to be innate in most Negroes might well be investigated; this rhythmic genius, which is apparent in their sculpture as well as in their music and dancing, is possibly just one of the media whereby they are able to keep in such extraordinarily close communion with the concrete and with life.

This quality of being instruments instead of pure effigies, which seems to be a feature of African Negro statues, is also to be noted in their masks; these are components in disguises

---

[1] *Arts de l'Océanie*, Paris, Editions du Chêne, 1948, p. 126.
[2] "Niam n'goura ou Les raisons d'être de Présence Africaine", *Présence Africaine*, No. 1, Paris, October-November 1947.

whose wearers are supposed to abandon their usual personality
to embody symbolical or emblematic beings belonging either
to the human realm (an ethnic group, a social class) or to the
animal kingdom (and in some cases the vegetable kingdom,
or the inanimate world) or to the spirit world, the whole often
making up, in Professor Marcel Griaule's words,[1] a "veritable
cosmos" with a very strong emotional content. In this case,
too, the sculptor is obviously not making a literal copy of
the being the mask is supposed to represent. Although regarded
as a ritual instrument, there is a definite element of spectacle
in the mask and in its use, since masked dances are always performed before an audience, whether small or great; and there
is often evidence in certain features of the mask's manufacture,
of a desire to awe and terrify. We may also ask whether the
group hysteria in which the solemn performances of masked
dances usually take place—performances whose frequency
varies from case to case but in which there is generally an
intense outpouring of that sense of festivity which is so striking
in most African Negroes, who seem to possess, in much higher
degree than Western peoples the capacity to let themselves go
while remaining within certain ordered bounds, and whose
very life, depending on the cycle of the seasons, seems to be
punctuated with feasts or ceremonies marking the major stages
in the passage of the year—we may ask, I say again, whether
this enthusiasm (in the etymological sense of the word) is not
a factor conducive to the creation of types of masks whose
fantastic lineaments indicate a deliberate departure from
everyday reality. Aside from these extreme cases, it should be
noted that the mask—a traditional piece of theatrical property
but also a factor in an esoteric system (linked as it is with
initiation, which may be defined as the group of rites whereby
the elders pass on the nucleus of tradition, in secrecy, to the
young)—has to serve as a medium by which the immaterial
may be controlled, and is often designed to establish a direct
communication between its wearer and the being he conjures
up by his costume and gestures. It is thus clear that masks
must follow tradition, at least in their general lines, and must
fulfil a definite symbolic function, as well as satisfying spectacular requirements. All these considerations combine to

[1] "Masques dogons", *Travaux et Mémoires de l'Institut d'Ethnologie*, Vol. XXXIII, Paris, 1938, p. 790.

thrust into the background, as in the case of statues, all concern for any but a conventional resemblance, limited to what is regarded as the essential minimum. Here we shall find again that the complete absence of "naturalistic" concerns helps finally to give greater solidity and consistency to things created not as works of art but as instruments.

Whether we are concerned with masks or with religious statues—which are utilitarian to the extent that they have a function to fulfil in rites which are themselves linked, in the last analysis, with practical life—we find that art, among the African Negroes, is almost always associated with some other aim. It would therefore be even more difficult, in this case, to draw a clear dividing line between art and utility than it is for the products of our own civilizations. While masks and statues, which seem to us to be objects of art, may from the African point of view be regarded as objects of utility, on the other hand many things which we should consider to be mainly utilitarian (receptacles, agricultural implements, weapons, etc.) are also objects of art, even though they may be quite undecorated. Such things are made by hand, and it never enters the craftsman's head to spare either time or effort in the creation of something which will be, as it were, an extension of himself (or, at all events, a sort of human organ involving nothing mechanical which might alienate it from its user); they show clearly that the individuals who fashioned them were never so exclusively concerned with the mere satisfaction of practical ends as to put aside, in their manufacture, all idea of beauty, at least so far as beauty consists in harmony of form and perfection of finish. Moreover, as among the African Negroes who have not yet felt the effects of European colonization to any great extent, religion is closely associated with even the most common everyday activities (since there is always the risk of setting loose dangerous forces or, at least, forces which must be conciliated if anything useful is to be done), the Negroes use many objects adorned with figures or designs which originally had a ritual significance but which often, in the process of time, have become purely decorative. Many utensils therefore have an added decoration whose symbolic significance is not necessarily appreciated either by their users or by the craftsman who fashioned them. Certain other domestic objects—such as the goblets in the shape of a human head found among the Bakuba, the seats supported by one or more figures seen, for instance, in Dahomey and the Belgian Congo, or certain musical instruments made to resemble a man or an animal—are in fact sculptures, even if it is not appropriate to speak of decoration, in the strict sense, in connexion with them.

In spite of the considerable complexity already existing in African civilization before the time of European settlement, technical, economic, legal and religious manifestations of life among most of the African Negroes are still too intimately associated to make it possible to draw a clear dividing line between these various spheres. We do not find among them the strict division of the various activities into at least theoretically specialized branches, which is the hall-mark of our industrial civilization. Although it is quite evident that anything like the idea of "art for art's sake" is still more or less completely alien to the African Negro who has felt little or nothing of the influence of European civilization, and although it is unusual to find examples of works of art, in the strict sense (apart possibly from such objects of state ceremonial as are to be found in the treasuries of chiefs or notables, though, even there, the idea of prestige comes into play and the concept of economic value is more apparent than it is in connexion with pictures and other collectors' pieces sought after by European art-lovers), it is to be noted that many Negroes are perfectly well able to appreciate their own sculpture from a disinterested artistic standpoint.

According to Mr. Carl Kjersmeier,[1] "decorative statuettes are often found" among the Baoulés. "They are placed in native huts not solely because of their religious significance but because people think they are pretty. A Baoulé does not think only of the religious importance of a statuette or a mask; he is also concerned with aesthetic considerations. Usually, when a Baoulé is asked why he buys some particular prettily carved article, he will answer: 'We bring them out on feast days and feel happy'. Art plays a great part in the life of the Baoulés; beautiful young women find it flattering to sit as models to a famous artist and will even pay to have their statues carved in wood. When a man leaves the country, he often has his likeness carved to leave it behind as a keepsake for his family and friends."

---

[1] *Centres de Styles de la Sculpture Nègre Africaine*, 4 vols. Albert Morancé, Paris, and Illums Bog-Afdeling, Copenhagen, 1935–38, Vol. I, p. 33.

Among certain peoples in Dahomey, the attitude of the group towards the artist is slightly reminiscent of what we find in our own societies in this respect. According to Professor Herskevits,[1] a Dahomey artist may be admired for his gifts, but there is a marked tendency for him to stand apart from society; the artist is respected for his art but at the same time regarded with some scorn, because of his lack of interest in the quest for riches and honour which are the ambitions of most of the people of Dahomey. "They are nice people," a Dahomey woman would say, "but they are not good husbands. Months and months go by without their taking any interest in anything but blocks of wood." On another occasion, when a sculptor was taking longer than was customary to execute an order for a chief, and was asked whether, when Dahomey was independent, such a delay would not have cost him his head, he replied: "What good would my head have done the king? You don't find artists everywhere!"

Admittedly the Baoulés, who also make very fine materials, are particularly gifted artistically. In the case of the people of southern Dahomey quoted by Herskevits, very considerable allowance must be made for the influences to which these people have been subject; they are among the West African tribes which may be considered to be most open to European culture and, apart from any question of outside contacts, account must also be taken of the high level of civilization and social differentiation already reached before they came under European dominion. There is no doubt, however, that, among peoples who have been far less affected by colonization and whose political organization is far less developed, objects made primarily for religious purposes may also be judged on their artistic merits. The Dogons of Sanga—who belong to the peoples described by their Moslem neighbours as *Habé*, i.e. "pagans" or "infidels", which implicitly suggests that they are little open to outside influences—acknowledge that the people living in certain villages, or certain individuals, are specially gifted for carving masks; in Sanga, indeed, such masks as those from the Wazouba region are legendary for their beauty, and one particular mask in the shape of an antelope's head with long tapering horns, brought back from

[1] Op. cit., p. 61.

Sanga in 1931 and now exhibited in the Musée de l'Homme,[1] was attributed to a certain Ansêgué, who was said to have been an excellent sculptor of masks before he was killed in a punitive military expedition carried out by the French. Similarly, among the Mandingos (these admittedly had a period of political greatness under such rulers as the famous Gongo Moussa, who was responsible, in the first half of the fourteenth century, for spreading the architectural style in which mosques and other puddled clay buildings are still designed in the French Sudan) there was a craftsman named Tamba, belonging to the caste of the smiths, who also enjoyed some local reputation in the Kita district in 1931 as an expert in wood carving.[2]

Even where art seems to be scarcely separable from religion, therefore, and where what we call "art for art's sake" obviously does not exist, it would be a very great mistake to assume that there is no conscious care for the beautiful in the manufacture (itself frequently "ritual") of objects necessary for the accomplishment of rites. We cannot help noticing however that, from the point of view of art itself, the development of this aesthetic awareness and, in particular, what we might call its acquisition of independence does not necessarily represent an advance. While there seems to be good reason, indeed, for speaking of a sort of "Negro miracle", of which certain Western artists suddenly became aware about the time when cubism first began to develop, there is no doubt that, generally speaking, African secular works make a less radical impression than the works which reveal, in all its sudden purity, that religious feeling implying a capacity in man for communion with other creatures or things around him—a capacity we have lost exactly in proportion to the extent to which we, in contrast to the peoples who until quite recently were still regarded as "savages", have allowed our activities to become much differentiated and split up into distinct sectors having little or no contact with one another.

Since 1920—the year in which *Action* published its collection of opinions on Negro art, and the year which marked the

---

[1] Item No. 31.74.2025 (Dakar-Jibuti expedition).
[2] Documents of the Dakar-Jibuti expedition.

beginning of a post-war period which gave grounds for some optimism and appeared to offer hope that the cessation of hostilities was to usher in a time when, in one way or another, the world would be knit into a single whole—there has been a great change in the position occupied by the arts of the African Negroes and their derivatives in the life of the white heirs of a civilization centred around ideas and standards drawn from the Hellenic and Judaeo-Christian worlds. This change is less obvious in relation to sculpture, which is still little appreciated outside fairly advanced intellectual circles, than in relation to music, where we now find jazz—which, though including other elements, is undoubtedly derived in essentials from Africa—playing a great part in the entertainment of town-dwellers in nearly every country, including the partly Westernized yellow nations, and of many country people also. This triumph gives grounds for thinking that it may be rooted in a need, felt more or less obscurely by the Western peoples, to recover—by surrendering to the power of compelling rhythms which have moulded the descendants of African Negroes and which still retain an echo of the times when the aim of music was encouragement, incantation or a sort of hypnosis—a sense of fuller life which their own mechanized civilization gives them too few opportunities of achieving in their day-to-day existence. In the same way, the fact that Negro sculpture offers an opportunity of refreshment by contact with something preceding the development of pure aestheticism, and that many specimens of Negro sculpture, with a fascinating rhythm of their own, are models of classic art in their severe simplicity, may account for the attraction it has for contemporary artists and art-lovers.

Going back, then, to what was said above about the convergence between African art and twentieth-century Western art —a convergence which obviously applies only to form, since the religious or ritual aims of African sculptors are entirely different from those pursued by such artists as the cubists in their strictly aesthetic experiments—we still have to decide what it was that our artists had to learn from this African sculpture which had such a strong attraction for them.

The first thing which this sculpture demonstrated was probably that a certain superficial naturalism may be contrasted with a profound realism, resting not on mere external imitation but on the creation of symbols whose evocative power depends less upon a "photographic" resemblance to the things represented than on an equivalence with the idea entertained of their essence, or, more accurately, with our conception of those things derived from the multiple relationships between us and them. A second point on which this sculpture may have seemed to bear out their arguments objectively was that, to achieve such realism, it is necessary to excise "anecdotage" or, at least, not to allow oneself to be dominated by what is purely fortuitous and without essential relation to what one knows of the creatures or things chosen as subjects—that it is vital, in short, to reduce everything to essentials instead of allowing oneself to be swamped by a multiplicity of details. That it is vital, too, to achieve coherence of form, or, in other words, to ensure, though the actual means employed are of little importance, that there is a visual connexion between each part and each other part, distinct from the mere logical connexion due to the fact that the thing represented is a whole in its own right—such as a human being or an animal.[1] A final point which could be clearly illustrated by this sculpture was that, if there is a golden rule for the artist, it is, when all is said and done, that his work should be "genuine"—a term which is difficult to define but which may be regarded as consisting essentially in the belief in the necessity for the work's creation (a necessity bound up with religion and the life of the community, so far as the African sculptor is concerned, but purely personal and individual for the Western artist of the time of which we are speaking), and in the fact that the work is created not simply out of a desire to please— or, alternatively, to shock—nor out of a desire to display skill. On the strictly technical side, moreover, these artists saw that the Africans had solved, intuitively, several of the practical problems which were occupying their own minds, such as how to represent volume other than by sculpture in the round (or by an imitation of it, in the case of the two-dimensional art of painting) ; how to treat the parts of a work both for themselves and in relation to the whole (it may truly be said that each one of the constituent parts of an African sculpture has a life of its

---

1 This question of coherence of forms, of the connexion, by contrast or analogy, between them, of their balance and equilibrium, is partly linked with the obscure question of rhythm, which always implies continuity in spite of the breaks introduced by the rests between the accented notes.

own, as well as its place in the unity of a whole, which also has a life of its own); how to create symbols which will be all the fuller of meaning for not being copies—e.g. in the masks from the lower Ivory Coast of which we spoke above, the representation of the eyes by two cylinders standing out from the head, which seem to be the very materialization of the glance.

What Jean Cocteau, in 1920, called "the artistic crisis about Negro art" has thus proved to be far more than the superficial and transitory phenomenon that term would suggest, even though Negro art, an important factor but only one among others, has not been quite the "fertilizing sperm of twentieth-century intellectual life" which Paul Guillaume would have it. Beyond the strictly artistic sphere, we must, as we continue our rapid survey, mention the fact that whereas the Africans, like the coloured peoples of America and the West Indies, had for hundreds of years known none but an oral literature (which, incidentally, was very rich),[1] there has been, during the last century, a development of written forms of expression by poets and prose writers belonging to the Negro race but of French, British or American language and culture, several of whom have deservedly won a reputation in cultured Western circles. A poet like Aimé Césaire (a native of Martinique) and a novelist like Richard Wright (a native of the southern United States)—to mention only these two—are now acknowledged writers who, in widely differing types of literature, both bear out Léopold Sedar Senghor's statement that "the Negro is, above all, a lyricist with a deep appreciation of verbal images and of the rhythm and music of assembled words".[2] Both of them, following their own genius, are becoming the spokesmen of the black race in its growing awareness of the oppression to which it is subjected. It should also be noted—although in this instance the writer is one of those who have not been appreciated as they deserve—that the biographical novel about the

---

[1] This literature is found in every department of social life, in the form of myths and legends, stories, songs, poems, riddles, proverbs, etc., all of which are traditional, at least in some degree; in addition to stories about animals (the characters in which represent types) and didactic or moral fables, a great variety of different types of literature is found, ranging from the epic, through war-songs, love-songs or working-songs, to the panegyric or the satirical poem. Many survivals of this oral African literature may be noted among the West Indian Negroes (e.g. in Haiti, the cycle of Bouqui and Malice) and among those of America (e.g. Brer Rabbit in the folklore of the southern United States).

[2] "Vues sur l'Afrique Noire ou Assimiler, ne pas être assimilés", *La Communauté Impériale Française* by Robert Lemaignen, Léopold Sedar Senghor, Prince Sisowath Youtevong, Paris, Editions Alsatia, 1945, p. 94.

Zulu conqueror, Chaka, written in Sotho by the South African, Thomas Mofolo, and considered by some to be one of the truest masterpieces of world literature, has now been translated into French.[1]

In these troublous times, when so many Western people are made restive by the over-mechanization of their life and when a complete rebuilding of our civilization in every sphere seems to many to be necessary, there can be little doubt that the Africans and their descendants in the West Indies and the Americas have a message to give, and far more than a merely local audience ready to listen to them. Although they may be less sophisticated than most Westerners belonging to the governing classes, broadly speaking, the Negroes seem so far to have preserved the possibility of a more direct contact with the natural environment (which may account for the special realism and the rhythmic qualities which are generally a distinguishing feature of African sculpture); they have also preserved a certain faculty for relaxation (very apparent in such festivals as the carnival, which, outside Africa, is still so vital and alive in the West Indies) and, together with that wonderful lyric gift which, in so many Africans and descendants of Africans, is ever ready to enliven speech, an incomparable aesthetic ability (a sense of style, in general, which is reflected even in the formality of everyday relations, and even in many of their gestures and attitudes); in short, they possess the constituents of a sort of *savoir vivre* (in the wide sense of the art of living, the way of enjoying life and living it as an art), which is certainly of inestimable importance at a time when the most obvious progress being made is decidedly in the direction of the arts of destruction, constraint and torture. If all this is true, the Negroes would deserve to be considered, by those of the white races who are concerned to preserve a certain humanism, as examples to follow in more than one respect, being the guardians of a certain number of virtues from which

---

[1] Thomas Mofolo, *Chaka, Une Epopée Bantoue,* Translated direct from Sotho by V. Ellenberger, formerly a missionary in Basutoland. Paris, Gallimard, 1940. The English edition was published in Oxford in 1931.

Mofolo was born in the village of Khojané in 1875 (i.e. nearly a hundred years after the birth of the man whose biography he has written, which is well deserving of the term "epic" in the sub-title of the French edition); his parents were Christians and Mofolo himself was brought up in the Protestant faith and served as a teacher for some time. His first work, *Mooti oa Bochabola* (The Pilgrim from the East), apparently bears some resemblance to Bunyan's *Pilgrim's Progress.* The second, *Pitsèng,* won him a large audience among his countrymen.

we tend to be diverted by the pragmatism which is the dominating trait of our civilization. There is admittedly no reason
for saying that such virtues—prompt reaction to external
stimuli, aptitude for establishing forms to be observed in
festivity and etiquette, as well as in the arts properly speaking—
are not purely ephemeral, linked as they are with ways of life
which are constantly changing as the technological and economic circumstances of the Negroes alter, and representing, in
any case, only one aspect (the pristine freshness which many
Westerners are inclined to attribute to non-industrialized
peoples because they themselves more or less consciously
hanker after a non-industrialized culture); or, more accurately,
they represent a section of the life of Africans and their
descendants, selected by sociological study and direct experience.
Nevertheless, the survival of the features we have just noted
among the descendants of slaves living in the New World may
be regarded as an encouraging sign by those who attach value
to such things; it is not inconceivable that this survival typifies
something which is strong enough to endure, in one form or
another, through all vicissitudes.

Since 1920, progress has undoubtedly been made in our
knowledge of the coloured peoples, who are now nearer to
being understood and appreciated as they deserve. We must
remember however that, despite the illusions which may have
been cherished before the last war, racial prejudices are not
merely survivals from a past state of affairs, but are nourished
by antagonisms which become more and more acute as the
coloured peoples succeed in making their voices heard; they
represent the defensive reaction of people of the white race
who are aware that their privileges are daily being more
seriously threatened. We must bear in mind, too, that many
people free of such prejudices still have only a conventional
idea of the African in their minds and that, while they are
already a little disturbed to see the present-day African
gradually breaking free of this convention, they would find
it still harder to accept the idea that he should take council of
himself alone in deciding his future fate.

There have been some among our social scientists and our
technical experts on colonization—whose good faith is not
to be doubted—who have given thought to the special features
which a European may discover in African civilizations and

to the things which it seems desirable to preserve from the revolutionary changes which the introduction of the modes of thought and action characteristic of our modern capitalistic civilization brings about in a colonial society. It is evident however that, unless history can be brought to a halt, nothing can be done to prevent the decay of tradition, and in practice any attempt to prevent this decay is equivalent to opposing the development of political maturity; the people would thus be kept to their old ways on the pretext of safeguarding them against the influence of our civilization, which, at least in certain respects, is judged harmful. It is equally obvious that, if anything deserves to be saved among the ways of life and systems of procedure of the peoples who have so long been subject to those traditions, this salvation cannot come from without, since the people concerned are themselves, by definition, the only persons qualified to recognize their true vocation.

From the purely artistic point of view—and no other can be adopted here—various attempts have been made, by services directly controlled by the colonial powers or by missionary bodies, to arrest the deterioration of regional arts which the introduction of a new type of economy and the transformation or weakening of beliefs combine to deprive of the stimulus on which they depend. But all the efforts made to safeguard the work of native sculptors by directing it into channels better fitted to cope with the new circumstances and with the previously undreamt-of markets thereby opened up have, generally speaking, produced very poor results, as regards the intrinsic value of the works thus produced. This is no doubt because the best that can be hoped for is a compromise when the artist is guided from without instead of being left to follow his own standards, and because, in any case, the work is done for a commercial purpose instead of in response to a deep inner impulse.

It is, therefore, no sign of particular pessimism to forecast that the immediate future will see an accelerated degeneration of African Negro sculpture, whose falling-off is already to be observed in many respects. This tendency is likely to develop as the introduction of ways of life based on Western ones gradually sever from its intellectual and emotional roots an art which has grown up in close association with the life of small farmers, working without the plough, grouped together in communities based on the family, and practising religions associated with what we have agreed to call animism, whose primary purpose is to ensure the maximum vitality in the group.

While it is true that among other examples of sculpture showing a European influence—and leaving out of account the countless products of the applied arts made to meet the demands of local European settlers—certain specimens whose manufacture shows some trace of the old quality are still found in Africa (whether they be statues, groups of figurines portraying subjects taken from the Scriptures, or figures representing Europeans, sometimes made with a satirical end in view),[1] there are no real grounds for serious hopes of a renaissance of African Negro sculpture. Moreover, among the descendants of Africans transplanted to the West Indies and the Americas, it is to be noted that, while music and dancing have developed in a wonderful way, the same cannot be said of sculpture, which has hardly ever been practised since the terrible ordeal of slavery.[2]

Let us, however, consider a piece of African sculpture such as the famous statue of the god Gou, representing a Dahomey deity of arms and war, which was brought back to France in 1894 after the capture of Abomey.[3] This statue is made entirely of iron and, although it includes many constituents of European origin (sheet iron from a whaler to form the base, nut and screw to fix the god's head-dress, etc.), it is nevertheless undeniably one of the finest known specimens of African Negro art. It may be thought that, in a work of this sort, which was made prior to the conquest, any European influence exercised on the artist can only have been by way of borrowing. Certain methods (I should almost like to say certain dodges) characteristic of Europe were used deliberately by the artist, without any inducement due to foreign intervention in his ethnic environment. In these circumstances, the motive impulse was in no way altered for the worse, and the resultant production

[1] On the question of the representation of Europeans in "primitive" art in various parts of the world, see Julius E. Lips, *The Savage hits Back*, New Haven, Yale University Press, 1937.
[2] An example of applied art coming under the heading of sculpture and carving may possibly be found, however, in the everyday objects in carved and incised wood made by the bush Negroes and Boni in the Guianas; these people are the descendants of runaway slaves, leading a life very similar to that of their African ancestors.
[3] Collection of the Musée de l'Homme, Item No. 94.39.1 (presented by Captain Fonsagrives).

was not an indeterminate hybrid but an object whose mixed composition gives it an added strangeness making it still more solemn and imposing.

When, moreover, we consider how vitally the genius of the Negroes transplanted to the United States of America has found expression in jazz, which was developed in deplorable conditions, when slavery was still scarcely abolished, by individuals who had no other aim in view than self-expression or self-amusement, taking their materials as they found them—Western musical instruments and themes which, in this instance, served in much the same way as the fragment of the whaler, the nut, the screw and similar items in the statue of the god Gou—when we consider that jazz has quite recently branched out along new lines (as we can see in the so-called "be-bop" style, whose firmly modernistic trend contrasts with the old New Orleans style), we may well feel inclined to place great hopes in the artistic future of the Negroes, even if the circumstances of their life come to differ greatly from those in which the styles of sculpture with which we are familiar were developed.

After all the upheavals through which they have passed in the course of their history, at the hands of Islam and the slave-traders, and later under the colonial domination of the European peoples, may not the African Negroes have been so far prevented from showing what they can really do in the fine arts? Whether this is so or not, one can conceive the possibility of a revival of Negro sculpture comparable with what jazz has represented in music. But it is doubtful whether such a revival can be brought about from above, under the concerted impulse of the colonial administrators and by channels which, being artificial, would inevitably have an academic taint. If such a revival does one day come about, we may be sure that it will be on the initiative of the Negroes themselves, as it was for jazz, and that it will take, as jazz did, a form very different from those handed down by tradition and showing very little respect for the suggestions of those Westerners who are so prone to regard themselves as the acknowledged pundits of civilization. Thus, when all is said and done, the possibility of a renaissance of African sculpture seems to lie in an emancipation of the Negroes which, like any form of emancipation, the people concerned must themselves accomplish.

351

The Problem of Negro Culture

by

MARCEL GRIAULE

The staunchest upholders of the cultural superiority of the West are precisely those who, unlike the racialists, proclaim the equality of all mankind and the futility of a qualitative classification of cultures. This egalitarianism can and should, in their view, be interpreted only as a recognition of the right and duty of all mankind to attain to the standard of living and to accept the ways of thinking of the Western societies.

This is no doubt due to the fact that the European, and the American too, even when he has got rid of his superiority complex with regard to coloured people, cannot abandon his devout attitude to science, regarded on the one hand as the prerogative of his culture and on the other as an entity outside mankind with a life of its own, blindly subjecting stars and infusoria alike to its laws, and inevitably leading to organized happiness.

In the view of "civilized" people this vast seismic convulsion, science, constantly expanding in its movement towards progress, breaks down and covers over the subtleties and peculiarities which distinguish individuals and nations.

The fact that a man has such and such an idea of his gods, his future, his family or the life-force is then of small importance; all his beliefs and traditions have respectfully to give way before the advance of science, which is essentially a mechanistic advance, mistaken for an ideal culture.

In a word, the anti-racialist only throws overboard the prejudice of racial hierarchy to deny that the so-called inferior peoples are handicapped in the race, a race which they not only can but must run to attain culture, from which has sprung science. He would consequently regard as a dangerous reactionary anyone who, while paying science due reverence, declared that it was desirable for its altar to be approached by various paths or even for special temples to be built to it in each distinct cultural territory, with the possibility of edifices on uniform lines being planned later on.

It mean that science, the only thing in which the West is indisputably superior, and the only one—dangerous as it may be—that belongs by right to all mankind, is strong enough and sufficiently independent of places and people to exist in any cultural environment. Thus an excellent doctor may be a Mohammedan; a ballistician, a Japanese believing in ritual suicide; a brilliant physicist, a practising Catholic; a systematic ethnographer, a Negro devoted to ancestor worship; a famous geneticist, a free thinker.

It is precisely this which is not recognized, particularly in regard to the so-called backward peoples, and I should like to emphasize the point. The great cultures of the world are, it seems to me, able by their very weight to hold their own. I do not believe that the British, French or Russians are in danger of seeing their spiritual edifice suddenly collapse from the impact of the Nambikwara or the Galla; and, even if that could happen, there would be grounds for hoping that something of their civilization would survive for a very long time; even if nothing remained but books in libraries, that would still be satisfactory from a scientific point of view, since the ultimate victors would be able to study the vanished past.

The converse, unfortunately, does not apply. Cultures which, backward as they are in terms of mechanical progress, have to their credit, in other fields, noble achievements of which mankind can be proud, are doomed to disappear if the upholders of the mechanized civilization are not objective.

And they are not invariably objective. Who would have the temerity to tell a Yemenite or a Hindu that his beliefs and traditions stand in the way of his intellectual development? No scruple restrains anyone from saying such a thing to a Sudanese who puts the first fruits of his field on the family altar, or lights torches at the winter solstice.

The fact is that the Westerner's ignorance of the real intellectual attainments and behaviour of the so-called backward peoples, and the astonishment or contempt which unfamiliar customs arouse in him, lead him to deny that they possess any culture whatever. And since he recognizes the equality of man, he can only hope that the whole of mankind

353

will be raised to the eminence upon which he stands himself, which he believes to be the only dignified and endurable position.

Whereas the racialist bases his views on pseudo-scientific evidence, the charitable egalitarian supports his mistaken belief with arguments and data which, though genuine in themselves, are not as a rule founded on any contact with the people concerned.

Thus he will be uncompromising on the subject of languages. Simple reasoning, supported or not by faulty observation, causes him to declare that the Negroes are culturally inferior because, for example, tropical Africa possesses hundreds of dialects and an unknown number of subsidiary dialects or varieties of pronunciation. Quite without grounds, he regards each group as isolated in its own system of oral symbols, and hence in a narrow system of traditions from which it must be charitably weaned. For he believes that it is not here a question of sufficient knowledge but of traditions, and of traditions which do not extend beyond the limits of the dialect under consideration.

That, however, is manifestly incorrect. A few Negro languages that are widely or fairly widely used are beginning to be known. They possess a much richer vocabulary than one is led to suppose by dictionaries compiled by amateurs or by hurried specialists; the use of the verb is often ingenious, much more play is made with roots than in other languages, and the view that these Negro languages cannot express abstract ideas is definitely false. All the native languages provide a means of expressing a wide range of knowledge, much of it real and exact and having a coherence which demolishes certain brilliant theories propounded by sociologists. Moreover this system is not simply built up from a complex of logically related symbolic correspondences; it is linked with the systems of the neighbouring peoples. Thus the Sudan, far from being a mosaic of many coloured and multiform elements, is a whole made up of peoples whose reciprocal parts in it were distinguished, if not actually played, according to the accidents of history, in the remote past.

The retirement of a Negro people within itself is therefore a pure fiction, especially since every one of them, in these countries, is polyglot. The very diversity of the dialects, which sometimes show considerable variation from place to place, demands the open ear and mind, and hence leads to salutory exertion and fruitful interchange.

The situation of the Negroes of the Niger, for example, whether it is a question of the Bozo fishermen, the Dogon mountaineers, the Samogo of the hills or the Bambara of the open plains, is almost comparable with that of Switzerland, where a few million people have four official languages and where 22 cantons jealously guard their own customs and dialects. And here "almost comparable" means that the situation of the Negroes is manifestly less complex than that of the Swiss.

The most stable and united country in Europe, with no doubt one of the most brilliant military histories, has found a harmony among its differences and antagonisms which many countries could envy. The fact that the Swiss, like the Negro, is often polyglot does not mean that he is inferior; to listen to a foreign language is to open one's ears to a new world. It is correct to say then, unlike many enthusiasts, that a highly civilized language must stand on the same footing as all the others; it can enrich "backward" peoples, but not take the place of their own means of expression; while the use of certain African or Asiatic languages is bound to open up to mankind horizons wider than that which an amazing stroke of fortune created north of the Mediterranean.

Language is not the only field into which Western teachers must venture with caution. The fields of religion, law and art, still less familiar, make up with language and others what we know as a particular society's culture. Expansionist modern civilization, proud of its scientific heritage, with which we are not concerned in this context, has never taken more than a mild interest in American, Asiatic, African or Oceanian cultures, except for purposes of theoretic speculation. But these cultures, arising largely from the unconscious, affect it in their turn. Whatever interferes with them is likely to harm the unconscious. To hustle them in order to get through stages of technical development more quickly, and to make a clean sweep of institutions and beliefs on the grounds that they impede progress, is to create repressions and traumatisms which may have catastrophic results for whole nations.

When a Sudanese says that man is the seed of the earth, he

connects him with the primordial stirring of the minutest seed as well as with the planet Earth itself. He refers also to the fact that man bears within him seeds whose quality, order and numbers give him his personality not only among his own people but in relation to neighbouring ones. He is his own granary, from which he symbolically draws the seed that is essential to agriculture.

No wonder, then, that he sees and feels his actual harvest differently from the white man, to whom the economic aspect is the only one. The white man, calculating the number of half-starving people and assessing the coming crops, suddenly orders the creation of reserve granaries, which seems only to involve questions of administration, collection and mud walls. But the Negro feels coerced and supervised in his subsistence, which is his substance, his very self. He will submit for years to this rational and possibly useful dominion. But as soon as he sends representatives to the Assemblies at Paris or Versailles he gives them categorical instructions to vote for the abolition of those same granaries.

Yet these are largely technical matters. Imagine what individual and collective ravages are caused when, in the name of public order and "morals", a blind authority causes the arrest in the open market-place of totemic priests whose function is to prophesy after putting themselves into a psychic state which we, in the poverty of our vocabulary, call trance. The traumatism is incomparably more violent than that produced in a patient by a clumsy psychoanalyst, for its effect is not confined to a single individual; it has repercussions on the whole society, which is stricken to its very core, to those depths where social stability is engendered. The priest is not just a man who happens to have adopted the career for personal reasons; he is also the vessel of an obscure and collective feeling of the unconscious; he is the collective self of a group, and on its behalf acts a definitely laid down part, the successive stages of which the spectators follow with a rational anxiety, in the belief that they are present at a scene that epitomizes life, a critical moment of destiny, wherein past, present and future intermingle.

When ingrained complexes are clumsily or brutally suppressed, they sooner or later break out in unexpected forms, on economic or religious pretexts or without any pretext whatever. Deprived of mask rituals, those canalization systems created by the patience of the people's ancestors, these complexes only go to ground in order to work for the eventual overthrow of the usurpers. Questioned about the supposed disappearance of Negro customs and metaphysics, one of the wisest and best known African Members of Parliament in the French Union replied: "Custom may hide, it may bury itself beneath the feet of the newcomers, but it is all the more alive for that."

This remark gives food for thought. In the first place it shows what a thin veneer the imported culture is. In military parlance, it is like a screen put up to deceive the enemy. In the large majority of cases it remains a debased culture, merely satisfying the vanity of an *élite*.

In the second place, custom is obliged to hide because of an inferiority complex saddled on its devotees by the teacher. This complex sometimes becomes so intense that the subject actually denies his ancestors, and even his skin. One young Negro, who did not know his country, hungry for politics, ensnared by an education which did him injury, went so far as to say at the last Rencontres de Genève: "When I am no longer a Negro I shall be a man."

A similar case has been quoted by a famous Negro woman dancer who, making a hobby of anthropology, studied an urban sect in the United States of America. The fundamental rite performed by the high priest of these Negroes consists in holding the hand over a bowl of water and calling out three times: "I am a white man; if I put my hand in the water it will come out white."

Half way to these extremes is messianism, the policy of unlimited claims, and practices of daemonic possession aping after a fashion the tried institutions of East Africa and the Arabian Peninsula, which institutions are factors of equilibrium, helping to restore the balance of the personality.

Such poor buoys would nevertheless permit temporary rescues if the Westerner did not see as plots to disturb the peace certain apparently disorderly rites which are really a desperate attempt to use rationally a valuable fund of mental reactions which the Westerner interprets as pathological phenomena.

For the fact that custom, as the wise Negro said, buries itself

357

in order to keep alive, means that it is holding itself in reserve, fully prepared, complete in its salient features and slightest details, ultimate body of an unconscious which, meanwhile, thrusts as best it can through the borrowed cultural crust.

But this tactical position to which the harried society falls back in order to launch later counter-attacks is, when all is said, a sign of decadence. It is a preparation for the disintegration and death which will follow when the rubble and dust left by the ancient edifices are cleared away.

Of the peoples who have recently taken their place in the world community, special attention must be paid to those of the African continent, particularly the Negroes. The general public and scholars alike have formed a conventional picture of Negro Africa, as they did for so long in the case of Greece. But while there was unbounded admiration for Greece, the Negroes have been looked upon as the most backward and degenerate of peoples.

For a long time it was thought, and many still think, that the Negroes have not even the merit of incarnating a very ancient stage of man's evolution, which at least would arouse scientific interest in them. The theory was, indeed, that Negroes were degenerate, owing to the climate and a certain lack of mental endowment, as proved by the fact that their rudimentary techniques had remained unchanged for centuries.

These views have set the tone for contacts between Westerners and Negroes since the beginning of the colonial period. The moral and material life of the conquered peoples has had to be reshaped so that, by adopting their conquerors' mentality, they might play their part in the economy of the governing nation. Compromises were of course accepted when no vital interests were involved, and no objection was raised to the consolation afforded by a few scraps of folklore.

This attitude is attributable not only to the superiority complex developed by any civilization once it feels able to make its influence felt in the world. It may also be explained by a certain reluctance to make the effort required to grasp human problems, and, where the effort is made, by the white man's impatience with unfamiliar customs.

Lastly, one of our gravest errors has been to discount any new facts that would show the Negroes in their true light as one of the formative influences in the shaping of the individual and of the human spirit. It is as if any increase in esteem for the coloured peoples detracted from the prestige of what we call civilization.

In all justice to Westerners, it must be conceded that it is far from easy to assemble ethnological material enabling them to face up to the problem of contacts. One obstacle is the diversity of the various groups in Negro Africa, which form as it were a mosaic of heterogeneous elements, each demanding lengthy study. But the greatest difficulty is still the inscrutability of the Negro world which, while willing to reveal the outward aspects of its institutions and techniques, is at pains to conceal its philosophy and metaphysics, i.e. its inner thought, the only factor that is of any ultimate significance for the organization of the world of today.

Whatever the reasons or excuses for this lack of curiosity, this indifference or reticence towards one another, one fact remains—the lack of any spiritual communication between white and black, of any give-and-take where the exchanges are not the monopoly of the more technically advanced.

The most urgent questions today are, then: Is there any basis for that spiritual communication, and, if there is, can it be built up and organized?

The first question must be answered in the affirmative: far from being "big children", whose activities are purposeless, whose customs are incoherent or loathsome, the Negroes have systems of thought akin to those of the Mediterranean and Asiatic worlds; and these systems shed light on the thought of antiquity that we know only through scattered allusions in a literature which, by definition, could not and was never intended to go to the root of things.

An English writer, Dennett,[1] had already drawn attention to these systems at the beginning of this century. In addition to scrapping the absurd notion of "fetishism", a word which in itself reveals our ignorance, Dennett demonstrated that the world was a single whole, and that there was a link between universal life and social and religious life. Owing to its faulty presentation, however, Dennett's work was never taken seriously. And the whole subject remained in abeyance until

---

[1] R. E. Dennett, *At the Back of the Black Man's Mind, or Notes on the Kingly Office in West Africa*, London, Macmillan, 1906, xvi + 288 p., 8 vo.

recently, when research carried out by specialists on the black races produced information which completely changed ideas hitherto accepted, and revealed the inadequacy of our knowledge.

This research shows that the traditional religions as well as the social and legal structure and the technical crafts of the black races emanate from a single, rigid system of thought—a system which provides an interpretation of the universe, as well as a philosophy enabling the tribe to carry on and the individual to achieve a balanced life, both personally and in relation to the group.

This means, first and foremost, that religion, previously regarded as a dominating or even an all-pervading force, is really only one aspect of a civilization, on a level with social and technical factors. It is not true, for instance, to say that forms of craftmanship, or the organization of the land property system, are permeated with religious significance; that the black races are still living in the shadow of the supernatural, or that action takes place within a ritual framework. We should say, rather, that their religious, legal, technical and social practices all reflect a metaphysical interpretation of the world; and that, on the other hand, every act, fact and object may well constitute a juxtaposition of several of these different aspects of their civilization.

Two examples will help to explain this:

When children of the Bambara tribe, at nightfall, exchange their ordinary garb for a toga-surplice of white cotton, they are performing a simple act called, in popular parlance, "changing themselves". What they are doing in effect is to mark the transition from day to night by throwing off the toil and sweat of the day, and donning spotless white. And this change of clothing is ordained by the rules of a society which is itself subject to the alternation of night and day.

But why must the toga be white? Because white is the colour of the day, day is the realm of the universal Monitor, and his kindly influence must be extended beyond the twilight hour. To dress in white is to clothe oneself in light.

By donning these uniform garments, moreover, children of all ages demonstrate that they are all the offspring of this same Monitor, the father of humanity, and that they form compact units of society.

This common act thus represents a juxtaposition of several different, though partially overlapping, planes of behaviour, of which not all the actors are equally conscious. In fact, whereas the practical significance of the act is recognized by all, its religious meaning is understood only by some, whilst the metaphysical significance escapes all but a few. Indeed, we may say that if excess of religion did result in rigid thinking, this would be detectable only in the intellectual *élite*, the popular masses, on the contrary, being "liberated"— a fact which contradicts generally accepted ideas on the matter.

A second example illustrates another aspect of the question: the fact that the various different interpretations of a custom are found to have the same metaphysical substratum.

The Dogon weavers of the Nigerian crags cease work and fold up their material at the precise moment when the sun reaches the western horizon. The explanations given for this are as follows: it is the normal end of the working day, the danger of blindness must be guarded against, it is forbidden to sing or rattle the shuttles after sundown. It is also thought that a weaver working at night would weave a strip of silence and shadow, since it was by day that the universal Monitor revealed this craft. All these explanations, though at first sight dissimilar, are in fact connected with the idea, first, that words (and noise) and light (and sight) partake of the same nature; and secondly, that the gaps between the warp (which represents the rays of the sun) and the woof (whose zigzags suggest the vibration of matter) contain the words of the tribal ancestors, sung by the weaver. Consequently, it is considered that weaving is daytime work, and that infringement of that rule would provoke cosmic disturbances. Thus, all the explanations given for this custom are, in the final analysis, based on a metaphysical principle.

Examples could be multiplied. The two we have quoted were chosen deliberately, because they relate to simple, unimportant acts appearing at first sight to have no ritual significance. We could give others, relating to religious or legal customs, where the great measure of underlying spiritual significance is more obvious. Before outlining that significance, we must make it clear from the outset that neither ignorant superstition nor poetic fantasy is involved.

Various Sudanese tribes, and in particular the Bambara, the Dogon and the "international" Forgeron group, believe that the world was created by and is impelled by vibration, a primordial phenomenon which, they think, existed before the spirit.

The Bambara people believe that the categories of living beings and objects in the world are the result of the 22 "prototype vibrations"; and that the universe was created by an ever-expanding vortex.[1]

The Dogon people see everything in terms of a spiral vibration, which they depict on their buildings and their tools, and which for them is the essential "path" of water, light, speech, heat, smell, and copper, the primary metal and primary matter. On the basis of this vibration, they interpret the connexion, first, between the various phenomena and, secondly, between the phenomena and life itself. Thus the initial act, anterior to and animating matter, the spirit and the creative god himself, takes the form of a movement, depicted as a vertical spiral, a simplified projection of the spiral on a single plane. But this refers, so to speak, to the internal movement of beings and objects within the universe, the universe itself being animated by an everexpanding spiral-conical movement.

It is doubtless fascinating to find the black races of modern times holding beliefs some of which we meet with in Anaxagoras of Clazomenae. But this is not, it seems, the most interesting point. The Greeks handed down to us various systems peculiar to certain schools of thought or individuals—which is not to say that they failed to evolve a general explanation of society and the universe—but, although they left some coherent theories, their political and private life was based on other principles, completely alien to us. As opposed to this, the Negroes of modern times present us with a universe based on simple metaphysical principles. And these principles are by no means confined to the speculations of the intellectual *élite* or of individuals, but are applied to what we call the supernatural, as well as to everything tangible.

In other words, the Bambara, the Dogon, the Forgeron or the Kurumba fits everything, from God to a gesture of the fingers, from justice to a pair of wooden clogs, into a single,

---

1 See G. Dieterlen, *Essai sur la Religion Bambara*, Presses Universitaires de France, 1953.

coherent system. For him, moreover, every being, object or act contains in itself, as it were, the essence of all other beings, objects or acts; thus men, animals, objects, dancing, work and music are all a summing-up of the essence of the universe.

For the maintenance of cosmic order, therefore, order must be maintained in every element; not only because each plays its part in the functioning of the whole, but also because, since each element is an image of the whole, disorder in any one would presage disorder throughout the universe.

Thus the Negro, far from being confined to his own small circle or absorbed by material considerations, feels that he is intimately bound up with creation, which he sees as a continuous progress—this progress being expressed, both concretely and in the abstract, by the development of new skills, which provide the material basis for the most elaborate system of knowledge.

The Dogons, to take one of the tribes about which most is at present known, think that progress resides in three skills which were revealed to man, one after the other, by a Monitor, who thus acts as a kind of redeemer or repairer of chaos. The first of these skills is the use of fibres for clothing, the fibres falling from the belt in spiral strips, and bearing the imprint of the vibration of the universe, their form thus corresponding to that of the word pronounced by the Monitor. Fibres and word became inseparably intertwined, so that man, possessing the one, also acquired the other. Thus equipped with a first skill, crude as the matter in which it was contained, man lived until the chaos he had introduced into nature called for a second revelation. This time, a more elaborate skill, weaving, became the bearer of a second, more explicit word, contained in the line of crosses formed by the woof passing to and fro across the warp. The cloth issuing from the lips of the Monitor became the bearer of the word; and indeed, in common parlance, the words for "cloth", "word" and "seven" (the teacher's number) all have the same root. Finally a third word, the word of the modern age, was contained in a cylindrical instrument, the drum, with stretchers adjusted in accordance with the method of weaving.

These images of the three skills denote different conceptions: first, a crude plant-strip, consisting of a fibre, damp with sap;

second, a surface of interwoven threads, with the warp symbolizing the rays of the sun; third, a sound emitted by skin
and copper thongs. This myth, illustrating a metaphysical
system based on vibrations (of which the above is only a very
brief summary) tells the tale of an increase of dimensions,
phenomena and materials alike.[1]

The Bambara are equally explicit in their material representation of technical and spiritual progress. Their shrines display
objects testifying to the age and glory of their civilization,
including tools ranging from the most primitive implements
to modern hoes.[2] The first of the series is simply an all-wood,
spear-shaped instrument, which was used for loosening the
soil around wild plants. Next comes the stone axe which, after
a long period of time, came to be fitted with a handle, which
also bore a kind of wooden hoe-shaped plate. And, to complete
the series, the iron axe and hoe. Thus some of the Bambaras'
shrines afford a brief history of their society from ancient to
recent times; and the young men are introduced to these
shrines at their initiation ceremony, the idea being both to
imbue them with respect for their forefathers and to inspire
them to carry on the tradition.

A craftsman's tool, also, is the object of the rites which are
performed in the event of calamity or chaos. When dyeing
cloth, the Bambara beat it, to allow the dye to soak in, with
an egg-shaped wooden block, which, according to them, was
the first tool; for it was older than fibre, the original material,
which was softened by heavy beating. This block, the "mould
of perfection", is the prototype of all tools and all skills, which
emerge from it one by one. as man's needs increase. On the
day when the village is struck by some disaster one such block
is taken out and laid at the crossroads (symbolizing the centre
of the world), where it is beaten with millet-stalks to force it
to emit a healing skill, capable of restoring order.[3]

Since knowledge embraces the whole of the universe, it is
not surprising to find that all the tribes we have studied have
a complete system for classifying animate and inanimate objects. Men, animals and plants, in particular, are classified in

---

1 See Griaule, *Dieu d'Eau*, Editions du Chêne, 1948.
2 See G. Dieterlen, *L'Arme et l'Outil chez les Anciens Bambara*, Africa, London, Oxford University
Press, Volume XVIII, April 1948.
3 See G. Dieterlen, *Essai sur la Religion Bambara*.

logical series which are more than bare lists. Every item has its history, and its place in the universal scheme; and it is associated with rites and beliefs that link it up with other items. In certain cases, the information dates back to prehistoric times, sometimes even to the earliest beginnings of life on earth. Thus the *Digitaria digitata*—a harmful, very hardy plant, which chokes the millet fields and heads the weed category, forms the subject of extensive rites which indicate that in very far-off times, before the emergence of farming, it was used as food.

As regards animals, the Bambara believes that certain of them have, since their creation, undergone substantial changes; this indicates considerable speculative imagination, none the less striking for being embodied in a series of complicated metaphysical-religious myths.

As regards the classification of human beings, all the Sudanese have theories which many Westerners, living in ignorance of their neighbours, might well envy them. Not content with maintaining relations with adjacent tribes, each Sudanese group has carefully-regulated relations with other groups on a scale which, for Africa, must be considered vast. There exist, moreover, societies of an international character, like the Forgerons, living in partnership with other, to all appearances, very different peoples. Such relationships, which are frequently of a ritual nature, also naturally have their place in the general pattern of life.

We may well wonder how so complex and polyvalent a scheme of thought could have been, and still is being, propagated in civilizations having no system of writing. It is done firstly by the spoken word, and secondly through materials on which the thought is recorded and transmitted in a multitude of different ways.

These peoples do not look on the spoken word as a haphazard means for handing down customs. On the contrary, the word is itself one of the purest manifestations of cosmic vibration, and they would never dream of using it arbitrarily in instruction regarding the functioning of the universe. For this reason, teachers and students are always well prepared; and moreover, the solemnity of the occasions on which communications are made well-nigh preclude any serious deviations or deliberate omissions.

As opposed to this, writing, and its corollary, reading, are accessible to everyone, and there is no check either on the writer or on the reader, who may in his turn also take to writing. This leads to indiscriminate dissemination of knowledge, a fact which was understood by the ancients; the latter considered it dangerous, with the result that writers like Herodotus or Plato wrote only such things as could be popularized, but renounced the pen when it came to serious subjects.

Another factor making any embroidery on or gaps in the oral tradition unlikely is the extensive use of the second of the above-mentioned means of transmission, recording on materials.

The Sudanese possess a wide variety of materials which they use for all kinds of different purposes, not even the simplest shape, the simplest piece of ornamentation being without its own special significance. Whether he is speaking of the most intricate mask or the simplest piece of wood, the Negro will always say "there is a reason for everything". Every detail of colour, design and material has its own particular meaning. The shepherd's crook, with its 22 copper rings, represents the 22 categories of objects. The sacrificial axe represents a sun, drawing from the victim jets of blood resembling the sun's rays. The shroud of the dead depicts the high façade of the family house (full of living beings) and tilled fields (full of crops). The shroud is thus the symbol of resurrection.

Wooden shoes, the seats used by the women and the weaver's shuttles all represent canoes to save man from future floods; baskets depict the shape of the universal system, or the work of the Creator; sandals the descent through the seven heavens, and the arrival on earth of a new order.

The Sudanese express their mythology and their metaphysical theories through the medium of ritual objects and common utensils, using signs and strokes equivalent almost to writing, as well as numbers.

Numbers are indeed the ideal symbol for the abstractions of the invisible world—which for these people is as real as the visible world—and the abstractions of all living beings and acts. In particular, the Creation, according to the Dogon and Bambara peoples, was based on a numerical progression which not only explains it but also, as far as our information goes, engendered it, in a way accessible to human understanding.

Thus it is not as the "one god" that Amma creates. Being one, he expresses not only the beginning of being, but the whole of what is to be. Within the One is contained the whole series of numbers, obtained by an endless process of adding the One to himself. Thus, within the One, everything is contained. But this implies a certain stagnation, which Amma counters by a series of additions in the form of movements, the prototypes of the dances men are called on to perform. Thus Amma, in the course of seven days of "dance-work", created 28 earths and heavens, this number expressing his own plenitude and the plenitude of creation. It is as though the Creator and his work progressed in number, were the number and were expressed by the number. The quality of work and beings is governed by the quality of the numbers, which themselves overlap. In this way, every number, in addition to its own particular character, also contains the elements of the numbers of which it is composed.

For example, since three is a male number and four a female number, the sum of the two expresses the complete being, i.e. a double being, partaking of both sexes (every being having two souls, one of either sex). This indicates that the true unit is composed of a couple. But this couple, although complete, cannot be perfect unless it possesses the primordial Word, the promoter and Monitor of creation; and this Word is represented by the figure eight, i.e. the couple seven with the addition of the One. This unit goes back to the beginnings of numeration, and possesses the qualities mentioned above. Occupying the eighth position, it represents the beginning of a new series, hence recommencement. Eight is the symbol of the movement imparted to animate objects by the speaking couple.

But arithmology is not confined to speculating on symbols: in the calculation of time, in particular, it is constantly being confirmed by the course of astronomical phenomena. Computations are based on factors connected with the qualities of the various numbers: the great year of 60 years, similar to Oenopides' year, corresponds to a number of days related to the classification of the universe. And the year itself is marked by a series of sacrifices whose dates are fixed in accordance with rules about which information is still very incomplete; yet the dates are arranged more evenly throughout the year than is sometimes the case elsewhere.

These calculations are based on an ingenious system in which abstraction and the polyvalence of symbols are so highly developed that it is difficult for a Westerner to follow.

A few examples suffice to suggest that this system of numerology is very closely akin, in spirit, to the Pythagorean system. And there is the advantage that it can be studied not only in extensive mythologies and cosmogonies, but also in equipment which, though technically fairly primitive, is nevertheless extremely varied in form and decoration.

This is the place to speak of Negro art which, according to myth, made its appearance at the moment when death first struck at immortal man. As long as forms, the receptacles of the life forces, enjoyed eternity, there was no need either to reproduce them or, by such reproduction, to depict the laws of the universe. Once, however, men and objects became transitory, it became essential to impart to life an artificial, man-made repetitionary process.[1] Nor did man's anxiety stop there. Not content with sculpturing significant forms in renewable if not actually imperishable material, the Negro went further, and attempted to mould his material both to act as the bearer of natural forces, and to serve as an indication of the laws and principles governing the movement of those forces. And we find these laws and principles again, not only in ritual objects, but reflected in common tools and utensils as well. Thus certain painted wooden objects, placed in a specific order, tell the "tale" of the stages of the creation of the world; or a collection of clogs may be used for the same purpose.

Art is thus, *inter alia*, the projection, in ritual or everyday objects, of myths and cosmogonies. It is a kind of depiction, for the initiated, of a certain conception of the world, whose continuation it thereby ensures.

Nor is it through the medium of objects alone that these ideas are conveyed. The whole of man's behaviour, his every movement, has a symbolic significance; even his most elementary acts have cosmic repercussions. The weaver's warp is like fallow land ready to be worked on by the weft of human labour; weaving is like farming, like bringing progress to life and water and purity to desert regions.

And what of the blacksmith? His movements to and fro in

---

[1] See Griaule, *Arts de l'Afrique Noire*, Editions du Chêne, 1947.

the smithy symbolize the course of the sun; he is the sun itself and, as such, must perforce enter by the east and go out by the west. His anvil is the constellation of the Pleiades, with the four horses of Pegasus around it. Every stroke of the smith's hammer sends up a shower of sparks to form a new world of stars.

On the basis of this necessarily very incomplete survey of the question (investigation is still continuing, and will continue for a long time) it is safe to say that the Negro world is governed by a set of coherent systems which constitute not only and not mainly a religion, but a system of knowledge and metaphysics, and a theory of the universe.

Far from being hidebound, the Negro, to judge by such technical skills as he possesses, appears to have a burning desire to understand the mysteries of the universe and establish contact with the rest of the world. He became aware at a very early stage of his position in the cosmic system without, incidentally, placing himself at the centre of that system.

Interpreting every phenomenon in terms of the 22 categories and their functions, he could not subscribe to anthropocentrism; quite the contrary, he regarded man merely as a cog, no more and no less important than a beetle or a drop of rainwater. It is this that explains the practice of human sacrifice, a practice which the Westerner finds repellent except in the cause of technical progress, when personal responsibility is absolved, but which, for the Negro, is merely a demonstration of man's complete identification with the cosmos; and some Negro initiates, by comparison with the ritual human sacrifices they remember from former days, tend to look with scorn on the profitless "mass sacrifice" of our war dead.

The fact of being so identified entails, in our opinion, serious disadvantages, notably technical stagnation and lack of freedom. As regards the first, it must be admitted that the Negroes have fully exploited such vital discoveries as weaving or forging, which even became the bearers of new "words", thus, finally, being integrated into the pattern of material and spiritual progress. The subtleties of these crafts are analysed and incorporated in rites no whit less elaborate than those of the Greeks or the ancient Chinese. In fact, there is no doubt that mechanical progress has been hampered by the Negro addiction to interminable speculation on both the general and the particular; excess of piety has sapped practical energy and, as the gap between thought and action has steadily widened, matter has sometimes been completely paralysed by mind. And yet, by a curious paradox, the intelligence has delved so deeply that the smallest details, every one reflecting the image of the universe, have afforded rich material for long years of contemplation: the infinitesimal is a gateway to the infinite.

Here, clearly, is one of the explanations for the industrial backwardness of the black races. The fact is that, having apprehended and possessed the cosmos from the very beginning, they saw no need to increase their material wealth; the aim of human life had been attained, and they had nothing further to learn from investigation in any direction.

As a natural consequence of this situation, the Negro is, as it were, a captive to a set of rules which, though admittedly universal in scope, nevertheless regulate his everyday life down to the minutest details. Interdicts, in particular, are so stringent and so numerous that they rule out any kind of freedom of thought or action. Indeed, it would be practically impossible to enumerate all the interdicts relating to killing, eating, seeing, speaking and hearing that every Dogon accepts for himself and others. Moreover, closer investigation shows each interdict to be but the symbol of a whole series of others which now no longer exist except in theory. Thus, the few animals and plants which form the object of a totem cult are merely the first items of the eighth part of creation, every man belonging to one of the eight primordial families. Originally, the interdicts applied to a large number of beings or actions, and symbolism was used to limit the scope of their application and concentrate their effects. Nevertheless, the system of interdicts is still very rigid, and must, it would seem, exercise a very restricting effect. It is not, however, looked on in that way. On the contrary, the Sudanese feels nothing but pity, mingled sometimes with scorn, for those who live without any kind of regulations, eating as they wish and drinking from every spring. He regards the interdicts to which he is subject not as a restriction, but rather as protection against impurity; he even discerns therein lofty spiritual motives, which he will depict on the façades of his shrines. He no more resents them than a medieval nobleman would have resented his coat of arms or his royal ancestry.

We begin to see how complicated all these questions are, and how cautiously they must be approached. In any case—and this is the conclusion suggested—a common meeting-ground for the ideas of whites and blacks does exist. There is, in fact, nothing to prevent the Westerner from meeting the Negro on an equal footing in the fields of philosophy and sociology, two of the most important branches of knowledge, having repercussions on all educational and teaching systems.

But it is not enough to assert that a common meeting-ground exists; it is our responsibility to organize contact between our societies and those of the black races.

What method should be adopted to this end, and what steps taken?

As regards method, the problem should be approached in three stages, i.e.: learning about the black societies; learning to appreciate the system of values of those societies; learning how those values can be utilized.

The first problem in this connexion is to obtain information. This admittedly, is very difficult; but we shall be failing in our duty if, in our scientific age, we fail to make the utmost effort to extend the sum of our knowledge of civilizations which are changing, maturing and dying before our eyes.

Anthropologists, ethnologists and sociologists are all, today, experiencing this thirst for knowledge. Up till a few years ago, specialists in the human sciences concentrated on problems of the origin of influences—on chronology. They discussed whether certain rites preceded certain myths, whether one society was older than another. Now all that has changed. Scholars today realize that their key theories are based on incomplete information, and that the first task is to apply all the modern methods of investigation available to the various branches of science—technology, psychology, psychoanalysis, sociography, anthropography, history, etc.—for the purpose of drawing up an inventory of the spiritual treasures of mankind.

It will not be a case of concentrating on certain practical problems, both more accessible and more "profitable" in that they attract the attention of the public authorities; nor yet of picking out those factors in native civilizations which, on superficial observation, appear to offer the most promising points of contact. In other words, information about native manpower, standards of living and, in a general way, all such facts as can be assessed by assistant specialists should form only a part of the survey.

The organizational and religious institutions of any society, like its structure, are merely epiphenomena, pointers leading to the gradual understanding of the psychological make-up of a people.

What we must do, therefore, is to make a "total" study of man, without dismissing archaic material, *a priori*, as useless, or regarding the Rohrschach test as arbitrary; and not treating cultural data as alone worthy of our attention. All aspects must be studied, by every possible means. Moreover, it is imperative that the old traditional institutions of Negro societies, so valuable as a key to Negro mentality, should be investigated immediately, since they are in the process of dying out.

Since the field of study is immense, however, investigations will have to be limited to a reasonable number of societies which are either characteristic of larger groups or which, on the other hand, present anomalies. We could thus, by careful selection, assemble a body of information applicable to regions larger than those which can actually be studied within a reasonable period of time.

The second stage, after the information has been collected, will be to select those moral values which are of merit and should be preserved. This stage will be no easier than the first, since sympathetic understanding does not always go hand in hand with mere perception.

This being said, the criterion to be applied in deciding what institutions and what systems of thought should be preserved and propagated in Black Africa is the extent of their prevalence. No scientific investigation can be of real value if it covers only limited areas.

The first question is that of language—assuming, that is, that we discount the attitude of those white people, and of certain black people as well, who dismiss the African languages and dialects as doomed to extinction.

The Negro's inferiority complex in the face of European culture, of which French or English is the vehicle, leads him to scorn the languages of his compatriots. In this he is encouraged by the colonial authorities, who prefer to have the native make the effort to learn their languages, and who are far too busy to apply themselves to the study of complicated African tongues.

Moreover, those who are sufficiently interested to undertake a serious study of the Negro languages are frequently disappointed by the results of their investigations. These bear mostly on short fables and other texts which, while of the greatest interest if placed in the setting of the whole cultural unit to which they belong, are in themselves insignificant. Riddles, proverbs and fragments of poetry abound. From time to time, the writer's fancy will lead him into some intricate byway of native custom, from which however he will emerge at once without throwing any light on the mysteries of native practices and rites.

A literature that is fragmentary and immature does not help to enhance the prestige of the language amongst those who speak it; on the contrary, it is regarded as proof of the alleged inarticulateness of the Negro.

This situation is due to the fact that few trained linguists ponder on the abstruse problem of language. They are moreover all too apt to concentrate on morphology, syntax or semantics; and, having little contact with ethnographers, may tend to treat the texts available rather as examples of expression than as means of expression providing a key for deciphering a system of thought.

Another obstacle is the vast number of native languages. This difficulty, however, is not insuperable, since what looks like a cloud of dialects is really a series of families of languages.

This is not the place to enter into the discussions which have been taking place in linguistic circles on the classification of the African languages; suffice it to say that those discussions tend to concentrate rather on the relative importance of the various languages than on the links between them. When Sir Harry Johnstone maintains that *Bambute* is a Sudanese language akin to *Mbumba-lese*, and P. Schebesta, on the other hand, affirms that it is a pygmy language adopted by the Sudanese,[1] it should be noted that neither of these two scholars for a moment questions the fact that the two problems are connected.

---

[1] P. Schebesta, "La Langue des Pygmées", *Zaire*, Vol. III, No. 2, February 1949, p. 119.

A similar conclusion emerges from the remarkable work of Miss Homburger, who is best known as the author of the theory that the modern African Negro languages are retarded forms of ancient Egyptian.[1] Whatever be the fate of this theory, or of another even bolder one advanced by the same author, that African is related to Dravidian, her work has shown that the languages of Black Africa, for all their apparent diversity, can in fact be arranged in several groups. One or more of the main languages of each major language group could be selected for use by the Africans, who would thus retain their own vehicle of expression, side by side with the modern European tongues.

This process of absorption of the minor dialects into a few major languages, gaining ever wider currency, would have to be carefully controlled, the natives having access to expert European advice on the subject. They must, in other words, be brought to know their own language; and here we may recall a curious objection which is frequently raised both by emancipated Negroes and by members of certain constitutional assemblies:

"Why should people have to be taught their mother tongue? Does not a Baoulé speak Baoulé as soon as he is born?"

It seems hardly necessary to reply that English and French children, from a very early age, attend organized schools where they learn the rules of the English and French languages, and that contemporary society requires that those rules be adhered to.

Anyone who objected that the Negro was indifferent to beauty of language, images and subtleties of expression, would be making a serious mistake. When using his mother tongue, he will criticize the language used by the person with whom he is speaking; and he will know, out of a family of idioms, which group is held to be correct and elegant. Thus the purest Bambara is spoken by the people of Segou, the ancient capital of the kingdom; while the most elegant dialect of the Dogon group is Dyamsay, which is spoken in the Gondo plain and is generally recognized to be very old.

Assuming that the language problem has been solved, the next step will be to assess the human value of the various social

---

[1] L. Homburger, *Les Langues Négro-Africaines*, Payot, Paris, 1941.

374

or philosophical systems, judging (as in the case of languages) according to their prevalence, and also taking into consideration their usefulness as social "cement".

Special consideration should be given to all institutions which have promoted the development or at least the survival of societies throughout the ages, and in adverse circumstances. Those which appertain both to craftsmanship and to religion must be retained, not perhaps for their intrinsic importance, but in order to assist in the transition to a new way of life.

Certain "social security" measures taken by the natives serve to illustrate this point. In the case of the Bambara, the "Komo" societies, as they are called, hold communal reserve granaries containing the finest grain, for seed, and grain of lower quality, for sale. The money received from sales constitutes a "working capital fund", from which the head of the society makes loans at interest, thus increasing the capital. So much for the adults. The children and other young people have their own reserve, fed by jointly farmed land.

But there is a deeper significance attaching to this custom. Depicted on the granaries are the figures of the tribal ancestors, with the tools they invented; and these buildings are regular educational centres where the people learn the intricate technical skills of the society, its rules, and the rights and duties of its members.

Against this background, it is easy to imagine the psychological reaction of these people to the introduction of official reserve granaries, in charge of guards. It meant the complete overthrow of a system where the notion of germination was closely linked with the ancestor cult. The new system was so unpopular that it was referred to by a coloured deputy as "forced labour".[1]

If the problem had been studied seriously, it would have been realized that the only possible solution, in this particular case, was to recognize and confirm the native practices which had proved their value down the centuries.

This example proves—if, indeed, proof were needed—how essential it is to consider every aspect of the native customs, and to take account of the ideas underlying them.

It is in fact these ideas which constitute the essence of native

1 "*Journal Officiel de la République Française*", Débats de l'Assemblée de l'Union Française, 6 Mar. 1948, p. 209.

metaphysics, cosmogonies and philosophies; and all these systems must be preserved, just as scholars preserve the systems of the Greeks and Romans, of Descartes and Sartre. The Negro systems have, moreover, the advantage of forming a coherent whole reflecting the actual life of the people; and they are capable of revitalizing, perhaps even reshaping, the metaphysical patterns of Western civilization.

We come now to the question of how to utilize the wealth of imaginative thought present in the black world.

This, it is sometimes alleged, cannot be done, and for two reasons: firstly, the rapid evolution of native customs; and secondly, the apparent lack of interest shown by certain emancipated Negroes.

The first objection may be discounted: after all, Western civilization has evolved very far since the time of Pythagoras or Cicero, yet Greek and Latin still form the basis of classical education. Only in the face of vigorous protest have Greek and Latin been eliminated from certain syllabuses, and even those responsible for taking this step have admitted that the general intellectual standard has been lowered as a result. There is no reason, therefore, why education should suffer as a result of adding the study of Negro civilizations to school curricula, even though those civilizations may belong to the past.

As for the apparent lack of interest of certain emancipated Negroes, this is the result of that kind of "leading astray of minors" which all colonial powers have indulged in. The way to train experts on native psychology is not to take a child at a tender age, uproot him from his environment, prime him with foreign theories, preach scorn for everything outside the Western world, and let him grow up virtually out of touch with his own people. On the contrary, that method is eminently calculated to give the Negro an inferiority complex, and drive him to slavish imitation of the defects as well as the virtues of Western civilization.

It would be useless, therefore, to turn to these "expatriates" for advice. They are not competent to advise on the subject; moreover, since they respect only white civilization, any advice they gave would inevitably reflect the teaching of their chosen mentors.

There is of course nothing to prevent the Negro from receiving a European education in a language other than his own, or attaining the same intellectual and technical level as that reached by the European. But if the Negro simply forsakes the verses of his native bards for the poems of Victor Hugo and the cosmogonic theories of his ancestors for the philosophy of Plato, the result will certainly be an impoverishment both for himself and for human thought. In fact, once he feels that the world no longer disparages his native wisdom, the Negro himself will turn to it and show the world what he can do. When he sees that European scholars prize it as highly as the culture of the Chinese and the Babylonians, he will begin to take pride in his ancestry and the original cultures of the tropical races. He will have the satisfaction of knowing that he is the equal, on the spiritual plane, of the European, who also has his merits in this respect. And, being also adept at the somewhat inferior form of imitation known as assimilation, he may well acquire two cultures, an achievement not often found amongst those he is all too apt to regard as his superiors.

The children must receive education in Negro culture concurrently with their education in European culture, and it must be given in the vernacular. For this purpose, the traditional authorities might be called on to help, just as the Moslem authorities help in the teaching of the Koran. Primary education, in its curricula, should pay increasing attention to local factors; while higher education should place increasing emphasis on the teaching of African wisdom and philosophies.

Parallel to this development in overseas territories, the syllabuses of European schools should also include a considerable measure of teaching about Negro civilization; it is here, indeed, that the new policy can be most easily and speedily initiated. There is no reason why the study of Negro philosophy and civilization should not be introduced into the curricula for the *agrégation* and the French university philosophy courses. And the study of Negro languages could be encouraged at all levels of education.

In this way, the ground could be prepared for better relations between Europeans and Africans, based on closer mutual understanding and the ability to share their past and present experience.

Any such alteration of university curricula is obviously a matter for decision on the governmental level. Such spasmodic attempts as have so far been made in this direction have clearly been handicapped by lack of real knowledge of the subject.

The point is that, except in a few cases, most attempts by Europeans to study African civilization have been isolated ones. Until quite recently, ethnographical research was left to individual enthusiasts, whose work the public authorities admired but did not understand. It is still difficult to make a career as a student of the institutions and customs of the coloured peoples. Moreover, the recent war disorganized efforts and systems in the field of intellectual exchange, and governments have found themselves faced with urgent practical problems demanding all their attention and financial resources.

The study of the African peoples, and the assessment of their spiritual values, is therefore eminently a task for Unesco. Without concerning itself with the details of internal organization and administrative structure, that international body could suitably promote the scientific study of African cultures, inform the general public on problems related thereto, and encourage the various governments to adopt an enlightened policy towards the peoples of non-self-governing territories.

Humanism of Tomorrow
and the Diversity of Cultures

*Final Statement of the Committee of Experts
convened by Unesco*

This statement is issued by the undersigned group of experts brought together by Unesco to consider the problems presented by the contacts and relations of cultures in the world today

The cultures of the world have been affected profoundly by technology, war and political change. The customs and beliefs of peoples who had lived as their ancestors lived, are being rapidly transformed by changed material conditions and external influences. The aspirations of peoples who have long sought political independence and autonomy, are being suddenly realized. The ideas and ideals of nations have been affected by contact with those of other nations, with whom they have previously had little or no relation; and from the efforts to treat economic, social and political problems which are recognized as common, there have arisen tensions which threaten the fundamental values of civilization. The crisis of our times is a crisis of cultures as well as of economics and politics; and what happens to the values of art, science, literature, philosophy, and religion affects, and is affected by, what happens to the material conditions of life and the international relations of nations. Unesco is itself a sign and acknowledgment of the important use to which the instruments of education, science, and culture can be put in advancing peace and the welfare of man.

This committee of experts assembled from various countries to discuss the problems presented by cultural contacts and cultural changes is impressed both by the urgent need of increased attention to and study of the cultures of the world and of their interrelations, and also by the contribution which cultural instrumentalities may make to the solution of economic and political problems. In spite of the fact that we represent many different points of view, we are in agreement on the following propositions which we consider to be of great practical and theoretical importance:

1. The effort to extend the benefits of industrialization and technological advances to all peoples must inevitably be accompanied by profound cultural dislocations. The problems presented by these abrupt alterations of traditional ways of life are of two sorts—practical and theoretical; and step by step with the execution of programmes of technical improvement, courses of action should be planned and carried out, to ensure the cultural stability of people acquiring new technical skills and to increase our knowledge of the relations of men and cultures. As new methods of agriculture, sanitation, and medicine are acquired, as fundamental education is extended to more peoples, and as machines and industrial techniques are acquired by them, it is important that they should not be faced by the blank alternative either of struggling to preserve traditional values or of acquiescing in accepting alien values. They must rather be given the means to develop, under the new conditions, values comparable to those which they had previously achieved. Parallel with this practical problem is the problem of acquiring and preserving knowledge of many cultural elements—of languages, customs, crafts, arts, folklore, beliefs—which are rapidly disappearing and which constitute important data concerning men and societies, their developments, and their interrelations.

2. Many of the peoples of the world have acquired political independence during the past few years and others are in the process of becoming self-governing. The Philippine Islands, India, Pakistan, Burma and Israel are now valued members of the United Nations; Ceylon is a member of Unesco, and many other peoples are moving rapidly toward autonomy and self-government. The revolutionary significance of this process by which hundreds of millions of people have acquired political independence in a few years is in the fact that the transition could be made within the framework of the United Nations with remarkably little violence. Not only does the United Nations provide the means by which international political problems may be solved, but it also constitutes a *milieu* in which these newly

constituted nations may take their just, proper, and dignified places among the nations of the world. Unesco should contribute to this process not only by making available educational and scientific techniques and materials needed by these nations, but also by assisting their peoples to study and understand their own pasts, to preserve the monuments of their ancestral achievements, and to spread the knowledge of, and respect for, the values of their cultures among the other peoples of the world.

3. Progress in technology and increased speed of communication and transportation, finally, have brought the nations of the world into close contact. Common social, economic, and political problems have necessitated co-operation among all nations and have made clear the effects of the actions of individual nations on the ways of life, customs, and ideas of the peoples of other nations. A world community of shared ideals and aspirations is slowly emerging which may serve as a basis for international political institutions and international economic exchanges. If the nations achieve mutual understanding, confidence may replace fear and tension; and, within the framework of understood values and recognized motives of action, economic co-operation and political agreement may proceed to successful and effective consummations. If that cultural framework is abandoned or destroyed in the rapidity of change which threatens the evolution and adaptation of values, material advances and selfish interests are likewise endangered. To promote mutual understanding the nations of the world should acquire and disseminate, through Unesco, knowledge of the different hierarchies of values esteemed in the various cultures, of the variety of means employed to achieve those values, and of the diversity of material circumstances which condition the conception and pursuit of those values.

4. These are the three stages of the problems of cultural relations in the world today: the problems of the cultural equilibrium and the evolution of values of peoples brought in contact by technological change; the problems of the readjustment and the dignity of peoples who have recently acquired their freedom, and of the understanding and respect due them by other nations; and the problems of

the mutual influences, tensions, and misunderstandings of the nations of the world which have only recently become aware of their dependence on each other and their common interests.

The problem of international understanding is a problem of the relations of cultures. From those relations must emerge a new world community of understanding and mutual respect. That community must take the form of a new humanism in which universality is achieved by the recognition of common values in the diversity of cultures. The nations of the world cannot achieve that community through their ministries of information and cultural relations, for even when the purposes of those agencies are disinterested, their activities are interpreted as the expression of a single culture or even as propaganda. An international agency like Unesco, however, may bring the forces of education, science, and culture to the formation of such a humanism by revealing, in the particularities of expression, common values and common meanings. The achievement of international understanding and a new humanism is necessary for the success of the political adjustments of men; but understanding and humanism are important ingredients in the pursuit of knowledge, in the cultivation of values, and in the good life for which economic and political institutions are but preparations and foundations.

N. K. Sidantha.
C. C. Berg.
S. Buarque de Hollanda.
M. Castro Leal.
L. Febvre.
M. Griaule.
R. P. McKeon.
Yi Chi Mei.
H. E. Mostafa Amer Bey.
J. M. Romein.

BIO-BIBLIOGRAPHICAL NOTES

BHIKHAN LAL ATREYA, M.A., D.Lit., K.C., K.T., M.T.A., born 1897, Judah, District of Saharanpur (U.P.) India.
Professor of Philosophy, Benares Hindu University; Head of the Department of Philosophy, Psychology, and Indian Philosophy and Religion, Benares Hindu University; Joint Secretary, Indian Philosophical Congress.

Principal works: *The Philosophy of Yogavasistha and Modern Thought; Elements of Indian Logic; Philosophy and Theosophy; Teaching of Religion in Post-War Schools.*

FRANCISCO AYALA, born 16 March 1906, Granada, Spain.
Professor, Universidad del Litoral, Buenos Aires, Argentina (1941–43); Honorary Member, Instituto de Sociologia, University of Buenos Aires; Member Instituto Argentino de Filosofia Jurídica y Social.

Principal works: *Cazador en el Alba*, 1930; *Indagación del Cinema*, 1929; *El Problema del Liberalismo*, 1941; *Oppenheimer*, 1943; *El Pensamiento vivo de Saavedra Fajardo*, 1941; *Histrionismo y Representación*, 1944; *Los Políticos*, 1944; *Tratado de Sociologia*, 1947.

EDGAR SHEFFIELD BRIGHTMAN, Ph.D., born Holbrook, Mass., U.S.A., 1884.
Professor, Boston University; President, Eastern Division, American Philosophical Association; Fellow, American Academy of Arts and Sciences; President, American Theological Society.

Principal works: *An Introduction to Philosophy*, 1925, revised 1951, translated into Chinese, Spanish, Portuguese; *A Philosophy of Ideals*, 1928, Spanish translation; *Moral Laws*, 1933; *A Philosophy of Religion*, 1940; *Metaphysics*, 1951; and numerous book reviews and articles in philosophical journals in the U.S.A. and abroad.

PEDRO BOSCH-GIMPERA, born Barcelona in 1891.
Ph.D. (Literature and History), University of Madrid; Doctor Honoris Causa, University of Heidelberg; Director, Archaeological Service of Catalonia, 1915–39; Director, Archaeological Museum of Barcelona, 1921–39; Professor, University of Barcelona, 1916–39; Dean of the Faculty of Letters, 1931–39 and Rector of the University of Barcelona, 1933–39; Lecturer, Oxford University, 1939–40; Professor, University of Mexico and National School of Anthropology appointed 1940; Professor in Guatemala, 1945–46; Lecturer in European and American universities; Honorary Member of the Royal Anthropological Institute of Great Britain and of the Society of Antiquaries of London; Head of the Division of Philosophy and Humanistic Studies, Unesco, 1948–52; Member, National Council of Prehistoric and Protohistoric Sciences; "Gastprofessor" Berlin 1919; "Rhind Lecturer" Edinburgh 1936; "Sir John Rhys Memorial Lecturer" of the British Academy, 1939; Raoul Dusseigneur Prize of the Académie des Inscriptions et Belles Lettres.

Principal works: *Prehistòria Catalana*, 1919; *Etudes sur le néolithique et l'énéolithique de France*, 1927; *Etnologia de la Peninsula ibèrican*, 1932; *Articles sur la Préhistoire de l'Espagne et de l'Occident de l'Europe dans le Reallexikon der Vorgeschichte de M. Ebert et dans la Enciclopedia Italiana; L'art Grec a Catalunya*, 1937; *Two Celtic Waves in Spain; El Poblamiento y la formación de los pueblos de España*, 1945; *Historia de Catalunya*, 1945; *Historia de Oriente*, 1945–51; *Los Iberos*, 1948; *Mouvements celtiques*, 1952.

SUNITI KUMAR CHATTERJI, M.A. (Calcutta) D.Lit. (London), F.R.A.S.B., born Sibpur, Howrah, near Calcutta, 1890.
Khaira Professor of Indian Linguistics and Phonetics; Head of the Department of Comparative Philology, and Lecturer in the Departments of Sanskrit, Pali, Modern Indian Languages (Bengali, Hindi, Urdu, Assamese, Oriya), English, French, and Islamic History and Culture, University of Calcutta. Honorary Member of the École Française d'Extrême-Orient, Hanoi, Viet-Nam.

Principal works: *Bengali Self-Taught*, 1927; *A Bengali Phonetic Reader*, 1928; *Languages and the Linguistic Problem*, 1943; and a number of papers, and monographs in English, Bengali and Hindi, on linguistic, literary, historical and art topics.

SHIH-HSIANG CHEN,
Professor, National University of Peking; Professor, University of California since 1945.

Principal works: *Modern Chinese Poetry*, 1936; *Literature as Light against Darkness*, 1949; *Chinese Literature*, 1951; and other articles and reviews in Chinese and English.

ALAIN DANIELOU, born Paris, 1907.
Attracted to India in the course of his researches on musical theory in 1932 and settled in Benares in 1937; learned Hindi and Sanskrit and studied Hindu music and the traditional philosophy of India; has established a unique collection of Sanskrit manuscripts on music; Director of Researches at the Hindu University, Benares.

Principal works: *Introduction to Musical Scales*, 1943; *Northern Indian Music*, 1950; *Yoga, the Method of Reintegration*, 1949; *Yoga, Méthode de Réintégration*, 1951 and numerous articles on philosophy, art and Hindu religion (in Hindi, English and French).

MARCEL GRIAULE, born, 1898.
Professor at the Sorbonne; École Nationale des Langues Orientales and École des Hautes Études; Member of the Assembly of the French Union; head of several scientific missions in tropical Africa.

Principal works: *Livre de recettes d'un dabtara abyssin*, 1928; *Silhouettes et Graffiti Abyssins*, 1928; *Jeux et Divertissements Abyssins*, 1929; *Masques et Dogons*, 1930; *Jeux Dogons*, 1930; *Les Flambeurs d'Hommes*, 1934; *Les Sao Légendaires*, 1941; *Arts de l'Afrique Occidentale*, 1947; *Dieux d'Eau*, 1948.

E. STUART KIRBY (B.Sc., Ph.D.), born Japan.
Professor of Economics and Political Science, University of Hong Kong; Oriental linguist; President of the United Nations Association, Hong Kong;

Various publications on economic and historical subjects in Japanese and Chinese, and articles in Western periodicals; has made current researches on economic history of China (Rockefeller Foundation) and on problems of Asian industrialization.

MICHEL LEIRIS, born Paris, 1901
Director of Research at the National Centre of Scientific Research, Paris; Member of the African Department, the Musée de l'Homme, Paris; participated in the Dakar-Jibuti expedition (1931–33) under the direction of Mr. Marcel Griaule.

Principal publications (apart from literary works): *L'Afrique Fantôme*, 1934; *La Langue Secrète des Dogons de Danga*, 1948; *Race et Civilisation*, 1951; and numerous articles in various reviews.

RICHARD MCKEON, born Union Hall, N.J., U.S.A., 1900.
Professor of Philosophy and Greek, University of Chicago; Fellow, Medieval Academy of America; American Academy of Arts and Sciences; Adviser to the United States Delegations to the First, Second and Third Sessions of the General Conference of Unesco.

Principal works: *The Philosophy of Spinoza*, 1928; Editor, *Selections from Medieval Philosophers*, Vols. I and II, 1929–30; *The Basic Works of Aristotle*, 1941; *Introduction to Aristotle*, 1947; *Democracy in a World of Tensions*, 1951.

JOHN SOMERVILLE, born New York, N.Y., U.S.A., 1905.
Professor, Hunter College, New York (Department of Philosophy); Visiting Lecturer: Cornell and Stanford Universities and the University of Michigan; Cutting Fellow, Columbia University; Senior Fellow, Hoover Institute Stanford, University.

Principal works: *Methodology in Social Science*, 1938; *Soviet Philosophy: A Study of Theory and Practice; Philosophy of Peace*, 1949; etc.

SILVIO ZAVALA, born 1907, Merida, Yucatán (Mexico).
Doctor of Law, University of Madrid; Contributor, Centro de Estudios Históricos, Madrid, 1933–36; Guggenheim Fellowship, 1938–40; Director, Centro de Estudios Históricos du Colegio de México, from 1940; visiting professor Columbia and Princeton Universities, and the Universities of Pennsylvania, Puerto Rico and Havana; lecturer at various American and European universities; Founder and Director of the Revista de Historia de América, from 1938; Director of a working group at the Unesco Seminar for the Teaching of History, Sèvres, 1951; Member, International Commission for the Scientific and Cultural History of Mankind; Member, Academia National de Historia y Geografica de Mexico et de l'Academia Mexicana de la Historia.

Principal works: *Los intereses particulares en la Conquista de la Nueva España*, 1933; *La instituciones jurídicas en la Conquista de América*, 1935; *La Enconmienda Indiana*, 1935; *La "Utopía" de Tomas Moro en la Nueva España*, 1937; *De encomiendas y propiedad territorial en algunas regiones de la América Española*, 1940; *Idearío de Vasco de Quiroga*, 1941; *New viewpoints on the Spanish Colonization of America*, 1943; *Servidumbre natural y libertad cristiana según los tratadistas españoles de los siglos XVI y XVII*, 1944; *Ensayos sobre la colonización española en América*, 1944; *La Filosofia Política en la Conquista de América.* 1947; *América en el espíritu francés del Siglo XVIII*, 1949.

LEOPOLDO ZEA, born Mexico, D.F., 1912.

Ph.D., National University of Mexico; Professor in the Faculty of Philosophy and Letters (Chair of Philosophy and History) University of Mexico.

Principal publications: *El Positivismo en Mexico*, 1943; *Apogeo y Decadencia del Positivismo en Mexico*, 1944; *Ensayos sobre Filosofia en la Historia*, 1948; *2 Etapas del Pensamiento en Hispanoamérica*, 1949; *La Filosofia como Compromiso*, 1951; *América como Conciencia*, 1951; and articles in various reviews in Mexico, the United States and South America.